Library Service to the Deaf and Hearing Impaired

by Phyllis I. Dalton

 ORYX PRESS
1985

117178

The rare Arabian Oryx is believed to have inspired the myth of the unicorn. This desert antelope became virtually extinct in the early 1960s. At that time several groups of international conservationists arranged to have 9 animals sent to the Phoenix Zoo to be the nucleus of a captive breeding herd. Today the Oryx population is over 400 and herds have been returned to reserves in Israel, Jordan, and Oman.

Copyright © 1985 by
The Oryx Press
2214 North Central at Encanto
Phoenix, Arizona 85004-1483

Published simultaneously in Canada

Printed and Bound in the United States of America

Library of Congress Cataloging in Publication Data

Dalton, Phyllis I.
   Library service to the deaf and hearing impaired.

   Bibliography: p.
   Includes index.
   1. Libraries and the deaf.   2. Libraries and the hearing impaired.   3. Deaf—Books and reading.
4. Hearing impaired—Books and reading.   I. Title.
Z711.92.D4D34   1985   025.5'2776'63   83-43242
ISBN 0-89774-135-8

To my husband,
Jack M. Dalton

Table of Contents

Preface

By Parents of a Deaf Daughter Who Are Librarians and Educators

The deaf are a difficult and challenging clientele for the library to serve. For them, most libraries hold no particular attraction. Profoundly deaf children have a severe learning disability. They are poor readers because they have never heard words nor have they been clued into word conceptualism through hearing. The deaf community lives in another world. Dealing with the everyday world gives them the handicap of very limited speech communication with all its problems; yet the deaf do speak, sign, write, and use telecommunication devices with individual degrees of competence. Many librarians and other people with understanding and sensitivity are reaching out and learning sign language. Present and near-future applications of technology, especially in the areas of microprocessor teaching, electronic publishing, and TDD computer terminal development, will help libraries more easily serve the deaf and the hearing impaired. Libraries may not always hear appreciation of their services, but it is there, starting with the deaf, their teachers, parents, families, and social and business contacts.

This much-needed book discusses the *whys, wheres* and *hows* of library service and programing for the deaf and hearing impaired and their associates. It addresses comprehensively and in depth the considerations required for success in establishing and continuing these programs—from advocacy and pilot programs to the international coalition of information networking among all professional groups serving the deaf and hearing impaired.

The author of this pioneering work is Phyllis Dalton. As a librarian and high-level administrator, she believes in relevant and quality library service for all. Within this context, she has always remembered the needs of special users. Her pervasive writing and speaking talents plus her professional expertise have made her a top-notch designer, implementer, and supporter of many "extra" library services with spin-off advantages for all library patrons. How fortunate the deaf and the hearing impaired are to have Phyllis Dalton now championing library services for them!

Michael and Doris Sadoski
Parents of Cynthia Sadoski
Class of 1983, Gallaudet College

Foreword

Morris Polan, the California delegation chair, and 37 other delegates and alternates attended the White House Conference on Library and Information Services in Washington, DC, November 15–19, 1979. These people came from a state that is emphatically pluralistic, and their delegation reflected that by including three Asian Americans, seven Hispanics, nine Blacks, two Native Americans and ten disabled individuals. They were proud that the strong, united voice of Californians had influenced the passage of several important key resolutions on behalf of special constituencies, eliminating some of the barriers that had separated them from library and information services.

Among the disabled delegates from California were Marge Klugman of the Los Angeles area and John Darcy Smith of the San Francisco area, both of whom are deaf. Because of their persistence and sincerity, a resolution to establish statewide clearinghouses on deaf services and to enact a National Library Service for the Deaf under the auspices of the Library of Congress was passed. Rev. Roger Pickering, who came from Philadelphia to present testimony through an interpreter, Betty Irgens (an alternate delegate from Michigan), and I (a delegate at large), had also done our best for the success of the resolution.

Delegates, speakers, and other participants made it clear at the conference that they believe that access to information is power and that, in our democratic society, the people themselves want to decide how to use that power. Generally, people want accurate information to guide them in making intelligent decisions about issues that concern them. They want to know how and where to find the government or community services they need to solve their problems. They want information on how to adapt to the rapid changes taking place in their environment. They want to expand their knowledge and the range of their options through education. It was a very exciting week, and we all have never learned so much! Most of us returned home with a better understanding and a renewed sense of what "We, the People" implies.

During the last 25 years, Americans were not prepared for the anger and actions of different special interest groups—all parts of "We, the People": bus boycotts; freedom rides; strikes in the lettuce fields and vineyards of California; riots at the Attica Prison; seizure of the tiny village of Wounded Knee; marches by the Gray Panthers, the National Gay Task Force, and Equal Rights Amendment supporters; and sit-ins by deaf and other disabled people in Washington, DC, and San Francisco. Such widespread, popular movements have resulted in the enactment of several new federal laws and regulations affecting all Americans.

Theodore Roosevelt, in his first annual message to Congress about 80 years ago said, "The American people are slow to wrath, but when their wrath is once kindled, it burns like a consuming flame." The library was also touched by these "consuming flames": issues involving the rights and needs of Black people, Jews, Spanish-speaking people, gay people, women, blind people, as well as people of Vietnamese origin, etc. All of these issues have been raised at American Library Association (ALA) conventions; thus, groups or individuals representing these special interests have become watchdogs at the ALA.

The National Association of the Deaf (NAD) has come a long way.

It was during the week of the 100th anniversary of the ALA conference in Chicago that ALA's executive board and council were first touched by deaf advocacy. Representatives from the District of Columbia Public Library, with Molly Raphael in charge, had arranged a meeting on July 6, 1976 for anxious ALA members about a need to change the organizational structure with the ALA to better fit the needs of people with hearing impairments. Present were Irene Hodock, a librarian at the Indiana School for the Deaf; Alexander Nobleman, then of Gallaudet College Library; myself; and all deaf ALA members, who were also joined by visitors from the Chicago area, including three nationally well-known deaf leaders (Frank Sullivan, president of the National Fraternal Society of the Deaf; Larry Forestal, then vice president and now president of the NAD; and Herbert Pickell, now on the board of directors of the American Coalition of Citizens with Disabilities).

Eighty-five years earlier, in 1891, when the ALA was only 15 years old and the NAD only 11 years old, Edwin A. Hodgson, the second NAD president, who had just completed his term in 1889, published the book *Facts, Anecdotes and Poetry Relating to the Deaf and Dumb*.[1]

It was published "with the aim and the hope that it would correct many erroneous impressions concerning the deaf." The book provided readers with interesting and true facts about deaf people, their amusing experiences, their literary and artistic contributions, as well as their other accomplishments.

Hodgson wrote in his preface, "It is hoped that those of the public who may peruse these facts will disseminate them, and thus help along the cause of truth and justice towards a class whose real condition is so often misunderstood."[2]

The American Library Association (ALA) has come a long way.

Dr. T. Alan Hurwitz, the 23rd president of the NAD (1982–1984) echoed the concerns of the past presidents at the NAD's biennial convention in St. Louis in the first week of July 1982. However, this time he emphasized strongly a need to build a positive image of deaf people in the media and the right of deaf people to have the freedom of choosing whichever communication method they feel most comfortable with for communicating with others—whether deaf or hearing.

President Hurwitz is coming closer to home than anyone has ever done in the past.

The main priority of the ALA, a nonprofit educational organization of some 38,000 librarians, educators, trustees, and other public-spirited citizens, is to assure that every individual has "access to information" at the time needed and *in a format the individual can utilize.* This objective has been at the core of library service and of the ALA since it was organized in 1876.

Since 1880, the NAD, a nonprofit consumer organization—the oldest and largest such organization of disabled in the United States with some 17,000 members—has been in the forefront in ensuring that deaf and hard-of-hearing people enjoy the same rights and services that hearing Americans do. Their particular emphasis has always been on public awareness about deaf needs. At the 1982 NAD convention, delegates voted to make the issue of TV access the NAD's top priority.

NAD and ALA are coming close to moving forward together.

Author Donald F. Moores, in his book *Educating the Deaf: Psychology, Principles and Practices*,[3] said that when he was in a training program to become a teacher of the deaf, he was taught that the major problem of the deaf was poor speech. A few years later, the consensus changed to the position that the biggest problem was language—a position Moores could not accept fully because deaf people *can* learn. He came to believe that "the major obstacle facing deaf people is well-meaning but misinformed hearing individuals."[4] The same is true for anxious hearing people who are endlessly confronted with well-meaning but misinformed deaf individuals who themselves often lack knowledge about deafness, deaf service, and deaf heritage and who, therefore, do not realize their responsibility for supporting their own community needs. The realization of this lack of knowledge among deaf and hard-of-hearing people is one reason why the new *Red Notebook*[5] concept came into existence and is well on its way to becoming the information and referral network on deaf accessibility in every corner of America. The *Red Notebook* is a depository of information about deafness, services for the deaf community, and library services that encourage deaf and hard-of-hearing people to learn facts about themselves that they can share with hearing people.

To create results, we must first see more involvement in library associations at all levels—state, regional, and national—by professionals from deaf communities who specialize in literacy, publishing, collection of print and nonprint materials, open and closed captioning for TV, broadcast and cable TV, preservation of deaf history, advocacy, outreach services for those in isolated places or with additional handicapping conditions, employment, and careers of disabled people in information-related jobs. Advocacy groups like the NAD, the American Coalition of Citizens with Disabilities, and others may participate in "Friends of Libraries, USA," a group within the ALA that works for legislative action.

There is also a growing number of people with hearing impairments who not only cannot afford a videotape player or even a TDD but who still have to achieve the survival skills for independent living which the library can help provide, no matter where these individuals live.

Professionals interested only in their own specialties who are willing to let ALA or state library associations assume the responsibility for improvements in library legislation, funding, standards, and technical and professional developments are getting a free ride. Their special interests *can* fit into their overall library programs.

Administrators, staff, and consumers at hospitals, colleges, schools, TV stations, businesses, prisons, and other places in the mainstream of society deserve good librarians. The effort to keep deaf and hard-of-hearing people in the mainstream requires the *continuing* understanding and involvement of librarians to help others be more sensitive to the communication needs of people—deaf or hearing. Librarians also deserve the spiritual support of deaf communities, where information specialists can gain skills that will make them effective facilitators in the information environment, both in and out of the library, maintaining the appropriate formats and smoothing the way for users to cope with limitless amounts of knowledge and information.

ALA 1983–84 President Brooke Sheldon said that "we are still a long, long way from achieving even the first of the detailed recommendatiions outlined in the 1979 White House Conference to promote access for the 36 million handicapped Americans."[6]

In this book, Phyllis Dalton will not be able to give us a simple step-by-step procedure for creating ideal library services for those with hearing impairment, but she will make it clear that we can all begin by first examining our own role in the community—either as public servants or as library users—and that we can learn from past experiences and current activities. Public servants—deaf or hearing—need not be specialists in deaf education or have deaf family members. Administrative people do not need direct contact with deaf or hard-of-hearing individuals. But they all do need a belief in public services—for *all* people to have access to knowledge and information.

We finally arrive! NAD and ALA get together for the first time.

During the ALA midwinter meeting in Washington, DC, in January 1981, the NAD gave a reception. Dr. Albert T. Pimentel, executive director of NAD, said then that ALA was to be congratulated upon obtaining a separate section within its own structure to focus on deaf needs.

Move over, Melvil Dewey.

Without the spiritual support and encouragement for full services to deaf communities of the District of Columbia and the nation by Dr. Hardy R. Franklin, director of the District of Columbia Public Library, we would not be here. Marie Davis, deputy director of the Free Library of Philadelphia and a very active ALA leader, now retired, and Molly Raphael, former librarian at the Martin Luther King Memorial Library, now assistant to the director of the DC Public Library, will be long remembered in the history of both ALA and the NAD for their pioneering work in starting library services in the area of deafness. Phyllis Dalton, who has been with us since the beginning, has greatly contributed toward this end by writing this very valuable book. Not only should it be useful for libraries and deaf communities, but it is valuable also for members of the various professions who need to understand why and how this lack of information power and knowledge has afflicted society, holding back our silent minority for the past 200 years.

This is a beginning, and we are now moving in the right direction. Yes, we are moving!

Marge Klugman, John Darcy Smith, Betty Irgens, Rev. Roger Pickering and I, as well as others who participated in the White House Conference in 1979, will be patiently waiting until everyone becomes involved.

Alice Hagemeyer
Librarian for the Deaf Community
District of Columbia Public Library

NOTES

1. Edwin A. Hodgson, *Facts, Anecdotes and Poetry Relating to the Deaf and Dumb* (New York: Deaf Mutes' Journal, 1891): preface.

2. Hodgson, preface.

3. Donald F. Moores, *Educating the Deaf: Psychology, Principles and Practices* (Boston: Houghton Mifflin Co., 1978).

4. Moores, 151.

5. National Association of the Deaf. *Communicating with Hearing People: The Red Notebook*, orig. Alice Hagemeyer (Silver Spring, MD: National Association of the Deaf, [1980]). (Loose-leaf.)

6. Brooke Sheldon, "6th Path: 'Removing Barriers'." In *Access to Information—Six Paths to Achievement: An Agenda for 1984 and Beyond*. 1982–1983 EDB #79- Position Paper (Chicago: American Library Association): 6 under 6th path.

Acknowledgement

So many people have assisted in the writing of this book that it is impossible to list them all. I am especially appreciative of the assistance received from members of the Library Service to the Deaf Section of the Association of Specialized and Cooperative Library Agencies of the American Library Association. Individual libraries were most generous in sharing their materials and their experiences with library programs of service to deaf and hearing impaired people. Members of associations of libraries and librarians of and for deaf and hearing impaired people also shared information with me. Governmental agencies with responsibilities for services to deaf and hearing impaired people responded to my requests for information on a variety of subjects. Then there were the many, many individuals who responded to requests for information and/or offered information, advice, and counsel freely. To all I say "thank you" with the hope that this book will bring together information and ideas which will further advance library service to people who have a hearing loss.

Phyllis I. Dalton

Introduction

The idea for this book originated through continuing work with libraries, with activity in the development of library service to the deaf and hearing impaired, as well as with an active advocacy for the establishment of the service. From a background of libraries serving the adult blind, to library service to all people who are blind, to the physically handicapped and to people with other disabilities, it was a natural step to consideration of library service being universally available to nonhearing people and to those with any type of hearing impairment.

The awareness of this need has been obscured by the attitude of the public, the invisibility of the disability, and the lack of understanding of the many aspects of deafness. Because of these barriers, the movement for providing service to the deaf and hearing impaired was slower in its emergence in libraries than it should have been. These factors hampered the development of programs which ensure people who are deaf or hard of hearing of the availability and accessibility of these services. Often, now, it is the lack of knowledge of this availability and accessibility by persons with hearing impairments which stands as a barrier to their use.

It has now become universally recognized that deafness, in many instances, is also a handicap to reading. There has not been in existence and is not, at the present, a nationally coordinated library service provided to deaf and hearing impaired individuals. Such a national effort in the development of programs in libraries related to deafness would be of immeasurable value. Because the reading preferences of this population cannot be distinguished on a national basis from those of the hearing population, the overall basic approach would be of assistance, also, to all people who are interested in the subject of deafness in all of its aspects.

Available figures indicate that there are more than 14 million persons in the United States with some hearing impairment. About 2 million suffer from deafness; among these, about 400,000 lost their hearing in their teens or were deaf from birth. The consequences of impaired hearing vary according to the age at which hearing loss occurs and the degree of that loss. Hearing loss at an early age has a profound effect on the development of language skills and the ability to use traditional library programs. Yet, all persons who are deaf or who have any degree of hearing impairment need information to function effectively in everyday life and to enhance their quality of life.

Librarians are recognizing the varied requirements of people who are deaf or who have any type of hearing impairment, but equal access to programs of services and resources in libraries does not presently exist. There is little indication that this will change in the immediate future without a special effort by the library profession, deaf and hearing impaired individuals, and the community in general. The availability of service programs and of resources is not universal because the services, resources, and policies of individual libraries are not coordinated. People who are deaf or hearing impaired, as is so with other special populations, make up a scattered population and need to receive service where they live. Without a local or a regional service readily and universally available, these individuals remain, as a group, unserved or underserved by libraries. A coordinated, bibliographic approach for bringing together the common knowledge necessary for the development of a total program of library service for people who are deaf or who have other hearing impairments will be considered throughout this book.

A difficulty exists in developing programs in an individual library or on a network library basis because of the present fragmentation of the effort to provide the required resources and services. A variation also exists in types of programs that are capable of being implemented by individual libraries or by networks of libraries. For a program to be effective, planners of the library services and resources available to the deaf and hearing impaired, at first inception, should consider the following:

1. What are the effects of deafness and other hearing impairments on the individuals? Considering the wide range of differences among these individuals, how can a program of library service be effectively designed? To develop a program designed with and for the deaf community, an overview is needed of the relationship of deafness to reading as well as a knowledge of the efforts which have been made to bring together the library, the hearing, and the nonhearing population into a viable program.
2. A review of the services available to support library programs for the deaf and hearing impaired on all levels of reading and services is the foundation upon which the service is developed. Although a basic library for the entire population living in the

library service area is the beginning of the program, the assessment of other supplemental services available or potentially available in the community ensures that the resulting design will truly meet the needed service. The integration of support services related to this special population is an integral part of the entire consideration of the program.

3. An assessment of resources available is required to ensure an immediate impact on the service and to maintain its continuing effectiveness. Again, the availability of resources needed by the general population is the foundation for the program. The special resources and materials, personnel, and equipment determined as necessary by the library and the people served requires special and continuing study.

4. A program of service to the deaf and hearing impaired naturally looks to the future, but the dynamics are such that the promise of today may be radically changed by the realities of tomorrow. It is a growing, ever-changing service which must, to maintain effectiveness, be monitored by the library and the recipients of the service.

Collectively, these 4 elements should be regarded as providing assistance in planning, implementing, and maintaining a library program. While the experiences of others in the development of such programs can be of value, they must be examined carefully before they are utilized in the development of service for a specific community. While some elements of a program remain constant, others bear little resemblance to each other when a service is finally in place. Even the date on which a program is originally established has a distinct effect on the elements of that service and their applicability elsewhere. At the same time, the sharing of experiences among the providers of the service by the beneficiaries can be of untold value.

Of course, a program of service to the deaf and hearing impaired will never be perfect and will be subject to many and various pressures. Constant evaluation is an element of any library program. Flexibility of action in thought and deed is a must in the program throughout its entire life. An effective clearinghouse of ideas, results, successes, and failures would be of the greatest benefit to all of these programs. Such a resource would be an asset to prevent the recurrence of mistakes, to capitalize on successes, and to evaluate a program.

The following pages provide a general mapping-out of how a library program for the deaf and hearing impaired can be established and continued with the promise of success in its philosophy, goals, and

ultimate objectives. Specifics are minimized and flexibility is emphasized because we work in an ever-changing library world. With library
service in this specific area being especially susceptible to the vagaries
of change, what is effective one year is often outmoded the next.

This text is not intended for a specific type of library or a specific
type of community. The library may be a large metropolitan library,
a small community library, or a library within the educational system;
it may have a general clientele or a special clientele. This book attempts
to deal with the elements that will help ensure that people who are deaf
or have any hearing impairment will be able to participate fully in library service at any point in life and in any geographical location.

Finally, because it is recognized that no one text can include all
aspects of library service programs, references are made to other existing sources of information. Emphasis is also placed on being especially
attuned to the future developments in libraries, in deafness itself, and
in other hearing impairments. Librarians along with the people served,
must constantly scan the field for new, innovative, and effective ways
of providing library service to deaf and hearing impaired persons.

Part I: Overview and Historical Context

Chapter 1
From Awareness to Action

Library service to the deaf and hearing impaired was brought before the general public as the result of a rush of awareness on the part of libraries in the 1970s—awareness that they could possibly provide and maintain high-quality service to this special population. This awareness is comparatively new, but it has rapidly progressed to an understanding of the situation, followed by action.

HISTORY OF LIBRARY SERVICE TO THE DEAF AND HEARING IMPAIRED

Libraries have existed in schools for the deaf for many years, although they varied in the availability and quality of service, resources, and adequacy of staffing. Examples of these libraries are the school for the deaf in St. Augustine, Florida and the California State Schools for the Deaf in Fremont and Riverside. The resources and services in school libraries for the deaf are, primarily, designed to meet the program needs of the students.

Where such a need was recognized, programs were sometimes made available in public libraries. One such program was developed at the Lansing, Illinois Public Library where a teacher of the deaf brought her class of children to the public library for story hour. However, this was an isolated instance. On the whole, little awareness of the need for general library service to the deaf and hearing impaired existed until the early 1970s.

GALLAUDET SEMINARS

Awareness of this need began on a nationwide basis when, in 1974, Gallaudet College in Washington, DC held seminars on library service to the deaf. It was appropriate that Gallaudet College should have held these seminars because of its position as the only accredited liberal arts college for deaf students in the world. The college invited participants to attend the seminars; those attending for each state included a representative from the state library, a representative from the state library association, and a member of the deaf community in the state. Through the seminars, a plan was developed for each participating state by the representatives from that state for the establishment and/or improvement of library service to the deaf and hearing impaired.

The attending librarians either became acquainted with deaf persons for the first time or they had their acquaintance and understanding reinforced. They learned about the many aspects of deafness and the materials needed to serve the deaf; they had the opportunity to examine resources and to use equipment designed to serve people who are deaf. When they left the seminars, they were ready to pass on this information to other people.

As a result, library service to the deaf and hearing impaired developed rapidly in the remaining years of the 1970s. One immediate result was publication of brochures describing library service to the deaf and hearing impaired. For example, the Virginia State Library produced such a brochure which was then used as a model by many other libraries. The Ohio State Library, in its *News from the State Library: Ohio Libraries Reach Out to the Handicapped*, carried a story about the seminars written by Eunice Lovejoy, a participant from Ohio.[1] This information acquainted many libraries with the activities of the Gallaudet seminars and described what libraries can do to provide service to people who are deaf or who have any type of hearing impairment. Hawaii was in the unique position of having the opportunity, because of its organizational structure, to carry out plans for the library service in many types of libraries and to many types of patrons. The library system in Hawaii also had a total media program which was of assistance in developing a program of library service, since it followed through on the ideas presented at the seminars and those that were presented by the deaf community in Hawaii.

In 1974, the California State Library, the deaf community, and the California Library Association collaborated on the first of 5 yearly programs at the California Library Association Conference in San Diego. The program was designed to raise the awareness of those attending the conference as far as library service to the deaf and hearing impaired was concerned. The program was videotaped so that it would be available nationally to anyone interested in this program of service. An offshoot of that meeting was the development of a proposal by the

Metropolitan Cooperative Library System, in the Los Angeles area, for library service to the deaf and hearing impaired. The program was initially federally funded through the Library Services and Construction Act (LSCA). The library system worked closely with the Greater Los Angeles Council on Deafness, Inc. (GLAD), and gained nationwide recognition and influence during the life of the project.

Also resulting from all of the activity in California was the formation of a chapter on Library Service to the Deaf and Hearing Impaired in that state's Association. The Florida Library Association formed a deaf caucus as the library service to the deaf and hearing impaired action began and the awareness spread. At the 1974 American Library Association conference in New York City, 2 significant events took place following the Gallaudet College Seminars. One of them was a social gathering of seminar attendees and other interested people that, for the first time, brought deaf and hearing impaired and other seminar attendees together to interact. The second important event was the passage of a resolution by the ALA Council at the conference that would provide interpreters for the deaf for both midwinter and annual ALA meetings. All of this activity created a favorable environment for the development of a section within the Association of Specialized and Cooperative Library Agencies (ASCLA), a Division of the American Library Association. This new section was to be called the Library Service to the Deaf Section (LSDS). Alice Hagemeyer, librarian for the deaf, District of Columbia Public Library, was elected the first chairperson for the section.

This section provided the first national, permanent vehicle for the development of library service to the deaf and hearing impaired in all types of libraries. One of the section's purposes is to foster deaf awareness both in the library community and in the deaf and the hearing populations at large. Another purpose is to work on legislation which relates specifically to library and information service for deaf persons in libraries. The section is also concerned with promoting the employment of deaf persons in libraries and in providing career opportunities to them. LSDS works to provide materials in formats readily accessible to deaf persons as well as to assist libraries in programing and in collection development. Finally, the section is concerned with programs of library service to the hard of hearing.

The awareness of need stimulated by the Gallaudet seminars and the gaining of knowledge about deafness and about persons who are deaf was the beginning of a dramatic action program throughout the United States. The Library Service to the Deaf Section in ASCLA epitomized that movement as a new strong, energetic force in future developments. Internationally, the Section on Library Services to Hospital Patients and Handicapped Readers is developing a working group on library service to the deaf. This section is a part of the International Federation of Library Associations and Institutions.

STATE INVOLVEMENT

Within the states, the program of library service to the deaf and hearing impaired developed rapidly, with fast responses coming from individual libraries.

A strong impetus to this development was the availability of federal funding through the Library Services and Construction Act. Because the programs of library service to the deaf and hearing impaired were, for the most part, inadequate, new, and/or innovative, they were eligible for funding. As knowledge and awareness grew among libraries, their grant proposals became better developed and reflected the philosophy, goals, and objectives of the best in library service.

GROWTH IN SCHOOLS

Libraries in schools for the deaf were experiencing many changes as well. Through Title IV B, Library Services and Construction Act funds had been made available to schools for the deaf since 1966. These funds provided the impetus to libraries in schools for the deaf in many states, resulting in program expansion. Media resources developed along with an improved book collection and staffing. Story telling programs, databanks, captioned films, resource sharing, and the use of new technologies have all become a part of libraries in schools for the deaf.

Another change, occurring in 1964, was the establishment of the Registry of Interpreters for the Deaf (RID). The goal of RID is to promote recruitment and training for interpreters. In July 1965, a set of guidelines and a code of ethics were established for all interpreters. In 1979, a revised code of ethics was developed. The basis of the code consists of 3 elements: confidentiality, impartiality, and professional demeanor. The establishment of interpreting as a profession has been of inestimable value in the development of library programs and in communication.

Through legislation in the 1970s, the climate became more favorable for people with a hearing loss. Section 504 of the Rehabilitation

Act of 1973, which was amended in 1974 and again in 1978, states that no otherwise qualified handicapped person should, solely by reason of a handicap, be denied benefits or suffer from discrimination under any programs or activities that receive federal funds. The implementation of this act was a catalyst in the development of library programs for people who are handicapped by a loss of hearing.

A second law, which favorably affected library service, was Public Law 94-142, the Education for All Handicapped Children Act, enacted in 1975. This law ensures that disabled children have the right to the same education as all children have. As children with the handicap of a hearing loss became a part of the mainstream as a result of P.L. 94-142, libraries again began to meet the challenge of providing the needed resources and services to meet the needs of children who are deaf.

Such action did not come easily, however. Although the need for the service had finally been recognized, still no service existed outside of the schools for the deaf. This lack of service illustrates that the awareness and understanding which occurred was just the first step in the process of obtaining action. Remarkably, however, the 1970s proved to be a decade of progress in deaf services, providing some stability in action and a foundation on which to build. This library service thus became not the result of chance but the product of choice—choice supported by determination, hard work, and an ever-increasing knowledge and understanding. It was not a service for which the world could continue to wait but one which had need of reaching fruition as soon as possible.

NOTE

1. Eunice Lovejoy, "Ohio Libraries Reach out to the Handicapped," *News from the State Library of Ohio* (153) (September 9, 1974).

REFERENCE LIST

Akron-Summit County Library. *Awareness Day: The Hearing Impaired and Deaf Adult*. Akron, OH: Akron-Summit County Library, 1975.

American Instructors of the Deaf. *Standards for Library Media Centers in Schools for the Deaf: A Handbook for the Development of Library Media Programs*. Washington, DC: U.S. Department of Health, Education and Welfare and Captioned Films for the Deaf, 1967.

California State Library. *California State Library Statistics*. Sacramento, CA: California State Library, 1982.

Dalton, Phyllis I. *Library Service to Florida State Institutions: A Long Range Plan*. (For the Florida Library Association, Tallahassee, FL.) Sacramento, CA: Phyllis I. Dalton, 1975.

————. *Library Service to the Hearing Impaired*. (For the California Library Association Conference, San Diego, CA.) Sacramento, CA: California Library Association, 1974. (Cassettes.)

————. "Library Service to the Hearing Impaired, Gallaudet College Workshop." *AHIL Quarterly* IV 3–4 (Summer–Fall, 1979): 17–18.

————. *Library Services and Construction Act: An Evaluation*. Honolulu, HI: Hawaii State Department of Education, 1975.

Hagemeyer, Alice. *Deaf Awareness for Public Libraries*. Washington, DC: District of Columbia Public Library, 1976.

"Hearing Impaired Classes at Loussac Library, Anchorage, Alaska." *Sourdough* 12 (5) (August 1975): 11.

Holcomb, Marjoriebell S. *Interpreting Services Handbook for Deaf Consumers*. Fremont, CA: Regional Interpreters Training Center, Ohlone College, 1981.

Jensen, J. C. "The House of Many Books." *Illinois Libraries* 55 (1) (January 1973): 37–38.

Kantor, David. *A Survey of Libraries and Library Services in State Institutions of Florida*. Tallahassee, FL: Florida State Library, 1967.

Lovejoy, Eunice. "The Ripple Effect: Library Service to Deaf and Hard of Hearing People in Ohio." *O L A Bulletin* 52 (3) (October 1982): 29–34.

Public Administration Service. *Library Services in California State Institutions*. Chicago: Public Administration Service, 1967.

Register of Interpreters for the Deaf, Inc. *Code of Ethics*. Silver Spring, MD: Register of Interpreters for the Deaf, Inc., 1979.

Sangster, Collette. "Library Service and the Hearing Impaired." *The Bookmark* 35 (2) (Winter 1979): 59–63.

Smith, Laura. *After Three Years: A Further Survey of the Library and Library Services in State Institutions of Florida*. Tallahassee, FL: Department of State, Division of Libraries, 1979.

Chapter 2
Advocacy and Library Service to the Deaf and Hearing Impaired

Involvement of the community has been a moving force in libraries' achieving progress in serving the deaf and hearing impaired population. It is essential that deaf, hard- of-hearing, and hearing impaired individuals and their families and friends begin or continue to have an impact on library service. To achieve this goal, a strategy is needed for impacting the library, the total community, governing bodies, and lawmakers at all levels of government. An advocacy program is vital to the gaining of this power base. Four ingredients are basic to this program of advocacy:

1. Awareness. Many people are not yet aware that a unique service, different from a traditional library service to a hearing population, is required; many do not realize the extent of the problem of obtaining library service that this part of the population faces. A true perception of the numbers of those who are not natural users of any library does not exist. Thus, *awareness* is a high priority in an advocacy program.
2. Knowledge. Information about deafness, hard-of-hearing problems, the difficulties of the hearing impaired elderly and of those who are beginning to acknowledge a hearing loss, is not widely disseminated. Books, magazines, films, and other media discussing this subject or providing background information are not readily available to all people who need to be informed. *Knowledge* is a part of awareness.
3. Understanding. *Understanding* follows naturally after people achieve an awareness of the problem, recognize possible solutions, and gain information concerning the negative impact on people in their inability to utilize a communication center—the

library. Understanding includes the realization that many of the resources and services in a library are not usable by people who have a hearing problem, a low reading level, and a communication mode which is non-English or is otherwise not compatible with that of the hearing world of the library.
4. Action. The ultimate goal of the 4-pronged advocacy program is the setting up of a relevant library service which is used profitably by the potential clientele—a service designed to meet the needs and desires of the consumer. It is a service that becomes a natural part of the daily lives of people who are deaf or hearing impaired and of their families and friends. *Action* represents the achievement of the goal of advocacy programs.

DEAF AND HEARING IMPAIRED PEOPLE AS ADVOCATES

The efforts of those involved in providing library service for deaf and hearing impaired people can make the difference in an advocacy program when they direct their energies toward that goal. Leaders in the organizations of the deaf and hard of hearing, along with concerned hearing people, can ensure that information relating to the kind of service needed is communicated to librarians, support staff, and library trustees. They can discuss the issues with those responsible for libraries and explore with them the problem areas. Possible solutions for deaf people's needs—both societal and technical—can be highlighted. By understanding and considering the present difficulties and frustrations of those who will use the service, a recommended library program can result.

Because libraries are an integral part of the community they serve—the public, the students, faculty, parents, and special clientele—support from that community is a vital impetus for moving the program from recommendation to actuality. A community, through advocacy, begins to understand the isolation of the deaf and hearing impaired and the part a library can play in alleviating the severity of that isolation. Because of the invisibility of a hearing loss, people in the community, as a whole, do not realize the severity of the communication barrier which results when, through that loss, many people are unable to participate fully in the society in which they live. Advocacy in the community includes the involvement of the people in the solution. Family, friends, and social, religious, civic, and other groups can provide back-up support to those who have a hearing loss.

Questions about the attitudes of the public, of the services needed, of the present isolation, and the need for independent living have prompted many concerned people to join with the deaf and hearing impaired. Rehabilitation personnel, architects, librarians, doctors, psychologists, research groups, and members of the media, among others, give special attention to the needs and desires of people who have a hearing loss.

Although the deaf, the hard of hearing, and others with a hearing loss differ in attitudes, backgrounds, tastes, lifestyles, opinions, and concepts, just as any other members of a community, they have a common concern—that of breaking down the communication barrier. They are first and most importantly individuals in the community; they have made progress through becoming assertive and insistent. However, more remains to be done through advocacy of groups in the community in support of library service for people who have any degree of hearing loss.

LEGISLATION AND LIBRARY SERVICE FOR THE DEAF AND HEARING IMPAIRED

Along with the movement toward growing awareness in the community and of the library profession is the need for awareness among governing bodies at all levels of administration. Because a library is a part of a larger organization, it is necessary that those who have a responsibility in government realize that the library plays an important part in ensuring that deaf and hearing impaired persons enter into the mainstream of life on a permanent basis.

Gaining support from public officials may result from securing support from the community. Public officials differ, however, from the general public they serve in that they have a responsibility to the electorate. The advocacy by deaf and hearing impaired persons and their hearing companions is needed to enable libraries to set up new services and have them funded. Because members of governing bodies have heavy pressures from many groups, they may overlook the library needs of the deaf and hearing impaired people unless they are made aware of what is now being provided by libraries and what is still needed and possible. Emphasis should be placed on the potential benefits of such service to the community in terms of rehabilitation, personal growth, increased employment opportunities, and constructive use of leisure time that can result. It should be pointed out that the community in general will gain because of the increased self-reliance of the deaf and hearing impaired and the resulting well-informed public.

This kind of advocacy is required to establish new library programs and to maintain those presently in existence. Myths and misconceptions still exist concerning deafness itself and the abilities and capabilities of people who are deaf or hearing impaired. These can be dispelled by making public officials knowledgeable about hearing loss. Such knowledge will also ensure that public officials will not make assumptions concerning the information needs of the deaf and hearing impaired. Support for library services should come from *informed* public officials. They should know that people with a hearing loss must have communication barriers removed to allow access to the library and to allow them to live in a world of knowledge, communication, and ideas.

Because no one person or group of persons can reach this goal alone, it is important that a cooperative approach is undertaken to ensure that public officials—governing bodies— are supportive of and active in providing library services to the deaf and hearing impaired.

Advocacy in the area of lawmaking is a natural outgrowth of this kind of advocacy. It is through the informing and supporting of the cause of the deaf and hearing impaired that much of the improved societal climate for persons with hearing losses has come. This is especially true of advocacy on the national level. Services in all types of libraries are influenced by lawmakers' attitudes and actions at all levels of government. Advocacy is concerned with improving the quality of life—in this instance, through library service. Whereas politics and government may appear complicated, the communication of a deep concern of an individual or a group to a lawmaker is a simple and direct process. It is made easier because those engaged in developing and enacting legislation encourage the imparting of views, information, ideas, and concrete suggestions in meeting the needs of the electorate.

Advocacy in the area of lawmaking is a continuing process. Once a law is passed, it must be implemented. If it is a good law with effective regulations, it must be maintained; if not, it must be amended or repealed. Also, effective legislation requires updating and strengthening through additional action. With leadership from the community of the deaf and hearing impaired and the concerned hearing community, effective legislation at all levels of government can be enacted. The library, as part of the community, is affected by the legislation and is a part of the political process. The coalition of the deaf and hearing impaired and other advocates, including the library, can build up strong political power for achieving the kind of information, knowledge, recreation, and interaction that effective library service can provide. The power structure in the community is an important factor in gaining the kinds of legislation needed by the library and the deaf and hard of hearing communities. No one of the groups can be as successful alone as can a mutual effort to secure the support needed on the local, state, or national level. Informed advocacy provides a key to the attainment of library service to the deaf and hearing impaired.

REFERENCE LIST

Bowe, Frank. *Rehabilitating America*. New York: Harper and Row, 1980.

Dalton, Phyllis I. "The Library in the Political Process." In *Local Public Library Administration*, edited by Ellen Altman, pp. 29–37. Chicago: American Library Association, 1980.

Du Bow, Sy. "Communicating with Your Legislators." *The Deaf American* 34 (3) (1981): 34–35.

Hagemeyer, Alice. "Deaf Awareness at the Library." In *Communicating with Hearing People: The Red Notebook*, by the National Association of the Deaf. Siver Spring, MD: 1980. (Loose-leaf.)

Harris, T. L., and Updegraff, D. R. *Understanding the Political Process*. Washington, DC: Gallaudet College, 1981.

Harvey, Michael. "The Psychological Effects of Frustration on Advocates." *The Deaf American* 34 (5) (1982): 14–15.

Josey, E. J. *Libraries in the Political Process*. Phoenix, AZ: Oryx Press, 1980.

Nickelsberg, Barry. "Section 501 and Deaf Self-Advocacy." *The Deaf American* 34 (4) (December 1980): 16–17.

Norley, Delores B. "The Care and Feeding of Legislators." *The Deaf American* 35 (2) (1982): 9–11.

Social Issues and Attitudes. Los Angeles: California Conference on Handicapped Individuals, 1976.

White House Conference on Aging. *Report on Elderly Hearing Impaired People*. Bethesda, MD: Self Help for Hard of Hearing People, Inc. (SHHH), 1981.

Witt, Jill, and Ogden, Paul W.. "Politics and Deaf People." *The Deaf American* 33 (10) (June 1981): 5–8.

———. "Politics and Deaf People." *The Deaf American* 33 (11) (July–August 1981): 3–8.

Chapter 3
Legislative Influence on Programs of Service

Through legislative programs at all levels of government, the attitudes of society toward all disabilities have improved during the last 15 years. This improvement has had a positive effect on the lives of people who are deaf or who have any hearing loss. Legislation has had a positive effect on libraries as well, with the combined benefit resulting in the provision of library service to the deaf and hearing impaired.

Change has come as the result of advocacy—sometimes by a special interest group and sometimes by a combination of many such groups joined in a common cause. It has come from many years of planning and even more years of advocacy and constant monitoring of both the legislation and implementing of regulations, along with amendments to the original legislation.

FEDERAL LEGISLATION

A law that brought many library benefits to the deaf is the Library Services and Construction Act (LSCA), (P.L. 88-269, as amended), which grew out of the Library Services Act of 1956 (P.L. 84-597) and was passed in 1964. The 1966 amendments (P.L. 89-511) added a priority for services to the physically handicapped under Title IV B. In 1970, amendments under P.L. 91-600 consolidated Title IV B with Title I, Library Services, creating the law in its present form. Under Title IV B, resident schools for the deaf began to apply for grants to improve their library services. When Title IV B was consolidated with Title I, public libraries presented grant proposals for library service to the physically disabled. Among the grants applied for and received were those that assisted libraries in beginning or improving library service to the deaf and hearing impaired.

The purpose, in part, of LSCA is to assist the states and territories in the extension and improvement of public library services in areas which are without such services or in which such services are inadequate. To be eligible for an annual allotment, a state or a territory must submit a program for the use of the funds. The funds are administered by the legally authorized state library administrative agency.

A review of the programs for the deaf and hearing impaired in public libraries shows that, in almost all programs, some federal funding was utilized. Reports on the funding of library services to the handicapped under LSCA indicate that funds have been granted on a continuing basis to institutions for the deaf and to public library programs for people who are deaf or hearing impaired. LSCA is indispensable legislation in the development and extension of library service to the deaf and hearing impaired. These funds have challenged creativity in the library community and ensured the continuation of progress in the development of these services. Because the programs developed were designed to be continued with local tax support when the funds were no longer available, grant proposals were realistically as well as creatively oriented.

During the same period, other legislative programs were being enacted which had an effect on the deaf and hearing impaired and the library services available to them. The Architectural Barriers Act of 1968 (P.L. 90-480) was one of these. The thrust of this law is that any building constructed in whole or in part with federal monies must be accessible and usable to the handicapped.

The passage of the Architectural Barriers Act of 1968 marked the first concrete federal legislation affirming handicapped Americans' right of access to and use of public buildings and facilities. This law was followed by the Rehabilitation Act of 1973 (P.L. 93-112), finally implemented in 1977. Title V of this act has been described as a "Bill of Rights" for disabled citizens. Its purpose is to ensure that no handicapped person who is otherwise qualified shall be excluded from any program or activity, solely because of a handicap. This law applies to programs and activities that receive federal financial assistance.

Although other sections of Title V of the Rehabilitation Act of 1973, as amended, are vital in the lives of disabled persons, Section 504 is of particular interest to libraries and to people with hearing disabilities, who are positively affected by this legislation because they are included in the act. As a result of Section 504, libraries receiving federal financial assistance are obligated to take steps to ensure that handicapped people are included as participants in and are the beneficiaries of programs, resources, and services offered by libraries. The passage of Section 504 of the Rehabilitation Act of 1973, the amendments of 1974 (P.L. 93-516), and the amendments of 1978 (P.L. 95-602) all mandate equal rights for disabled people. In effect, the Rehabilitation Act of 1973 was the first major civil rights law for handicapped individuals, addressing employment, accessibility, education, transportation, and a variety of other subjects which directly or indirectly affect libraries.

More specifically, standards were needed for making buildings accessible to persons with physical disabilities. The Easter Seal Society, together with the President's Committee on Employment of the Handicapped, played a major role in setting the first design standards for accessibility approved by the American National Standards Institute (ANSI) in 1961 (ANSI A 117.1) and reaffirmed in 1971. In 1980, a new standard (ANSI A 117.1 [1980]) was developed by ANSI and announced by the ANSI Secretariat, composed of the National Easter Seal Society, The President's Committee on Employment of the Handicapped, and the U.S. Department of Housing and Urban Development (HUD). The standards play a major role toward achieving a barrier-free environment.

Another step forward occurred when Congress, in order to enforce the Architectural Barriers Act of 1968, created the federal Architectural and Transportation Barriers Compliance Board authorized by Section 502 of the Rehabilitation Act of 1973. The board began operating in March 1975.

Enacted by Congress soon after the Rehabilitation Act of 1973 was the Education for All Handicapped Children Act (P.L. 94-142) in 1975. Appropriate education in the least physically restrictive environment was guaranteed to every child in America by this act. The law was a landmark in that it acknowledged federal responsibility for the education of handicapped children. The mandates of P.L. 94-142 were of interest and concern to libraries and to media centers then and now. One of the aspects of the act was of special interest to librarians—that of the Individualized Educational Program (IEP). Mainstreaming brought together not only deaf and hearing children, but also brought together library and media center resources of all types in order to serve all children in their educational programs. Because cooperation is a vital key in the individualized program, libraries and media centers must work together.

Deaf and hearing impaired students are a part of the student body who are served by the library and especially by the media resources. Their inclusion in the mainstream of education has had an effect on the types of materials provided in the educational program. As a result, one type provided by the library is high interest-low vocabulary reading materials. The media center provides captioned films. Interpreters are used for effective communication.

Legislation affecting library service to the deaf and hearing impaired has been enacted on the state, as well as federal, level. For example, under a law passed in California in 1979, a new section (2831) was added to the Public Utilities Code that mandates that the California Public Utilities Commission design and implement a program in which each telephone company would provide a telecommunication device, with a single party line, for the deaf or severely hearing impaired individuals. This service was phased in over a 4-year period and is provided at no additional cost to the certified subscriber. Such a system emphasizes the need for telecommunication devices in the library as well.

WHITE HOUSE CONFERENCE

Interest in mainstreaming the deaf or hearing impaired into society was further heightened by 3 White House conferences. The first was the White House Conference on Handicapped Individuals, held in May 1977. The conference was authorized by P.L. 93-516 with 3 purposes in mind.

- To provide a national assessment.
- To generate a national awareness.
- To make recommendations to the President and Congress.

The topics considered at the conference were health concerns, social concerns, educational concerns, and special concerns including service delivery systems. Librarians were among the state, regional, and national delegates who participated in overall conference planning and implementation. There is tangible evidence that the White House Conference on Handicapped Individuals has had a positive effect on the awareness, understanding, and action in providing library service to this special population.

In 1979, the first White House Conference on Library and Information Services was held. It was authorized by P.L. 93-568. Among the issues addressed were access and special constituencies. "Access" refers not only to access to library and information services programs, facilities, and materials but also access to library positions and boards. Deaf and hearing impaired persons are included in the "special constituencies" designation.

Some of the goals and objectives discussed at the conference which especially affect the deaf and hearing impaired were:

- A national information policy, which would guarantee equal
  and free access to publicly funded library and information services.
- A national policy for free access without charge or fee to the
  individual to information in public and publicly supported libraries.
- Access to library and information services by special populations, which include the people in the population who have a
  hearing loss.
- Public awareness to ensure that special constituencies—nonusers, those who are underserved, or those who are
  not aware of the services available to them—be served adequately.
- Special constituencies awareness that will ensure library service
  to the deaf and hearing impaired.

A specific concern relates to the information needs of the deaf and
hearing impaired. Included in the resolution supporting this issue were:

- Training of personnel in library service to the deaf and hearing
  impaired.
- Establishment of a State Library Committee for the Deaf under
  the auspices of the State Library Commission or its counterpart
  in each state, with each committee including deaf individuals.
- Establishment of a clearinghouse to act as an information and
  referral service in the state, with its purpose to be in assisting
  libraries and the general public on information needs related to
  deafness and interlibrary loan services for the deaf.
- Enactment of a National Library Service for the deaf under the
  auspices of the Library of Congress, to be planned and developed by a board of deaf professionals, deaf consumers, library
  personnel, and laypeople.

Specifically, access to library programs and facilities is to be ensured through implementation of Section 504 of the Rehabilitation Act
of 1973. Program accessibility is to be encouraged through use of videotapes and captioned films. Special communication devices are to be provided wherever possible. The Library of Congress and publishers are
encouraged to provide materials suitable to the needs of persons with
learning disabilities. Technology for information storage and retrieval
is recommended, which would eliminate inequities caused by resources
that are inadequate or inaccessible because of geographical or architectural barriers.

Librarians, library-related people, and the general public participated in this conference through local, state, regional, and national meetings. The results of the conference were positive; the conference raised the awareness of people concerning library needs of the deaf and hearing impaired. Implementation of the conference resolutions is an ongoing process with completion the ultimate goal.

The third White House Conference relating to deaf and hearing impaired individuals was the White Conference on Aging, 1981. This conference evolved out of the 1981 White House Conference on Aging Act. Issues discussed at the conference included: "Economic Security," "Physical and Mental Health," "Social Well Being," "Older Americans as a Growing National Resource," "Creating an Age-Integrated Society within Societal Institutions," and "Research." A number of recommendations generated from these issues have an impact on hearing impaired and deaf elderly individuals.

A related conference was that convened by Shhh, Inc., "White House Conference on Aging, Mini-Conference on Elderly Hearing Impaired People." The issues of this mini-conference included: "Research Areas," "Hearing Health Care Services," "Environment," and "Social Access." Libraries are directly included in the recommendation relating to "Public Awareness, Information, and Education" and indirectly included in many of the other recommendations. While the gains made for deaf and hearing impaired individuals in the White House Conference on Aging were not that substantial, the conference did focus attention on many of the needs of the aging, including those aged individuals who are also deaf or hearing impaired.

Taking place concurrently with this last of the 3 White House Conferences was the declaration by the United Nations that made 1981 the International Year of Disabled Persons (IYDP). The year was designated to focus attention on the living conditions and needs of disabled persons. The American Library Association expressed a direct interest in this declaration and expressed its concern that libraries demonstrate their commitment to meeting the library needs of the disabled population.

The central theme of IYDP was full participation and equality for all. Its 5 main objectives were:

- To help disabled persons to adjust to society.
- To promote efforts to provide disabled people with proper assistance, care, and guidance as well as opportunities for work.
- To encourage study and research projects designed to facilitate the practical participation of disabled people in daily life.

- To educate and inform the public on the rights of disabled persons.

The slogan for the year was "Meeting the Challenges through Partnerships."

The American Library Association Council issued a resolution in support of IYDP. The Association of Specialized and Cooperative Library Agencies (ASCLA) spearheaded the observance of the year through the appointment of a committee made up of ASCLA members. Each section, including the Library Service to the Deaf Section, was represented, as well as each division in the association itself. The purpose of the committee was to raise the awareness of libraries and librarians in making services and resources accessible and usable by persons who are disabled.

Elizabeth Stone, president of the American Library Association, set forth a 4-point program to be accomplished during IYDP:

- Cooperation with other national and international organizations participating in the celebration.
- Increased availability of information about technical advances for the handicapped.
- Availability of advance braille copies for the blind of major ALA agendas and papers for Midwinter and Annual Conferences.
- Sponsorship of a symposium concerned with the curriculum in library schools in order to prepare new professionals to serve the disabled better.

All 4 objectives were accomplished in some degree during IYDP.

Through the work at the national level and the community partnerships formed at the local, state, and regional levels, libraries and deaf and hearing impaired people participated actively in the celebration of IYDP. New library programs were begun to serve deaf and hearing impaired persons or were expanded or actively maintained during IYDP.

Because so much had been initiated toward full and equal participation in society by disabled persons but had not been completed by the end of IYDP, 1982 was declared the National Year of Disabled Persons (NYDP). The designating resolution was passed by Congress, and the declaration of the year was made by President Ronald Reagan. The slogan for NYDP was "Continuing the Momentum." To carry out the objectives of IYDP, the IYDP Committee of ASCLA became the NYDP Committee and actively continued its work with libraries and with persons who are disabled. The privately funded National Organization on Disability coordinated the national, state, and community activities. During NYDP, activities were geared toward securing a declaration by the United Nations for the designation of 1983–92 as the Decade of Disabled Persons. On December 3, 1982, the General Assembly of the United Nations proclaimed the period of 1983–92 as the Decade of Disabled Persons. On January 12, 1983, the Council of the American Library Association passed a resolution supporting the Decade of Disabled Persons. The United States Congress, on July 25, 1983, passed a concurrent resolution that resolved that the President of the United States should take all possible steps to implement, in the United States, the objectives of the decade and should report to Congress annually on the progress made. "The National Decade of Disabled Persons: A Proclamation" was issued by President Reagan on November 28, 1983. The ALA council passed a supporting resolution on June 26, 1984.

The international aspect of IYDP was emphasized by libraries throughout the 47th Annual Conference of the International Federation of Library Associations and Institutions (IFLA), held in Leipzig, East Germany. In her opening address, IFLA President Else Granheim highlighted IYDP; Jes Petersen, library advisor, State Inspection of Public Libraries, Copenhagen, Denmark addressed "Libraries and the International Year of the Disabled." The thrust of his remarks was that one of the most important goals for IYDP was to work together toward equal access to the social and cultural life and activities of the community; that one of the most important responsibilities of libraries is to remove the barriers which deny people who are disabled access to their services and resources.

The legislative influence at all levels of government, from city and county to national and international, has had a profound effect on the development of programs of services and resources of libraries for the deaf and hearing impaired. Legislative action has ranged from the passing of resolutions providing inspiration and impetus to assist this population in participating fully in all aspects of society to the acquiring of civil rights, educational opportunity, and funding. The legislative bodies helped to establish an environment in which the programs of library service to the deaf and hearing impaired could develop and flourish.

REFERENCE LIST

Association of Specialized and Cooperative Library Agencies. *Celebrating the International Year of Disabled Persons.* (American Library Association Annual Conference in San Francisco, 1981.) Chicago: American Library Association. (Cassettes.)

Becker, Marjory. "Handicapped Notebook." *Las Vegas Sun* (April 5, 1982): 4.

"California Implements State Law Providing Telecommunication Devices for the Deaf." *Shhh* 2 (5) (November–December 1981): 14.

Calovini, Gloria. "Implications of Public Law 94-142." *Illinois Libraries* 59 (7) (September 1977): 468–69.

"Conference on Aging: ALA Prepares for White House Conference on Aging." *Interface* 3 (1) (Fall 1980): 5.

Dalton, Phyllis I. *Alaska Conference on Library and Information Services: An Evaluation.* (For the Alaska State Library.) Sacramento, CA: Phyllis I. Dalton, 1979.

Estle, Margaret S., and Christensen, Cheryl R. "Teacher Centers and PL 94-142: A Unique Opportunity for Cooperation and Resource Utilization." *Illinois Libraries* 59 (7) (September 1977): 486–88.

"Federal Funds and Library Development in Illinois." *Illinois Libraries* 62 (6) (June 1980): 514–22.

"504 What's New?" *The Nevada Informer* (Summer 1980): 11.

"The 503 and 504 Legislation." *Gallaudet Alumni Newsletter* 12 (6) (Special Edition, June 15, 1978).

Gallaudet College. *Education: Parents Guide. I.E.P. Public Law 94-142.* Washington, DC: Gallaudet College, n.d. (Leaflet.)

Granheim, Else. *Opening Address.* Paper presented at the 47th Conference of the International Federation of Library Associations and Institutions. Leipzig, East Germany, 1981.

Greenberg, Joanne, and Doolittle, Glen. "Can Schools Speak the Language of the Deaf?" *New York Times Magazine* (December 11, 1977): 50–102.

Hagemeyer, Alice. "IYDP Update." *Interface* 4 (2) (Winter 1981): 11, 12.

"International Year Becomes National Year." *Gallaudet Alumni Newsletter* 16 (10) (March 15, 1982): 2.

"International Year of Disabled Persons." *Interface* 3 (3–4) (Spring–Summer 1981).

"Legislative History." In *Interpreting Services Handbook for Deaf Consumers,* prepared by Marjoriebell S. Holcomb, pp. 15–25. Fremont, CA: Regional Interpreter Training Center, Ohlone College, n.d.

Lewis, M. Joy. "IYDP or Initiatives You Did Promise: Imagination and Ingenuity Overcome the Obstacles." *Library Association Record* 84 (3) (March 1982): 105–07.

Merrill, Edward A., Jr. "International Year of Disabled Persons—A Rare Opportunity to Invest." *Gallaudet Today* 11 (3) (Spring 1981): 10–11.

National Easter Seal Society. *Design for Accessibility.* Chicago: National Easter Seal Society, n.d.

———. *How and Why the 1980 ANSI Standard for Accessibility Was Developed. Some Background Information.* Chicago: National Easter Seal Society, 1980.

National Office on Disability. *Comments Received in Response to Survey on the Prospective "Decade of Disabled Persons" and Its Potential Value to the United States.* Washington, DC: National Office on Disability, 1981.

Noaks, Phyllis, and Partington, Wylva. "IFLA and Handicapped Readers: A Summary of Relevant Papers Presented during the IFLA General Conference, Leipzig, DDR." *IFLA Journal* 8 (3) (August 1982): 291–95.

Petersen, Jes. *Libraries and the International Year of the Disabled.* Paper presented at the 47th International Federation of Library Associations and Institutions Conference, Leipzig, DDR, 1981.

Pimentel, Albert T. "The Need for a Comprehensive Network That Would Allow Organizations of the Deaf to Work Together on Legislative Matters." *The Deaf American* 35 (4) (1983): 1–6.

"PL 94-142 and Deaf Children." *Gallaudet Alumni Newsletter* 12 (16) (Special edition, June 15, 1978).

President's Committee on Employment of the Handicapped. *Guilty Buildings.* Washington, DC: President's Committee on Employment of the Handicapped, n.d.

———. *A Librarian's Guide to 504. A Pocket Guide on Section 504 of the Rehabilitation Act of 1973.* Washington, DC: President's Committee on Employment of the Handicapped, n.d.

"Public Libraries and 504." *Interface* 3 (1) (Fall 1980): 5–6.

"Sources on PL 94-142 and Section 504: A Bibliography." *HRLSD Journal* IV (1) (Spring 1978): 4–5.

U.S. Architectural and Transportation Compliance Board. *About Barriers.* Washington, DC: Architectural and Transportation Compliance Board, n.d. (Brochure.)

Volin, Larry K. "If You Get Federal Money You Must Know about 504." *HRLSD Journal* IV (1) (Spring 1978): 2–3.

The White House Conference on Aging. *A Guide to the 1981 White House Conference on Aging.* Washington, DC: White House Conference on Aging, 1981.

White House Conference on Handicapped Individuals. *Report of the California Conference on Handicapped Individuals.* Los Angeles: White House Conference on Handicapped Individuals, 1976.

The White House Conference on Library and Information Services. *Update.* Washington, DC: National Commission on Libraries and Information Science, 1979.

"White House Conference on Library and Information Services (WHCLIS)." *Newsletter. District of Columbia Public Library for the Blind and Physically Handicapped* 8 (1) (Spring 1980): 2.

Chapter 4
Two-Way Communication

Libraries, as providers of information, are centers of communication; as recreational centers, their services involve communication. Resources in libraries may be in many formats, both as information and recreational sources. Vocal interaction with those who use the library is indigenous to library service. Informing nonlibrary users about available library programs, through many types of communication, expands the horizons of the library programs. The discussions with people concerning wants and needs in library activities keep the programs current, strong, and relevant.

Within the service to children, storytelling is an important aspect. Conducting a reference interview is an integral part of ensuring that a user is receiving the requested information accurately and clearly. Group meetings for all age levels and special library programs entertain, instruct, and inform. Great Books discussion groups provide an interaction of ideas, telephone reference provides a valued service for busy or homebound people, and television programs enable people to be entertained and to be current with and live within the world of information. All of these activities enhance the value of a library in whatever community it serves. Each activity is a part of communication among and between people.

The effects of deafness or any hearing impairment on communication are most apparent on the use or nonuse of libraries and on the library itself. This situation is particularly true for the deaf user. Because libraries primarily provide an exchange of ideas, the inability to hear is a serious communication barrier. Because deaf and hearing impaired individuals constitute only a small minority within the general population, libraries have accommodated the large group— the hearing. Even though impaired hearing is the single most prevalent chronic disability in the United States, that disability still remains a serious barrier to communication in the use of libraries. The barrier is a 2-way obstacle—

people in the hearing world do not communicate with those in the non-hearing world and vice versa.

To provide library service to people who are deaf or who have any hearing loss, both the library and the public to be served are finding ways to overcome this barrier and to establish the communication basic to opening the library to this segment of the population. Because each library user or potential user is an individual, various means of communication are required. As librarians become more aware of the special library needs of people who are deaf, hard of hearing, or who have any hearing loss, they have become conscious of the present lack of effective communication methods.

COMMUNICATION MODES

Deaf and hearing impaired people have many ways of communicating with each other that hearing people need to understand before they can be comfortable communicating with them. Hearing losses can be described in several ways to explain the need for various modes of communication. One simple and effective division is as follows:

1. Persons whose hearing loss is *prelingual*. These people were deaf at birth or very early in infancy. When this degree of hearing loss occurs, the person is not only deaf but has also been deprived of the opportunity to acquire normal speech and language patterns. The problem in communication is linguistic as well as aural.
2. Persons whose hearing loss is *postlingual*. These people sustain a hearing impairment after the acquisition of normal speech and language patterns. Included in this group are those whose hearing loss is the result of injury, illness, or old age. The problem in communication here is aural rather than linguistic.

There are many different degrees of hearing loss. They range from an impairment which presents minimal difficulty in understanding speech—for example, those who must ask for conversation to be repeated—to the most severe loss which allows recognition of only very strong aural vibrations. A person who cannot hear and understand connected speech is said to be deaf. A hard-of-hearing person may understand connected speech with or without amplification. Hearing tests measure the amplitude level and the frequency range. These levels are then developed into a chart which shows the relationship at various coordinate points. By connecting these points, an *audiogram* is developed which indicates the hearing range of the individual and may also indicate the pockets of hearing. Scores (in decibels) are as follows:

- 0–20 normal
- 20–60 mild to moderate loss
- 60–90 severe loss
- 90–100 profound loss.

Many types of communication modes are presently in use. Those based on the English language are:

- Oral Method. Uses speech-reading and amplification of sounds, along with speech. Gestures and signs are not used.
- Cued Speech. Uses 8 hand configurations in 4 different locations near the mouth to clarify all of the sounds of speech.
- Finger Spelling. Uses 26 different positions of the fingers to represent the 26 letters of the alphabet. Fingerspelling is a part of the Rochester method.

The language used by the deaf, a formal language separate and distinct from English, is American Sign Language (ASL), also called Ameslan. ASL is the third most frequently used non-English language in the United States. It is a specific language system developed by deaf people to convey concept information. Another system is Manually Coded English (MCE), a system that borrows signs from ASL and puts them into English word order so that it follows English grammatical structure. Included in MCE are Signed English (SE), Seeing Essential English and Signing Exact English (SEE and SEE II), and Linguistics of Visual English (LOVE). Pidgin Sign English (PSE) uses both English and ASL. It has become a common form of signing and communicating. PSE is also know as Signed English (SIGLISH), an ASL-based system modified to English syntax and word order. AMELISH, another system, is similar to ASL but uses more finger spelling. Speech-(LIP)-Reading incorporates the sounds of words, the position of the lips, and the total facial expression and body gestures to facilitate communication. Simultaneous Communication (SC) denotes the combined use of speech, signs, and finger spelling. Total Communication (TC) combines all of the above techniques, along with reading, writing, and the media. Total Communication is a philosophical approach rather than a method in itself. The Auditory-Verbal method utilizes residual hearing and amplification; speech and listening are emphasized in this method.

Communication with persons who have lost their sight as well as their hearing changes the means of interaction. Because a deaf-blind person cannot rely on the visual sense as can the sighted person with a hearing loss, communication takes a tactile approach. Through the printing of simple block letters on the palm of the hand of the deaf-blind person, accurate information can be transmitted. The letters are printed with a pause after each letter and a longer pause at the end of a word. Faster communication can be accomplished with a deaf-blind person who knows the one-hand alphabet. The finger positions of the manual alphabet are formed within the cupped hand of the deaf-blind person. (From the brochure, *The Cuyahoga County Public Library*.)

Sign language classes offered by the library can assist in bridging the gap between the hearing and nonhearing communities. Such a program not only teaches signing for improved two-way communication but also highlights the program of library service to those with a hearing loss. Continuing instruction in sign language and the offering of both beginning and advanced signing classes will help to ensure that the skills gained are not lost through disuse. Libraries can, through a community program of signing, provide a learning opportunity for the public and the library staff with the important interaction between those who hear and those who have a hearing difficulty. In a large library system, providing such a program, not only at the headquarters library but throughout the service area, enables all to have the opportunity to attend. If the classes are open to both hearing and non-hearing people, the community and the library involvement will widen

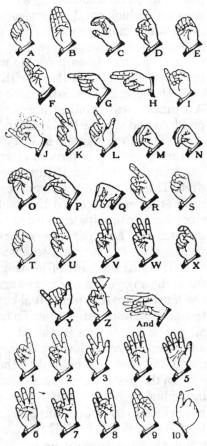

Manual Alphabet used by the Deaf

the knowledge of and the interest in the library program. A second type of class which is also of value in communication is that of lipreading. The classes are helpful for those who have a hearing loss or who need to supplement failing hearing.

ATTITUDES TOWARD LIBRARIES

Within the program, to help to ensure its success, is the important need for awareness of the use that deaf and hearing impaired people can make of a library. Training in this area is vital to the development of an effective service. To enable staff members to use communication methods, more than skill in manual, oral, or written means is required. The interaction among people who are deaf, hearing, or hearing impaired and communicating within a nonwork situation improves the ease with which the 2 groups can work together. Fluency in total communication may not result from the combination of skills and positive attitudes, but it does ensure that the library staff members can communicate comfortably with people who are deaf, the hard of hearing, the impaired elderly, and those with failing hearing.

The formation of attitudes begins early in childhood development. Attitudes toward nonhearing people can be established early in hearing children and vice versa. Concurrent with the development of children's attitudes is their interest in story telling. Libraries have the unique opportunity of both entertaining and presenting a positive approach to children through signed story hours for hearing and nonhearing children. Thus, the interaction and ease of communication will begin naturally at an early age. To the deaf and hearing impaired children, the story hours can initiate a love of reading and contribute to their interest in libraries. The experience of participating in story telling will communicate, also, the stories available for their independent reading.

To assist the hard-of-hearing person, auditory aids are often helpful in the enjoyment of records and audiocassettes. Through these aids, the hard-of-hearing individual can utilize audio materials for both entertainment and instruction. To meet additional communication needs, all public telephones in the library can be equipped with easily used amplifiers; several devices/equipment for meeting rooms to assist in communication are helpful to those who are hard of hearing.

In the past, telephone communication has presented a problem for individuals who are deaf which seemed insurmountable. Technology has helped to overcome this barrier through telecommunication devices for the deaf (TDD). TDD service enables a person who is deaf to communicate with another person using a TDD to type messages which are transmitted by telephone. When a teletypewriter is the kind of machine used to send and receive messages, it is known as a TTY. Through the installation of a TTY/TDD in the library, deaf persons can receive the same telephone service now available to hearing persons. The TTY/TDD number is then available for people who are deaf and can be listed on library publications and on its letterhead along with the voice number.

For group meetings sponsored by the library, the use of interpreters makes communication with all deaf and hearing impaired people more easily accomplished. Interpreters can make a group tour of the library a pleasure and unfold the wealth of information and the variety of services available.

Closed-captioned television programs in libraries enable people who are deaf or hearing impaired to enjoy many programs. Telecaption devices (decoders) attached to television sets that allow display of captions on the screen enable such communication. Captioned film showings in libraries provide both entertainment and education for those with a hearing loss; captions which are clear, concise, and understandable are appreciated and enjoyed.

An effective program for library service to the deaf and hearing impaired relies heavily on the visual sense; visual cues are important. Clear, understandable, and readable directional signs promote self-reliance and ease of use. Short instructional signs reduce the need for asking questions and enable the deaf and hearing impaired to function more independently. There are other ways to communicate information to this population. A regular newsletter can provide details of services and resources currently available. Audio-dogs (hearing-ear dogs), which are trained to alert their owners to specific sounds which are important can also be used as a communication link between the librarian and the deaf patron.

COMMUNICATING EFFECTIVELY

Because approximately 14 percent of the general population is to some degree affected by hearing loss, it is important that such programs be available. But it can be a challenge for a hearing person to communicate with a deaf person. While deaf people may understand each other 100 percent of the time, the information they receive in their communication with hearing persons is fragmentary. This means that the deaf person may only receive 30 to 70 percent of information communicated by a hearing person who uses speech or has just learned sign language.

Library staff members can facilitate communication with people who have a hearing loss by following these suggestions in one-to-one communication:

- Speak slowly and clearly but do not exaggerate pronunciation of words that could distort lip movement. A clear view of the mouth should always be maintained.
- Look directly at the person when you speak.
- Communicate on paper when necessary.
- Maintain eye contact with the person even when an interpreter is present.
- In case of difficulty in communicating, rephrase the sentence.
- Use mime, body language, and facial expression to assist in communication.
- When approaching a person with a hearing loss, especially a deaf-blind person, a simple touch will indicate proximity.
- Always be sure the person understands the information being communicated. This is especially important with a deaf-blind person.
- Rely on natural courtesy and common sense in all communication.

In group communication:

- Avoid standing in front of a window or other light source.
- Aid the deaf and hearing impaired persons, when applicable, with an outline, summary, script, or printout prior to a meeting.
- In a session where many new terms are being used, provide the new vocabulary in written form prior to the session.
- Make use of visual aids as much as possible. Be sure they can be clearly seen from all points in the room.
- Face the group when speaking and avoid any unnecessary moving about when talking.
- Slow down the pace of speaking and speak clearly.
- Provide typed copies of any necessary instructions or explanations for use during the session.
- Repeat questions or statements from the audience before answering or commenting.
- If interpreters are used, make sure the interpreter is positioned well, with enough space and lighting available to be understood easily.
- Depending on the format of the program, provide special seating for persons with a hearing loss so that they can see the speaker's face and read captions.

Not only is there a barrier when hearing people attempt to communicate with the deaf but also when the deaf attempt to communicate with hearing individuals. Because this is a problem of communication rather than of physical access, this population could very well be considered an ethnic minority rather than a disabled group. Levels of communication may vary among this group using the library. Some may have no knowledge of sign language but will speak or use speech-reading. Others might use ASL or be bilingual and be fluent in both English and ASL. These latter 2 groups may or may not use speech. Still others may not yet acknowledge a hearing impairment. Some may use amplification. The deaf-blind person will communicate tactually or through an interpreter. Some may have little knowledge of any language but will use personal signs. English is considered to be the first language of some but the second language of others. There are, of course, individual variations among all of these groups.

Deaf or hearing impaired persons, as individuals, will communicate differently. Their ability to communicate should not be underrated. They will use every possible way to communicate with a hearing person. Such communication is not easy and some of it involves guesswork, making accurate interaction between the 2 groups difficult. In some instances, the person may be accompanied by an interpreter, facilitating the process. This is especially true of people who are both deaf and blind.

A loose-leaf book entitled *Communicating with Hearing People: The Red Notebook*[1] was developed in 1980 by Alice Hagemeyer, librarian for the deaf, District of Columbia Public Library. It is distributed by the National Association of the Deaf. *The Red Notebook* was developed to provide a central depository of information on deafness which could be easily updated. It helps people who are deaf and their families to communicate their library needs.

When staff members who are deaf or hearing impaired are employed by the library, 2-way communication becomes a daily occurrence. Communication is more than sign and speech. It is a means of getting along with others. Hearing staff members and those who are deaf or who have a hearing loss should mutually work out the best communication mode available to them. This will ensure a continuing smooth relationship. It will ensure, also, that the 2-way communication is accurately given and received.

Learning about the deaf, deafness, the hard-of-hearing person, the hearing impaired elderly, as well as hearing in general will facilitate 2-way communication. Understanding is basic to any effective interchange. Today's technology is offering increasing opportunities to allow hearing, deaf, and hearing impaired people to participate in both a working and a social exchange. The United States has been the prime mover in this field. In addition, interpreters are being used more frequently than in the past. The success of 2-way communication relies on an outgoing attitude and an aggressiveness that cannot be daunted by frustration. The media is assisting in providing more exposure to auditory problems through television, the theater, films, and books. Although it is no easy task, striving for effective communication continues to challenge librarians. Communication is the key to good library service to the deaf and hearing impaired. It is the heart of the service—both transmission and reception. The hearing, the deaf, and hearing impaired persons need to understand and to be understood within the library setting.

NOTE

1. National Association of the Deaf. *Communicating with Hearing People: The Red Notebook.* (Silver Spring, MD: National Association of the Deaf, 1980).

REFERENCE LIST

Broberg, Rose Feilback. *Over Fifty Nifties.* Washington, DC: The Alexander Graham Bell Association for the Deaf, Inc., 1975.

"Communications." *The Deaf American* 34 (3–4) (1981).

Communications: What's It all About? Rochester, NY: National Institute for the Deaf. Rochester Institute of Technology, n.d. (Leaflet.)

Dalton, Phyllis I. "Are You Listening?" *Illinois Libraries* 57 (7) (September 1975): 473–75.

Flournoy, Mary, et al. *Signs of the Times: Library Programming for Deaf and Hearing Impaired Audiences.* (Library Service to the Deaf Section Program at the American Library Association Conference in Dallas, TX.) Chicago: American Library Association, 1984. (Cassettes.)

Froehlinger, Vira J., ed. *Today's Hearing Impaired Child: Into the Mainstream of Education.* Washington, DC: The Alexander Graham Bell Association for the Deaf, Inc., 1981.

Hagemeyer, Alice. "Deaf Awareness at the Library. In *Communicating with Hearing People: The Red Notebook,* by the National Association of the Deaf. Silver Spring, MD: National Association of the Deaf, 1980. (Loose-leaf.)

———. "Library for Deaf Action." *The NAD Broadcaster* 6 (3) (March 1984): 7.

Helen Keller National Center for Deaf-Blind Youth and Adults. *Guidelines for Helping Deaf-Blind Youth and Adults.* Sands Point, NY: Helen Keller National Center for Deaf-Blind Youth and Adults, n.d. (Leaflet.)

HELP! Libraries and the Hard of Hearing. Library Service to the Deaf Section, American Library Association Conference at Philadelphia, PA: Chicago, American Library Association, 1982. (Cassettes.)

Hopkins, Karen. *The Deaf Patron in the Library.* Speech given at the Library Service to Patients and Handicapped Readers program at the International Federation of Libraries and Institutions Conference in Montreal, Canada. 1982.

Hurwitz, T. Alan. "Use of an Interpreter: A Deaf Person's Perspective." *The Deaf American* 34 (4) (1984): 22–25.

National Information Center on Deafness. *Deafness.* Washington, DC: Gallaudet College, n.d. (Leaflet.)

Peterson, Betty. "Newborn Testing, the Young Deaf, Audiology, Hearing Aids, Aural Programs." In *Library Institute for Service to the Deaf. Report of Proceedings*, by Doris Sadoski. Fullerton, CA: California State University at Fullerton, 1978.

Stone, Howard E. "Shhh in its Origins." *Shhh* 2 (8) (November–December 1981): 6–7, 13.

"Techniques for Library Service to the Deaf and Hard of Hearing." *Interface* 4 (1) (Fall 1981): 2–3.

"Telephone Tips: Speaking Aids." *The Source Book for the Disabled.* Edited by Glorya Hale. New York: Paddington Press, 1979, pp. 27–33.

Turner, Alison. "Cued Speech as a Tool for Older Users." *Shhh* 5 (1) (January–February 1984): 5–6.

Velleman, Ruth A. "Architectural and Program Accessibility: A Review of Library Programs, Facilities and Publications for Librarians Serving Disabled Individuals." *Drexel Library Quarterly* 16 (2) (April 1980): 32–47.

Chapter 5
Philosophy, Goals, and
Objectives of the Program

The philosophy of library service to the deaf and hearing impaired is based on the philosophy of library service in general. This service is based on the concept that the library is an information agency serving a total community; that it is also, and perhaps more importantly, a place with open doors to its community where people can borrow its materials freely. A library may serve many other purposes as well, which are equally designed for the public good. The support of libraries is broad because it is based on the principle that a library serves all of its constituencies. As a result, its services will mirror its community. In realizing this goal of service to all members of the community, the library relies, in measuring its service, on quality as well as quantity. In accepting the concept that library service should benefit all members of its population, the library makes the crucial decision that it is worth the time, effort, and funding necessary to ensure service.

The philosophy of service to deaf and hearing impaired individuals builds on this general approach to library service. The goal encompasses the concept that all library services are available and usable by people who are deaf or hearing impaired. To meet this goal requires both an administrative and a staff commitment. The people who make up the deaf and hearing impaired population are diverse. They range from those who are regular library users to those nonusers to whom the library is a formidable institution. While such diversity is true of the general population, it is more pronounced in this population group. Among the users are hearing parents of deaf children, deaf individuals who have learned how to use a library, newly deaf people, the hard of hearing, and those with a minor hearing loss which they may not have acknowledged. Among the nonusers are the prelingually deaf. With this wide range of people to be served by a new but continually developing program, a desire to meet the need is not enough—a commitment is required.

OBJECTIVES OF THE SERVICE

An important objective that must be reached in order to provide satisfactory service to this population is to identify the consumers to be served and to involve them in the planning of the program from its inception. Another important objective is to achieve an acceptable level of service usage. An "acceptable level" should be measured in terms of quality as well as quantity; that is, the library should not only measure the number of individuals using the service (quantity) but should also examine whether they are using the services fully, taking advantage of all services offered (quality). It is important that such measurement be made over a longer period of time than that of an established, less complex service. Specifically, objectives to meet the goal of providing accessible service to all people with any type of hearing loss are:

- Using local contacts to reach all people in this segment of the population.
- Making a wide range of resources available in suitable formats and reading levels for deaf and hearing impaired people.
- Making a wide range of services available to attract users to the library for use as an information and a recreation source.
- Providing personalized service when required to adequately serve the person with a hearing loss.
- Using a variety of communication modes to ensure 2-way understanding.
- Making a temporary service available when needed on a short-term or emergency basis.
- Making collections, services, and programs available which are designed for parents of deaf children and for others concerned with people who have hearing losses.

Responsibility for reaching these objectives and the ultimate goal of library service to the total community is one which is shared among libraries through a network of services, programs, and resources.

THE DEVELOPMENT OF A NEW SERVICE

In structuring a new service to a special group of potential users, the pattern may take several forms. The 2 which are most realistic are development of a special service or development of an integrated service. The following are the characteristics of special services programs developed as projects with the ultimate goal of becoming permanent.

- Funding by special monies. This is often accomplished through federal funds and/or grant funds. The funds are provided on the basis of a proposal that sets forth the goals and objectives of the special program, the time span of accomplishment, and the steps to be taken for implementation. Included also in the grant proposal are the method to be used in evaluating the project, the method of funding when the grant period is completed, and the direction the service will take at the end of the project. at the end of the project.
- Inclusion of a special program worked out with the deaf community and with those who have any type of hearing loss. Because the period for the accomplishment of results is necessarily short, assessment of needs and program planning with the people who will receive the service is intense and comprehensive.
- Inclusion of specially trained staff. Both librarians and support staff are included in this designation. Because special projects are supported by funds that are additional to those appropriated for ongoing library support, the library staff is augmented to handle the additional service. Requirements for the staff members in a special project for the deaf and hearing impaired include the ability to communicate with them. A proficiency in sign language, lipreading, interpreting, or a special ability to communicate, in whatever mode that brings positive results, is necessary.
- Inclusion of special materials in suitable formats and with specialized subject content beginning with the inception of the project. Because of the time constraint of the project, the materials may be located in the building in which the project is based and made available from that location to the entire community. To be effective, the collection is made up of materials by, about, and for deaf and hearing impaired people.
- Inclusion of equipment to facilitate the service and to ensure the success of the entire program. As with the materials collection, the special equipment for use by deaf and hearing impaired people is essential from the very start of the project. For example, a TTY/TDD enables the library to provide the same service to deaf and hearing impaired individuals that it does through the telephone for the hearing population.
- Inclusion of an intensive information program. Because use of the services is their only reason for existence, it is important to acquaint potential consumers with their existence and with how

to access them. Meeting with the population being served by the project, providing them with attractive information materials, and assuring them that the program is designed by them and for them is also high on the list of priorities for this program.

- Personal attention. The quality of service received is one of the criteria for whether a special project will be suported by general funding at its close. Because the service will be new to many of the deaf and hearing impaired people, extra time is needed for orientation. New consumers are a constant element to deal with throughout the life of the project.
- Evaluation of the project. Such an assessment is essential to its continuance through general funding. With a special project, evaluation is built into the project from the beginning. Evaluation takes into consideration the quality of the service given as well as the quantity. The nature of the program makes it inadvisable to use the usual quantity measurements to determine the level of success. Quantity will be a measure but only in conjunction with quality. The per capita cost will undoubtedly be higher than the general per capita cost in this unique project of library service to the deaf and hearing impaired.

When a special project begins, it must be determined where in the organization the service should be placed. A special project of serving the deaf and hearing impaired can logically be placed in several areas of the library organization. Because the service provided is a total service to the population of deaf and hearing impaired, it can be placed directly under administration. Because it is a community program, it can be placed with other community programs. Because it provides service to people who have a disability, it can be placed with other special library service programs.

In making this placement decision, the library administration must consider where it can most readily meet its goals and objectives. Probably an even more important decision for the success of the project is where it is physically placed in the library building. A readily accessible and pleasant environment is a strong factor in the success or failure of a program such as one involving the deaf and hearing impaired.

One of the most crucial moments in the development of a special project is that time when the decision must be made concerning continued funding and integration of the service into the overall library program. Options include:

- Continuing the program at the project level of service.

- Continuing the program at a lesser level of service—lesser in either breadth or depth or in both.
- Discontinuance of the program.

These 3 options have several suboptions also. The decision made has a dramatic effect not only on the library and the consumers but also on the entire national and international movement aimed at providing library service to the deaf and hearing impaired.

INTEGRATION INTO AN EXISTING SERVICE

The second method of providing library service to the deaf and hearing impaired is to develop it from the beginning as an integrated service. Such a plan requires an immediate decision concerning the location of the service within the organizational structure. Another option available in this instance is that of integrating the program by age levels. Whatever place is selected, total staff training/development is essential in reaching individuals who are deaf or hearing impaired.

An integrated service moves more slowly than a special project and has, in all probability, a lower level of funding because of the continuing life span of the service. All aspects of library service in an organization are affected when the decision is made to reach deaf and hearing impaired people as a part of the ongoing library program. The addition of a coordinator for the program assists immeasurably in an adequate development of the service.

With an integrated library service, deaf and hearing impaired individuals have an opportunity to become a part of the total group of library users. They have an opportunity to see the entire spectrum of knowledge available to them in a library. While this is an advantageous situation, it may also be a confusing one to people who are not accustomed to using a library and who have the additional problem of communicating with hearing persons. The specially trained staff can assist the deaf and hearing impaired in using the total library.

To inform consumers about the many services available to them requires an intensive public information program and a community service involvement. Continuing evaluation and a testing of the successful use of the service is a necessity. Through this assessment, the flexibility of the program is maintained. If the goals and objectives are not being reached, the service can be modified in such a way that it will have the potential for success.

Both special projects and integrated programs are needed to serve people who are deaf or hearing impaired. Special projects allow an unusual opportunity for creativity and the trying of new approaches. They have the potential for moving the service to deaf and hearing impaired people ahead faster than an integrated program. When the program does become integrated as an ongoing part of library service, these potential consumers have the opportunity to use library service along with that which is available to nondeaf people. Through library service, the deaf and hearing impaired will find their isolation is lessened as they move into the mainstream of society.

OVERALL GOALS FOR THE SERVICE

All local programs for this group affect the national goals as well. National goals and objectives are a strong stimulus to local programs. Because deaf and hard-of-hearing people are a part of every community served by libraries, every library needs to be able to serve them. It is essential that the national focus on this disability service be maintained on a continuing basis through programs to achieve national goals.

Along with this continuing program is the need for research to determine the library service needed at every age level, what the potential is for national networks, the potential of TTY/TDD for implementing a network, how publishers or film producers can enhance the materials utilized by libraries for the deaf and hearing impaired, and the potential of television in the library program and what can reasonably be expected. These are all long-term objectives but, with an acceptable integrated program, time is available for continuing research. Whatever program is developed, all of the elements of the special project are required: services, resources, staff, equipment, public information, and community study and involvement.

A goal which is emphasized by every group concerned with library service to the deaf and hearing impaired is the development and operation of a clearinghouse of information on services to this population. Its purpose is to assist libraries in their programing and in development. The concept of a clearinghouse is specifically a part of the purpose of the Library Service to the Deaf Section of the Association of Specialized and Cooperative Library Agencies. Also, in the recommendations from the White House Conference on Library and Information Services, the states are encouraged to establish clearinghouses for information about the deaf. The memorandum developed by the Board of the Health and Rehabilitative Library Services Division (HRLSD) and the Association of State Library Agencies (ASLA) [later merged into the Association of Specialized and Cooperative Library Agencies (ASCLA)], concerning the appropriate permanent location for library service to the deaf unit in the American Library Association, emphasized the operation of a clearinghouse. A clearinghouse would not only act as a collection and distribution point for information and materials of library programs already in existence but would actively seek out resources. Deaf awareness remains a constant national goal. Awareness by the deaf and hearing impaired population of the library services available to them is a goal of national importance also. This total awareness is important, not only in the development of the services, but also in the education and training of librarians in this area of librarianship. Such awareness affects the basic education in graduate schools, continuing education, and inservice training.

A national goal also involves the greater availability, accessibility, and scope of resources. Included in these resources are captioned films as well as new ventures in producing films, filmstrips, and other video resources suitable for deaf and hard-of-hearing consumers. Access to all resources in compliance with Section 504 remains a national goal as does access through suitable equipment and environmental access.

Evaluation and a survey of the services available to deaf and hearing impaired individuals throughout the United States is a national goal. Overall planning for these services on a national basis is presently lacking. Individual goals can be accomplished on a state-by-state basis to ensure that the unique characteristics of each population group are met. The national goal can be reached through a melding of the state plans into an overall national plan.

In order to achieve many of the national goals, an intermediate goal has been set to try to obtain appointments of people who are deaf, hard of hearing, or have any type of hearing loss to boards and commissions at the local, state, and national levels. Such involvement will help to ensure that the programs developed really meet national goals. The ultimate goal, of course, is accessibility by all deaf and hearing impaired people to the resources of the library.

REFERENCE LIST

"Breaking Down Barriers: Information Services for Disabled Persons." *Illinois Libraries* 63 (7) (September 1981).

Dalton, Phyllis I., moderator. *Awareness, Understanding, Action.* Annual Conference, California Library Association in San Francisco, CA, 1977. Sacramento, CA: California Library Association. (Cassettes.)

Da Rold, Joseph, and Bray, Betty. "Service to the Deaf." *News Notes of California Libraries* 71 (1) (September 1976): 5–20.

Deaf Pride. Washington, DC: Deaf Pride, Inc., n.d. (Brochure.)

Hagemeyer, Alice. *The Public Library Talks to You.* Washington, DC: Gallaudet College, 1975.

Langevin, Ann Thompson. "WHCLIS and IYDP." *Interface* 3 (3–4) (Spring–Summer, 1981): 3–4.

"Library Service to the Disabled." *The Bookmark.* 40 (1) (Fall 1981).

Memorandum. Appropriate Permanent Location for Library Service to the Deaf Unit within ALA. January 13, 1978. Chicago: American Library Association.

Pennsylvania School for the Deaf. *Deafness Means More Than Not Being Able to Hear.* Philadelphia, PA: Pennsylvania School for the Deaf, n.d. (Brochure.)

"Special Library Services." *Illinois Libraries* 50 (9) (September 1979).

Chapter 6
Community Involvement in
Program Development

To achieve an effective service to deaf and hearing impaired people, the library must learn from present and potential consumers what the design and content of the program should be. In defining this service, a library cannot wait until a request comes but, rather, needs to take an aggressive approach. Because people who are deaf generally do not have a pattern of library use, they will not, in most instances, make the first move to instigate a program. The feeling of isolation, common to many people who have a hearing loss, is also a deterrent to their being assertive about their library needs. Also, communication with the hearing world, of which the library is a part, can be difficult for nonhearing people. These are among the reasons why the library program will become a reality only if the librarians take a strong initiative in establishing communication with those who are deaf and hearing impaired.

A program that is developed independently from the consumers in the community may be well-designed but unused. The deaf and hearing impaired population must share in the planning of such a program. However, ideas, concepts, and broad designs of the program can be pre-developed by the library to help establish a base for interaction. This approach is especially effective if some of the staff members involved in the planning process have hearing losses themselves or have had experience with those who have.

The number of people with hearing losses in any given community will vary from a very large number in a metropolitan area to very few in a rural environment. It is estimated that one person in 10 in the United States has some degree of hearing loss. The services will vary in relation to the number of people to be served but all should have one element in common—community involvement.

KNOWING THE COMMUNITY

As a starting point, the library needs to identify the deaf and hearing impaired population in its service area. This can be done successfully in a variety of ways. Vocational/ rehabilitation agencies at the state level can help identify the population to be served. Other state offices—especially those concerned specifically with deafness and hearing impairments—can be helpful. A breakdown of the number of deaf and hearing impaired individuals should be available from these offices. It will not include all who should be involved in a library program, however. Because deafness and hearing impairments are invisible disabilities, complete identification and census on a statewide basis are difficult to achieve.

The schools are valuable, not only in identification of the deaf and hearing impaired persons, but also in identifying the parents of children who have a hearing loss. To know the parents is essential to the development of services and resources to which they may turn for information. Parents are often the most eager of the population to have information about deafness and hearing impairment and may seek out the library to gain this knowledge. Community colleges and 4- year colleges and universities can also assist in identifying those nonhearing and hard-of-hearing individuals.

In some areas, regional resources for locating deaf and hearing impaired people exist. Often groups concerned with employment of the handicapped have knowledge of this segment of the population. Chapters of national and state organizations that have a concern with deafness and hearing impairments could be helpful. Some of these organizations are made up of deaf, hard-of-hearing, and hearing individuals so that the pattern of interaction and communication is already established.

Professional organizations that are made up of parents, educators, administrators, and others who are interested in promoting education of children who are deaf or hard of hearing also exist within communities. Other organizations are action groups developed to improve *all* services to people who are deaf or hearing impaired. Social clubs have been formed in many areas of the United States; they not only provide a meeting point for deaf adults, but they also work toward improving services for the deaf. Senior citizen centers are a beginning, too, for locating the hearing impaired elderly. Many of the elderly are difficult to locate because they do not identify with any one group. Churches are an aid, also, as are speech and hearing clinics.

When cooperation in library programing is the established mode of operation, various types of libraries in an area are usually involved—public, school, community college and university, special, and the state library. By involving such a group of libraries, the chances of locating the total population are much greater than that of any one single library. In some instances, where the community is small, identification can be made on a one-to-one basis. In a library of any size, the staff members will know deaf and hearing impaired people, will have family members who do not hear well, or will themselves have a hearing loss. Any person identified as belonging to this group is an important means toward total identification. A library is committed to serve all people in its service area—identifying the deaf and hearing impaired will be, for the most part, identifying a part of the population that is not presently served.

National organizations, while removed from the locality, can still be helpful. Many have chapters within a state or region, members within a locality, or can give practical suggestions on how to locate people who are deaf or who have any hearing loss. Telephone directories are helpful in identifying sources for follow-up. Newspapers, through news stories, letters to the editor, calendars of events, and other features, can keep libraries in touch with the day-to-day life of the community, including the activities related to deaf and hearing impaired people. Associations that secure volunteers for many types of community activities can also provide assistance in the search.

After identifying the population to be served and the groups that have the potential for program development, the library should next be concerned with involving these people and organizations in the process of setting up a library program which will be of use to everyone in this population group. Meeting with the identified groups, as a participant or as an observer of a program, enables a librarian to make contact with the deaf community and involve them in the library. Inviting deaf and hearing impaired people or groups of people to the library to discuss, express, and explore views, and to plan is also a beginning in involvement. The importance of personal contact cannot be overestimated for both the library and the deaf and hearing impaired. It may be slow in developing, but if carefully and personally done, it will be built on a solid base. In following through on a commitment to serve all, the library must accept the responsibility of maintaining the program being developed as an ongoing, well-conceived service.

RESPONSIBILITIES OF THE DEAF AND HEARING IMPAIRED

Responsibility for program development rests also with the deaf and hard-of-hearing communities, with the elderly hearing impaired, and with others who have a hearing loss. Their roles should not be passive but should be to seek out the library to determine whether it can be of service to them. If it can, the services should be used to the fullest extent needed; friends and relatives should be told about the resources and services available. If it cannot accommodate their needs, they have a responsibility to let the library know that they have not been included in the development of library programs. The library will have some program available for use as a beginning to a more complete service. *The Public Library Talks to You* by Alice Hagemeyer[1] is a publication that is of assistance to the deaf and hearing impaired in their first use of a library or in the expansion of their use. Among this population are those who have long been library users and who are sophisticated in the utilization of its services and resources.

The public library serves *all* of the community just as other types of libraries serve *all* of their clientele. People who are deaf or hearing impaired are a part of that community or clientele and can make good use of the library within the limits of its resources. Any library needs not being met should be brought to the attention of the library for inclusion in the overall planning process. Without this information, the library will be less equipped to include people who are deaf and hearing impaired.

The interaction between the library and organizations for deaf and hearing impaired persons and between the staff members and these users and potential users will enable the librarians to act on accurate information rather than on assumptions. Full involvement of all people who have hearing losses will result in a relevant and actively used service. The identification of community leaders and their involvement in library activities, including planning, will enable the library to direct its efforts effectively without wasted motion. Although every effort made by the hearing and by the nonhearing population may not be successful, a continuing program of community involvement will eventually result in a positive 2-way responsiveness.

People who are deaf or hearing impaired can find out about library services available through the libraries themselves, from friends, or from library associations. They can gain information on programs nationwide through *The Red Notebook* and national organizations concerned with library services. Many publications describe library programs; some of this information may be available through the library itself even though the program is not locally offered. The involvement with the library can effectively begin before any specific interaction with the planning occurs.

By reaching many people, librarians will be better able to reach people who are deaf or hearing impaired. The International Year of Disabled Persons, 1981, proclaimed by the United Nations, developed an effective means of involving all types of organizations and a variety of people in its programs. The United States Council on the International Year of Disabled Persons was set up as a nongovernmental, nonprofit organization with Alan A. Reich as its president. This council successfully promoted community partnership programs throughout the United States. Libraries were, as part of the community, very much involved in reaching the goal of full participation in society of all people with disabilities. Library programs for the deaf and hearing impaired were begun or further developed during that year. To continue that momentum, the United States Congress declared 1982 the National Year of Disabled Persons. The National Office on Disability, later the National Organization on Disability, was a successor to the U.S. Council with Alan Reich continuing as president. The United Nations proclaimed 1982–1992 as the Decade of Disabled Persons. People in the community who are deaf or hearing impaired, along with the library, became partners in the total development of community programs which involved both groups. These dedicated years provided an opportunity to mutually develop programs of service which assist in achieving full participation of the deaf and hearing impaired in society. Awareness by the people who have a hearing loss and by the hearing may be just as important as the library service specifically established. All problems are not solved by these dedicated years because the goal is not to produce an action plan only but to develop an awareness leading to understanding and action.

The communication in this library development program is 2-way as are the relationships; each needs to be allowed to develop a rapport with the other. Mutual and active participation leads to mutual community involvement with positive results. All librarians need to learn all they can about the possibilities of providing this service. The planning cannot be done in a vacuum. At the same time, those who are deaf or otherwise hearing impaired need to communicate how a library can best serve them. Libraries can then make the effort to provide the service. Many of their needs are unique and that uniqueness requires careful consideration. All persons must be involved—the deaf, hard of hearing, hearing impaired elderly, parents of deaf children, children of deaf parents, professional people who work with the deaf and hearing impaired, and all others who have any hearing loss at all—and hearing people. Some of the people involved will move easily in both the hearing and nonhearing worlds; some will be less comfortable; some will be well-educated; some will have a 5th-grade reading level or less. The variety provides a challenge to all involved to accomplish a meaningful program.

COMMUNITY RESOURCES

Many sources exist to assist in identifying people who have a loss of hearing; several sources are available to people who are deaf or hearing impaired concerning services possible for a library to provide.

RESOURCE LIST

Groups that can assist the library with community involvement include:

Alexander Graham Bell Association for the Deaf, Inc.
International Parents' Organization (IPO)
3411 Volta Place, N.W.
Washington, DC 20007

American Athletic Association of the Deaf (AAAD)
3916 Lantern Drive
Silver Spring, MD 20801

American Deafness and Rehabilitation Association
814 Thayer Avenue
Silver Spring, MD 20910

American Society for Deaf Children
814 Thayer Avenue
Silver Spring, MD 20910

Helen Keller National Center for Deaf-Blind Youths and Adults
111 Middle Neck Road
Sands Point, NY 11050

Lions International, Inc.
Hearing Conservation and Work with Youth
York and Cermak Roads
Oak Brook, IL 60521

National Association of the Deaf (NAD)
Junior National Association of the Deaf (JR. NAD)
814 Thayer Avenue
Silver Spring, MD 20910

National Easter Seal Society for Crippled Children and Adults
2623 West Ogden Avenue
Chicago, IL 60612

The National Information Center on Deafness
Gallaudet College
7th and Florida Avenue, N.E.
Washington, DC 20002

Quota Club International, Inc.
1828 L Street, N.W.
Washington, DC 20036

President's Committee on Employment of the Handicapped
(PCEH)
1111 20th Street, N.W.
Washington, DC 20210

Self Help for Hard of Hearing (SHHH)
P.O. Box 34889
Bethesda, MD 20817

Types of groups that can assist the library with community involvement
are:

Adult education classes

Churches

Community colleges, colleges/universities

Governor's committees on employment of the handicapped

Professional organizations

School districts

Senior citizen groups

Service clubs

Social clubs of the deaf

Speech and hearing clinics

State and local offices of rehabilitation and resource centers

State school superintendent offices

State schools for the deaf

In addition to the other groups already listed, some other sources which can assist the deaf and hearing impaired to involve the library in their information and recreation needs are:

Library Service to the Deaf Forum
Association of Specialized and Cooperative Library Agencies
American Library Association
50 East Huron Street
Chicago, IL 60611

Libraries—college, public, school, special, university

State and local library associations

State libraries

NOTE

1. Alice Hagemeyer. *The Public Library Talks to You* (Washington, DC: Gallaudet College for Continuing Education, 1975).

REFERENCE LIST

Amdursky, Saul J. "To Reach the Deaf." *Illinois Libaries* 57 (7) (September 1975): 467–70.

Clark County School District (Clark County Deaf and Hard of Hearing Program). *Clark County Directory of Services for the Hearing Impaired*. Las Vegas, NV: Clark County School District, 1981.

Center on Deafness. *Directory of Services*. Denver, CO: Center on Deafness, 1979.

Gorski, Robert. "The International Year in America." *Shhh* 2 (3) (May–June 1981): 14–15.

Hagemeyer, Alice. "Library for Deaf Action." *The NAD Broadcaster* 4 (10) (October 1982): 9.

Higgins, Paul C. *Outsiders in a Hearing World*. Beverly Hills, CA: Sage Publications, 1980.

Levin, Louis. "Hearie's Corner." In *Communicating with Hearing People: The Red Notebook*, by the National Association of the Deaf. Silver Spring, MD: National Association of the Deaf, 1980. (Loose-leaf.)

Meeting the Challenge through Partnerships. Washington, DC: U.S. Council for the International Year of Disabled Persons, 1981.

Spradley, Thomas,and Spradley, James P. *Deaf Like Me*. New York: Random House, 1978.

Stark County District Library. *PALS Project: People in Action*. Canton, OH: Stark County District Library, 1982. (Leaflet.)

Thomas, Roberta. *Handbook-Directory for Families with Deaf Children*. Philadelphia, PA: Action Allicance of Parents of the Deaf, 1982.

Part II: Services in Support of Serving the Deaf and Hearing Impaired

Chapter 7
Library Programs of Effective Service

Based on the statistic that one person out of 14 has some degree of hearing impairment, this special group of deaf, hard-of-hearing people, and those with some hearing loss is a large one. Children represent 20 percent of hearing impaired people; one out of 4 elderly people has a hearing loss problem. Thus, the people in this group represent the full range of ages in the population.

All people are entitled to the services of libraries; these services are to be available and accessible to everyone through such precepts as those declared by the National Commission on Libraries and Information Science (NCLIS), established by Public Law 91-345 in 1970. The White House Conference on Library and Information Services (WHCLIS) passed many resolutions pertaining to the accessibility to library services for all. The follow-up committee to that conference, the White House Conference on Library and Information Services Task Force (WHCLIST), is implementing those resolutions as one of its priorities. Libraries and information services are looking forward to a second White House Conference on Libraries and Information Services, a conference which, in all probability, will strengthen these commitments.

SURVEYS OF LIBRARY SERVICE PROGRAMS

The statements, resolutions, implementation, and planning are of utmost concern to librarians and library-related people who are interested in the deaf and hearing impaired because these consumers make up a neglected group. A survey was made of state library agencies by Harris C. McClaskey and Katherine Brewer in relation to library services provided to people who are deaf. These 1974 results showed that not much was being done, at that time, to provide library services to the deaf outside of state institutions for the deaf. The survey found, also, that, although the *Standards for Library Functions at the State Level* includes the statement that captioned films should be made available for the deaf, over 95 percent of the state library agencies were not members of Media Services and Captioned Films. There were a few outstanding public libraries with active programs for service to people who were deaf but 79.55 percent reported no active public library programs. A conclusion of the study was that this lack of programs was not an intended oversight but rather a lack of awareness about the needs and the implications of the specific disability as it relates to library service.

A second survey, made in 1980, was also concerned with library services to the deaf. This survey and report was made by the Deaf Resource Center of the Metropolitan Cooperative Library System with headquarters in the Santa Fe Springs City Library, California. A questionnaire was sent to each state library asking about services to the deaf being offered by that library and by the public libraries in the state. No attempt was made to include schools for the deaf or other special service agencies. Four of the states questioned did not respond. Eight of the responding states were not providing or establishing service for the deaf. The questions to the state libraries covered the following services:

- Signed story hour
- Public access TTY/TDD
- Reference TTY/TDD
- TTY/TDD loan
- Sign language classes
- Newsletter
- Captioned films
- Video
- Staff use of sign language

The results of the survey showed that in 5 of the responding states, the state library provided library service to people who are deaf. The largest number of public libraries providing services in any state was 16. In some states, only the state library provided the service. The largest number of services being offered by any one state was 8. The smallest was one. The 2 services most frequently offered were reference TTY/TDD and the use of sign language by the staff. Those least frequently available were video and TTY/TDD loan. Several libraries offered services, not specified, which were not covered by the questionnaire. The survey results indicated that, at the time of the reporting, while some few libraries were providing a fairly wide range of services to people who are deaf, others were not providing any special services for them. Only the traditional library services were available which they may or may not be able to utilize.

PARENTS IN THE SERVICE PROGRAMS

Traditional library service can be used by people who are deaf or hard of hearing but, because of their disability, they require a modification of the services to make them readily usable. Such a modification can be integrated into the traditional services to include deaf and hearing impaired people through varying the approach to meet their specific requirements. Among this population, the parents of children who are deaf need, on a continuing basis, information on deafness and on services available to them and their children. The library can make contact with parents through parent clubs or a group within a parent-teacher association or other educational groups. Parents have many questions the library can assist in answering. Among these are how to determine if a child is deaf; where to obtain information concerning deafness; what communication mode options exist for the child; what the characteristics of each method of communication are; what type of education is available to a child who is deaf; where should the child be placed in an educational setting; what are the advantages and disadvantages of a residential school, a day school, and public school; how to handle problems which arise during the education of the child; what education is available after high school; and what career opportunities are available.

The information received by parents is one of the most important factors in the positive development of the deaf child. Because 90 percent of deaf children have hearing parents, the hearing parent group is a large one. The librarians working with parents can not only learn of their individual needs but be guided in the services provided by those expressed needs. The meetings of the parent groups can be scheduled into the library on a regular basis with the resources and services of the library available to the parents as a part of the ongoing library community program. Libraries can help parents by providing every bit of information that can be found about the subject of deafness and at as many levels as possible. Libraries can effectively widen the horizon for parents of children who are deaf.

The parents are a resource in the support of a program in the library for the children who are deaf or hard of hearing. The firsthand knowledge which they have in their experience with their children is invaluable in the development of services to the children. Few librarians have had firsthand experience with children who cannot hear, who have difficulty with hearing, who may not be able to speak clearly or who utilize a visual or written means of communication rather than or in addition to oral communication. The mutual effort of the parent and the librarian is invaluable in designing an effective program of children's services.

Parents of deaf or hard-of-hearing children who are themselves deaf have library needs both for themselves and for their children as do deaf parents of hearing children. An important part of the life of the child is the learning of good vocabulary and reading skills. Through the sharing of books and stories and other library materials with children, parents can show children that books, films, and other media are important, fun, and worthwhile. Libraries can provide, along with their standard services, simple stories and books without words which are developed especially for vocabulary and language building. Books, cassettes, films, and story hours can be made available for use by deaf, hard-of-hearing, and hearing children with the advice and assistance of their parents.

TRADITIONAL LIBRARY SERVICE

Children's services in a traditional library setting require a modification of the book selection and the acquisition policies to include suitable children's materials for loan and reference. In addition, an important program is that of offering a story hour which, by its design, can be enjoyed by children who are deaf or hard of hearing as well as by hearing children. Some modifications are needed when stories are told. The stories should be signed, visual aids should be used, and books with a simple vocabulary and with colorful realistic pictures and movement should be selected. Special attention should be paid to the seating of the children because those who are deaf need to be able to see the storyteller and the interpreter. Because some of the children may read lips, it is important that they be able to see the storyteller clearly in order to do so. Children who are hard of hearing need to be able to sit where they can make the most use of their hearing abilities. Good results can be obtained through a story hour group made up of deaf, hard-of-hearing, and hearing children. This type of story hour can become a regular part of the standard services provided for children.

Among the services of greatest value are matinee and evening programs showing captioned films. These programs are of great interest to children, young people, and adults who have a hearing problem. The films are on a variety of subjects and are produced both for entertainment and for education. The films are available from many services. Some are loaned free, some are available on a rental basis, and others can be purchased. Silent films that were captioned when produced are also enjoyed by deaf, hard-of-hearing, and hearing people of all age levels. The captioned film programs can become a part of the library's regular programing. If the film showing is available during daytime hours as well as in the evening, a wider audience is reached. The scheduling of the programs in all of the branches or on a similar geographic basis allows more people to attend. Involving people who are deaf and hearing impaired in the program development and implementation helps to ensure a larger and more interested audience when the captioned films are shown.

COMMUNICATING

A library offering a traditional program can expand that service dramatically for people who are deaf by providing a public access teletypewriter (TTY)/telecommunication device for the deaf (TDD). Through this medium, they can communicate with other deaf people, with government offices such as the Internal Revenue Service, with airlines, public utilities, other libraries, investment houses, and with many other enterprises. In this way, people who are deaf have an opportunity to achieve the same type of independence that hearing people have through the telephone. Some people who are deaf have a TTY/TDD in their homes, but others do not. A public-access TTY/TDD makes the service available to all. The number of machines needed differs from one locality to another. Having the machines located geographically throughout a library system enables those who need them to have easy access to them. There are many types of machines from which to choose. Again, feedback from the people who will use them will prove helpful in their selection. Public-access telephones that amplify sound are needed for people who are hard of hearing. The users of these telephones can best advise on the kind best adapted for their use.

By installing a TTY/TDD in the reference sections of libraries, that service becomes available to people who have machines in their homes. All reference services then become available to deaf people through the TTY/TDD. In this way, the reference TTY/TDD helps to ensure access to information by people who are deaf. It is an application of a new technology to information for a group of people who, heretofore, found it impossible to access information at a distance. Although the most frequently offered service appearing in the report of the 1980 survey of services to people who are deaf was that of a reference TTY/TDD, many libraries do not provide that means of communication. The TTY/TDD can be used for many purposes. Among these are to inquire about a specific title, to call for information, to reserve a book, and to secure answers to reference questions. With a TTY/TDD at library headquarters, at branches, and at bookmobiles, people who are deaf can have ready access to the library. A TTY/TDD is also useful when a deaf person is expecting an important message and does not have a machine available or if s/he wants to communicate with government offices or other agencies concerning matters affecting them. A call/relay service by means of the TTY/TDD and the telephone can be provided by a library to meet emergency situations and other needs.

Another communication service that can be offered by the library is sign language classes. Such classes are invaluable in training deaf people as well as librarians and other professional people who need to communicate with the deaf. Others to be included are parents of deaf children, children of deaf parents, ministers, and the general public. Because people are usually at different levels of expertise in sign language, both beginning and advanced classes are needed. Besides teaching this skill, the classes bring people together who have a common interest in working and communicating with people who are deaf. The class provides an opportunity, also, for recently deaf people to become a part of a group which is interested in their new communication need.

Librarians and other library staff members who attend sign language classes acquire the ability to communicate with the deaf people who come into the library. If it is not possible for them to attend library-sponsored sign language classes, they can attend classes sponsored by a community college, other educational institutions, or by an association of people who are deaf. To become and remain proficient in the language requires practice and use. With several staff members receiving the training concurrently, they can interact with each other to maintain their language skill. When the library employs people who are deaf and who communicate through sign language, use of the language becomes an everyday occurrence.

Because some people who are deaf do not communicate in sign language but read lips, lipreading classes are also needed. Lipreading enables library staff members to communicate with more ease with people who are deaf or who have any hearing impairment. Many people who are losing their hearing are interested in becoming proficient in lipreading to enable them to continue to function in society. The scheduling of both sign language and lipreading classes during the day and in the evening increases their availability as does using several geographical locations. The classes can be a part of the regular program of the library.

A group of hard-of-hearing and deaf people who may not be identified easily are those whose hearing loss is a result of aging. Some, prior to becoming deaf or hard of hearing, may have used the library but began to avoid it as their hearing loss became more pronounced. Others have never used the library and have become further removed from that possibility as they retreat from society into isolation. For many, coming to the library is not possible because of a physical impairment in addition to a hearing loss or because of a lack of transportation. A program of service to elderly people who are hard of hearing or deaf can be integrated into the ongoing program for the deaf. The modification of this standard program involves, primarily, the materials selection activity and the inclusion of communication skills so that the staff members in the program can relate effectively to their special patrons.

People who are deaf and hearing impaired at any age have been deprived of hearing news programs which are available to hearing people. Although some television news has been signed and other news programs captioned, many news programs on television are not available to people who cannot hear or who are hard of hearing. The decoder for television sets now makes more of the news programs understandable. Such viewings can be supplemented by the library's providing of news through a TTY/TDD. A newsletter can also provide local and national news relating to activities for, by, and about the deaf and hearing impaired.

While some libraries provide service effectively to deaf and hearing impaired individuals without special communication training, library staff members who have this skill increase the probability of successfully communicating with this group of users. The goal of the training is understanding. Training also emphasizes the importance of receiving accurately the information given and ensuring that the information received by the user is accurate despite the possible communication barrier. Training includes sensitizing staff members to communication problems of the deaf and hearing impaired and discussing how they can best minimize them. Those who can provide the most practical information for the library staff are people who are deaf or hard of hearing; interaction between the hearing and the deaf or hard-of-hearing people in a training atmosphere benefits all 3 groups. Many possible problems disappear as everyone interacts.

A program resulting from this training or one set up independently is that of library orientation training in library use for people who are deaf or hard of hearing. This orientation can consist of special, interpreted programs which emphasize those library services especially designed for the group. These programs can also be developed for the general public or for the students in an educational setting or clients of a special library. In this case, they are interpreted for the deaf and designed so that hard-of-hearing people can understand the tour leader or the trainer.

A captioned film showing of the library is a good supplement to such orientation tours. After seeing such a film, deaf people are more knowledgeable about when to ask questions and what questions to ask. Video is important in the library for deaf and hearing impaired people at all age levels and on all subjects. Those who are deaf require video materials which are captioned; those who are hard of hearing require amplification of sound with audiovisual materials. These can be included in the ongoing audiovisual programs. Amplified receivers can be included in the equipment provided by the library for its users.

A breakthrough for the deaf and hearing impaired was the availability of the use of the decoder with closed-captioned television programs. Libraries have an opportunity to participate in this service by providing decoders with their television sets used within their library, or by lending decoders. Deaf or hard-of-hearing people who are interested in television programs need to have their own decoders. Lending decoders will enable individuals to decide whether they wish to purchase one for personal use. Such a lending program also enables people to view particular programs of interest to them.

Once the services have been developed and are in place, the continued involvement of the consumers is most important. They not only need to know that the services are available but to use them successfully. The standard publicity methods, with some modifications, can be used to make those services known. Information can be included in the library's newsletter. If this method is used, the distribution policy must be modified to ensure that the deaf and hard-of-hearing residents find out about programs developed for their use. Newsletters for this group can be distributed to clubs of and for the deaf and hearing impaired, schools for the deaf, public schools, churches, professional people working with the deaf and hearing impaired, and individuals in the community who have been identified as having a hearing loss.

In addition to a newsletter, library public information efforts can include using newspapers, calendars of events, feature stories, and editorials. Church and club newsletters provide another channel for information as do booklists and bookmarks. Within the general program of issuing bibliographies, reading lists can be included. The lists will be well received if they are visually attractive and informative. Reading lists designed for parents of deaf children and including information on specific titles will increase the chances that parents will come to the library for additional information. Parents of deaf and hard-of-hearing children are also interested in reading lists which are available for the children. The variety of books is increasing for the preschool child who is deaf as well as for deaf children in general. Because communicating with children through story telling is important to their development, parents are interested in reading lists that include stories that have proved to be successful with deaf and hard-of-hearing children. In general, all visible forms of public information are possible sources of informing the special public about these special programs.

PLANNING

Because modification of standard library service results in a special service within a traditional one, the plan for such service becomes a plan within a plan. The following list can be used as a guide when forming the special service.

Plan of Library Service for the Deaf and Hearing Impaired

1. **Potential Consumer Groups.** Description of the deaf and hearing impaired population in the community for which the plan of service is being developed. Who are the people and where do they live?
2. **Advisory Group.** Determination of the makeup of the group and the role of the potential consumer as an advisor in the planning and implementation process. How will possible members be identified? How will they interact in the planning process?
3. **Purpose.** Statement of why the service is being planned. What is the reason for its development?
4. **Goal.** A definition of the goal of the program. What is to be accomplished?

5. **Scope.** Identification of the people to whom the service will be offered. Who are the potential consumers of the services being planned?
6. **Objectives.** Establishment of several objectives. What objectives must be accomplished in order to reach the goal?
7. **Criteria.** Identification of measurements for the evaluation of the implementing of the plan of service and progress under the plan. How much should be accomplished and when should it be accomplished?
8. **Alternatives.** Description of the possible alternatives for achieving the goal. What are the different ways the objectives can be accomplished in the serving of the deaf and hearing impaired?
9. **Decision.** Selection among the alternatives. Which alternatives will best achieve the goal?
10. **Action Steps.** Description of the activities to be developed to reach the goal. What are the priorities?
11. **Resources.** The detailing of the resources needed to support the action steps. What are the resource needs in terms of people, materials, finances, facilities, cooperative activities, and advisors?
12. **Implementation.** The outlining of the step-by-step implementation of the action segment. In what order will the action steps be taken to achieve the objectives and the goal?
13. **Evaluation.** Determination of how the program will be evaluated. What information is needed from whom and when in achieving an effective qualitative and quantitative evaluation of the program?
14. **Organization.** Description of the placement of the service within the library organization. Where will it be located and what level of staff position will have the ultimate responsibility for providing the service?
15. **Financing.** A determination of what the cost will be and how the service will be funded. What is the estimate of the cost per capita? What percentage of the funds will be local? State? Federal? Private?
16. **Staffing.** Description of the staffing of the service. How many staff members are needed? Professional? Technical? Clerical? Volunteer?
17. **Services.** Description of the services to be offered. What 5 major services will be available to people who are deaf or hard of hearing?

18. **Service Outlets.** Description of the services in relation to their availability. What types of library outlets will provide the service to the deaf and hearing impaired? Where will they be located?
19. **Physical Facilities.** An outlining of the physical facilities required. What are the standards for the physical facilities which each type of service outlet must meet in providing the services?
20. **Public Information.** Description of the public information programs needed. What means will be employed to publicize this program?
21. **Other Considerations.** Review of the plan of service to determine other needed considerations. What other factors should be taken into consideration in planning and implementing this kind of an effective program of library service?

SERVING THE PEOPLE

A companion document to the plan of service—a checklist of services—is required in designing a program so that full library service is available to the deaf and hard-of-hearing people. This checklist includes the following:

1. Familiarizing the deaf and hearing impaired with the informational, recreational, social, and cultural resources of a library.
2. Providing specialized assistance in the use of these resources.
3. Promoting awareness of this population among the general public.
4. Providing telecommunication devices for the deaf (TTY/TDD) for public access, for reference service, and for loan.
5. Providing telephones with amplified volume control for those who are hard of hearing and other amplified audio equipment so that hard-of-hearing people can use the services.
6. Including interpreter services for library programs as needed for people who are deaf.
7. Providing a special sound system for library programs for the use of hard-of-hearing people.
8. Developing library programs designed to meet the social, vocational, recreational, and everyday needs of the deaf and hearing impaired.

9. Offering library tours for information, orientation, and instruction.
10. Making available research, reference, and information services.
11. Providing access to programs for children, young people, and adults.
12. Ensuring the availability of staff skilled in sign language, lip-reading, and total communication.
13. Providing magazines, newspapers, pamphlets, slides, maps, and other library materials.
14. Providing books, magazines, films, and pamphlets on the subject of deafness and other hearing disabilities.
15. Making accessible information and referral service.
16. Providing captioned, signed, and silent films for use in library programs and for loan.
17. Providing books by mail services for people who cannot come to the library because of an added disability.
18. Offering signed children's books and high interest/low reading-level books for children and adults.
19. Making meeting rooms available for groups interested in the well-being of deaf and hard-of-hearing people.
20. Making available large-print books for people with a visual impairment in addition to a hearing disability.
21. Providing communication with people who are deaf/blind as well as supplying materials in suitable formats for their recreation and information needs.
22. Offering sign language classes at different levels of proficiency.
23. Displaying information on deafness and other hearing disabilities through appropriate exhibits.
24. Making available electronic decoders for closed-captioned television programs in the library and for loan.
25. Installing auditory aids helpful to hard-of-hearing people and listening stations for phonorecords, audiocassettes, and other audio formats with amplification controls.
26. Installing a listening system in meeting rooms for people who are hard of hearing.
27. Observing special occasions such as "Deaf Awareness Week/Month" and "Better Speech and Hearing Month."
28. Providing visual kits on library instruction.
29. Making available visual aids in libraries to assist in library orientations for the deaf and hearing impaired.
30. Providing a news service for people who are deaf by means of the TTY/TDD and/or newsletters.

This checklist covers some of the basic services which can be made available through a modified traditional library service and meet some of the needs of people who are deaf or hard of hearing. In each community, a local advisory group of deaf and hearing impaired persons can help to choose among the services listed. They can include all of the above items or substitute, delete, and/or add library services to accommodate the characteristics of this special population group within the entire population.

Although a reliance on the traditional aspects of library service is inadequate in addressing the services to be used by the deaf and hearing impaired, librarians can use these services as a base for modified services. The modifications required to make all services readily available to deaf and hard-of-hearing individuals will, many times, improve the availability and accessibility to *all* who use the library. Those services that are specifically designed for people with a hearing loss are basic to providing the option to use the library's other services. Through these modified services, the library becomes one of the few public institutions that can be used by deaf and hearing impaired people because it is a place that accommodates their special needs.

THE SERVICE AS A SPECIAL PROJECT

A special project approach to providing such services requires funding beyond the modest increase available in most library budgets. Funding in the form of a grant based on a proposal developed by the library and the deaf and hearing impaired people themselves is the basis for a special project. In order to ascertain its effectiveness, such a program requires a 4-year time span because the people for whom the service is developed are slow to make use of it. The potential consumers are people, who because of their disability, are (1) isolated, (2) have severe communication problems, and (3) are unaccustomed to including the library in their everyday lives. While the population to be served is a diverse one, these 3 characteristics are common among the deaf population in any community that has not previously offered such a program.

To get the deaf and hearing impaired population to use the library, the library must, as its first priority, employ a staff that can communicate adequately with these patrons. A coordinator of the services to be planned and offered can assist immeasurably in ensuring that the project reaches its goal in the time span provided. The coordinator needs to have considerable administrative and organizational skills. In addition, the position requires a person who is empathetic and interested in service to deaf and hearing impaired people. Considerable skill in communicating with nonhearing people is a requirement as well as the ability to work easily and effectively with community organizations, especially those related to the deaf and hearing impaired. Support staff in the project with similar special qualifications is essential in achieving the goals and objectives of the programs in the project.

A program designed especially for this specific population requires the allocation of a specific physical area in the library even though the service uses the entire library. The objectives of the project itself require that the specialized services be self-contained in an accessible location in the library. Many diverse activities take place in the service area of the project with use of other areas of the library, as needed, to provide a complete service. Both the special and the general service locations can receive active use; however, the designation of one area where special services to the deaf and hearing impaired are available lessens the confusion associated with locating service in an area where many diverse activities are taking place. Successfully using the library can, in a contained situation, hasten the time when the person with a hearing loss can participate successfully in library services in a complex setting.

The special project, with its staff, designated area, and planned services, can provide special training in the use of the library services being offered. It can serve as a program for children in special school classes and their parents, for teachers who need materials for use with deaf and hard-of-hearing children, for story hours presented orally by the librarian and signed by the class teacher or the librarian, and as a center for the collection of special materials.

SURVEYING THE POPULATION TO BE SERVED

When a special project is set up to serve the deaf and hearing impaired, a survey of that population assists in developing sound planning. The survey should be conducted before the resources are acquired and the activities begun, so that the project develops from basic and sound data. Such a survey takes time and staff but serves as a valid foundation for all project activities and for the entire future of the service. In addition, a summary of the status of the services being provided is of assistance in the planning process. The total study provides an estimate of the population to be served and its characteristics. The following important statistics should be included in this summary.

1. The total population of the service area of the library.
2. The size of the geographical area served, in square miles.
3. A determination of the population characteristics in relation to the percentage of urban and rural users.
4. The number of libraries in the service area participating or cooperating including total number and breakdown by public, public school, private school, vocational school, academic, residential school, institutional, and other.
5. Estimate of the population in the area in relation to deafness, hearing impairment, and a census of the current library services provided to the deaf and hearing impaired in the service area by type of library and general characteristics of the population in the area of service.

Although the estimates of the size of the deaf and hearing impaired population on a national basis vary widely, a local estimate can be made initially, assuming that 5.5 percent of the population is profoundly deaf and that 20 percent of the population is hearing impaired. Many deaf and hearing impaired people congregate in large metropolitan areas because communication is easier. If the area to be served is predominately urban, the estimate should be increased.

The general characteristics of this special population include that the reading level of deaf and hearing impaired people is lower than the average reading level. The 12-year-old child who is deaf reads at an average of 2.58 grade level. This can be compared with the level of a hearing 12-year-old child who reads at the 6 to 6.9 grade level.

To know the population to be served by the project in a more detailed and personal way, the project director and staff can make an extensive survey of the population to determine its size and characteristics. To achieve valid results requires a staff that works equally well with both hearing and nonhearing people. This ability is crucial in the initial survey and in the development and implementation of a many-faceted program. Such a survey can vary in structure from one locality to another, but some statistics are universally necessary. For example, identification of the agencies, organizations, and individuals most likely to have information concerning the number, location, and characteristics of the deaf and hearing impaired population is essential. This study includes, but is not limited to:

- Libraries in the area of service.
- Associations of people who are deaf and hearing impaired.

- Teachers and administrators in public and private schools and in day and residential schools for the deaf and hearing impaired.
- Public and private agencies serving people who are deaf and hearing impaired.
- Individuals who are deaf or hard of hearing.
- Other groups or individuals in a locality having direct knowledge of hearing impaired and deaf persons.

These individuals and groups can be contacted by personal visits and/or by telephone and TTY/TDD interviews initially. An interpreted meeting relating to the proposed services is also effective in ascertaining the services needed and in acquainting the people with the library and its present and potential services. The use of an audio system for hard-of-hearing people facilitates discussions in this type of meeting. Conferences of librarians throughout the area to be served increase the probability of identifying people who are deaf or have any type of hearing loss.

A representative survey of households in the area of the project can be made. To be of the most value, the survey should be based on personal interviews. A supplemental, brief written survey adds more information to the base of the project and offers additional input. A short reply form published in the local newspapers throughout the project area can be of value. A similar form published in organizational newsletters can also assist in identifying individuals and in learning their present and potential interest in libraries. Through the contacts made, not only the number and location of the individuals to be served will be determined, but also the characteristics of that population will emerge. Interested individuals will be located through the survey and from this knowledge an advisory committee and other project committees can be developed.

A group of people who will be identified during the detailed survey are the parents of deaf or hard-of-hearing children who are themselves deaf or hard of hearing. When this group of people has been identified and interviewed, many potential project committee members will be located for general and special services.

DETERMINING SERVICE

As the identification of the population to be served develops, so does the determination of the level of service to be provided by the project. The details of the service depend, to some extent, on the kinds and levels of service already being provided in the community. The goal of this special project is to reach the level of service equal to that available to all other segments of the population. To ensure that deaf and hearing impaired people are in the mainstream of library service is also an important goal as is the establishment of the library as an important public agency responsive to the needs of deaf and hearing impaired people. In general, the goals of a special project include the following specific elements:

- A staff that can communicate effectively with people who are deaf, hard of hearing, or have any type of hearing loss.
- A strong working relationship with community organizations and agencies related to the needs of the deaf and hearing impaired.
- Development of a program that meets the needs of the population to be served and raises the awareness of the hearing community to the characteristics and needs of deaf and hearing impaired individuals.
- Creation and maintenance of an ongoing public information program, reaching not only the deaf and hearing impaired, but the hearing community as well.
- Establishment of a center for communication, resources, basic library services, and information purposes.
- Establishment of referral, information, and interlibrary loan TTY/TDD service.
- Motivation of deaf and hearing impaired individuals to use the resources and facilities of libraries.
- Development of video programs and audio programs with sound amplification.
- Availability of high interest/low vocabulary materials.
- Formation of an advisory committee to assist in the development and implementation of the project and to monitor the ongoing progress of the program as well as to evaluate the project at determined intervals.

Among the services that can be provided in both breadth and depth for special projects designed especially for the deaf and hearing impaired are:

- Computer-based instruction, information, and interaction.
- Development and use of visual media within the library such as films, filmstrips, flannel boards, and transparencies.
- Provision of a library kit for parents of children who are deaf to use in helping their children through play.

- Development and distribution of a directory of all library services that are available in the project area and where those services are located.
- Employment of deaf and hard-of-hearing people as library staff members.
- Publishing of a newsletter and other informative materials in both print and nonprint formats.
- Development of a videotape on the establishing of library services for the deaf and hearing impaired for use with other libraries.
- Previewing of captioned and signed films considered for purchase. People who are deaf and hard of hearing are included in the rating of the films as are hearing people. The evaluation is done on special forms developed to result in effective ratings.
- Making a continuing survey concerning the ways in which the library can provide the most effective services.
- Showing captioned programs on dedicated television sets in the library.
- Development of a slide program showing the library services offered.
- Making the project a clearinghouse for other libraries needing information on the development of a library program serving deaf and hearing impaired individuals.
- Offering, on a daily basis, computerized TTY/TDD news including such items as special features, weather, local events, announcements, and personal items. This program would be designed specifically for the use of people who are deaf.
- Compilation and distribution of a directory of services provided by the library for people in the community who are deaf or hard of hearing.
- Development of programs on issues of deafness and of other hearing losses designed for the deaf, hard-of-hearing, and hearing public on subjects such as detection of hearing problems in infants and children, legal rights of the deaf, coping with hearing loss, employment of deaf and hard-of-hearing people, hearing-ear dogs, signed poetry, and signed songs.
- Presentation of story hours with follow-up activities such as creative dramatization, illustrations of the story through filmstrips, slides, collages, and the making of posters and videotaping.
- Development of a bookmobile program to include services for deaf and hearing impaired people and including stops where the services can be used, such as schools for the deaf and community

programs and clubs for deaf and hard-of-hearing people as well as centers for elderly people.

- Development of information kits for the library on services for the deaf and hearing impaired. The kits can include both services in general of the sponsoring library and special services for deaf and hearing impaired people. A special kit for children is helpful.
- Presenting of programs and other information to the hearing public on deaf awareness and what it means to be hard of hearing.
- Development of songs for signing for children's programs.
- Relaying TTY/TDD and telephone calls between deaf and hearing people on request.
- Presenting of workshops on library service to the deaf and hearing impaired.
- Availability of scripts at the library for plays performed in the community for the duration of the play.
- Celebration of special birthdays throughout the year such as the birthday of Dr. Edward Miner Gallaudet, former president of Gallaudet College, Washington, DC, in February; Alexander Graham Bell, inventor of the telephone and educator of the deaf, in March; Anne Sullivan Macy, teacher of Helen Keller, in April; Helen Keller, deaf-blind lecturer, writer, and scholar, in June; composer Ludwig von Beethoven, partially deaf at age 32 and completely deaf at 46, in December; and Laurent Clerc, the first deaf teacher in America to teach deaf children; Laura Dewey Bridgman, the first deaf-blind person to be educated formally; and Thomas Hopkins Gallaudet, founder of the first permanent school for the deaf, all in December.
- Introduction of TTY/TDD TEL-MED to provide prerecorded information on health through telephone lines to people who have TTY/TDD equipment.
- Issuing of a calendar by the library that includes special occasions in relation to deaf and hard-of-hearing individuals to highlight "Deaf Awareness."

These and many other programs can be fully developed during the life of the project.

SURVEYING THE SERVICE

A survey of the deaf community can ensure the relevance of the project to the needs of the deaf. Such a survey should stress the communication and services required to obtain the best results from library use. An assessment of the level of the services will be a by-product of the survey. Another benefit of a periodic survey will be to provide to the deaf and hard-of-hearing people information concerning the services available. The survey forms can be mailed to individuals, be available at the library, at churches, and at organizations of and for the deaf and hearing impaired. Through a study of the answers to the survey, the library and the advisory committee can identify specific areas which require special attention.

Although the survey questions will vary from time to time as the program progresses, some of those which should be included are:

- Name and address.
- TTY/TDD number.
- Telephone number and whether the telephone sound is amplified.
- Knowledge of sign language, lipreading, and the level of skill.
- The use of a decoder for television.
- The need for large print.
- Knowledge and use of braille for TTY/TDD and/or for reading.
- Any other needs because of additional disabilities besides being deaf or hard of hearing.
- Present use of library, including identification of library/libraries used, frequency of use, type of use, and kinds of materials used.
- Level of satisfaction with services offered and ease of access to those services.
- Suggestions for improvement of services.

After the survey results have been tabulated, they can be made available to deaf and hard-of-hearing people, who can also be kept informed of the changes that are made in response to their answers. In addition to the general survey, a special study can be carried out on present services such as captioned films, story hours for children, public meetings, and available resources. The forms should be brief and be confined to one type of service only, with the level of use and the level of satisfaction as the information to be acquired.

A result of the ongoing assessment is a valid evaluation of the entire project at the end of the timespan allotted to the project. An additional assessment which can assist in the total evaluation is that of asking the users of the service to help determine the priorities for the continuing services. In doing this, the services can be listed in a questionnaire and the users asked to arrange them in priority order with the opportunity to add services not listed and to comment in general about the program.

In the overall assessment of the project by the advisory committee, the library administration, and the library staff, much of the information gained from the patrons can be used. Interviews with users can supplement the written data as well as oral and written comments from the staff, outside organizations, and the community in general. Results of programs of service for deaf and hearing impaired people developed in other libraries can assist in evaluation of a project program as well. Another good idea is to review professional field visits, professional meetings, and detailed questionnaires.

The results of the evaluation can assist in determining which programs are to be incorporated into the ongoing library program and at what level of funding. At the same time, the library and the advisory committee can determine which programs can be carried on by other agencies within the community. Survey results also indicate which services can be enhanced through closer cooperation with other agencies and community organizations.

Decisions reached concerning the services offered in the project at the close of the project can assist in making a smooth transition from a special project-type program to one which is a part of the ongoing library services. Both the planning and the public information relating to the changes in the breadth, depth, and placement of the services which may occur are vital to the use of the library on a continuing basis by deaf and hard-of-hearing individuals. In the phasing-in of the project as a part of the general library service, it is essential that the momentum, both in service and in use, be maintained.

THE SPECIAL SUBJECT PROJECTS

A second type of service, which can be developed to serve people who are deaf or have other types of hearing losses, is a special subject project, financed by special funds, with emphasis on one aspect of the program of library service. Such a project can be in addition to a traditional library program, a modified traditional program, or a special project of full services financed with outside funding. Such a special subject project can provide the opportunity to fully use creative ideas, innovation, and experimentation by both the library staff and the people who are deaf or hard of hearing. Because of the emphasis on one facet of the program, a 2-year time span only needs to be allocated to the project for achieving the objectives of the service.

Any of the services can be selected for emphasis as a special funded project. The following are examples of such special subject projects.

Awareness Program

With the number of people in the United States who have a hearing impairment of any kind reported in 1977 at 16.2 million (a rate of 76.4 hearing impairments per 1,000 persons), an awareness program becomes a priority in libraries. All age levels of the population are affected with such an impairment or loss. The largest number is among the elderly—385.5 per 1,000 for persons 75 years of age or over compared with 14.3 per 1,000 for persons under 17 years of age. The other age group statistics per 1,000 persons are 40.2, 17–44 years; 123.7, 46–54 years; and 204.6 for 65–74 years. The purpose of an awareness program is to alert libraries to the size and nature of the deaf and hard-of-hearing population requiring services to meet their needs, to inform people with a hearing loss about the present and potential services available to them currently and in the future, and to increase the awareness of the general public.

Awareness of the deaf and hard-of-hearing world among the hearing, and being involved with it, is as important as the services established for that segment of the population. Some of the activities which can be emphasized in the awareness program include:

- Conferences on library service for people who have a hearing loss. The emphasis in the conferences can be on the meaning of a hearing loss and its effect on using library services, along with an emphasis on communication. A segment can be included on what the public can do to help bring deaf and hearing impaired people into the mainstream of society. The inclusion of interpreters for the deaf as participants as well as interpreters for the program can assist in developing the linkage between the deaf and the hearing worlds.
- Seminars for people who are deaf or hard of hearing centered around the subject of "How Do We Rate with You" can raise the awareness of deaf and hearing impaired people concerning

what a library is and what it does. With emphasis on rating done by consumers, 2 publications can be used effectively as the focal point of the program: *The Public Library Talks to You* by Alice Hagemeyer,[1] and *Communicating with Hearing People: The Red Notebook.*[2] The concept of *The Red Notebook* was originated by Alice Hagemeyer.

- A weeklong workshop on awareness, developed and implemented by the entire community. The sponsors and facilitators can be, in addition to libraries, educational agencies (including schools for the deaf), teachers of the deaf-blind, civic organizations, the Junior League, Lions Club, Quota International, and the Sertoma Club. The purpose of this workshop can be to develop an awareness by the general public of the abilities, needs, and desires of people who are deaf or hard of hearing and of the attitudinal and communication barriers which exist in our society. The activities of the workshop will help to dispel the restrictive attitudes, replacing them with awareness. Through the interaction, the hearing can learn more about deafness and the non-hearing can improve their skills in communicating with hearing people. Hearing impaired participants can learn, also, about the libraries and other services available to them in the community. They have, in addition, an opportunity to communicate to the library and other agencies the special kinds of program needs suitable for them. The workshop may result in the formation of an advocacy group to work politically to meet the needs of deaf and hearing impaired people. In addition, to provide concerted and continued actions by the participants in the workshop, they can select areas of their own particular interests in problems of the deaf and hearing impaired such as communication barriers, educational opportunities and educational barriers, culture and heritage, the arts, employment opportunities, laws and legislation, and library opportunities and barriers. They can caucus according to their interests, develop a plan for continuing action, and develop concrete plans for that action.
- An "Aware Fair," developed by the library and other service organizations and agencies. Library services and programs to deaf and hearing impaired individuals can be exhibited in a shopping mall, convention center, or other areas which the public regularly visits.
- An open forum in which the library and other service organizations can present to the public the services currently being provided and those that they wish to provide in the future. Included

in the program of the forum can be a panel of legislators and other public officials to inform the hearing, deaf, and hard-of-hearing attendees about the present laws and regulations relating to deaf and hard-of-hearing people and those contemplated for the future. Such a panel provides a 2-way communication in raising the awareness of the public. It can also dispel many myths and misconceptions relating to the subject of hearing loss and its effect on the lives of people.

Such activities provide positive steps, through awareness, to remove as many barriers as possible to the use of library service by deaf and hearing impaired people. At the close of the awareness project, the library can maintain the momentum through the activities of a community awareness committee composed of people who have been involved in the activities of the project, along with other interested people in the community. In this way, awareness of all people can be raised and continued on an ever-increasing level.

A second special subject project for development is that of intensive utilization of visual materials and services. Because most aural materials and programs are inaccessible to the deaf and hearing impaired, emphasis is placed on the visual. The purpose of the special project is to bring materials to the people in a visual format.

One group of visual materials of great importance to deaf and hearing impaired people is that of captioned films. These films, captioned for the deaf, are available from several sources for loan, rental, or purchase. In addition, the classic silent films are useful as are subtitled foreign films. Some nonnarrated films are available as well as those which use sign language. The subjects range widely to cover all interests and age levels. Saturday matinees are possible as well as evening showings. Where no social clubs or local chapters of major deaf organizations exist, the captioned film program provides a place where deaf and hearing impaired people can meet at a social event. To publicize the films, flyers are effective when they are sent out to individuals, to schools, and to organizations serving deaf and hearing impaired people. The flyers can carry announcements about other related events in the community. Press releases can be sent to all local newspapers and magazines; special subject features are also of benefit in such a program. The library can become a community resource center for captioned films.

A part of the visual project should include locally produced videotapes. Libraries which have video equipment can explore ways in which it can be made available for producing the tapes for and with people who are deaf and hearing impaired. Such material can be developed and used on a cooperative basis among the libraries in the community and with related organizations. The videotapes can be captioned or signed; people who are deaf or hard of hearing can appear as actors in the videotaped programs.

The Multi-Level TV Captioning Project, a federally funded program, researched the best method of captioning programs so that young deaf children with limited reading skills can read and enjoy them. From this research came the multilevel captioning system. This system offers captioning at 3 levels of difficulty:

1. Sentence construction.
2. Vocabulary and idiomatic expressions.
3. Inferential or implied information.

Also, the rate of presentation of the captions is controlled to allow for comfortable reading time. At each of the levels, elements of language are considered. A resulting benefit from the project is a *Captioning Reference Manual*[3] followed by *Readable English for Hearing Impaired Students*[4] which allows others to replicate the process and techniques of analyzing and controlling components of language at 3 levels of increasing complexity.

A valuable program for deaf and hearing impaired people in the visual services project is that of captioned television programs. A service to be enjoyed by many people is an in-the-library activity of captioned programs on a closed-captioned television set with a discussion session at the close of the program, when appropriate. Making closed-captioned decoders available becomes an increasingly valuable service as more television programs become closed-captioned.

The usefulness of the visual materials in the project can be determined by circulation, audience statistics, and audience reaction. A video committee assisting in the development of the video program is also useful in determining its effectiveness and in the decision concerning those aspects of the project to continue in the ongoing program.

A third special subject project for development with special funding is that of heritage. An important part of this project is emphasis on history, culture, and folklore. Such a program is of value both to the hearing and nonhearing because there has been a lack of deaf writers and a lack of materials on deaf culture, language, and history in libraries in the United States. The book *Deaf Heritage*, by Jack Gannon,[5] provides a basic foundation for the project with the program built around it. Another publication of value in the project is *American Deaf Folklore*, by Simon J. Carmel,[6] included in *The Red Notebook* collection. In addition, book lists and brochures enable the general public, as well as deaf and hearing impaired people, to learn about heritage. In developing and implementing the project, it is essential that people be included on the advisory board who are knowledgeable in the contribution that deaf people have made to American history and culture. Such planning enables the entire project to maintain its special focus in its workshops, programs, filmmaking, poster development, and other activities developed as a means of taking the program to the people.

Another facet of the heritage project is the making of the arts accessible to deaf and hearing impaired people because the arts enhance the quality of life. The deaf, hard of hearing, and hearing individuals can all participate in a poetry series. In such a series, the sign language interpreter works with the poet or reader to ensure a poetic interpretation. Interpreted theater productions can also be included.

Because museums and art galleries are responding to the challenge of serving the members of their audiences who are deaf or hard of hearing, they can also participate in the project. In the past, deaf and hearing impaired people have found it difficult to take advantage of the opportunities to learn about American history and culture through museums and galleries. A number of large museums and galleries are captioning films, slides, and videotapes and providing amplification of sound systems. Some are rewriting printed materials in simplified English and using interpreters. Some are employing guides who have a hearing loss and using deaf or hearing impaired volunteers. Because of these activities, visits to museums and art galleries can be incorporated into the special subject project. Notices of programs of museums and galleries carried in library publications will reach the project audience. In addition, if the library supplies advanced printed material such as scripts or synopses, the visits are more interesting and understandable. Because museum and gallery collections usually illustrate the significance of language, they can do much to break down the communication barrier which isolates many people.

Visits to museums and galleries can also be planned to enable groups of people with limited hearing to enjoy lectures and film showings. This is possible when the museum or gallery installs amplification systems in the meeting rooms, uses captioned films and slides, interprets the programs, and provides materials prepared in simplified English. Some museums at historic schools for the deaf illustrate deaf heritage—the history of deaf culture. Gallaudet College in Washington, DC contains nineteenth century buildings in a National Register historic district. Maryland School for the Deaf in Frederick commemorates events of American and deaf history at the historic Hessian Museum. The California School for the Deaf, Fremont, formerly at Berkeley, has a heritage collection which includes photographs taken by one of its early graduates, Theophilus Hope d'Estrella. Also part of the school's heritage is a statue, "The Bear Hunt," by Douglas Tilden, another early graduate. Deaf history and art can be brought together in museums and art galleries. Because of the growing accessibility of museums and art galleries, people who are deaf or hard of hearing are showing great interest in both deaf and general history. Historical programs are becoming highly popular.

Through the heritage project, people who are deaf or hard of hearing gain information along with hearing people as to their history and their culture. Such a project provides not only the special subject project information but also plans for the future through videotapes, slides, and films produced during the project. Printed materials also can be developed during the project. At the close of the project, the advisory group can assess it and develop an ongoing plan so that the heritage project materials and programs become a part of the library's program for the people of the community. Because of the specialized nature of the heritage project, people who are deaf and hearing impaired must be involved at all levels of planning and participation.

Many other special subjects of library service to the deaf and hearing impaired people can be explored for special emphasis on a 2-year grant basis. Each project, if carefully planned, results in expanding horizons for the library as well as for the consumers. Each project brings the deaf and hearing impaired further into the mainstream of society.

TRAINING OF STAFF

To achieve positive results in establishing and maintaining library service to deaf and hearing impaired people requires special training of the library staff. Technical training is one aspect but probably more important is the sensitizing of staff members to the requirements of the users. Training can include such aspects as making the most and best use of video materials and equipment. Such training sessions emphasize the importance of video as an entertainment and learning format. Visual materials can be used individually or with groups, they can be used at a controlled pace, and they can, when in the public domain or by permission, be duplicated. Training is also needed for staff use of telecommunication devices for the deaf (TDD) and so that they can also teach people who are deaf how to use them. TDDs include TTYs (teletypewriters), CRTs (cathode ray tubes), and LEDs (light-emitting devices). Hands-on practice in the training session enables the staff members to use the equipment and to become proficient in instructing others.

Staff members can use training sessions to practice their sign language to communicate with those who express themselves through signs, they can practice speaking clearly for persons who lip-read, and learn to work smoothly with lipreading and signing interpreters. In addition, sensitivity training sessions and awareness programs are an essential part of the program. Emphasis in the training sessions is on the need to speak at a slower pace when being interpreted and, in discussion, to repeat any questions asked in speech through signing or in writing to the entire group and to direct the answers to the group. It is important to realize the need for the effective use of mime in communication and the avoidance of unfamiliar words and idiomatic expressions in communicating. Staff members learn alternative methods for communicating with deaf-blind people as well as deaf and hard-of-hearing people. They can learn how to use total communication.

During the training sessions, staff members can learn how common hearing loss is; that the effects vary greatly due to the difference in the severity of the loss and age of onset. In general, the greater the loss and the earlier it occurs, the less able a person will be to read and communicate effectively. The person, deaf or hard of hearing from birth, does not have a constant language experience so there is a greater effort needed for language and reading achievement.

Because special training includes providing books and other materials on the subject of deafness and the special needs of deaf and hearing impaired persons, these people must be included in the program. They will be able to give advice on criteria for materials on sign language, high interest/low vocabulary books, signed books, picture books, captioned films, and special-interest periodicals. Through an "Orientation to Hearing Loss" program, the staff will understand better the unique characteristics of hearing loss and the special needs of deaf and hard-of-hearing people. The trainers can be deaf or hard of hearing as well as hearing people. If the program includes staff members who are deaf and hearing impaired as well as hearing people, the group can better understand the difficulties faced by each group and how to overcome barriers.

Because little formal training is available for teaching people how to provide library service to people who are deaf or hearing impaired, libraries must necessarily provide the knowledge and experience through inservice training. To assist in tailoring the training to the specific needs of the community, the library can make a needs assessment of the deaf and hearing impaired in the community. As the sessions develop, the emergence of a general bibliography of literature on the characteristics of deafness and hearing impairment, library service to people with a hearing loss, and characteristics of this group of people in the specific community builds trainee awareness and understanding. The reading of the materials as a part of the training provides an invaluable background of information for an effective service.

Although both library staff members and library users need to make an effort to overcome the communication barrier, a few basic guidelines are helpful in the training information. The guidelines are especially important in meetings and conferences in which hearing, deaf, and hard-of-hearing people participate. A basic fact to remember is that people with a hearing loss cannot hear well enough, in most instances, to follow the discussion in any meeting; this is especially true of the question-and-answer period which is often included in a meeting or a conference. If the deaf and hearing impaired are included in the planning of meetings and conferences and in the discussion periods and if their advice is sought and listened to, all attendees will have the opportunity to participate in and benefit from the group. Also, having the meeting or conference interpreted lessens the communicative problems.

Staff members need to learn how to work effectively with an interpreter during the training session. Practice in conducting interpreted meetings of a group of hearing, deaf, and hard-of-hearing individuals helps the library staff member in many communication situations and improves 2-way understanding.

Training in the use of visual aids is important in developing effective communication, including the use of simple written messages to films, overhead projectors, diagrams, chalkboards, television programs, special outlines, vocabularly listings, and definitions for unfamiliar words.

In written communications, staff members' use of simple, short, written messages aids in communicating without the necessity of writing out each word. Short phrases or a few words are sufficient in an information transfer. Training in the use of the telephone can be a segment of a training session on communication. Some people with a severe hearing loss use a telephone with a built-in amplifier; some use a speaker telephone with an interpreter. In communicating through an interpreter, library staff members need to find out from the individuals involved what type of interpreter is required in each instance. The following are types of interpreting:

- Manual interpreting. The interpreter signs what the speaker says with some mouth movement—but does not mouth every word.
- Oral interpreting. The interpreter mouths what the speaker says (soundlessly) using gestures and facial expressions and translating the speaker's words for easier speechreading.
- Simultaneous interpreting. The interpreter mouths what the speaker says in English syntax.
- Reverse or voice interpreting. The interpreter speaks what a deaf person is signing and/or mouthing.

Meeting with the interpreter before sessions is important as well as introducing the interpreter to the group at the meeting. Practice can be provided with each type of interpreter in specific types of meetings to enable the staff members to communicate easily through a third person.

Staff members, deaf, hearing, and hard-of-hearing individuals need to learn patience with themselves as well as with the person with whom they are communicating. Because communication is 2-way, it is as important for the person to receive messages accurately as well as to send them. It is often necessary to ask a deaf person who is proficient in sign language to slow down or to repeat when the message is not fully understood by the hearing person. Practice in a public area is important in training staff members so that both the deaf and the hearing person become comfortable with all communication methods in real situations. When the group of staff members is made up of hearing, deaf, and hard-of-hearing people, the training sessions themselves become real communication situations for all. Those in the training session are encouraged to obtain all of the practice they can. This practice includes signing and reading signs. Such exercises improve not only the ability to send and receive messages but increase the signing vocabulary. Staff members need not strive to become experts; the ability to send and receive information accurately is a sufficient goal.

Librarians, in general, need to educate themselves about hearing loss and how to work with people who have a unique means of communication. In serving people who are deaf or hard of hearing, libraries have been deficient in this area of service. This has been due, in part, to a lack of awareness. The training sessions can reduce this problem if staff members:

- Realize that shyness exists in communicating in a means other than the usual communication methods.
- Remember that patience and understanding are basic to accurate communication.

- Learn one-to-one communication.
- Learn group communication.

The reasons that people who are deaf or hard of hearing give for not using a library are remarkably similar to those that hearing people give:

- I have never enjoyed reading.
- I do not know how to use a library, and I am too shy to ask for help.
- My friends and relatives do not use the library.
- It is much easier to buy books than to borrow and return them.
- My only experience with using a library was not a pleasant one so I have never tried again.
- I never really considered borrowing books for reading.
- I was not aware that the library had services I might use in addition to borrowing books.

Specific problems the deaf and hard of hearing often express in relation to the use of the library include:

- The library really does not know what to do when a deaf or hard-of-hearing person needs assistance.
- There are no employees who are deaf or hard of hearing who can help me, and no one knows how to communicate with me.
- The library does not have a TTY/TDD.
- People who have a severe hearing loss have not been trained to use a library when growing up and are now afraid to try. We need help.

These reasons should be treated as basic considerations in orienting people who are deaf or hard of hearing to the library. They are misconceptions to be dispelled by providing usable services but, more importantly, perhaps, by reversing the orientation of the potential consumers from nonuse to use. No one prescription enables this change to occur. Once the services are in place, designed by and for people who are deaf and hearing impaired, the library is faced with convincing this population to make the library a part of their lives.

To solve this problem, libraries can make staff time widely available in the beginning months of the service to serve deaf patrons on a one-to-one basis. Staff effort will focus on programs, discussions, classes, announcements, and any visual means which can be effectively used to arouse interest in the use of the library services. One-to-one communication, while costly in time, is a good means of explaining services that the library is providing and how these services can serve recreational, educational, or informational needs. Staff members with the necessary communication skills enable the deaf and hearing impaired to understand what the library can mean to them in their everyday lives. Staff members should definitely have:

- A complete knowledge of the library and its services.
- A dependable and continuing proficiency in communication skills.
- An understanding of how a hearing loss affects people in relation to library use.
- A sensitivity to the problems the deaf and hard of hearing have with library service and the patience for overcoming them.

Volunteers can supplement the library employees in this program. To be effective, however, the volunteers need to meet the above-mentioned criteria developed for library staff members working in the program.

A part of the work of the library staff is the reorientation of deaf and hearing impaired people to the library. Many elderly people who are deaf or hard of hearing were library users before they sustained their hearing loss. Because of their retreat from public contacts, they have cut themselves off from library use. The program for reorientation can stress the changes that have occurred in library attitudes and services which now make the library usable by people who have lost their ability to hear.

The results of both the orientation and the reorientation programs may come slowly. An orientation program that communicates the concept of the library and its services requires time, visual examples, and repetition. In the reorientation program, changing the stereotype of the library involves an explanation of the means by which the former barriers have been overcome. This can be accomplished, in part, through descriptions, visual aids, and actual visits to the library. The development of awareness through orientation and reorientation of deaf and hard-of-hearing people is just as important as the services established specifically for them.

PUBLICITY

In preparing informational publicity items, libraries can design materials for special segments of the deaf/hearing impaired population. For example, materials can be geared to individuals with a specific degree of expertise in communicating and in using the library. Therefore, the publicity needs to be diverse in type, format, and content. Some of the information can be integrated into the library's ongoing publicity developed for the general public simply by including the TTY/TDD number along with the number of the voice telephone and describing the services and resources for the deaf and hearing impaired. This type of public information is useful for those deaf and hearing impaired persons who are already library users and only need updates.

A second type of publicity is that which is developed especially for people who are deaf or hard of hearing and have a relatively high reading level but need to be made aware of the services available to them. The audience for this information also includes hearing people who are related to or interested in the deaf and hearing impaired. Another audience is those who are difficult to reach because of their isolation, their lack of reading ability, and lack of interest and experience in using library services.

All media can be used to publicize library services for deaf and hearing impaired people. Because this group is so diverse, some of the people will be reached by information regardless of the format or the language level. The printed word reaches and is understood by many of the deaf and hard of hearing in addition to the library's usual audience. In addition, if different types of publicity material are produced, with the language adapted to at least 2 other levels, the audience reached is greatly enlarged. One level which maintains a simplicity of language for a beginning reader will have a wide appeal; a second level with a more complex grammatical construction and with a larger vocabulary further improves the chances that the information will be understood and acted upon.

Included in the special publicity for people who are deaf or hard of hearing and others who are interested in hearing loss are brochures, leaflets, and bookmarks which include subjects such as:

- Services for the handicapped.
- Description of services, activities, and resources.
- Description of the library as an information, recreation, and education resource for deaf and hearing impaired people.
- Listing of library resources for understanding disabilities.
- Explanations of what libraries can do.
- Deaf awareness.
- Listings of library services and resources for parents of deaf children.
- Understanding deafness.
- Services to handicapped children.
- Overcoming barriers.

- Interpreting for the deaf.

Some publicity items which can be understood by all if they are written in simple language with much visual interpretation are publications which include:

- Stories for signing.
- Songs for signing.
- Information on using the library with your child (for deaf parents).
- Listings of services for people who are deaf.
- Instructions on how to use the telephone (TTY/TDD) to call the library.
- A monthly or weekly calendar of events at the library designed for deaf and hearing impaired individuals.
- A library calendar/date book including descriptive materials as well asspace for the days of the month for recording current library events.

Another factor to be considered in issuing publicity pieces on new and continuing services is ensuring that the people receive the materials. The type of distribution used will vary with the type of library but, with all libraries cooperating, many communication channels are available. The type to be used at any given time depends on the audience. Again this is something that deaf and hearing impaired people should have a major part in determining.

NETWORKS

Networks of information for the deaf and hearing impaired can be established through the regular communication systems developed by libraries for all types of service. As services for deaf and hearing impaired people are developed, they can become a part of the network of library service. Just as no one library can be self-sufficient in general services, it cannot be in services to people with a hearing loss. Through networks of information, services, and resources for people who are deaf or hard of hearing, they can receive services equal to those received by the general public. With each library designing its local services in relation to the needs of its community and with the help of the consumers themselves, the networks provide a wider scope and a deeper resource than would otherwise be possible, ensuring that this group will have adequate and usable services available to them on a national basis.

NOTES

1. Alice Hagemeyer, *The Public Library Talks to You* (Washington, DC: Gallaudet College, 1975).

2. National Association of the Deaf. *Communicating with Hearing People: The Red Notebook* (Silver Spring, MD: National Association of the Deaf, 1980).

3. Jill Shulman, ed., *Captioning Reference Manual* (Boston: The Caption Center, WGBH-TV, n.d.).

4. Jill Shulman and Nan Decker, eds., *Readable English for Hearing Impaired Students* (Boston: The Caption Center, WGBH-TV, n.d.).

5. Jack Gannon, *Deaf Heritage* (Silver Spring, MD: National Association of the Deaf, 1981).

6. Simon J. Carmel, "American Deaf Folklore." In *Communicating with Hearing People: The Red Notebook* (Silver Spring, MD: The National Association of the Deaf, 1980).

REFERENCE LIST

Bergman, E. *Arts Accessibility for the Deaf.* Washington, DC: National Access Center, 1981.

Brewer, Katherine, and McClaskey, Harris. "Survey of State Agencies." *HRLSD Journal* II (1) (Spring 1976):3.

Brown, Dale. "Access for All: Theaters Begin Playing to Everyone." *Disabled USA* (Winter 1982): 22–24.

The Caption Center. *The Multi-Level TV Captioning Project.* Boston: The Caption Center, WGBH-TV, 1982.

"Captioning: Performance Not Promises." *Caption* (Summer 1982): 1.

"Closed Captioning: Questions and Answers on the Process, the People." *NCI News* (March 1982). (Leaflet.)

Communicating with Hearing People: The Red Notebook. Alice Hagemeyer, originator. Silver Spring, MD: The National Association of the Deaf, 1980.

Cornelius, D. A., ed. *Barrier Awareness: Attitudes toward People with Disabilities.* Washington, DC: George Washington University, 1981.

"Courses and Equipment Aid Deaf at Library." *Library of Congress Information Bulletin* 34 (18) (May 2, 1975): 176–78.

"Current Services to the Deaf Being Offered in Public Libraries in the United States." *Fingertips Newsletter* 7 (3) (July–September 1981):8.

Deaf Action, Deaf Pride, Deaf Culture, Deaf Heritage. Washington, DC: District of Columbia Public Library, 1978. (Leaflet.)

"Deaf and Hearing Participants in Poetry Series." *Access* (January 1982):2.

Esteves, Roberto. "Video Opens Libraries to the Deaf." *American Libraries* 13 (1)(January 1982):36–38.

"The Hearing Impaired." *The Crab* 4 (1) (August 1974): 6–8.

Myhre, Margaret. *The Heritage of Deaf People.* San Francisco, CA: San Francisco Public Library, n.d. (Brochure.)

"News from the Deaf Awareness Workshops." *Keystone* 9 (3) (June–July 1980):1.

"1981—International Year of Disabled Persons." In *America, The Library Has Your Number*. Chicago: American Library Association, 1981: 25–27.

Putnam, Lee. "Information Needs of Hearing Impaired People." *HRLSD Journal* II (1) (Spring 1976): 2–13.

Resource Center, Library Service to the Deaf and Hearing Impaired. *Programming Primer*. Santa Fe Springs, CA: Metropolitan Cooperative Library System, n.d.

"San Francisco Library Project." *DCARA News* (October 1982): 3–4.

San Francisco Public Library. *Deaf Services*. San Francisco, CA: San Francisco Public Library, n.d.(Brochure.)

Songs for Signing. Cleveland, OH: Cuyahoga County Public Library, n.d.(Booklet.)

Sources of Video Materials by and for the Deaf. San Francisco, CA: Cooperative Services for the Deaf. San Francisco Public Library and Oakland, CA Public Library, n.d. (Leaflet.)

Stark County District Library. *Let's Have Fun!! Signs, Stories, Songs*. Canton, OH: Stark County District Library, n.d. (Booklet.)

Virginia State Library. *A Guide to Concepts, Activities, Resources. Library Services with Deaf People*. Richmond, VA: Virginia State Library, n.d.(Leaflet.)

Westerville Public Library Services to the Deaf Community. Westerville, OH: Westerville Public Library, n.d.(Brochure.)

Chapter 8
Professional Associations and the Service

In general, library associations have as their objectives promoting the development and use of libraries and promoting and improving library service and librarianship. They have been and are continuing to be, at the local, state, national, and international levels, a strong influence on and impetus to the development of library service to deaf and hearing impaired populations. Such has been true of general library associations with specialized units and of special library associations.

Activities of library associations which affect library service to the deaf and hearing impaired extend from education and advocacy to workshops to scholarships and intellectual freedom. The conferences of the associations themselves can be educational as far as library service to deaf and hearing impaired people is concerned. Professional associations are adapted to providing educational opportunities for preservice, inservice, and continuing education for their members. The association may act in a coordinating role or assume responsibility for the actual implementation in programing and development. The association can take the responsibility to ensure that educational programs are available for service to the deaf and hearing impaired and encourage library association members as well as nonmembers to take advantage of these opportunities. A related service provided by many library associations which is of value to deaf and hearing impaired persons is that of job placement in libraries. Other association activities which positively affect deaf and hearing impaired people include development of standards of service, public relations, and the emphasis on maintaining the freedom to read.

Librarians invest their time and talents in organizations with objectives they consider worthwhile. The associations are built around the needs of people who have common goals and objectives. They exist in answer to a need or to promote the welfare of an affected population in an effort to establish the common good. The professional associations, among their many activities, provide leadership in serving the members of the association, setting standards, developing programs of education, promoting intellectual freedom, training in the planning process, increasing the prestige of librarianship, and seeking out populations without service or with inadequate service.

An association is involved in the many facets of librarianship and has an impact on those areas of librarianship which the leaders and the members decide to emphasize. A progressive and flexible association membership uses many joint efforts to enhance and stimulate the work of the association in meeting current and changing needs. Through these efforts, an association has an impact on developing and providing library service far beyond its membership.

ACTIVITIES OF THE ASSOCIATIONS

Although library associations have always had an interest in institutional libraries and library service to people who are disabled and/or elderly, it was not until the 1970s that associations became visibly concerned about service specifically for deaf and hearing impaired people. This interest manifested itself through programs and publications developed for the deaf and hearing impaired population. In carrying on this activity, associations have held seminars and workshops on the subject of deafness and other hearing losses, often in cooperation with other organizations and agencies. Several state associations have a unit within their organization with the specific purpose of establishing and/or improving library service to deaf and hearing impaired people. Usually such groups are formed through caucusing or petitioning. Usually, also, deaf and hearing impaired librarians are among the group of librarians establishing the unit. In some of the associations, the deaf and hearing impaired are included as a part of a larger group devoted to specialized library services.

Within the American Library Association, the Association of Specialized and Cooperative Library Agencies (ASCLA) took the lead in developing library service and other related activities for the deaf and hearing impaired. This activity has been centered in the Library Service to the Deaf Section (LSDS). It was only after a thorough review of the American Library Association and its organizational structure that the study group decided that ASCLA was the suitable division in the association in which to locate the section. An ALA press release in March 1979 announced the formation of the LSDS. The section immediately

established a leadership role in the association. Its activities have resulted in development of services and in advocacy for services to the deaf
and hearing impaired. In addition to promoting library and information
services, the section is concerned with legislation relating to library and
information service for deaf and hearing impaired persons. Its membership is concerned with the stimulation of the production and distribution as well as the collection of library materials which are in formats
that are readily accessible to deaf and hard-of-hearing persons. The section is also concerned with the accurate portrayal of deaf and hearing
impaired persons in the media. LSDS has been developing relations
with organizations outside ASCLA which are also concerned with people who are deaf or hard of hearing. An occasional publication, *LSDS
Review*, has been issued which is primarily devoted to reviews of books
concerning library service to the deaf and hearing impaired and other
related subjects. This material is also, at times, published in *Interface*.[1]

Within the American Library Association, several units have co-
operated to produce programs and services of interest to the LSDS. An
effective preconference program was developed and presented in 1982
in Philadelphia. "Challenge: Serving Deaf and Hearing Impaired Children, Young Adults and their Parents" was sponsored by the Association of Library Service to Children, Association of Specialized and Cooperative Library Agencies, and the Young Adult Services Divisions,
all divisions of the ALA. During the International Year of Disabled
Persons, 1981, the National Year of Disabled Persons, 1982, and in the
Decade of Disabled Persons, 1983–1992, interunit cooperation was and
is essential to the success of the dedicated years and to the decade. The
cooperation of the divisions in working toward a single goal has been
and is dramatic. A valuable program developed during IYDP involved
not only the American Library Association through ASCLA but also
the Library of Congress through the National Library Service to the
Blind and Physically Handicapped; the School of Library and Information Science of the Catholic University of America; and the National
Rehabilitation Information Center (NARIC). This cooperative effort
resulted in a "Symposium on Educating Librarians to Provide Information to Blind and Physically Handicapped Individuals" in San Francisco in 1981. Education for library service to the deaf and hearing impaired was one of the considerations of the symposium.

An effective partnership effort among associations and agencies
during the International Year of Disabled Persons was the reception
held in 1981 in Washington, DC to honor books written by, about, and
for disabled persons. Cooperating in this observance were the American
Library Association through ASCLA, the Library of Congress through

the National Library Service for the Blind and Physically Handicapped, the International Federation of Library Associations and Institutions, the World Federation of the Deaf, the World Council for the Welfare of the Blind, the President's Committee on Employment of the Handicapped, and the U.S. Council on the International Year of Disabled Persons.

The International Years/National Year of Disabled Persons, 1981–1982, brought forth the best in communication and partnership. The IYDP/NYDP Committee, spearheaded by ASCLA, was composed of a representative of each division in ALA. The committee not only developed activities which it sponsored but also stimulated awareness among the library and membership of ALA. The highlights of this program are brought together in a report compiled by the chairperson of the committee. Many of the activities highlighted relate to the development of library service to the deaf and hearing impaired.

The Special Libraries Association has shown interest in services to the deaf and hearing impaired by publishing an article by Kieth Wright[2] on resources for deaf and hearing impaired people in the association's publication *Special Libraries*. Library associations in other countries are also promoting library service to this population. The International Federation of Library Associations and Institutions (IFLA) is developing a working committee devoted to library service to the deaf and hearing impaired. Papers on service to this group of people have been presented at the annual meetings of IFLA.

Although library associations have functioned effectively in the area of library service to the deaf and hearing impaired, the number actually participating in this activity is small compared with the potential level of participation and when measured against the need for the service. This type of library service has unique aspects which require an interest by professional associations to ensure that the service becomes universally available. The programs and activities undertaken by library associations have, for the most part, continued to provide positive results. However, some have declined in quality and in momentum because they have lost their high-priority status to other library interests and activities. With making library service available to all people a library objective, library associations need to reemphasize services to those who have been neglected by libraries in the past, including the deaf.

EFFECTIVENESS OF LIBRARY ASSOCIATIONS

Library associations are a potent force in the development of libraries and in promoting and improving library service and librarianship. To assist in the developing and maintaining of library service to the deaf and hearing impaired, library associations have brought together desirable principles to be followed in the form of standards and guidelines. In developing these standards, special attention is required to maintain flexibility because of the changing elements in this particular area of library service; standards require constant updating. Meeting standards leads to new, higher standards being set. If the standards are set too high at first, they can/should be broken down into stages and accomplished step by step. The use of standards of library service is valuable in the development of the service program as well as in its evaluation.

STANDARDS AND GUIDELINES

In establishing such standards, the professional association should call upon deaf and hearing impaired librarians to help ensure that the services developed to meet the standards will be helpful to the consumer. In addition, involving the consumers themselves in the development of basic standards and guidelines will result in quality, usable programs. A continuing, objective review of standards by others ensures that the standards and guidelines do not limit the service but rather provide for its continual progress in both breadth and depth.

Standards for library service which relate specifically to the deaf and hearing impaired are of relatively recent origin. In 1967, the U.S. Department of Health, Education and Welfare developed standards for library media centers for the deaf. These standards were considered when the *Standards for Library Services in Health Care Institutions* were developed in 1970. The *Standards for Library Functions at the State Level*, as revised in 1970, include the statement that captioned films should be made available for people who are deaf. Progress was made in the area of standards/guidelines for library service to the deaf and hearing impaired in 1981 when ASCLA published *Techniques for Library Service to the Deaf and Hard of Hearing* [2] in the fall issue of *Interface*. These guidelines for all types of libraries were developed by the ASCLA Standards for Library Service to the Deaf Subcommittee. Included in the guidelines are statements concerning communications, resources, publicity, programs, and staff. The purpose of these guidelines is to assist libraries in making all of their resources and programs available to all people who are deaf or hard of hearing. Emphasized under "Communications" are:

- Using sign language, lipreading, and note taking.
- Using directional and informational signs and all available means of communication.
- Having interpreters available at library-sponsored public programs and classes.
- Training library staff members to communicate with deaf and hard-of-hearing persons.
- Having a TTY/TDD available for reference, information and referral service, and for public access with others available as needed.
- Using sound amplification of auditory materials and of public access telephones.
- Equipping library television sets with decoders.
- Improving communication through a physical environment suitable for 2-way communication.
- Equipping buildings to ensure the safety of the deaf and hard-of-hearing user.

The "Resources" recommendations include:

- Providing a broad range of reading interests in a variety of formats.
- Including high interest/low reading level; well-illustrated print materials; film and electronic video, including captioned and noncaptioned; material developed especially for people who are deaf or hard of hearing.
- Collecting and displaying current information on deafness and hearing impairments. Making information on medical, legal, and educational materials available.
- Providing information and referral on organizations, institutions, and individuals providing service for deaf and hearing impaired people.
- Ensuring accessible and widely available library service.

In the areas of publicity and programs, guidelines include:

- Publicizing library service to the deaf and hard of hearing and also services provided by other organizations.
- Including TTY/TDD number on library publications and stationery.

- Including captioning or interpretation of any library programs on television.
- Making interpreters available for library programs.
- Including nonnarrated and captioned films as a regular part of the library film programs.
- Making library programs available to deaf and hard-of-hearing people with multiple handicaps.

"Staffing" recommendations include:

- Recruiting representatives of deaf and hard-of-hearing people for committees, boards, and volunteer groups.
- Involving deaf and hard-of-hearing persons in planning and implementing of programs being developed for the deaf and hard-of-hearing population.
- Training library staff members to communicate with deaf and hard-of-hearing people and to coordinate services to them.
- Considering the contributions deaf and hard-of-hearing people can make as employees.

The techniques, themselves, are specific and necessary for use in any stage of the development of library services to the deaf and hearing impaired. The full text of these techniques provides an important guide to libraries, librarians, and to deaf and hard-of-hearing people as they develop the design and implementation of the service.

Many of the other more general standards and guidelines which have been developed also have an effect on library service for deaf and hearing impaired people, although not as specifically. One such set of standards is that of the American National Standards Institute (ANSI), ANSI Standard A.117.1 (1980), "Specifications for Making Buildings and Facilities Accessible to and Usuable by Physically Disabled People." *Programming for Children with Special Needs* [4]by the Association for Library Service to Children, a Division of the American Library Association, was not developed as standards, but provides criteria for programing. The criteria address children with all types of disabilities and include specifically a section on deaf and hearing impaired children. Suggestions of examples for programing include using:

- An interpreter for the children when needed.
- An induction loop.
- Carpet to reduce distracting noises for hearing impaired children.
- Captioned films and stories which relate to current themes, are repetitious, are concerned with familiar themes, and are signed.

Program examples for serving deaf and hearing impaired children include:

- Family night programs.
- Visual aids such as large flannel boards.
- Activities such as dancing, pantomime, and dramatics for encouraging nonverbal communication.

One example of organizational rules for the general public in communicating with hard-of-hearing individuals is that presented by The Suzanne Pathy Speak-up Institute, Inc., New York, which is a member of the International Federation of the Hard of Hearing. The concept of the rules for speaking to an individual with a hearing loss include:

- Speaking clearly and slowly and at a normal level.
- Rephrasing sentences when they are misunderstood.
- Conversing away from a background of noise.
- Standing in a lighted are.
- Facing the person.
- Keeping mouth clear of all obstructions.
- Asking the person's advice on what you might do to make the conversation easier.

These rules become important in light of the fact that one out of every 2 individuals has some type of hearing impairment at some time.

CONTINUING EDUCATION

A related activity of library associations and other organizations is that of continuing education. A part of this education is carried out effectively at conferences sponsored by either one organization or by a group of several organizations. The American Library Association's 1982 preconference, "Challenge: Serving Deaf and Hearing Impaired Children, Young Adults and their Parents," brought 3 independent ALA divisions together to produce an educational program. The resulting continuing education had, as its objectives, providing information and experience to increase librarians' understanding of the information needs of the parents of deaf children, the several approaches available for educating deaf and hearing impaired young people, the impact that prelingual deafness has on language comprehension, and the special needs of the deaf and hearing impaired young adults.

At the same conference in Philadelphia, a program on libraries and the hard of hearing provided education on the subject of hearing loss and what it means to be hard of hearing, special problems encountered by hard-of-hearing people, accessibility aids for serving hard-of-hearing library users and working with staff as well as demonstrations of accessibility aids for hard-of-hearing people. The program was cosponsored by the Association of Specialized and Cooperative Library Agencies' Library Service to the Impaired Elderly and Library Service to the Deaf Sections; Reference and Adult Services' Library Service to an Aging Population Committee. Other ALA conference programs have included a "Swap and Shop" program in which library materials, ideas, and equipment for working with deaf and hearing impaired people were exchanged, presented, and discussed; the use of video for people who are deaf has also been presented at an ALA conference.

Educational programs of this nature have been presented on a local and regional basis but not on a regular schedule. They have been included in many of the general programs and in programs presenting library service within the community. Because of the lack of available education in such service, state and regional library associations become most important as vehicles for providing an educational opportunity for people who do not regularly attend ALA conferences, although some of the ALA programs are recorded on cassettes and are available for purchase.

Continuing education can also be provided through conferences of associations of and for the deaf and hearing impaired. An example of such a conference is "A Workshop for Deaf Consumers and an Interpreters Training Workshop," which was sponsored by the Nevada Association of the Deaf, the Nevada Bureau of Vocational Rehabilitation, the Ohlone College in Fremont, California, and involved the California School for the Deaf in Fremont. The workshop was held in Las Vegas (Clark County) and had as its intended audience deaf persons, beginning interpreters, advanced interpreters, and other interested persons. It actually brought together staff, students and parents involved with the Clark County School District Deaf and Hard of Hearing Program; librarians; deaf consumers; interpreters for the deaf; members of the sponsoring groups; and other interested individuals. This workshop enabled participants to interact with national leaders involved with deaf issues.

Continuing education programs sponsored by associations are important because few librarians and support staff have had the opportunity to learn about aspects of service to deaf and hard-of-hearing people. The associations, at any level, can make this educational opportunity available to all, and the results are especially effective when the library association and an association for/of deaf and hearing impaired people make a cooperative effort in making continuing education available. The ASCLA Library Service to the Deaf Section can act as a model for state and regional associations, not only in continuing education programs, but in all types of activities involving deaf and hearing impaired people. Although the section has many activities, it has had a profound effect on educating librarians in the many aspects of providing library service to the deaf and hearing impaired. Through its work with other organizations, the section has spread its knowledge and expertise to a wider clientele than would otherwise be possible. It has also encouraged others to recognize their responsibilities to the deaf and hearing impaired in their programs of continuing education.

Publications of national, regional, and state associations are also a source of educational information and are widely available. Included in this group are the publications of library associations and associations of/for deaf and hard-of-hearing people. ASCLA's publication, *Interface*, has carried news of the Library Service to the Deaf Section as well as examples of services, guidelines for service, employment of deaf and hearing impaired people in a policy statement, and resources and information related to the subject of deafness and other hearing loss. The unit also acts as an information source concerning other organizations to contact for further information and assistance. In most instances, associations issue a regular publication and/or have educational materials available on both a purchase and a free basis. The Library Service to the Deaf Section has assisted in the developing and providing of an annual information packet for *The Red Notebook*, through receiving materials, organizing a resource file, and in promoting library activities for people who are deaf. Both *Interface* and *American Libraries* carry information and reviews of publications related to the deaf and hearing impaired. Bibliographies and filmographies including materials relating to the deaf and hearing impaired are published in *Interface*. Information which is useful in continuing education is included in publications of associations of the deaf and hearing impaired. An example of this type of information is that included in a column on library service by Alice Hagemeyer in *The NAD Broadcaster*, a publication of the National Association of the Deaf. State library association publications carry information on library programs for deaf and hearing impaired persons. One such example is that of the Maryland Library Association publication, *The Crab*. Information included in such publications provides educational information as well as a clearinghouse of information for those interested in serving the deaf and hearing impaired.

Associations function, also, as an information channel to educate the public as well as librarians in the areas of deafness and hearing impairment. In October 1982, when the Public Broadcasting System aired the documentary, "To Hear," the American Library Association provided library directors and others with information concerning the broadcast and a colorful poster relating to the program. Library directors and staff were urged to promote "To Hear." The program was concerned with hearing conservation and the pleasures and hazards of sound as well as deafness and hearing impairment.

Library associations are also active in providing scholarships for the continuing education of people already in the library field. The grants may range from a substantial amount to mini-grants of a lesser amount. They can be used for many purposes, including education in library service to deaf and hearing impaired people.

Throughout the development, expansion, and improvement of library service to the deaf and hearing impaired, professional associations have played an important part. These associations provide a forum for people who wish to work together in a common endeavor and to acquaint others with whom they work of the need for service and the possibilities and potential of its development. They provide, to a certain extent, a clearinghouse of ideas, services, resources, and equipment. Professional associations promote and provide continuing education through the many channels available to them. They are truly a most important means through which the objectives of effective library service to the deaf and hearing impaired can be reached.

NOTES

1. *Interface*, quarterly publication. Association of Specialized and Cooperative Library Agencies, American Library Association, Chicago, IL.
2. Kieth C. Wright, "Deafness Information Center." *Special Libraries* 66(2) (February 1975):74–78.
3. "Techniques of Library Service to the Deaf and Hard of Hearing," *Interface* 4(1) (Fall 1981):2-3.
4. Association for Library Service to Children, *Programming for Children with Special Needs* (Chicago: American Library Association, 1981).

REFERENCE LIST

American Library Association. *Handbook of Organization, 1983–1984.* Chicago: American Library Association, 1983.
———.*Standards for Library Functions at the State Level.* (Revision of the 1963 edition.) Chicago: American Library Association, 1970.

————.*Standards for Library Services in Health Care Institutions.* Chicago: American Library Association, 1970.

Association for Library Services to Children; Association of Specialized and Cooperative Library Agencies; Young Adult Services Division. *Challenge: Serving Deaf and Hearing Impaired Children and Their Parents.* Chicago: American Library Association, 1982. (Brochure.)

Dalton, Phyllis I. "IYDP at IFLA." *Interface* 4 (3) (Spring 1981):10.

————. "IYDP Reception." *Interface* 5 (2) (Winter 1982): 6-7.

————.*Libraries in the United States and the International Year of Disabled Persons: Highlights of the Year.* Las Vegas, NV: Phyllis I. Dalton, 1982.

Dickey, Marilyn. "Helping Others." *The Washingtonian* (October 1981): 131–39.

Hagemeyer, Alice. "Library for Deaf Action." *The NAD Broadcaster* 4 (11) (November–December 1983): 13.

"Library Association Administration." *Drexel University Quarterly* 3 (3–4) (July–October 1967).

Somerton, Cathy. *Welcome to the Contra Costa County Library: A Quick Guide for the Deaf and Hearing-Impaired.* Pleasant Hill, CA: Contra Costa County Library System, 1983.

The Suzanne Pathy Speak-Up Institute, Inc. New York: The Suzanne Pathy Speak-Up Institute, n.d. (Brochure.)

Symposium on Educating Librarians and Information Scientists to Provide Information on Library Services to Blind and Physically Handicapped Individuals. Washington, DC: National Library Service to the Blind and Physically Handicapped, Library of Congress, 1981.

Chapter 9
Community Relations and the Service

From the very beginning, libraries in America have been unique institutions, primarily because they have always developed in a different way from one community to another. Throughout the development of libraries, efforts have been continuously made to increase the quality of library services available and to increase the number of individuals who have complete access to the total range of library services. Libraries are committed to being freely available to all people.

COMMUNITY ACTION

Achieving these objectives, as far as the deaf and hearing impaired are concerned, requires the actual and realistic involvement of these people themselves. Libraries are presently confronted with the serious problem of having unusable and inaccessible services to offer to this group of people. Little training is available which provides library staff members with the knowledge of how to serve deaf and hearing impaired people. Libraries are not usable by some deaf people because of poor academic achievement; their use is also adversely affected because of communication problems.

The implication of these problems is tremendous. With this population spread throughout the geographical area served by the library, the staff must make an unusual effort to identify deaf and hearing impaired people. They will find that the people identified will range from those whose language and intellectual achievement are extremely limited to those who communicate effectively and have made outstanding intellectual achievements. Making libraries accessible to this group involves making library resources usable and accessible; the involvement of the deaf and hearing impaired people in the community in designing programs of service and evaluating is vital.

What can the deaf and hearing impaired contribute to a library program? What can parents do to help with programs for the children? They can supply advice and a perspective as individuals who are deaf or hearing impaired or are concerned with someone who is. When the library employs deaf and hearing impaired staff members, it has a continuing resource for such advice. With so much variety required because of the varied needs of deaf and hearing impaired people, no one library program will meet all requirements.

One of the most important steps a library can take in the development of a practical program is to meet the deaf and hard-of-hearing people on their own ground—at their local clubs or other organizations. In addition, inviting them to the library so that they can give their views on what is needed and what they feel is now available to them will provide valuable information. Also, both those with a hearing loss and those who are hearing will better understand problems encountered in designing a plan which will result in a usable and accessible library program.

Interpreters will be needed at these sessions. When meetings are held, they should be planned at several locations to ensure that people do not have to travel a great distance in a highly populated area. Active participation should be encouraged. A benefit received from this type of planning is the individualized programs which result. They are not simply those that imitate other library programs that have been successful. Programs based on the needs of the individual community have unique characteristics. Patience is needed in the development, as well as in the utilization, of the services. It takes time to develop a worthwhile library program and more time to achieve maximum use of it.

Care must be taken so that libraries do not become so involved in the service that they forget the most important ingredient of all—the individual deaf and hearing impaired user or potential user. The great potential of the individual is the most valuable resource available to the design of the library program. Many who work with the deaf believe that there are 3 broad categories of individual deaf and hearing impaired people. They are:

- The top achiever, which comprises 5–10 percent of this population. Individuals in this group have language skills and have been able to meet the requirements of college and technical schools.
- The middle achiever, which comprises 40–50 percent of the deaf and hearing impaired population. The language skill of individ-

uals in this group has not been developed far enough for functioning effectively in institutions of higher learning.
- The underachiever, which comprises 30–40 percent of the deaf and hearing impaired population. Their language ability has not developed to a high degree.

To achieve optimum results requires both individual and group advocacy. To achieve any degree of success in advocacy requires obtaining information about the program desired and information at the local level about the groups concerned. Successful advocacy for library service to the deaf and hearing impaired requires convincing the decision makers, the funding groups, and the library administration of the need for the service. They will require information to convince them that the allocation of funds for adequate services and resources to deaf and hearing impaired people is a high priority. At the state level, those advocating for service may turn their attention to the establishment of a clearinghouse of information on library service to deaf and hearing impaired people. At the national level, the effort may be made to establish a national library service to the deaf and hard of hearing.

To achieve progress through community action, it is necessary for both library staff members and the deaf and hearing impaired to become involved in the community. Such action may include the following:

- Publishing articles on deaf and hearing impaired people in newsletters and newspapers.
- Dedicating a scheduled event such as a fund raiser, a picnic dinner, a reception, or a special day of library programs for deaf and hearing impaired people.
- Inviting a speaker such as a representative of an agency or organization for/of deaf and hearing impaired people to address a regularly scheduled event.
- Encouraging the media to feature deaf and hearing impaired people in their work settings.
- Conducting advocacy training workshops.
- Developing a brochure highlighting the achievements of deaf and hard-of-hearing persons in the locality to raise the awareness of the general public.
- Producing a film, with the help of the media, based on an original drama written to make the community aware of the contributions, real and potential, of deaf and hearing impaired people. Such a production requires the involvement of deaf and hearing impaired people throughout the entire life of the project.

- Designing a month-long activity during May to celebrate "Better Speech and Hearing Month" and "Deaf Awareness Month."
- Holding a "Hearing Resource Fair" which includes demonstrations of lipreading, signing, and the latest technological advances in assisting deaf and hard-of-hearing persons; also include an exhibit of library resources available to them. Such a fair offers an opportunity for cosponsorship by many community agencies.
- Involving the business community in employment programs. A Job Fair could be held for deaf and hearing impaired people.
- Developing a directory of community services available to deaf and hearing impaired people. This directory can be a guide to all organizations, agencies, and professional groups providing services in the geographical area concerned.
- Observing "Deaf Heritage Week" by presenting activities by and for people who are deaf. Each year, the week could have a special focus such as recognition of the contributions made by deaf people in America, exhibits by deaf artists, recognition of deaf authors, or dedication of the week to people who are deaf-blind.
- Developing a transportation plan for and with deaf and hearing impaired people. One means by which this can be done effectively is through surveys asking whether the people need a ride or can give a ride to someone else. Through this plan, not only will more people be able to attend library programs, but valuable interaction can also take place among the attendees at library activities.
- Placing a suitable collection of library materials at the meeting place of social clubs of the deaf and hearing impaired or at other organizational meeting areas. Such a library collection provides a beginning link between the library and the consumer.

Involving deaf and hard-of-hearing persons in the design of library service is an ongoing process. This involvement provides interaction for library staff and for the potential and actual user. It is appropriate, during this planning period, to reach out to as many of the people as possible to get their thoughts and suggestions for making the library useful to them. Because their needs are ever-changing, such a review assists in the identification of specific areas in which changes should be made for program improvement. It will also indicate how much they use the library or have a definite knowledge of its positive influence on their lives. In most instances, when an overall survey is made of the use of the library by deaf and hearing impaired persons, the results are disappointingly small. The challenge is then to the consumers themselves and to the library to increase the use of the library as the program develops. One such survey was made in 1982 by Martha Sheridan, then of the Family Life Center in Columbia, Maryland. The deaf and hard-of-hearing people surveyed lived in Maryland. The purpose of the survey was to determine the extent to which they used the public library. The group surveyed was small; not all counties in Maryland were included. A total of 174 people responded. Of these people, 168 use telecommunication devices for the deaf; 161 know sign language; 152 have a TV decoder; 103 sometimes use materials at public libraries; 48 use them often; 21 never use the library; 2 rarely do. Although the number surveyed was not large, the responses are interesting because they indicate the kind of information which can be gained through a survey. Such a survey also has the additional value of involving people in developing a base for continued library planning.

In developing and implementing library programs for the deaf and hearing impaired, libraries are aware of the need to establish and maintain communication with legislative bodies. Because many of the people in this group have had little experience with advocacy, it is important that they have the opportunity to participate in educational programs concerned with the meaning of social action, democratic procedures, citizen participation, and how to be an effective advocate. The legislative committees of professional associations can play an important role in assisting with legislative workshops for deaf and hard-of-hearing people. Such workshops will be most effective if cosponsored by library associations and associations of deaf and hearing impaired people. Through such programs, these people can make themselves heard in local, state, and national legislative bodies. Knowledgeable advocates and leaders from among the deaf and hard-of-hearing communities are needed. Librarians can assist by doing as much as possible to advance leadership training, to provide access to information, and to maintain linkages with other organizations. Hearing people can help by assuming advocacy roles—by helping deaf and hearing impaired people to increase the awareness of the general public of their special needs.

One of the situations that often occurs in advocacy activities is that individuals who are deaf or hard of hearing are included in a grouping of handicapped individuals or special groups. These groups have a wide range of different interests in the area of library service and, as a result, the unique needs of people with a hearing loss can be lost in the many concerns which must be addressed with a larger group. In some instances, a deaf person's need for library service relates more to the needs of ethnic groups rather than to those of handicapped persons because some deaf peoples' problems of communication relate to a difficulty in reading and understanding the English language. Designating the deaf population as a separate cultural/ethnic group may make it easier to consider this group as a separate concern rather than part of a larger and more diverse unit.

Even though some libraries are serving the deaf and hard-of-hearing communities with videotaped information, signed or captioned films, and many of the new technologies, the average person in this group is probably not a library user. There is an identifiable need for them to have a better understanding of the library services available to them and how they can be used effectively. Their needs are specific and require specific attention through advocacy for deaf and hearing impaired people's library service.

In order to have factual information on which to base political or other related action, it is necessary to question deaf and hearing impaired persons. One means of receiving information is through a brief and factual questionnaire. Among the subjects that can be included for consideration by a library user are the following:

- Regularity of library use.
- Instruction received concerning library use.
- Determination of the priority order of information and referral service, research, captioned material, programs of entertainment, special library materials, education programs, increase in library services, utilization of sign language by the library staff, raising awareness of special services to the deaf and hearing impaired, and use of new technologies.

If the individual is not a library user, s/he can be asked which reason/reasons most accurately describe library nonuse:

- Not interested in reading.
- Staff cannot communicate with deaf and hard-of-hearing people.
- Do not know how to use the library.
- Do not know what a library can do for an individual.
- Other.

Through such a survey, the advocacy for library services to deaf and hearing impaired persons will have a base upon which all of the advocates can build an information file.

ADVOCACY FOR LIBRARY SERVICE

Libraries are places where people can turn to for information which has been accumulated and organized for rapid retrieval and for ease of use. It is essential that people with a hearing loss have access to an adequate program of information. The question which can be put to the decision makers by the advocates for such a service is: What will you do about ensuring that the needed service is available and what is the time frame in which it will take place?

Beginning an advocacy program is difficult. Some of the areas which can be addressed are:

- Prevention of hearing loss and speech difficulty.
- Early identification of hearing loss and intervention.
- Living and learning with the disability.
- Working and the disability.
- Library service to the deaf and hearing impaired.

Through the division, by subject, of the people working in the advocate program, each group can take one area as a task force. The library can provide a service to the advocacy through its staff, programs, resources, creative ideas, and technologies. By putting the work of each task force together, the advocacy group will find the areas in which it lacks coverage. The group can then work toward closing the gap between what exists and what is needed.

The necessity for involvement in deaf advocacy has greatly increased because of the pressing need for the instituting and/or expanding and upgrading of library service for this group. Added to this is the increasing pressures from all areas of society for a part of the tax revenue. The scope of involvement, particularly of the deaf and hearing impaired people, has taken on new and broader dimensions. As they have become more active and better informed on what a library can offer, they have become more able and more impelled to work toward the development of library service for themselves and for library service in general at all levels of government and in all types of libraries. Regardless of the locality and of the unique needs, some of the principles to be kept in mind by the advocacy group are:

- Work together to present a unified program.
- Identify the leaders in the community and work through them.
- Realize that advocating the service is a continuing program of public relations although the emphasis will change as the service develops.

- Present programs of action which are well planned with both continuity and flexibility.
- Adopt a realistic approach in the action and develop a patient outlook.
- Remember to express appreciation of all efforts on behalf of a program promoted whether successful or not.

In developing the program for action as an advocacy group, it is necessary to:

- Know the clearly defined goals and objectives.
- Have information on the goal, how proposed action will improve the current and the future situations, and what the estimated cost will be initially and for the ongoing program.
- Have a timetable developed for implementation, initially and ongoing.
- Prepare written material stating the goals, objectives, needed action, estimated cost, and time frame. This material should be prepared for distribution as needed.
- Secure as wide support as possible for the program.
- Make use of media, telephone calls, and personal visits.
- Make sure that all questions concerning the proposed program are answered.

The importance of library service to deaf and hearing impaired people needs to be explained to all governmental bodies by the consumers themselves and their hearing supporters. The proposed programs should have both long- and short-range objectives. The fact that the development of these services and resourcees requires financing is an important point to emphasize in presenting a plan. In developing and following up on the program of action, the importance of a thorough knowledge of organized groups in the community, especially those related to deaf and hearing impaired individuals, cannot be overemphasized. One of the most effective means of developing support for a program is through working with organized community groups. These organizations can provide support for an advocacy group for library service to deaf and hearing impaired people. The formation of a library committee within organizations of/for deaf and hard-of-hearing people can provide a new strength to advocacy. An example of such a group is that formed within the National Association of the Deaf called "Library and Information for Deaf Action" (LIDA). The goal of the group is to alert deaf and hard-of-hearing people about the services which public libraries can provide. Some of the state associations of/for the deaf have also formed library committees.

Governmental relations units within organizations can be effective in maintaining, enhancing, and making service universally available. To achieve these objectives, the unit can engage in varied activities such as analysis and dissemination of information concerning proposed and pending legislation, laws, governmental policies and procedures, and court actions affecting deaf and hard-of-hearing people. An important activity can be training advocates; an example of a workshop on advocacy is "New Challenges in Deaf Education," conducted in 1981 by the Public Policy Studies Office of the National Academy, Gallaudet College. In this workshop, the participants took the roles of state and federal legislators, lobbyists, special interest group experts, and concerned citizens. The goal was to increase the knowledge of the participants in the political process. Participants took active roles in simulated exercises in defining and identifying problems and determining needs as well as solutions on issues which affect the lives of deaf Americans. In the exercise, they developed and presented "expert" testimony to the role-playing "senators."

A power structure exists in every community regardless of its size or form of government. The advocates for library service to deaf and hearing impaired people should become well acquainted with the power structure so that they will succeed in their objectives. Among the "power brokers" will be those who are supportive of the purpose of the advocacy.

In addition to the recognition and utilization of the power structure, the advocacy should be broad-based. Educational institutions and religious, cultural, and business representatives should be included as well as those from rehabilitation groups. Where one group of individuals interested in library service to deaf and hearing impaired people cannot succeed, a coalition between or among 2 or more groups will achieve the objective. The library, its staff, board of trustees, and Friends groups plus organizations of/for deaf and hearing impaired individuals can form a coalition. The coalition members have a united advocacy group which can present justification for desirable action. It can also, on short notice, oppose, with documented testimony, any undesirable action which is proposed.

To help ensure that an informed population exists, the sponsorship of a statewide meeting such as a governor's conference helps to make such awareness possible for instant action. If regional conferences are held prior to or following the statewide conference, the information will be widely available on a local basis as well. While the public may appear to be apathetic as far as the needs of deaf and hearing impaired persons for library service are concerned, a part of that apathy can accurately be attributed to lack of information/awareness. The bringing together of people in a common effort enables them to realize their strengths and newly recognized abilities and to see the new opportunities for action open up to them. Probably the greatest benefits which will come from such meetings are that people will better understand the problems that deaf and hearing impaired people have with traditional library service and will recognize the shortcomings of present service. These concerns can be brought up with librarians, governing bodies of libraries, Friends of Libraries, vocational and rehabilitation professionals, the deaf and hearing impaired, interpreters, and the parents of deaf and hard-of-hearing children as well as to other interested participating citizens. Without such meetings, the exchange of ideas among these groups of people is almost impossible. Through regional and statewide conferences, advocacy groups can be developed for action on any level of government.

While one statewide conference will establish a momentum, the action needs to develop into a continuum. One conference can be followed up with current awareness programs which use the existing communication system to help to meet the needs of the deaf and hard-of-hearing people. The holding of periodic conferences on deafness and hearing impairment will help to maintain communication among all of the people involved. Probably the deaf and hearing impaired themselves can accomplish the most by working together in their own geographical area. Sometimes overcoming communication barriers is difficult; the challenge is to develop creative solutions.

TALENT AND LEADERSHIP

Throughout its involvement as described thus far, the library can also help in the search for talent and leadership among this group. Identification of talent and leadership among this group. Identification of talent and leadership will not only bolster the advocacy but will help bring these people into the mainstream of society. Special programs during Deaf Action Week, Deaf Heritage Week, Deaf Awareness Week and Month, and Better Speech and Hearing Month not only bring deaf and hard-of-hearing people together in their celebrations but also involve them in the programing. An opportunity is provided for them to be involved as participants both in the presentation and discussion periods.

People can be recruited for these programs in many ways. Information about the library programs to be held during these dedicated weeks and months can be disseminated through the local media and to deaf and hard-of-hearing members of organizations. If a request for help from the people is included in the announcement, the first step in talent and leadership identification is made. If the response is slight, the library can repeat the request, using a different wording and format. Asking deaf or hard-of-hearing people known by the library to assist in the search for people with present or potential talent and with leadership qualities will bring additional positive results. It is possible that people with a hearing loss will be hesitant to work with groups that include hearing people even though they have successfully worked with nonhearing people in similar programing situations. With the library's help, much of the reluctance can be overcome.

The development of exhibits and displays can result in the easy involvement of deaf and hearing impaired people in identifying capabilities. An arts and crafts exhibit in the library that uses only the work of people who are deaf or hard of hearing can involve many individuals in creative programing in a library. Those preparing the exhibit can identify and include as many local artists as possible. A reception for authors who are deaf or hard of hearing gives an opportunity for the public to recognize them and their writings. Local authors can speak about their writings during the reception. During "Deaf Heritage Week" or at other times when the library is presenting historical programs, deaf or hard-of-hearing speakers can talk about their heritage and any local history relating to the deaf and the hearing impaired. To emphasize the effectiveness and beauty of sign language, people who are deaf and proficient in signing can present songs, poems, and drama at a public program in the library. As deaf and hard-of-hearing people become proficient in effectively using the library, they become a valuable asset to the library and useful mentors for other deaf and hard-of-hearing individuals, as well as effective workshop and seminar leaders.

The search for talent and leadership involves people of all ages. Story telling programs allow children to participate in an enjoyable experience while developing the ability to cope with experiences in real life. The children can assist in the development of the story hour programs by providing the props to be used in the stories and becoming active participants in the telling of the stories. Those with acting ability can dramatize the story; others can illustrate the stories or engage in other activities of their choice. High school-age users can develop programs through dramatic adaptations of the classics. Video programs can be developed from material in the library by those who have technical capabilities, creative ideas, dramatic talent, and signing proficiency.

These children can best be reached through the schools and/or through special library classes.

To identify leaders in the community, librarians should investigate, in addition to the local deaf clubs, chapters of national associations. Two examples are the National Association of the Deaf and Self Help for Hard of Hearing Persons, Inc.(SHHH). The names of the officers of these chapters are available through local or national publications. Local officers can participate in library programs and become the communication link with other deaf or hard-of-hearing persons. In some states, local chapters of national associations have not yet been formed; in such cases, the national association should be contacted.

As the library program develops, a leadership workshop should be held for deaf, hard-of-hearing, and hearing individuals. The design of such a workshop may include one or 2 general sessions which everyone attends; using interpreters and visual materials is helpful. Several smaller discussion groups on subjects related to leadership should also be formed during the course of the workshop. These will enable the participants to pursue the subject of leadership in depth and allow all members to participate in the discussion. If the small group discussion sessions have agendas distributed in advance, the participants will have the opportunity to formulate ideas prior to the discussion and can then make recommendations for follow-up by the library and the participants.

In developing each program of library service to deaf and hearing impaired people, an advocacy committee from that group of people is necessary to succeed. A consumer advisory board helps to ensure that the program, throughout its life, is and continues to be relevant to the needs of the deaf and hearing impaired. For the most part, the group will provide advice and consultation on how the program should be designed and implemented. The size of the board will vary according to the size of the deaf and hard-of-hearing population and in relation to the type and size of the library. It is important, however, that the committee be representative of the users and potential users. Organizations of the deaf and hearing impaired can be included in meetings as ex-officio members. The same holds true for the library staff.

BOARDS AND COMMITTEES

In some instances, it may be difficult to identify those potential appointees who would comprise a representative group. One method might be to call a meeting of deaf and hearing impaired individuals, parents of deaf and hard-of-hearing children, and other interested people to determine the concerns that specific people have in relation to library service to the deaf and hearing impaired. Such a meeting would require extensive advance publicity and an easily accessible meeting place. In a large population area, more than one group and one location will be needed. The meeting place should be the library and its branches if all are located within easy access. Because it is difficult to reach all of the deaf and hearing impaired on a particular date, follow-up publicity about the need for representatives can assist in securing a committee of people who represent their constituents. A waiting period for response from others who were not in attendance at the meeting(s) will result in a larger group of people responding. Board members can then be selected by a combination of the people at the meeting, the representative organizations, and the library. Other interested persons should be told that the board meetings are open to all, that the board members are appointed for a set term, and that ad hoc committees will be needed as the planning and service progress.

The purpose of the consumer advisory board can be defined at its organizational meeting but, in general, the activities of the board will include the following:

- Advising the library on services, resources, and activities, on a continuing basis, which will best serve deaf and hearing impaired people of all ages.
- Serving as a 2-way communication link between the deaf and hearing impaired and the library.
- Deciding when there is need for such activities as in-depth studies of the services of the library in relation to the needs of the present and potential consumers; advocacy for library services; development of creative projects.
- Advising the library in the ongoing evaluation process to determine the effectiveness of the services, resources, and programs.

To ensure that there is complete agreement and understanding, the board can develop brief, concise, and clearly stated bylaws for its operation. Minutes of the board meetings should be recorded and kept on file. A summary of the actions and discussions of the board should be made available to all consumers, present and potential, for the purpose of information and for eliciting suggestions or comments from them. Dissemination of this information through the media will help raise the public awareness of the present library services available and of the future need.

Such an advisory board allows active participation in the development of a practical program. To distribute the responsibilities of board members, to involve the maximum number of people, and to use special talents, the advisory board and the library can appoint ad hoc committees as needed. These committees may or may not include members of the advisory board but should be responsible to and report to that board. The quality and quantity of service provided by ad hoc teams will vary but will be helpful in developing or exploring the need for particular program/project needs.

The members of the board and the ad hoc committees will gain a working awareness of the library's resources and services and of its potential. They will become a better and more communicative source of information; they will also provide relevant library service to the deaf and hearing impaired because they know their needs from firsthand experience. To enable the population to be served and the general public to get to know members of the advisory board better, a publicity piece with the background of each board member included can be published in newsletters and newspapers. On a continuing basis, profiles can also be published of ad hoc committee members. The consumer advisory board can be a valuable source of information. It is a means for direct community contact and will help to bring deaf and hearing impaired people into the mainstream of library and information service.

Library service to deaf and hearing impaired people is a reality in some communities. Through an exchange of ideas and plans, each service is improved in breadth and depth. The community relationships developed in one program of library service to the deaf and hearing impaired can extend the service so that it becomes a basic library service for all libraries.

REFERENCE LIST

Auton, Sylvia. *The Life of a Federal Advisory Council in Education*. Paper presented at the American Research Association Meeting in Washington, DC, March–April 1975.

Baskin, Barbara, and Cosel, Ronne. "The Librarian as an Advocate for the Patron with Special Needs." In *The Mainstreamed Library: Issues, Ideas, and Innovations* edited by Barbara H. Baskin and Karen H. Harris, pp. 241-73. Chicago: American Library Association, 1982.

Dansky, Yona. "Services for the Deaf." *Catholic Library World* 51 (1) (July–August 1979): 22–23.

"The Do's and Don'ts of How to Write to your Legislator." In *America, the Library Has Your Number*, by the American Library Association, pp. 37–39.

Francis, Janice C., and Waldman, Lester G. "Advocacy and Technology." *The NAD Broadcaster* 4 (10) (September 1982): 9–10.

Hagemeyer, Alice. *Pulling Together through the Use of the Red Notebook.* Paper that was partially presented at the workshop "Total Communication: Public Library Service to the Deaf and Hearing Impaired." New Carrollton, MD: New Carrollton Branch Library, 1982.

"Handicapped Panel Seeks Continued Funds." *Las Vegas Sun* (March 19, 1983): 3.

Henley, Vernon. "Deaf/Blind Coalition in Nevada." *The NAD Broadcaster* 5 (1) (January 1983): 7.

Safran, Daniel. *Evaluating Parent Involvement.* (Issue paper no. 1.) Berkeley, CA: Center for the Study of Parent Involvement, 1974.

"Senator-for-a-Day." *Gallaudet Alumni Newsletter* 15 (3) (March 1, 1981): 5.

U.S. 93rd Congress. Senate 2nd Session. "Educational Crossroads for Deaf Children." *Report of the Proceedings of the Forty-Sixth Convention of American Instructors of the Deaf.* Document No. 93-65, 1974.

"Workshop Emphasizes Political Involvement." *Outreach* (February 1982): 5.

Chapter 10
Service Organizations and
Program Planning

The International/National Years of Disabled Persons, 1981–1982, have demonstrated dramatically the impact that partnerships with a specific goal and with objectives can have for the common good. The Decade of Disabled Persons, 1983–1992, is carrying on the momentum achieved during the 2 dedicated years. These types of partnerships can and do achieve goals and objectives associated with library service to people who are deaf or hard of hearing. Throughout the history of library service to disabled persons, service clubs and other service organizations have provided an impetus.

ACTIVITIES

As a project, some service clubs participate for a set period of time to assist libraries in specific areas of disability programs. Others permanently make the issue of hearing impairments a total or partial concern. These contributions are invaluable to programs of library service to deaf and hearing impaired people not only as a show of support but also in the knowledge gained of the needs of deaf and hearing impaired people; their background experience can help guide libraries which are just embarking on a service program. Because the service clubs have local as well as regional, state, national, and international chapters, their outlook is broad but at the same time pinpointed to local situations. It is important to know that these service clubs are making services to the deaf and hearing impaired a priority.

Examples of service clubs working with people who are deaf or hard of hearing include Quota International Incorporated, a business and professional women's service organization whose major service project is "Shatter Silence." This project is designed to provide services to those people with hearing and speech impairments. It covers the full gamut of problems of the deaf and hearing impaired. The Quota Club members, through "Shatter Silence," have been and are involved with libraries in their work with people with a hearing loss. This involvement has resulted in many benefits to libraries and to the deaf and hearing impaired. Their activities have included the donation of a telecaption television set to a community library attached to a school having a special program for the deaf and hearing impaired and gifts of TTY/TDDs to libraries.

Service to persons with hearing and speech handicaps has been a major concern of Quota International since 1946; in 1972, this became a united service project for *all* Quota Clubs. In 1974, the "What is Silence?" program was developed worldwide. The club has adopted the title "Shatter Silence" for all projects concerning deafness and hearing and speech.

Among their activities in the area of communication are:

- Teaching courses in fingerspelling and sign language.
- Offering programs in speechreading.
- Donating amplification loop systems and telecaptioning units and TDD units.
- Creating special awareness in the community of the beauty and function of sign language through special gifted groups who tour with "sing and sign" programs.
- Promoting special "handicapped awareness" troupes such as "The Kids on the Block" and national theatres for the deaf.
- Raising funds to buy telecaptioning devices for libraries, schools, and other organizations and groups.
- Making available the "Shatter Silence" brochure to school libraries, local public libraries, and local college libraries.
- Establishing both manual and oral interpreted referral services.
- Distributing materials on hearing loss through libraries.
- Videotaping a series of signed sessions for class language lessons donated to the local library for the use of all.

These activities are only a sampling of the work of Quota International. Many of the activities in library programs can be carried on in conjunction with the projects of this organization.

The Lions Club USA has made assistance to the deaf a major priority. Among its activities have been the purchase of TTY/TDDs for libraries and the distribution of literature and information about closed-captioned television.

The Sertoma Foundation, through its "Local Action" programs carried out by its clubs, reaches many people with communication problems. Club projects include screening children and adults for hearing disabilities and providing hearing aids, devices and equipment, evaluation, and therapy, as well as professional and public education.

The Pilot International Foundation, an organization of professional and business women, was founded with the purpose of promoting full citizenship for disabled people. This international service organization, working through its local clubs, has benefitted library service to the deaf and hearing impaired by providing needed special equipment.

Local clubs of Zonta International, an organization of business and professional women, have assisted in promoting closed-captioned programs on television for the deaf. The American Legion/American Legion Auxiliary offered, in 1983, the first infant hearing assessment. This was accomplished through an agreement among the Washington Adventist Hospital in Takoma Park, Maryland, the American Legion/American Legion Auxiliary, and the Infant Hearing Assessment Foundation. The Telephone Pioneers of America, a service organization of senior employees of the telephone industry, also provides assistance in programs of service to the deaf and hearing impaired.

In addition to solving communication problems, many clubs, in cooperation with each other and with other organizations, develop programs of common interest to the deaf and hearing impaired. Many times they will be realizing a club goal as well as helping the library.

There are many guidelines to be observed in adapting a volunteer program to the needs of the library, especially in a program for service to the deaf and hearing impaired. Probably the most important point to remember is that volunteers are to be used to supplant or to displace established library staff positions or be used in lieu of new staff positions required in the future. Other guidelines to follow in adapting a volunteer program include:

- Prior planning by the administration with the staff and the governing body of the library as well as with the deaf and hearing impaired community.
- Providing of training, development, and evaluation for volunteers.
- Assigning of work in the program which makes use of the talents, experience, training, and interests of the people in the volunteer program. Volunteers should be assigned duties in which they feel most competent.

- Assigning a staff coordinator for the program of service to the deaf and hearing impaired to facilitate the work of the volunteers and aid in their effectiveness.
- Continued planning with volunteers to enable them to keep up to date with the program. This planning will also provide them with the opportunity to present their ideas for improvement and realignment of services.
- Attempting to build a group made up of a variety of ages and of both men and women as well as minorities. If possible, various types of hearing acuity should be represented, from profound deafness to normal hearing.

Some types of work that volunteers can do to expand the effectiveness of the program are:

- Stationing the TTY/TDD 24 hours a day so that the deaf will have communication links available to them.
- Serving as a liaison between the library and the "Hearing Dog" program.
- Teaching classes in communication to assist people with different hearing abilities to understand each other.
- Assisting in story telling to groups of children with various hearing abilities.
- Acting as a tour guide for the library and explaining the program of the deaf and hearing impaired to the general public.
- Presenting public programs on the subject of deafness and hearing impairment.
- Developing publicity materials relating to the programs for the deaf and hearing impaired.
- Developing collections of historical and archival materials relating to the needs of the deaf and hearing impaired.
- Providing library transportation for deaf and hearing impaired people who have transportation problems.
- Assisting in the book selection activity relating to deaf and hearing impaired people.
- Participating in the total program of volunteers for the entire library system.

Probably the greatest single benefit to libraries in beginning special programs for deaf and hearing impaired people is having volunteers. Many volunteers are members of service clubs and may be able to provide assistance with TTY/TDDs from an answering service to training people how to use new equipment. Volunteers can come as individuals who wish to use their time and talents to help others. Because there are so many groups that need volunteers, libraries are in competition with many other organizations and institutions. The recruiting of people with special abilities and interests in deafness and hearing impairment helps to match people with the work with which they are most happy and effective.

Volunteer activities provide ways in which people can learn and gain valuable on-the-job experience. There are many rewards and benefits in volunteering. Such experience can prove helpful when applying for a paid position. In some areas, volunteers are provided liability insurance coverage and reimbursement for travel expenses. Recognition of volunteers through receptions, luncheons, certificates, or other means gives people a tangible reward for their efforts. Such recognition events also provide an opportunity to publicize the volunteer program and to raise the public awareness of its existence and value. Such recognition often results in the recruiting of new volunteers to the program.

Beginning and/or expanding library service to deaf and hearing impaired persons may, at times, seem overwhelming because of its newness and because so many activities are taking place at one time. Volunteers are often the answer. They can complement the expertise of the staff members in providing a valuable link with the consumers and they can bring new dimensions to the program. People volunteer in programs of library service to the deaf and hearing impaired for many reasons. They may want to do volunteer work because of a desire to be of service, because of a special interest in libraries, or because of a special interest in deafness. Volunteers may include people who have a deaf or hard-of-hearing family member, parents and advocates for the deaf and hearing impaired, and people from the deaf and hearing impaired community itself.

Some of the qualities needed in volunteers are an interest in the library and its services and an interest in deafness and hearing impairment and its effect on library service. Also essential to successful volunteering is the ability and desire to accept ongoing responsibility and to have good judgment. Because the library has a responsibility to ensure that people with a hearing loss know of and use their facilities, they can offer training for people with a hearing disability which will enable them to volunteer successfully. As this is accomplished, people with a hearing loss will be encouraged to use the library. A more positive attitude will be developed through 2-way communication.

Volunteers often make the difference between having a very limited service and having an extensive, high-quality service. Sometimes the use of volunteers means that a program can actually be implemented rather than just remaining in the planning stages. Volunteers provide an extension of the library service in both breadth and depth.

REFERENCE LIST

Action Programs in Speech and Hearing: Sertoma Foundation. Kansas City, MO: Sertoma Foundation, n.d. (Brochure.)

Akley, Denise S., ed. *Encyclopedia of Associations*. (2 vols.) Detroit, MI: Gale Research Company, 1983.

International Year of Disabled Persons: The Story of the U.S. Council for the International Year of Disabled Persons. Washington, DC: National Organization on Disability, 1983.

"Lobbying at its Best." *The NAD Broadcaster* 5 (11) (January 1983): 10–11.

Lovejoy, Eunice. "Library Service to Handicapped People and the Role of the Advisory Committee." *Public Library Quarterly* 19 (4) (Winter 1979): 377–86.

"NAD Section Formed on Libraries." *Gallaudet Alumni Newsletter* 15 (12) (April 15, 1981): 1–2.

Naylor, Harriett H. *Volunteers: Resources for Human Services*. (Project SHARE. Occasional Paper Series.) Washington, DC: U.S. Printing Office, 1980.

Reaching Out. Pilot International Foundation. Macon, GA: Pilot International Foundation, 1982. (Brochure.)

Ruark, Ardis, and Nelly, Carole. "Volunteers in the School Library." In *Kangaroo Kapers: Or How to Jump into Library Service*, by the State Department of Education (Elementary and Secondary Education), pp. 23–25. Pierre, SD: State Department of Education (Elementary and Secondary Education), 1978.

Shatter Silence. Washington, DC: Quota International, Inc., n.d.

Sonnestrahl, Debbie, and Majewski, Jan. "Museum Volunteering." *The NAD Broadcaster* 4 (10) (September 1982): 9.

U.S. Council for the International Year of Disabled Persons. *Partners' Workshop Report*. Washington, DC: Gallaudet College, 1980.

"Volunteers." In *The Librarian and the Patient*, edited by Eleanor Phinney, pp. 192–95. Chicago: American Library Association, 1977.

Zonta International. Chicago: Zonta International, 1980. (Brochure.)

Chapter 11
Involvement of Other
Professional Organizations

In a program such as that of library service to the deaf and hearing impaired, librarians are at a distinct disadvantage if they maintain their independence from other professional organizations. The reverse is also true—professional organizations which provide services to this group of people expand their capabilities greatly when they work closely with libraries. What is needed is a type of organization such as a formal or informal network, a coalition, cooperative activities, complementary activities, or coordination. Such involvement means more than being aware of each other's activities and working together on an occasional project. It means working and planning together with the end result being a combined force of rehabilitation professionals and library professionals acting as information providers. Some work has been accomplished in this field through cooperative efforts, but more is needed in types of organizations and in geographic locations.

COALITIONS

The need for this kind of coalition arises because the deaf and hearing impaired have information needs which are the same as those of the general public. But, in addition, this group of people has information needs which are unique. It is because of this second set of needs that professional groups can play an essential role. Information requirements vary from one community to another. The library can take the lead in identifying the information needs and the available service agencies in its locality. It can then begin developing partnerships with these agencies to make the information readily accessible, available, and usable. Libraries can be a resource for these agencies as well. Even though providing information is not the same as providing the service, it does give the inquirer the first opportunity to secure the desired service, to determine the types of services available, or to receive a positive referral.

The Library Committee of the President's Committee on Employment of the Handicapped took a significant step toward bringing together rehabilitation professionals and library professionals at its 1982 annual meeting through a joint program sponsored by The Rehabilitation Information Round Table and the Library Committee on Employment of the Handicapped. The title of the program was "Delivering Information to Rehabilitation Providers and Disabled People." Subjects covered included:

- Library resources and information from the point of view of the rehabilitation professionals and the disabled persons.
- Information in relation to concerns for access and attitudes.
- A response to the statement "What Libraries Can Do."

Represented on the panel were people from rehabilitation services, library services, and from services concerned with barrier-free environments. Some of the presenters were disabled.

Many programs of this kind must be held in order to bring together information agencies for people with disabilities, with the library as an active partner and, in some instances, the focal point. Such cooperation among groups is invaluable to deaf and hearing impaired people as it reduces the number of agencies that must be contacted while increasing the quality of information received.

One of the chief problems the deaf and hearing impaired face is the communications barrier. Such a coalition helps to remove that barrier within a community. As one example, it demonstrates that libraries have a commitment to serve deaf and hearing impaired people and to treat them as individuals. Some of those who need this cooperative information flow the most are:

- Parents of deaf and hard-of-hearing children, other families with deaf or hard-of-hearing members, and the deaf and hearing impaired themselves. This group has a continuous need to learn more about the nature of deafness and of hearing impairment. This need relates to the services available as well as where the resources and services can be utilized.
- Health professionals and librarians. Because there is a need for so much information relating to deafness and hearing impairment and because of the importance of maintaining currentness,, the providers of the information are also clients of infor-

mation sources. Cooperatively, they can provide an exchange of information among themselves.

- Employers in business and industry. They are potential recipients of combined information resources. Information concerning the employment of people who are deaf or hard of hearing and job modification in that employment is constantly needed. Modification or design of buildings to eliminate architectural problems is important to deaf and hearing impaired people and to those who also have multiple handicaps. Government, as well as business and industry, has a need also as an employer, builder, and contractor. Many professional organizations also need easily available information concerning deaf and hearing impaired individuals.
- The general public. As deaf and hearing impaired people become a part of the mainstream of society, the general public has a responsibility for them and for information about their needs. As they mainstream, more interpersonal relationships between hearing and nonhearing people result. Each needs information on how best to work with the other. The availability of current and accurate information is essential to an effective ongoing communication system.

To facilitate the dissemination of information, publicity is needed so that people do not have to wait until they have a crisis to identify suitable sources. Bibliographies, information sheets, and brochures are some good ways to present information.

COOPERATIVE ACTIVITIES

In a cooperative setting, all types of programs are possible. One such example was presented during the International Year of Disabled Persons at the Clark County Library District in Las Vegas, Nevada. Through the cooperation of many professional organizations in a program presented by the library, professionals working with the deaf and hard of hearing were able to present some of their needs to the general public, people with disabilities, and legislators. The items presented on the "Wish and Want List" by professionals working with the deaf and hearing impaired included:

- Captioned and interpreted local news.
- The availability of TTY/TDDs for every person who is deaf and for all employers of this group of people.

- TTY/TDDs in more offices and agencies, including employment security, social security, and Employment Training Administration offices.
- Interpreters employed for colleges and trade schools.
- Improved access to local training facilities which will lead to better jobs.
- Hearing aids and batteries freely available for those who cannot afford to purchase them.
- TTY/TDD repair available locally.
- Expanded interpreting services.
- Expanded mental health and social service facilities staffed with counselors fluent in sign language.

With the partnership programs from the International Year movement going into the Decade of Disabled Persons, the environment for building a successful community partnership program in all localities is most favorable. When the National Year of Disabled Persons began, an advisory committee to the National Organization on Disability presented a community action workshop at the President's Committee on Employment of the Handicapped Conference which emphasized cooperation among professional groups. The committee panel was made up of representatives from business, industry, health services, government, rehabilitation services, and library services. The program was entitled "Community Programming Across America" and included the following subsections:

- Idea Exchange.
- Media strategies.
- Goal setting.
- Local business involvement.
- Identifying community needs and resources.

Such a meeting could easily be held on a local and regional level, focusing on deafness and hearing impairment with a strong action program following.

Communications among agencies by libraries should be continuously maintained to ensure that libraries are included in the community information and service program for the deaf. Probably the most important work that can be done in this area is the formation of a coalition, formal or informal, to provide effective information and services to the deaf and hearing impaired. In such a group, the various professional agencies can contribute their expertise, information, and services, sometimes together, and sometimes in turn.

A cooperative informational program among librarians and other professionals can turn into a solid service coalition. Not only would the people being served benefit, but the groups themselves would gain cooperative use of services, resources, and equipment. Each group can then spread its services and supporting activities that much further and develop a higher quality of service. Together, the groups can:

- Promote independent living.
- Help to ensure equal employment opportunities.
- Develop a barrier-free environment.
- Provide the necesssary supportive activities and services for employment opportunities.
- Ensure free and appropriate education of children.

Specific steps which can be taken by such a coalition include:

- Ensuring that TTY/TDDs are strategically placed throughout the professional services and easily accessible to the deaf and hearing impaired. If the library is unable to secure its own TTY/TDD, it may be possible for one of the other professional groups to ensure that the library has that equipment on an ongoing basis.
- Ensuring that each of the professional groups has the informational resources (books and other library materials) to provide needed information. It may be possible for the library to provide these materials to the other professional groups.
- Providing an exchange in training in the use of materials and equipment which will be helpful to the library professionals and to the rehabilitation professionals to ensure that both groups have expertise in all possible services.

A program which can have beneficial effects is one in which all professional groups work together on career opportunities for the deaf and hearing impaired. The program can include:

- Looking at jobs which will be available.
- Reviewing the training that will be necessary to do these jobs.
- Exploring ways to find qualified employees.
- Looking at how technology is creating new job trends and opening up more jobs to disabled individuals which will help deaf and hearing impaired people to start small businesses while providing them with information, advice, and opportunities.
- Publishing informative monthly newsletters on deafness and hearing impairment.

- Developing posters with the theme "Ability" showing deaf and hearing impaired persons in sports and in other activities, with radio spots to coincide with posters on subjects such as sports, barriers, employment, education, and libraries.
- Organizing the resources available through the many professional agencies in such a manner that one distinct segment of the series is stressed each 6 months and for a 6-month period. For each 6 months, a task force of the professional personnel, including libraries, can be formed and a chairperson selected. The group can hold meetings along with deaf and hearing impaired persons to consider ideas for the 6-month program. Each task force's responsibility can be to determine which of the subjects to address, to set objectives, to determine the community resources, and to decide on the activities to reach these objectives. Each task force can explore within itself the resources and strengths with the knowledge that community support is available. Suggestions for the themes are:

   1. Education, including library service, for all deaf and hearing impaired people at all levels and for all ages.
   2. Communication—a consideration of all means of communications between hearing and nonhearing people and how they can be improved.
   3. Employment—development of appropriate employment opportunities for poeple who have a hearing loss.
   4. Legislation/advocacy in the interest of providing assistance to people who are deaf or hard of hearing and prevention and/or repeal of laws that act as a hindrance.
   5. Transportation—how deaf and hearing impaired people can reach their places of employment, health care services, recreation and education facilities, and the library.
   6. Health care—what care is available, accessible, and affordable.
   7. Recreation—consideration of recreation which involves both deaf and hearing impaired people. Libraries are included in recreation as well as in education.
   8. Creativity—opportunities for artists, authors, and other creative people with a hearing loss to have recognition of their work by their community.
   9. Buildings that are adapted to the needs of the deaf and hearing impaired and with special attention to the multiple handicapped.

    10. Independent living for deaf and hearing impaired people so that they can become a part of the mainstream of society and, as a result, become less dependent on others.

A second type of program which can be effective is "Partners in Action," a program that uses professional services for the deaf and hearing impaired. Again, the large group can divide into committees with each group taking responsibility for one segment of the activities. Committees can be concerned with:

- Education and employment.
- Recreation and activity.
- Community awareness.
- Professional interdisciplinary activities.
- Promotion and publicity.
- Information and knowledge.
- Health and independence.
- Disabled rights and leadership.

To achieve even a modicum of success in a 6-month period, the task force/committee of rehabilitation professionals and library professionals and deaf and hearing impaired people needs to set goals. Priority goals might include community awareness with emphasis on children's awareness. One publicity tool might be the publishing of a special tabloid edition in the newspaper.

Schools are excellent allies for professional groups working with deaf and hearing impaired people. They can provide leadership through their library programs and by gaining community commitment to school library programs. By working with students, the professional group is ensuring the future of a better society for deaf and hearing impaired individuals and is also improving their current situation. There is no better place for such a program to exist than in a school library. It is the center of activity in the school and has the needed resources and information. A school library also is invaluable because it allows parents to be involved in the total program. The opportunity presents itself, also, to encourage a deaf or hard-of-hearing child to start a home library. Parents can also be encouraged to support their children's reading and to be involved in the total professional program through the library's involvement. The program can result in:

- The child being surrounded with books during the early years.
- Having appropriate books to read to and with a child.
- Building up an appropriate library.

- The parents becoming models for the children to follow in their reading experiences.
- Supplementing of the home library and a home atmosphere of reading and story telling.

Through this program, rehabilitation professionals and library professionals can work with parents and deaf and hearing impaired individuals to develop an effective program of service.

A valuable tool which can be provided by this group is a "Service Directory" for the deaf and hearing impaired. A directory must be very clear, both in language and in format, and have explicit instructions as to its use. Services listed in such a directory can include:

- Personnel (interpreters, counselors, physicians, social service workers, lawyers, audiologists)
- Programs (educational, multiple disabled, speech and hearing, deaf associations, state programs for the hearing impaired, sign language classes, parent organizations)
- Facilities (sheltered workshops, rehabilitation centers/summer camps, speech and hearing centers, centers for independent living, national organizations)

Such a directory has value not only in its accuracy but also in its currentness. It is invaluable for those who need such reference and information. Now, more than ever before, the rehabilitation community, the library community, and the deaf and hearing impaired consumer need to share quick, current, accessible, and accurate information. Such a directory is worthwhile because of the imbalance in numbers of the consumers who need specialized information provided efficiently, accurately, and quickly and the limited number of professionals available to provide that information. A pool of knowledge readily accessible is a very fine service to deaf and hearing impaired individuals.

A focus for the exchange of services between and among professional groups can be the Governor's Committee on Employment of the Handicapped in each state or its counterpart. The interests of that group are broad and encompass all aspects of employment of the disabled; the goals of library service blend well with the activities of the Governor's Committee. Some of the programs which can be coordinated by the Governor's Committee and which can include the library are those that:

- Encourage employers to give job opportunities to deaf and hearing impaired people and provide resources concerning the neces-

sary modification of jobs to be made so that they can be effectively performed by this group of people.
- Enlist the cooperation of the news media in working toward reaching the public with the awareness that deaf and hearing impaired people can and have become useful members of society.
- Educate employers and employment agencies on the abilities of deaf and hearing impaired individuals.
- Recognize outstanding nonhearing people for their contributions.
- Provide community, social, and recreational facilities and integrate individuals into these programs by implementing the following:

    1. Providing adequate transportation.
    2. Removing architectural barriers.
    3. Making adaptations in environment, activity, equipment, and instruction which provides true accessibility.
    4. Clarifying the meaning and extent of accessibility when a recreational/cultural activity is so identified.
    5. Providing an adequate number of interpreters for the deaf and hearing impaired.
    6. Organizing a group to oversee recreational facilities and their accessibility.

Other activities which can be carried out by professional groups are the development of a social services network of administrations to address the social integration of the deaf into all aspects of society and making deaf and hearing impaired persons aware of their legal rights, the social programs available to them, and the intricacies of the social service system. Some specific activities which can be pursued are:

- The improvement of life safety through such concerns as the intelligent use of elevators, enlargement of platforms, and accessible emergency exits.
- Qualified interpreters and TTY/TDDs accessible to emergency staff such as hospital, police, fire, and ambulance personnel.
- Development of networks to provide comprehensive and effective systems to meet the needs of health care and illness prevention for all age groups.

In any community, some professional groups exist with which the library can function in its service to the deaf and hearing impaired. The library's program for the deaf and hearing impaired will benefit from the support it receives from other professional groups and from deaf and hearing impaired consumers. The total effect will be input from the groups and a melding of the information, resources and services, and output which can be measured by the effectiveness of the program. The information gained by the library through the support of other groups of professionals results in a lessening of uncertainty in the development of the program. The consumers themselves and their involvement increase the confidence with which the library can proceed with its program. The deaf and hearing impaired individuals will benefit from the information about the library and its services. They will know more than they did before. The difference that having this information makes is a most important difference for people who can profit from it—the deaf and hard of hearing.

REFERENCE LIST

Alexander Graham Bell Association for the Deaf, Inc. *The Story of the Volta Bureau Library*. Washington, DC: Alexander Graham Bell Association for the Deaf, Inc., n.d.

Cross Roads of the State of New Jersey. Newark, NJ: New Jersey International Year of Disabled Persons, 1981.

Fitzgerald, Jean. "Partnership Program Notes. Community Partnership Program." *National Organization on Disability Report* (Spring 1984): 3.

Hagemeyer, Alice. "Accessibility at Libraries." In *Communicating with Hearing People: The Red Notebook*, Silver Spring, MD: National Association of the Deaf, 1982. Section on Library: 1–2.

I.Y.D.P. Report. Washington, DC: U.S. Council for the International Year of Disabled Persons, 1981.

National Organization on Disability. *Award Winners: 1983–84 Community Partnership Program. Decade of Disabled Persons, 1983–1992*. (Sponsored by Westinghouse Electric Corporation and the National Organization on Disability.) Washington, DC: National Organization on Disability, 1984.

Roth, Helga. "Information and Referral for Handicapped Individuals." *Drexel Library Quarterly* 16 (2) (April 1980): 48–55.

Vincent, Ruth. "A Library Program to Educate Students in Understanding the Handicapped." *The Bookmark* 39 (2) (Winter 1980): 308–10.

Chapter 12
Library Education for Library Service to the Deaf and Hearing Impaired

For the library to serve patrons adequately requires a specific knowledge of people, of materials they can use, of programs which will be effective, and of appropriate resources available. Formal education providing the knowledge, information, skill, and understanding of service to the deaf and hearing impaired has been totally lacking on a continuing basis in library schools, in continuing education, and in workshops and seminars. In the last several years, attempts have been made to promote this kind of education, but the movement has not been widespread enough to affect either librarians currently working in libraries or current library students. When such education *is* available, it is usually part of a course concerned with disabled individuals rather than specifically with people who have a hearing loss. The number of courses being offered in library schools is very small and their geographical availability limited. Continuing education courses, workshops, seminars, and related types of meetings are also sporadically offered and are limited in their geographical availability.

SURVEYS

In 1977, Merrillyn C. Gibson, reference librarian, National Library Service for the Blind and Physically Handicapped, Library of Congress, stated in her article, "Preparing Librarians to Serve Handicapped Individuals, "[1] that 75 percent of the American Library Association accredited schools were not offering courses in the field of library service to the disabled. At that time, there was a lack of courses addressing issues of the availability of programs, equipment, appropriate materials, accessibility, standards, employment of disabled persons, and information and referral sources for the disabled within the local community. In June 1976, the National Library Service for the Blind and Physically Handicapped, Library of Congress, conducted a survey to determine which accredited programs offered special courses, institutes, seminars, or workshops to serve disabled persons. Of the 67 accredited library school programs surveyed, 88 percent responded. Of those responding, 20 percent offered formal courses. Fifteen schools indicated that, although no separate course was offered, the discussion of this specialized service was included in other courses. However, 73 percent of the responding schools were not interested in offering courses of this kind in their programs. The program offered by the Catholic University of America, where a Post Master's Certificate could be earned, included a course on library service to the hearing impaired and related courses. Practicums were available and summer schedules were arranged to allow librarians from various geographical areas to attend.

The schools were resurveyed by the National Library Service for the Blind and Physically Handicapped in December 1978. The 63 American Library Association accredited programs were surveyed. One hundred percent responded to the request for information; 19 percent offered formalized and special courses of instruction to prepare librarians in providing library service to the physically disabled. Forty-eight schools reported that, although they offered no separate courses in the area of library service to the disabled, the subject was included as a part of other courses. Sixty percent of the schools not offering course work in this field indicated that they had no plans to incorporate courses relating to library services to disabled persons in their programs in the future. The Catholic University of America, Washington, DC, Department of Library and Information Science, included in its offering library service to the hearing impaired. Laboratory sessions for the teaching of American Sign Language were incorporated into the program.

In October 1980, the National Library Service for the Blind and Physically Handicapped conducted yet another survey to determine which American Library Association accredited library schools offered special courses, seminars, workshops, or institutions to prepare librarians to serve disabled clientele. The 61 library schools accredited as of March 1980 were surveyed. Of these, 43 percent responded. Of those, 27 percent offered formal and specialized courses designed to serve the physically disabled. Sixty-five percent of the responding schools that were not offering this type of course work in their programs indicated that they had no plans to include such courses in their programs in the future. Geographically, the 7 schools offering courses in the study of library programs and services to meet the special needs of the physically disabled readers, in 1980, were located in the eastern, southern, and midwestern parts of the United States. Fourteen of the responding schools reported they offered no separate course but included the discussion of service to disabled readers in other courses.

A review of the 1976 answers related to institutes, specialized independent study, seminars, and workshops shows that several schools offered this type of training. The University of Maryland indicated that a workshop was held on that campus on the subject of deaf awareness. Ninety-one percent of library schools participating in the survey indicated that they would be willing to sponsor special workshops relating to service to disabled persons. In the 1978 survey, several schools were offering workshops, seminars, special institutes, or independent study. The University of Denver offered a one-week course on "Library Services for the Handicapped" which included service to the deaf and hearing impaired. Ninety-five percent of the library schools participating in the 1978 survey reported that they would be willing to sponsor workshops on library service to the disabled. In 1980, 5 schools indicated that, although they did not offer formal courses, they had offered workshops, institutes, or seminars on library service to the physically disabled reader. Ninety-six percent participating in the survey reported that they would be willing to sponsor special workshops related to library services to disabled individuals.

The subject of education of librarians for service to disabled individuals has been considered carefully by both practitioners and educators. Significant discussions have taken place in the 1980s. In the April 1980 issue of the *Drexel Library Quarterly*,[2] Elizabeth Stone of the Catholic University of America wrote on the subject of the library's role in serving the disabled and its implications for the library science curriculum. She recommended that students be taught the facts about particular disabilities to develop an understanding concerning the special needs of the disabled and that they should learn about other agencies related to people with a special disability.

A second landmark discussion was a symposium held in July 1981 in San Francisco. Educating students to provide library service to people with disabilities was the subject under discussion throughout the meeting. Aspects discussed included: information needs, special requirements of librarians for the service, the library education curriculum to prepare librarians, and future trends in this type of education.

Among the information considered in the symposium were the following:

- At the Palmer Graduate Library School on the C. W. Post Campus of the Long Island University, New York, a course on "Library Service to the Handicapped" is offered. A part of the course is devoted to library service to the deaf as well as to deaf-blind individuals.
- Very little library literature directly discusses librarians' attitudes toward disabled persons. Neither does it offer specific suggestions as to how to develop positive attitudes.
- The general attitude of librarians toward disabled people is positive, according to the sample included in an attitudinal survey at Northern Illinois University.
- At Florida State University, the program on "Library Service to the Disabled" has 2 objectives: (1) to produce graduates with the skills, knowledge, and attitudes that will enable them to work effectively with people with disabilities and (2) to conduct research and demonstration projects in the field of library service to persons with disabilities.
- The program at the University of Minnesota was concerned with the user first—anyone temporarily or permanently impaired in any way. The primary concern was with the individual, with the emphasis on commonalities and not on differences.
- The philosophy of service should be based on the recognition of the disabled person's need for independence and self-reliance.
- Library school students need to know about specialized information centers such as the National Rehabilitation Information Center (NARIC), located at the Catholic University of America, and other sources of information of all kinds relating to disabilities.
- The San Francisco Public Library Communication Center serves people who are deaf as well as the blind and physically handicapped and the general public.
- In the practical process of providing library service to people with disabilities, attitudinal awareness is important, but it must be paralleled with an understanding of the needs of disabled persons.
- There is a need for financial assistance to provide more incentives for students to prepare for work with disabled people.
- There is no single type of job position for librarians serving people with disabilities.

- There is a need to be aware of trends, especially in technology, as they affect disabled persons and to consider these trends when library education programs are developed.
- Education in communications would help librarians to work with people who have an invisible communication disability.
- Libraries for library schools should ensure that the materials are available that are needed for courses taught by visiting faculty members in the area of library service to disabled persons.
- Attitudes are basic. They constitute one of the major barriers to library service to people with disabilities.
- A possibility in the field of education for library service to disabled persons is that of a specific telecommunication experiment in providing this training by interdisciplinary or interschool specialists in the area of library service to disabled persons. However, this is a cooperative and experimental venture only.
- The National Rehabilitation Information Center (NARIC) integrated rehabilitation with librarianship.
- ABLEDATA is a national database at the National Rehabilitation Information Center and provides information on adaptive equipment and devices designed for disabled people.
- Not every disabled person is going to be a library user.
- Schools for library education should teach more about the sources of information and services which are available to people who are deaf or hearing impaired.
- Library schools need increased budgets to begin a new program including funds for faculty, resources, and equipment. Practitioners and library educators need to work together on this problem.
- Teleconferencing is a possible method of delivering educational services to students in the area of library service to disabled persons.
- The International Federation of Library Associations and Institutions (IFLA) should consider using interpreters at its meetings, so that people who are deaf can attend IFLA conferences.
- Service to disabled persons should be a part of total library service, not a service apart.

Even with the work being done to provide educational opportunities to students interested in library service to disabled persons, library service to deaf and hearing impaired persons is being developed and provided by librarians with little or no formal education in this area of service. Many have not had the opportunity to attend any continuing education courses. However, effective programs of service have been and are being developed without special training. The experience of these innovators should be used by library educators and made available to their students. As libraries are increasingly developing programs directed toward all people and with appropriate services, resources, and equipment to serve them, the education needed to serve deaf and hearing impaired people becomes essential. Also, as more of these people elect a career in librarianship, faculty in library schools will need to be aware of the many communication modes being used.

Library education for serving people who are deaf and hearing impaired has basic ingredients that library school graduates need as a background for their actual work with these consumers. These ingredients include a basic foundation in librarianship plus a special knowledge of how the unique needs of deaf and hearing impaired people can best be met. Required are a general library education and a specialized library program. Included in the specialized library program should be the following:

- A basic understanding of deafness and hearing impairment and how this disability affects people's lives.
- A knowledge of the many communication modes used by people with a hearing loss and how to use them.
- A knowledge of the following: basic books required for a collection of materials on deafness and hearing impairment; types of books needed to meet some specific needs such as books without words, high interest/low vocabulary books, highly illustrated books; and sources for acquiring books designed for people with a hearing loss and a resulting English-language difficulty.
- A knowledge of media other than books which can be used by people with a hearing loss such as captioned films, signed video materials, and pantomimed materials. The specialized education should provide a knowledge of the sources for this media.
- A knowledge of specialized equipment required by the deaf and hard of hearing such as telecommunication devices for the deaf, induction loops and their counterparts, and volume-controlled equipment. The specialized education should include knowledge of the sources for purchasing the equipment.
- A knowledge of the periodicals available in the area of deafness and hearing impairment, both for the librarian and the consumer.
- Guidance in the purchasing of specialized resources and equipment should be made available to students in the form of criteria to be used in their selection.

- Basic principles on how to develop programs of service to deaf and hearing impaired people and how to involve the consumer in the design of the program should be developed. Such principles should evolve with the special requirements of nonhearing people taken into considertion.
- Information on how to survey a community to accomplish the following should be available: (1) identify deaf and hearing impaired persons; (2) determine the use of the library by this group; (3) identify the types of programs and services and resources which will be usable and accessible; and (4) evaluate the effectiveness of the activities of the library in relation to deaf and hearing impaired people on a continuing basis.
- Information on how to develop the types of publicity which can be most effective with nonhearing people.
- A knowledge of the types of organizations—professional, social, and service—that are concerned with the needs of deaf and hearing impaired people and how to interrelate with them most effectively.
- An understanding of how to develop networks of information among deaf and hearing impaired programs both with other libraries and with groups unrelated to libraries.
- A knowledge of how to develop an advocacy program for library service to deaf and hearing impaired people including how to work in the political process to achieve effective library service to the deaf and hearing impaired.
- A study of programs of library service already in place.
- A work/study period in at least one or more of the programs identified.

In addition to general basic library education and specialized information concerning the deaf and hearing impaired, some other considerations are helpful in the practical program of serving deaf and hearing impaired individuals. These considerations can also be adapted to other types of library programs. Some of the highlights are:

- A development of interpersonal skills and a knowledge of how to develop positive attitudes in others toward disabled persons.
- The use of technology in all aspects of serving people with a hearing loss.
- The knowledge of data banks which are especially oriented to disabilities.
- A study of the basic rights of people with disabilities as developed in legislation and in regulations.

- The development of research studies into the subject of library service to disabled people and/or as related to a specific disability.

Because a formal library education can provide only the basic information needed and because conditions are ever changing, librarians serving the deaf and hearing impaired need to take advantage of continuing education offerings, workshops, institutes, seminars, and any type of program that relates to deaf and hearing impaired people. These educational opportunities are few in number and random as far as geographic availability is concerned. Workshops on hearing loss designed for educators can assist librarians in broadening their knowledge. Such workshops are frequently available in a local community with specialists in the field presenting materials and information. Sign language classes offer a fine opportunity for librarians and other staff members to learn about deaf and hearing impaired people; librarians who are also interpreters are few in number. The classes are helpful in teaching librarians to sign and offer an opportunity to meet others concerned with the deaf.

Institutes for deaf and hearing impaired people that are open to other interested persons provide a broader dimension to the education of the librarian. The interaction between people with a hearing loss and hearing people is a valuable experience for both groups. Workshops for interpreters open to other interested people enable the librarian to understand the value of interpreters. The 2-way communication also provides valuable experience on how librarians and interpreters can work together most effectively.

Institutes, seminars, and workshops on the subject of library services provide information on building a program of library service to the deaf and hearing impaired. Three such effective educational opportunities have been held over the last decade. The 3 are:

1. Library Services to Hearing Impaired People. Two workshops of 4 days each held in 1974 by Gallaudet College in Washington, DC.
2. Library Training Institute for Service to the Deaf. A 2-week workshop held in 1978 at the California State University–Fullerton and funded by the U.S. Office of Education.
3. "Challenge: Serving Deaf and Hearing Impaired Children, Young Adults and Their Parents." A one-evening, one-day preconference of the American Library Association, cosponsored by the Association for Library Service to Children, the Library Service to the Deaf Section of the Association of Specialized

and Cooperative Library Agencies, and the Young Adult Services Division and held in 1982 at the Free Library of Philadelphia.

Each of these educational opportunities presented a different approach and different content; taken together, they offer an expanded knowledge of library service to deaf and hearing impaired people. The workshop at Gallaudet College provided both an overview of the service and an in-depth study in areas of library service to hearing impaired people. Subjects discussed included:

- What do deaf people really want?
- Causes of deafness.
- Simultaneous communication.
- Implications of deafness for education.
- Implications of deafness for employment.
- Programs available for the deaf and implications for the future.
- Organizations serving the deaf.

Throughout the workshop, various materials of special interest were on display and videotapes were shown. A book list on deafness was provided.

This workshop was designed to explore ways in which libraries can serve deaf and hearing impaired people more effectively. It was also designed to consider how libraries can function as a source of community information on hearing impairment and its consequences. A team approach was used in bringing together state librarians, heads of state library associations, and leaders in the deaf community. These teams planned and carried out workshops and programs for staff training in their own states on a regional and a local level. In addition, the participants had the opportunity to visit the campus of Gallaudet College and meet with students and faculty. The communication between hearing and nonhearing individuals helped to break down barriers and dismiss misconceptions. It also reduced hesitancies on the part of the participants in starting or in continuing a program of library service to deaf and hearing impaired people.

A workshop such as that held at Gallaudet College provided those who attended a base from which to work in developing library services to deaf and hearing impaired individuals. It also had the built-in regional and local training concept for those states participating. Another benefit was that participants acquired a knowledge of where to turn for information and resource people. Such workshops, held at regular intervals, would provide a continuing opportunity for those having no formal education in this area to secure a background. For those with an educational and experience background, it would provide an opportunity to update and expand that education and experience.

SPECIALIZED EDUCATION

Another type of education was provided in the library training institute for service to the deaf held at the California State University-Fullerton. The students for this 2-week institute were recruited from all types of libraries—public, school, special, university. They were selected on the basis of their ability to continue in-service training in this subject area with other librarians. The institute was a pioneer program with the purpose of extending the knowledge and sensitivity of the participants in relation to needs required to provide effective library service to people who are deaf. Specifically, topics dealt with the nature of the problem, library and media materials, and library equipment for the deaf. Considered also were specialized service techniques, public library service for the deaf, and technological possibilities for their education. Included in the sessions were presentations concerned with the following:

- Newborn testing, the young deaf, hearing aids, aural programs.
- Teaching signing to librarians, interpreting, and court interpreting.
- Teletypewriter (TTY) service in libraries and videocassettes.
- Vocational rehabilitation, social service agencies, college education, and employment.
- Sign language films, resource materials, and producing media for the deaf.
- Legal rights and laws affecting the deaf.
- Technological possibilities for the education of the deaf.
- Research possibilities for library service to the deaf.

The institute sessions presented a variety of demonstrations, and field trips were a part of the program. Instructors were both hearing and nonhearing or had family members who are deaf. Case studies were included in the sessions as well as the development of a plan for providing library service to the deaf.

The evaluation report on the institute concluded that the institute had succeeded in sensitizing the participants to the special needs of the deaf and hearing impaired and had motivated the participants to do something concrete about meeting those needs. Institutes such as this one offer (in the same, expanded, or tailored format) a cost-effective means of achieving the educational goals for providing library service to the deaf and hearing impaired. Each institute can reach only a small group of people on a limited geographical basis. If, however, the librarians attending return to their communities and become involved in training others, the effect of each workshop will be broadened.

A third example of workshop/institute training is that of the American Library Association preconference workshop in Philadelphia in 1982. As the title, "Challenge: Serving Deaf and Hearing Impaired Children, Young Adults and their Parents" indicates, the workshop was focused on one specific group. The sponsors were all concerned with children and young people and/or deafness and hearing impairment. Because of this specific focus on one group and the expertise of the cosponsors, the subject could be covered appropriately in the timespan of one evening and one full day. Subjects included in this program were:

- Deaf awareness for hearing people of all ages.
- The effects of prelingual deafness and hearing impairment on language comprehension.
- Education of deaf and hearing impaired children.
- "My Education Experience," discussed by a panel of parents.
- The deaf teenager.

The preconference included 3 workshops, each with 2 sessions on the subjects of:

- Establishing public and school library service for deaf young people and their parents.
- Print and nonprint materials for deaf young people including evaluation, selection, and use.
- Programs and special materials on sexuality and careers. Also included in the preconference were an exhibit of telecommunication devices and a book display.

A well-planned program such as this preconference, with time effectively used, can reach people from a wide geographical area, although the number in attendance is necessarily limited by the facilities, personnel, and resources available and by the number who can attend because of the travel and living expense involved. But, again, if each participant takes the training back to the local and regional areas represented, the effect of the conference will be felt much further than the training conference itself can reach. The opportunity to attend such diverse programs as these 3 provides a librarian with a knowledge of library service which is effective in both breadth and depth.

The education needed for working with deaf and hearing impaired people, in addition to the courses leading to a degree in librarianship, requires a basic and broad academic background (especially in the humanities and social sciences) and a background in the area of deafness and hearing impairment. Developing a structured professional reading program for librarians on this subject is important to ensure a basic background. Many excellent bibliographies are available to guide librarians. The subjects used in "Information on Deafness," a selective list of books for the use of those attending a workshop, "Listen: The Hearing Impaired Adult and the Public Library" at the Cleveland Public Library Outreach Services, 1974, reflects the needed reading of the librarian beginning in the program of service to the deaf and hearing impaired. Topics include:

- Sound and hearing.
- Deafness.
- Hearing aids.
- Means of communication.
- Mime.
- Personal accounts.
- Fiction.

These provide a reasonable breakdown of the subject so that the librarian will not be overwhelmed by the many aspects of it. A broad listing on deafness is that issued by the Pennsylvania Materials Center for the Hearing Impaired in 1981. Although this bibliography is directed toward educators working with deaf and hearing impaired students, it will help librarians to understand better the many aspects of deafness and hearing impairment. The first section of this bibliography is devoted to professional material; the second includes pamphlets and reprints; the third contains intructional materials; the fourth is devoted to institutional references; and the fifth lists audiovisual materials. Such a bibliography provides a wide selection of materials from which a librarian interested in self-education can choose.

Many institutes and workshops have been held covering a variety of subjects. In 1981, the New York State Library, in cooperation with the St. Mary's School for the Deaf in Buffalo, sponsored 3 regional workshops designed to assist librarians in developing a better understanding of deafness and its implications for library service. In these workshops, the needs of people with hearing impairments in public, college, or school libraries were considered, and telecommunication devices and decoders for captioned television programs were exhibited.

A workshop on public library service for the hearing impaired, cosponsored by the State Library of Florida and the Florida School for the Deaf and Blind in St. Augustine, Florida, was held in 1974. This meeting included in its program librarians, faculty from the School for the Deaf, and guest speakers who are authorities in the field of library service to the deaf and hearing impaired. A series of 3 Deaf Awareness Workshops was sponsored in 1980 by the Florida Library Association.

A combination of several agencies put together a one-day workshop on library services for deaf and hard-of-hearing persons in 1981 sponsored by The State Library of Ohio and held at Ohio Dominican College. The goal of the workshop was to make library personnel aware of the deaf and hard-of-hearing population and to provide them with information for serving this specific group. Alice Hagemeyer of the District of Columbia Public Library, Washington, DC, was the keynote speaker. Subjects included locating the deaf and hard of hearing, and resource and information needs.

These are examples of workshops directed entirely toward promoting library service to the deaf and hearing impaired. For those who have the opportunity to attend, they are invaluable. To provide adequate continuing education, librarians need to ensure that these workshops are more widely available to more people.

A continuing education workshop held by a group of people and agencies serving deaf people was held by the Nevada Association of the Deaf, Nevada Bureau of Vocational Rehabilitation, and the Interpreter Training Center at Ohlone College, Fremont, California, held in Las Vegas in 1982. A special invitation was issued to all staff, students, and parents involved with the Clark County School District Deaf and Hard of Hearing Program. The workshop was scheduled for an evening and the following day. Subjects covered included the effect of hearing loss on the person's everyday life, including social, educational, and employment implications; description of the several interpreting methods; and the use of interpreters for and by people who are deaf.

It is the responsibility of librarians to remain current in this area. One way to ensure an up-to-date outlook is to read each issue of the several periodicals published in the area of deafness and hearing impairment. Such information relates to current research, the arts, literature, scientific advances, technology, equipment, and attitudes, among other things. Library literature also provides some information on current library programs. Staying current in the field of the deaf and hearing impaired is essential in order to provide a continuing and useful service. A review of current articles is important for both the hearing and non-hearing.

Attendance at conferences of associations of the deaf and hearing impaired assists librarians in their awareness of trends in the field. This communication can become 2-way through the attendance at library conferences by people who are deaf or hard of hearing. Workshops within a conference of an association for deaf and hard-of-hearing people assist in this 2-way communication. Regularly scheduled visits to programs of library service to deaf and hearing impaired persons help to maintain currentness through an exchange of ideas and information. Programs in libraries of schools for the deaf and in public and private schools as well as public, academic, and special library programs should be included. Although the actual activities will have different priorities, the attitudes, communication, problems, equipment, and resources will be similar enough to add to the basic education and to the current awareness of librarians.

It is important that library schools not only provide a means by which librarians can be formally educated in library service to deaf and hearing impaired people, but that they also establish the concept that this library service is an integral part of the ongoing library program. Because the greatest number of library school students are hearing persons, they need to become aware of ways in which jobs can be modified to employ nonhearing people and they also need to become familiar with the equipment and/or modification of equipment available to assist in this process. Therefore, the total faculty in library schools needs to be aware of the requirements for the service and how deaf and hearing impaired people can be employed effectively. Because the greatest number of library school faculty members are hearing persons, they will initially need education in the field of deafness and hearing impairment and will then need to keep abreast of the current trends. The addition of deaf and hearing impaired individuals to the library school staff will assist in this currentness and will enable the faculty members to maintain a hearing/nonhearing interaction. It is important that graduates of library schools, as they begin their work with deaf and hearing impaired people, are able to rely on their training until they have the opportunity to add successful experience to that education. Interaction among deaf and hearing impaired people and a perception of possible library needs must necessarily precede successful practical service.

Throughout the education of librarians in library service to the deaf and hearing impaired, the state library can play an important part in each type of education activity—formal education, continuing education, workshops, seminars, and convention programs. The state library can work effectively with library schools in developing and maintaining programs for service to the deaf and hearing impaired; consultants are an important force in the continuing education of library personnel in this aspect of library service. State library staff and consultants must have some expertise in this area of librarianship. One of the resolutions of the White House Conference on Library and Information Services stated that, at the state level, libraries must train personnel in library service to the deaf. Also, in the recommendations of the San Francisco Symposium on library education to the disabled presented to the International Federation of Library Associations and Institutions (IFLA) in 1981, in Leipzig, East Germany was that state library agencies be involved in this field of librarianship.

Another type of education beneficial for librarians is symposiums which focus on recent developments in deafness, education, and research. Such symposiums have been held by Gallaudet College on a regional basis. Some of the areas covered which would be useful to librarians are:

- The latest use of media and computers.
- Parent involvement.
- Identification of leadership qualities in people who are deaf.
- Information on the resources and services offered, both on and off campus, that Gallaudet offers to the deaf and to advocates of the deaf.

A positive effort to bring deaf and hearing impaired people into library school education will bring the profession closer to providing library service to this group of people as a natural development of providing appropriate library service to all people. These librarians will be professionals first, but their disability can make them valuable resources as well as competent librarians. However, bringing them into faculty positions and the student body requires attitude changes in libraries and in the general public. It requires, also, the understanding of the need for possible accommodations in the job and action to make those accommodations. Even though Section 504 of the Rehabilitation Act of 1973 (P.L. 93-112) prohibits discrimination solely on the basis of handicap by those agencies receiving federal funds, more work remains to be done before such compliance is complete.

The White House Conference on Library and Information Services was concerned with the issue of educating library and informational services librarians in the resolution "Access to Library and Information Services" in which it was stated that institutions engaged in this education should assume the responsibility to address the needs of the consumers through their training and education. This resolution also emphasized that everyone, regardless of disability, should have a continuing access to information and materials and that library service be extended to persons in institutions for the disabled. Other resolutions in that conference were concerned with library service to the disabled and hearing impaired and with the special information needs of hearing impaired persons.

The programs of library education throughout the United States have a strong impact on the level and quality of services provided by libraries. Librarians are a product, to a great extent, of the educational background they receive in library schools. If libraries are to increase each person's access to libraries and the resources there, the awareness of that goal and the need for reaching it begin with the education of librarians. While many other factors play a part in the ultimate achieving of this goal, attitudes and expertise of librarians predominate. Deaf and hearing impaired people have not had that access to knowledge in a great many instances; programs of education in schools of library education can help to bring about a positive change.

NOTES

1. Merrillyn C. Gibson, "Preparing Librarians to Serve Handicapped Individuals," *Journal of Education for Librarianship* 18 (2) (Fall 1977): 121–30.

2. Elizabeth W. Stone, "Educating Librarians and Information Scientists to Provide Information Services to Disabled Individuals," *Drexel Library Quarterly* 16 (2) (April 1980): 10–31.

REFERENCE LIST

Casey, Genevieve M. "Education for Institutional Library Service." *Library Trends* 26 (3) (Winter 1978): 431–45.

"Continuing Education and In-service Training." In *The Librarian and the Patient*, edited by Eleanor Phinney, pp. 199–205. Chicago: American Library Association, 1977.

Ferstel, Kenneth L, and Gibson, Merrillyn C. "Training and Research in Librarianship." In *That All May Read*, by the National Library Service for the Blind and Physically Handicapped, Library of Congress, pp. 347–80, Washington, DC: National Library Service for the Blind and Physically Handicapped, Library of Congress, 1983.

Gibson, Merrillyn C. "Education for Service." *Interface* 3 (3–4) (Spring–Summer 1981): 4–5.

Hammet, Barbara. "Library Education and Disabled Readers." *Link-up* (17) (November 1982): 9–10.

Library Training Institute for Service to the Deaf. July 31–August 11, 1978. Narrative Report. Fullerton, CA: California State University-Fullerton, 1978.

Library Training Institute for Service to the Deaf. July 31–August 11, 1978. Report of the Proceedings. Fullerton, CA: California State University–Fullerton, 1978.

McNett, Jan, and Merchant, Diane. "Disabled Educators: Assets—Not Handicaps—to Good Teaching." *Today's Education* 70 (3) (February–March), 1981): 34GE–37GE.

The National Commission on Libraries and Information Science. *Toward a National Program for Library and Information Services; Goals for Action.* Washington, DC: The National Commission on Libraries and Information Science, 1975.

Pennsylvania Materials Center for the Hearing Impaired. *A Selected Bibliography of Materials to Better Understand the Hearing Impaired. A Guide for the Regular Educator.* Williamsport, PA: Pennsylvania Materials Center for the Hearing Impaired, 1981.

Schuster, Jack. *Library Training Institute for Service to the Deaf: An Evaluation Report.* Claremont, CA: Claremont Graduate School, 1978.

Stark County District Library, Children's Department. *Let's Learn Gesture and Mime.* (Jane M. Biehl.) Canton, OH: Stark County District Library, n.d.

Part III: Resources in Support of Serving the Deaf and Hearing Impaired

Chapter 13
Library Materials

An assumption on which library service to the deaf and hearing impaired (or a lack of it) has been based is that this group does not have any special difficulties in using traditional services and facilities. This concept is widely held by the general public. While some deaf and hearing impaired people, it is true, can fully use traditional resources and services, librarians cannot assume that this ability is common to all. No matter at what age the hearing loss occurs, the disability can bring severe changes to the lives of the people with this loss.

Some people who learned to use the library prior to developing hearing difficulties will continue to use traditional libraries. They will make their own accommodations as needed and compensate as they find it possible to do so. Students who have learned to use the library in elementary, secondary, and higher education can use the traditional services if their reading ability matches that of a hearing person. One inhibiting factor in library service for deaf and hearing impaired individuals is the communication barrier. Not being able to understand what is being said and being misunderstood sets up an immediate barrier between the nonhearing person and the library.

The full range of traditional resources and services available to hearing individuals should be equally accessible to the nonhearing. The accessibility will, however, vary as those with a hearing loss become more skilled in their language ability, more expert in using the library, and more effective in their communication. Eventually, the full range of library resources will be open to them. It is for this reason, primarily, that the resources should not be maintained permanently in a special services program to the deaf and hearing impaired but should be integrated into the total resources of the library. Deaf and hearing impaired individuals should have the opportunity and encouragement to use any of the resources.

But to be able to serve *all* deaf and hearing impaired people, the resources to support the service must be carefully developed to meet the needs of a very diverse group. As each person differs from others in the hearing population, so does each individual in the nonhearing population. Added to that difference in individuals is the difference in the severity of the hearing loss and its effect on language skills and communication ability.

Probably most libraries begin building resources for serving deaf and hearing impaired individuals from a near-zero base. The exceptions are those libraries in schools for the deaf, libraries in an educational setting where courses in deafness and hearing impairment are offered, or in other such special circumstances. Some of the resources are developed in response to the community's requests for materials. For example, as sign language classes are organized in the community for the public in general, books on sign language are added to the collection. As projects are developed with federal funds or with special funding, resources are purchased for use during the life of the program. Sometimes such acquisition is done without concern for overall development of the collection after the project has ended. There is an absence in traditional libraries of materials concerned with deaf pride, deaf history, deaf culture, and deaf heritage. Few materials are acquired on a nationwide basis on the contributions of the deaf to American society and their importance in the American social fabric. The deaf, in most instances, have not had a communication link with the past through materials and resources which depict their contributions.

COLLECTION DEVELOPMENT

A collection on deafness and hearing impairment can become a part of traditional library service if the library is supported as a public good. As such, it must maintain a broad base of support in the community it serves regardless of whether all people in the community use it. It must have resources available, accessible, and appropriate to the use of *all* people in the community. In such resource development, collections of materials on deafness and hearing impairment are considered to be neither special collections nor outreach programs. They are fundamental to and an integral part of the library program. Their budgeting and funding is part of the ongoing collection funding. Collections of materials have been, for the most part, oriented to hearing people, neglecting the nonhearing people in the process of selection and acquisition. Collection development, taking into account both the diversity of the deaf and hearing impaired in the community and their commonalities as well, will help to ensure that appropriate resources are available.

Such a program will also ensure that the resources are neither lost in the mainstream of a selection and acquisition program nor relegated to a permanent special status. A modification in the book selection policy may be required to make sure that books and other materials on deafness and hearing impairment are included as ongoing acquisitions. There are, however, no ironclad rules for selection of these materials. Guidelines may be developed, but the dynamics of the communication patterns as well as the behavioral patterns of deaf and hearing impaired individuals need to be considered in this area of selection and acquisition.

In developing the collection on an ongoing basis, the librarians should have a realistic approach to the acquisition of resources and should make sure that the materials are as representative as possible. When resources are being developed to support a curriculum, the approach will be ever-expanding as the curriculum expands. As new opportunities develop for deaf and hearing impaired people in education, employment, and in society in general, resources in the collection will encourage them to go into a wide variety of occupations. Of course, a wide range of reading levels in book selection, as well as a wide range of visual materials, should always be considered. When audiovisual materials are included, amplification of sound should be provided also. Research materials on deafness and hearing impairment should be included in libraries which normally include research materials.

The collection of books and other materials are the resources on which the services and programs are based. The selection of resources determines the information which is available and accessible to the user. The selection policies determine, also, the form in which the communication is transmitted. Although all of these considerations are a part of the selection for a traditional library collection, they become more critical when the needs of the deaf and hearing impaired are considered as well. The criteria for selection are not weakened in the process but rather expanded to ensure that this special population group is not overlooked. Expansion of the collections will be needed, but this can be done within the stated mandate of the library and without changing the mission of the library or its character. Required in the selection process will be expansion of the sources of materials, an expanded knowledge of some different types of resources, and consultation with advisory people not usually included in the selection procedure. Because the expansion of materials to be included on subjects relating to deafness and hearing impairment must often be done within the existing budget, care must be taken to choose materials which will best answer the needs of the consumers. It is important that the selection librarians make informed choices in selecting materials, by, for, and about the deaf and hearing impaired in any library setting.

SELECTION OF MATERIALS

A professional library on deafness and hearing impairment can be developed as part of the traditional library if the selection policy is modified. Included in this collection should be books, pamphlets, periodicals, microfiche, films, and government publications in the fields of deafness and hearing impairment. The field of special education should be included, also, as some of the deaf and hearing impaired have multiple disabilities. The collection should not only reflect deafness and hearing impairment but also other disabilities.

Hearing parents of deaf and hearing impaired children can also make good use of the traditional type of library collection acquired under an expanded subject policy. Materials of an educational nature are important to parents as well as to those who will help them with their problems. They need to have special support from experienced parents on how to cope with problems which arise. Materials reflecting this experience will be invaluable to them.

The determination of the materials included in the library collection depends on the community needs and on the proximity of other libraries with collections on deafness and hearing impairment. The materials should be general in nature and broad in scope. They should be representative of the many issues and concerns relating to hearing loss and deafness. They should also include materials illustrating the various methods used in communicating with deaf and hearing impaired people, such as sign language, fingerspelling, lipreading, and speech, as well as total communication. The subject of education of the deaf is an important inclusion in the collection as are major educational methods of teaching deaf and hearing impaired persons and the subject of mainstreaming children into regular classroom situations.

Many articles in periodicals contain current, as well as background, information. Encyclopedias include authoritative articles on deafness and hearing impairment and numerous periodicals and newspapers help to maintain currentness. Visual materials are helpful as are government publications, pamphlets, and ephemeral materials. Because one of the most important activities of a library is to distribute information, books on deafness and hearing impairment are essential to library service to the deaf and hearing impaired. Because one of the major problems in providing this service is attitudinal barriers, this information assists in promoting understanding of the problems, needs, desires, and abilities of this population. Only through mutual understanding and information can an entire library program be accessible and usable to deaf and hearing impaired persons. Many of the standard selection aids and selection guidelines are useful in selecting materials for the collection on deafness and hearing impairment in the traditional library service. New sources of selection for material on deafness and hearing impairment will, of necessity, be added.

The collection may be developed along many lines, The following are basic criteria:

- Sign language. Many members of the deaf community use sign language. As the third most commonly used non-English language in the United States, information is needed about American Sign Language.
- Fingerspelling. This technique supplements sign language. Books can range from manuals for the beginner to a complete guide for fingerspelling. In addition, they can relate the use of this communication method to sign language. These books can provide a dictionary of idioms, can analyze American Sign Language, and can relate the fingerspelling to ASL (Ameslan) as well as to other modes of communication.
- Speechreading. Usually people do not realize how difficult speechreading-lipreading really is. Books on the development and use of this skill will be helpful in understanding this problem and in becoming skillful at it. Materials may range in content from the teaching of speechreading-lipreading to materials on research which is being done on this subject.
- Audiology. The world of the deaf and hearing impaired is not a completely silent one. Many are able to perceive sound even though they are unable to hear and understand speech. Subjects covered in this field can provide information on auditory training, text material on the subject, a study of aural rehabilitation, and research in the field of audiology.
- Total communication. Because many people use total communication as a method of talking with other people, an understanding of its use and effectiveness is essential. Materials included should be related to using this method of communication skillfully and to discussing its value as a method of communicating.
- Historical background. Some of the history of the education of the deaf and hearing impaired assists in understanding the controversies in the methods of educating this group. Books in this field cover the history itself, the international viewpoint, personal accounts of how deaf people have been educated, and the re-

sults of this education. Included also should be information on the history of specific communication methods used in education and their results.

- Social and psychological aspects. The effects of hearing loss on the lives of people is important to the understanding of deafness and hearing impairment. Books may consider the entire subject of hearing loss in relation to the development of communication. They may be devoted to the subject of the intellectual, vocational, academic, and personal achievements of people with a hearing loss. Some of the problems to be considered include the problem of thinking without language, the effect on reasoning, or a total review of the psychological effects of a hearing loss on individuals and the resulting social implications.

- Parental understanding. Because most parents of deaf and hearing impaired children can hear, they usually have little initial knowledge of deafness and hearing impairment. They need to understand the problems involved and how to cope with them. Books in this area can provide information in handbook form and can describe the problems that parents face. They can also relate personal accounts of the effects of deafness and hearing impairment on the family, provide basic and fundamental information which helps parents to understand their children, and present how people overcome problems involved in a hearing loss.

- Education. There is a general need to have a knowledge of the special learning problems of the deaf and hard-of-hearing child. Books on education can range from teaching reading to the child from preschool through secondary education to a discussion of music for deaf and hard-of-hearing children. Included also can be the subjects of speech and hearing and the mainstreaming of deaf and hearing impaired children. Reading books on postsecondary education can provide information on schools to attend, admission requirements, programs of instruction, standards of excellence, academic standing, and availability of financial assistance.

- Careers. One of the most important aspects of life for the deaf and hearing impaired is the selection of a career. Books range widely in subject matter. Some discuss improved opportunities for deaf and hard-of-hearing persons—vocational, technical, and academic. Others assist this group in telephone training in a work situation; participating in the benefits of continuing education classes; discovering independent living skills; learning how to fill out a job application and how to find and interview for a job; and examining work regulations and workmen's compensation as it affects deaf and hearing impaired people.

- Older adults. To prevent isolation and withdrawal because of a hearing loss, the library can provide books on hearing loss for older adults and the elderly. Materials can include information about hearing aids and how to select and use them. Continuing education opportunities should be included as well as recreational activities available. Books should discuss volunteering, its usefulness to the community, and its benefits to the individual.
- Prevention and research. Progress is being made in the prevention of hearing loss and in its treatment; continuing research is being conducted and reported. Books can include information on the effects of noise on hearing, selection of hearing aids, the development of ear surgery, and how the ear functions.
- General sources. Because many people will not take the time to read extensively on deafness and hearing impairment, some of the areas which will assist in obtaining an understanding of the disability are deaf and hearing impaired authors writing about their own experiences as well as fiction concerning the experiences of deaf and hard-of-hearing characters; effects of technological and other advances and activities as they have affected and are affecting the lives of the deaf and hearing impaired; how the public library can be an asset to these people and how libraries, working together and with other organizations, can have a positive impact on deaf and hearing impaired people; bibliographies on several communication modes to provide easy access to this necessary information; the psychology of deafness and hearing impairment and the important relationship between mental health and hearing loss; and true personal narratives of family life and deafness and hearing impairment and of the problems encountered.

To make the library truly usable by deaf and hearing impaired consumers requires an expansion of the traditional library methods of selection and acquisition of materials. The mission of a library is to serve all people in its service area with appropriate materials; the selection and acquisition of materials for the deaf and hearing impaired is but one aspect of that mandate.

Because a severe hearing loss at birth or in early childhood causes difficulties in communication and impedes the development of language, the reading level of people in this group is usually below that of their intellectual abilities. This is generally true even with early intervention. As a result, vocabulary is small and the grasp of complex grammatical construction is not developed. People with such language difficulties are usually attracted to reading materials on subjects related to their age level rather than to their reading level. In selecting materials, librarians have a responsibility to accommodate their needs. It is important to ensure that materials are available that correspond to the age interests of the deaf or hearing impaired persons so that using the library becomes an enjoyable and rewarding experience. Soliciting input from deaf and hearing impaired youth and adults in the development of materials selection guidelines as well as in the selection of the materials themselves is essential.

SPECIAL MATERIALS

To meet the needs of this group of people, librarians will find that high interest/low language-level materials are appropriate. In this type of material, the content is more mature than the vocabulary or the sentence structure used. Because the reading skills of the individual are below average, it is incumbent upon the library to remove any language barrier between the consumer and the subject content. However, the interest level is vital to the motivation of the reader—it must be relevent to the interests of the potential consumer. In addition, the materials should have an attractive format—a format that is also appropriate to the age level. The subject interests represented in high interest/low vocabulary books will vary as much as they do with any group of books being selected for a large population. The only variation is in the complexity of the language used. Topics may relate to recreational activities and informational needs and interests as well, and to fiction and nonfiction.

Because some deaf and hearing impaired individuals with limited reading skills have difficulty understanding written language and abstract concepts, high interest/low vocabulary materials should be given special consideration in the selection of materials for this age group. A small vocabulary and a lack of reading achievement produce a barrier which must be overcome through a skillful selection of materials developed to meet that particular problem. This is due not only to a limited vocabulary but also because some deaf and hearing impaired individuals have difficulty with syntax, idiomatic expressions, and words with several meanings. Finding suitable material, however, and promoting its use is a very demanding job.

There are many publishers of books with a high interest level and written in vocabularies that are appropriate to the reading skills of the potential users. The books can be reviewed in relation to their interest level and their corresponding reading level. A knowledge of the needs, abilities, and interests of this group is essential if the books and other reading material selected are to be considered usable and attractive by the consumer. Materials that can be read easily yet have a more mature content are most needed by children with a prevocal hearing loss as well as those with a loss later in childhood, by the young adult and the vocational adult, and less by the older adult and the very elderly who have a hearing loss. Library materials with high interest/low language-level emphasis will provide access to fiction and nonfiction, and to information with the proper interest level content.

Because people with a hearing loss learn primarily through sight, most ideas, concepts, stories, and information must be presented visually to be understood. For this reason, well-illustrated books are needed in the library collection, including wordless books which contain pictures alone and those with some identifying words. Vocabulary skills can be raised through books containing pictures of common things in the environment and in the daily lives of people. Through identification of the pictures and through suggested answers, people with limited vocabularies can increase their reading ability. Some nonverbal books are so well illustrated that the meaning can be understood through the pictures alone. Nonverbal, well-illustrated books are useful in story telling for relating the pictures to the concepts and ideas. Children and young adults with a hearing loss can then relate this new information to their visual perception created by the illustrations.

Sign language books are available for library selection. Signed stories are valuable both for children with an early hearing loss and for a later one; they are also important for young adults, parents, and the elderly who have lost their hearing. Many of the children's illustrated classics, which have signs added to the text, are readily available. In some of the children's classics, the sign language-illustrated tapes with text are inserted above the regular print.

Collections of songs for signing are good additions to the collection. Some include the music, the lyrics, and the accompanying sign language. Picture books are also available with the story written in words and in signed English. Comic strip formats can provide a useful introduction into the use of sign language. Comic books without signs also have an appeal which encourages children to read. Also, *Sign*

Writer, a bilingual newspaper written in sign language and spoken language, is available.

Because learning by sight is so essential to people with a hearing loss, visual presentations of concepts and ideas through films, videotapes, and other such means become important in materials selection for the deaf and hearing impaired. Filmstrips, videotapes, transparencies, and posters appeal to those who have a hearing loss but can acquire information, learn skills, and enjoy recreation through visual skills. Videotapes are available for both loan and purchase on a wide variety of subjects. Some are captioned, some are signed, others are silent. Available on videotapes, also, are poetry collections which are signed or captioned. The majority are in color, but some are available in black and white. Included in the collection should be, in addition to videotapes, filmstrips, pictures, posters, charts, films, slides, videocassettes, transparencies, maps, prints, and microforms.

One of the greatest sources of information and recreation is the captioned film. As with all types of nonbook media, these films are enjoyed by all users of the library from the children to the elderly. Captioned films which are available on a loan basis include educational, theatrical, and general interest subjects. Many 16mm films have been captioned and are available on a free loan basis to groups of people who are deaf or hearing impaired and to agencies serving them. A library collection should include captioned films available by purchase, free loan, or rental.

The captioning of films for the deaf has a long history, and the results of the work have provided an excellent source of education, information, and recreation for deaf and hearing impaired individuals. Through the efforts of many, P.L. 85-905 was signed into law in 1958. The law, An Act to Provide for a Loan Service of Captioned Films for the Deaf in the Department of Health, Education and Welfare, became operational in 1959, although the funding to implement the law was initially quite low. In 1962, P.L. 87-715 amended and expanded the act and increased the funding and in 1965, P.L. 89-258 again expanded the original act providing for captioned films and increased the funding for successive years. Additional amendments increased the scope of the Captioned Films Act.

There are now several educational film depositories in different parts of the United States from which educational captioned films are distributed. Theatrical films, short subjects, and film documentaries are also available in captioned form.

The purpose of the program of captioned films for the deaf is to promote the general welfare of deaf individuals by bringing them the understanding and appreciation of films that play an important part in the culture of hearing persons, giving them the opportunity of being in touch with the realities of their environment, and enabling them to share a rewarding experience.

The Special Materials Project, a project of the Associations of Education of the Deaf, Inc. (under contract with the United States Department of Education), provides free loan of captioned films to certified groups.

A companion service to captioned films is captioned television. The continued progress in closed-captioning services gives the library an exceptional opportunity to provide resources within the library. It is important that the library provide resources which enable people with a hearing loss to gain information at the same time hearing people are receiving it. Captioned broadcasts provide information and recreation for all ages. Decoders allow such resources within the library and, through a loan service, people with this device can enjoy the captioning. Teletext is another closely allied resource which may be available to the deaf and hearing impaired through the resources and services of the library.

Another type of film important to many consumers is the training film. Some of these can be borrowed, others purchased, and some produced by the library itself. Some may be used to train librarians and other staff members, parents, teachers, and other individuals who work with the deaf and hearing impaired. Training and educational films for parents are many in both quantity and subject matter. They include subjects such as giving what-to-do solutions to the many problems involved in working with a hearing impaired or deaf child. Total communication and ways in which hearing parents can help their nonhearing child are included in training films. The exploration of the psychological effect of the condition of deafness or hearing impairment on the family situation is also a subject included in these films.

Some films are useful in the career training of the deaf and hearing impaired themselves. Career training films include subjects such as data processing job opportunities, careers in electronics, and attitudes in a work situation. Films also range in subject content from continuing education programs for deaf and hearing impaired adults to independent living skills. Some include basic information for people in the medical profession on caring for patients who also have a hearing loss while others are concerned with the relation of deaf and hearing impaired clients to their lawyers.

To ensure that all subjects needed are available on film, a program of resources can be developed in the library which involves the making of video programs by the library itself. Story telling programs can be captured on film for reuse or for exchange with other libraries. The filming of sign language classes can enable libraries to use these films with many groups. Local theaters of the deaf productions can be recorded for future viewing. A local history project can be a subject of interest to many deaf and hearing impaired individuals when presented in visual form.

Other materials a library can effectively include in its collection are kits which will provide practical advice to parents concerning their child's hearing loss. Kits can be put together simply by gathering all materials which provide information about deafness and hearing impairment and are of interest to parents. To develop the materials for these kits, a panel made up of specialists in deafness and hearing impairment, librarians, parents of children with a hearing loss, and deaf and hearing impaired people can make the initial selection of information to be included in such a packet. Included in the materials can be the following:

- Listings of local special services offered to the deaf and hearing impaired people for both the child and the parent.
- Annotated bibliographies on deafness and hearing impairment, including the broad overview and the special interest listings as well.
- Descriptions of laws relating to the deaf and hearing impaired such as the Vocational Rehabilitation Act of 1973 and the Education for All Handicapped Children Act of 1975 (P.L. 94-142).
- Instructions on how to be an advocate for the deaf and hearing impaired.
- Descriptions of possible home problems—with possible solutions.
- Travel suggestions—how to successfully meet problems which may arise in travel situations.
- Lists of the types of specific recreation which can be enjoyed by the deaf and hearing impaired.
- A referral directory for the local community. This will usually have to be developed locally, although some directories do exist on a statewide basis such as those issued by the Western Oregon State College for Alaska, Idaho, Oregon, and Washington.

These subjects can be enlarged through the purchase of packaged kits which contain material on such subjects as:

- Discovery of a child's hearing loss and the reactions to this knowledge.

- Language development.
- Child management.
- Development of learning skills.
- Social considerations.
- Effective note-taking.
- Bibliography on deafness and hearing impairment.
- Career information (education and employment).
- Trends in the fields of deafness and hearing impairment and predictions for the future.

The kits may be packaged in many ways, but an attractive packaging enhances their appeal to consumers. They may be used as a package and/or as materials from which selections can be made to develop an individualized kit.

The panel that develops the original package will have an ongoing responsibility to update the materials in the kits, to add materials as the knowledge about deafness and hearing impairment expands, and to delete materials as they become outdated. Such kits can be made up for various audiences such as the deaf or hard-of-hearing child, young adults, older adults, and the elderly. Also, specific groups of people can be provided with current as well as basic information they need about working with deaf and hearing impaired people. Included in these groups are librarians, medical and legal personnel, police officers, and firefighters. As the program expands, users will contribute information to be included in future kits.

The Red Notebook: Communicating with Hearing People can be used as a reference source by including in the notebook pertinent information on local services. Each library has the opportunity to add to this notebook by submitting pertinent information to be included because it has a scheduled updating.

In developing the concept of kits for the child who is deaf or hearing impaired, toys can be included in the library's collection of materials. Other materials, such as puzzles, games, pictures, posters, cassettes, filmstrips, puppets, records, and flash cards are also worthwhile additions. Creating variety in these kits will ensure appeal for individuals, ranging from the preschool child to the elderly. The library can provide attractive tote bags or some other means of carrying the material to and from the library.

Included in the total collection on deafness and hearing impairment should be materials relating to deaf-blindness, such as:

- Facts describing and defining deaf-blindness.

- Lists of educational and community resources for those who are deaf-blind.
- Stories of people who are deaf-blind and how they adapted to this condition.
- Discussions of salient issues of the psychological adjustments to deaf-blindness, the rehabilitation services available, and the social adjustments required.
- Guidelines on 2-way communication as it relates to people who are both deaf and blind.
- Information on interpreting for deaf-blind persons with special considerations for this type of interpreting and the methodology of various interpreting techniques.

The formats for the collection of materials are many and varied. Books are as basic in this service as they are to the service to the population in general. Pamphlet material is essential because so much information is included in brochure and leaflet form which is not available elsewhere. Pamphlets are attractive to the reader, also, because of the conciseness of the material and the fact that they usually address specific subjects. Government publications often provide material absent in other resources. They may range from proceedings of a conference on deafness and hearing impairment to the description of educational facilities available to the deaf and hearing impaired. Periodicals are essential to a collection. Many of the associations of and for the deaf and hearing impaired issue magazines on a regular basis. Other valuable information is contained in magazines which are independent of any specific organization but are devoted to deafness and hearing impairment. Periodicals of a general nature often carry articles on deafness and hearing impairment as well. This knowledge enables the nonhearing and the hearing, including the library staff, to remain current on the activities of the deaf and hearing impaired communities. Newsletters, both national and local, are a complement to periodical information. Some of the newsletters are devoted entirely to the deaf and hearing impaired. Others are directed toward all types of disabilities, including a hearing loss. Still others are concerned with one particular activity such as legislative action and regulatory activities which affect people with a disability, including a hearing loss. Indexes are invaluable in locating information on deafness and hearing impairments. These indexes cover specific information on deafness and hearing impairment, on disabilities, or are of a more general nature but include information on deafness and hearing impairment. Some of the indexes are in traditional book format while others have been automated. Captioned films may range from those produced especially for deaf and hearing impaired people to silent movies and foreign films which are captioned for audiences who do not understand the language that is spoken. Mime can be included in the collection through productions of theaters for the deaf. It can also be included in story telling and in the programs developed locally by and for deaf and hearing impaired groups of people. Visual media can include filmstrips, transparencies, videotapes, videocassettes, films, posters, and other visual means of communication. When audio is also included, amplification of sound is necessary. Kits provide a prepackaged collection of materials for specific groups or on specific subjects. They also provide an opportunity to allow people to develop individualized kits. Closed captioned television is a resource which can be used in the library or, through a program of lending decoders, can be enjoyed in the home of the user.

In addition to the materials on deafness, hearing impairment, and deaf-blindness are materials on other types of disabling conditions. So me deaf and hearing impaired people are multidisabled so that materials on all types of disabilities should be available. To ensure that the resources are accessible to the people for whom they are intended, the library needs to ensure that physical, as well as attitudinal, barr iers are eliminated. Deaf and hearing impaired people and parents of children with a hearing loss can also be helpful in selecting this type of material.

NEEDS OF THE CONSUMER

In developing resources for library service, all considerations should be reviewed to determine the extent and depth of the resources needed in this library collection. Libraries serve all people and, as stated in the legislative policy for the American Library Association in 1983, the association supports provision of library resources and services to disabled persons as well as the aged, those with learning disabilities, and people who have a limited skill in speaking and understanding the English language. To ensure that adequate resources are available, libraries need to determine that materials are readily accessible elsewhere before a decision is made for exclusion of a specific item in a specific library collection. Because of budgetary constraints for this service, as well as for all library resources, cooperation and coordinated sources of materials are vital to developing a broad collection. The types of materials and subjects included will depend on many other factors besides the selection and acquisition policies. Some of these considerations are:

- The size and characteristics of the deaf and hearing impaired population in the community served.
- The proximity of any specialized and accessible collections on the subject of deafness and hearing impairment within the service area of the library.
- The relationship among the libraries in the region as far as interaccessibility of materials is concerned and determination of the existence of that interaccessibility as a practical reality.
- The programs provided in the public schools for deaf and hearing impaired children and the resources available through the schools.
- The organizations and institutions serving deaf and hearing impaired children and adults and the extent, availability, and accessibility of their library resources.

Because the resources of a library support all other programs offered to the community, extreme care must be exercised in selecting materials for any type of library service and because most librarians have limited experience selecting resources for deaf and hearing impaired people on a national basis, they need to exercise special care that the resources are expertly developed. Education for librarians in this area will help to ensure that a library collection is useful and that the investment of funds has been wisely made. As programs are developed on a national and an international basis, the selection of resources in this area of service will be as natural as it is for traditional services. Because the American Library Association, in its 1983 federal legislative policy, declared its support for the establishment of a national library service for deaf and hearing impaired people, libraries will move closer to including resources for deaf and hearing impaired people in their collections. Because the International Federation of Library Associations and Institutions held its first open meeting of the Working Group on the Library Needs of the Deaf at the 49th Conference in Munich, Federal Republic of Germany, in 1983, selection of library resources and services for deaf and hearing impaired people will be approached on an international basis. Each such activity makes the development of a collection easier and more reliable in actually meeting the needs and interests of deaf and hearing impaired people.

REFERENCE LIST

American Library Association. "Equal Access to Library Service." In *ALA Federal Legislative Policy*, by the American Library Association, pp. 18–19. Chicago: American Library Association, 1983.

Association for Library Service to Children. *Selecting Materials for Children with Special Needs*. Chicago: American Library Association, 1980.

Association of Specialized and Cooperative Library Agencies. Library Service to the Deaf Section. *Basic Sources of Information on Serving Deaf Library Users*. Chicago: American Library Association, 1983.

Bramley, Gerald. "Library Service for the Deaf." In *Outreach Library Services for the Institutionalized, the Elderly and Physically Handicapped* by Gerald Bramley, pp. 211–17. London: Clive Bingley, 1978.

Baskin, Barbara H., and Harris, Karen H., eds. *The Mainstreamed Library: Issues, Ideas, Innovations*. Chicago: American Library Association, 1982.

The Special Child in the Library. Chicago: American Library Association, 1976.

Caviglia, Karen; Hopkins, Karen; and Ritter, Audrey. *Selected Bibliography Prepared for Libraries Establishing a Deafness Collection*. Rochester, NY: National Technical Institute for the Deaf, Rochester Institute of Technology, 1981.

"Disability Awareness, Hearing Impaired." *Higher Education and the Handicapped Resource Directory, 1982–1983*. Washington, DC: HEATH Resource Center, 1983.

Dodson, Marguerite A. "Bridging the Information Gap: A Brooklyn Public Library Kit for the Parents of Children with Special Needs." In *The Mainstreamed Library: Issues, Ideas, Innovations*, edited by Barbara H. Baskin and Karen H. Harris, pp. 269–73. Chicago: American Library Association, 1982.

Fader, D. N. *Hooked on Books*. New York: Berkeley Publishing Corporation, 1976.

Gallaudet Media Distribution. Washington, DC: Gallaudet College, n.d.

The Ideal Library for the Deaf. (California Library Association Conference, San Francisco, 1981.) Sacramento, CA: California Library Association, 1981. (Cassettes.)

"IYDP Filmography." *Interface* 3 (3–4) (Summer 1981): 6–8.

Lee Katz Memorial Collection. Hyattsville, MD: Prince George's County Memorial Library System, 1982.

Materials Useful for Deaf/Hearing Impaired: An Annotated Bibliography. Lake Oswego, OR: Dormac, Inc., 1976.

Myhre, Margaret, researcher and compiler. *The Heritage of Deaf People. A Collection of Books and Moving Video Image Video Tapes for Your Enjoyment and Enlightenment*. (A special publication of the San Francisco Public Library Deaf Services Department.) San Francisco, CA: San Francisco Public Library, 1982.

"Resource Materials for Audiologists, Special Education Supervisors and Parents of Hearing Impaired Children." In *Audiology, Education and the Hearing Impaired Child*, by Fred H. Bess and Freeman E. McConnell, p. 293. St. Louis, MO: C. V. Mosby Company, 1981.

Ritter, Audrey. "The College Library Serving Hearing Impaired Students." *The Bookmark* 40 (1) (Fall 1981): 21–24.

Ruark, Ardis, and Melby, Carole. "Bibliography of Wordless Books." In *Kangaroo Kapers or How to Jump into Library Service for the Handicapped* by the State Department of Education (Elementary and Secondary Education), Pierre, SD: State Department of Education (Elementary and Secondary Education), 1978.

Sadoski, Michael J., and Sadoski, Doris C. "Building Libraries to Serve the Deaf." *LJ Special Report* (6) 1978: 29–34.

"Services to the Deaf." In *Services to the Handicapped*. Metropolitan Cooperative Library System Workshop, Pasadena, CA. Santa Fe Springs, CA: Metropolitan Cooperative Library System, 1979. (Cassettes.)

The Sign Writer. Newport Beach, CA: The Center for Sutton Movement Writing. (Various issues.)

Spach, George. *Good Reading for Poor Readers.* New Canaan, CT: Garrard, 1974.

Special Materials Project of the Association for Education of the Deaf. *Catalog of Educational Captioned Films for the Deaf.* Silver Spring, MD: Association for Education of the Deaf, 1983.

Strang, Ruth G. *Readable Books.* Bronx, NY: H. W. Wilson, 1975.

Western Oregon State College. *Resource Directory for Deaf and Hearing Impaired Individuals.* (Separate issue for each of the following states: Alaska, Idaho, Oregon, Washington.) Monmouth, OR: Western Oregon State College, 1982.

Chapter 14
Cooperative Programs

An emphasis on the development and funding of multitype library networks is important to the success of library service to deaf and hearing impaired people. That no library can be self-sufficient in any type of library service is especially true in this specialized field. In some areas of deafness and hearing impairment, much has been published. In other areas, the publication of materials is just beginning. Materials are available in a variety of formats, and the potential exists for new formats to be created. Computer technology is continuing to have a positive impact on library service as it relates to information service for the deaf and hearing impaired. The population distribution of consumers to be served is uneven. The assumption is that the larger population concentrations of deaf and hearing impaired people are in the metropolitan areas; however, each community, no matter how small, will have within its geographical area of service some people who are deaf or have some type of hearing impairment.

Cooperative library programs are not new for overall library service but, for service to the deaf and hearing impaired, few such programs have been established. Of those which have been established, a few have continued, uninterrupted, on a nationwide basis. While some cooperative services have been provided, these programs have not had a continuing national funding source. Libraries have a long way to go to provide a walk-in service with a high probability of deaf and hearing impaired people and their associates being able to obtain the materials and services they need and desire. Libraries strive to reach their entire clientele, including people who are hearing impaired or deaf, but to do so requires the resources and programs to back up the effort. This means that libraries must strengthen and diversify their collections in content and format; they must modify and enlarge their programs of reference, research, and recreational and informational materials; they must accommodate people with a hearing loss at all age levels; they must provide story telling, theater programs, films, and other appropriate activities in which the visual aspect is emphasized; they must accommodate their new users through changes in communication methods as well as making active use of advances in technologies. Through participation in cooperative programs of multitype libraries, the library community can meet the diverse needs and desires of the deaf and hearing impaired population.

ELEMENTS OF A COOPERATIVE PROGRAM

The type of cooperative programs and the area covered is less important than the services and resources which can effectively be made accessible to users. Programs for people with a hearing loss which are in existence on a cooperative basis or which have been developed but not continued vary from citywide to a geographical part of a county, from countywide or regional to those which are statewide or interstate. In reality, some of the programs have approached the concept of service on a national basis with international possibilities.

Cooperative programs also vary from being planned and operated to serve one type of library to serving all libraries in the area as part of the program; they vary from including libraries exclusively to combining all kinds of institutions and services interested in or serving deaf or hearing impaired people. However, in all cases, the mission of the service remains the same—to serve the deaf and hearing impaired population with library service appropriate to their needs and desires.

The value of a cooperative program is demonstrated in the ability of libraries to provide service to the public through the sharing of all of the components that make up library service. Through such a program, deaf and hard-of-hearing people are able to obtain a wide range of service from the library. It provides a realistic means for making available a breadth of resources and programs and allows the possibility of increasing their depth. The economics of the cooperative programs vary according to each situation. The quality of the programs also vary, depending upon the components that make up the cooperative system and upon many other distinctive factors.

Cooperative planning is essential to cooperative programs. The guidelines used in overall library planning are helpful in this kind of cooperative planning. If the cooperative service is to become a part of the total library service, its inclusion in the overall planning process is essential. The basic difference in this kind of planning is the deep and constant involvement with deaf and hearing impaired people by the librarians, boards of trustees, support staff, and others associated with planning for libraries.

Another difference in cooperative planning from the usual overall planning is the necessity for data collection. An extra effort is required both initially and then on a continual basis to learn about the deaf and hearing impaired population, including their number and geographic location and their characteristics, such as the extent of hearing loss, extent of isolation, mobility, age levels, educational levels, prevalence of multidisabling conditions, language skills, and reading abilities. The social and service structures in the community as they relate to people with a hearing loss are important aspects to know about. Within cooperative programs, the findings in these areas will have a profound effect on the distribution of services, resources, and responsibilities throughout the agencies making up the cooperative network. User surveys to determine the amount of and satisfaction with the usage of the libraries are essential. Emphasis should be placed on the planning, development, and operation stages of the cooperative program because even the very small library has the potential to make extensive use of the services and resources of the entire program. Outlets, such as bookmobiles, may receive heavy use because of their direct service to varied population groups which will include, undoubtedly, people who are deaf, hard of hearing, or who have some type of hearing impairment. In all the planning, implementation, and usage of cooperative programs, deaf and hearing impaired people must be involved in every decision. Because this type of planning cannot be developed in a vacuum, the potential consumer must help guide its direction and redirection. All planning and data gathering must have a well-defined focus for the initial establishment and evaluation of cooperative programs of library service to the deaf and hearing impaired. This focus must be broad enough to include all salient facts but narrow enough to omit all data which are not significant to the design of the program.

One of the greatest values of a cooperative program is the possibility of having large collections of resources available. Parents of children who are deaf or hard of hearing will have easy access not only to basic materials but to strong collections in breadth and depth. Another strength is the rotation of services such as story telling, sign language classes, captioned film programs, and theater among the libraries which are part of the cooperative network. A third value of a cooperative program is the opportunity for an exchange of ideas. The program can operate in a limited fashion as a clearinghouse of materials and ideas. If feasible, professional assistance to libraries in developing programs of service can come from a central source. Such assistance can be provided by specialists in the field of library service to deaf and hearing impaired people and/or by professionals in general who work with the deaf, as well as deaf people themselves.

FUNDING SOURCES

State and federal funding is an important consideration in the realistic development of cooperative programs of library service to the deaf and hearing impaired. This is in addition to the local funds allocated for this purpose. Some states are providing funds to develop programs statewide; federal funds, administered by the states, have been an impetus to these kinds of programs which extend beyond the borders of one library jurisdiction. A federal, state, and local coalition which includes all types of libraries as well as nonlibrary agencies serving deaf and hard-of-hearing people will advance the service immeasurably. Because of the expense in both money and time in the development of a special program, expert planning is necessary. Inadequate or poor service from a cooperative program negates its existence. Cooperative programs which may not continue to exist are to be avoided if at all possible. While the programs themselves will, of necessity, change to meet new needs and improve the quality of service, the service itself should be planned as a continuing one developed for the public good.

Since the goal is to provide consumers with library service at all outlets in the community, it is essential that libraries in every community in the cooperative program, no matter what their size and the number of hearing affected individuals, provide appropriate services and resources. Within a cooperative program, every effort should be made to ensure that the service is of an even accessibility and quality. A standard, high-level quality of service, programs, and resources should be continually available to all people who have a hearing loss.

Both the development of the program of service and the strengthening of libraries in this field of service should occur simultaneously. Both are key elements in a multitype library network. Within a developing network or a cooperative program of any type, pilot projects can be developed with the assurance that the pilot project will remain in place and that it will be replicated throughout the system as it develops.

DESIGNING THE PROGRAM

Because library service to the deaf and hard of hearing looks outward as well as inward in the process of development, it will attract the attention of other agencies and organizations. A formal alliance is not essential; rather, the concern should be for how the service can be enhanced through these coordinated activities. Flexibility is a key ingredient to be emphasized at all times in cooperative efforts. As the program of service to the deaf and hearing impaired develops, coverage of a wider geographic area may become feasible. The combination of 2 or more networks can well be the basis for the delivery of the service. When a national plan of library service to the deaf and hearing impaired is developed, the approach can well be a regional service pattern with programs and resources provided at the appropriate degrees of breadth and depth at every library outlet in the region. The multitype library networks already in existence and providing library service to people who are hearing impaired or deaf can well provide the base for the planning and development of a nationwide system.

Deaf and hearing impaired people should have a continuing opportunity and responsibility for the design of these cooperative library programs and for their quality and quantity. They will know how new services can be provided, how the people can have access to them, and how the services can be strengthened. They will also be a strong element in securing the funding for these resources and services from both public and private sources. With cooperative programs of service available, potential consumers can help libraries with funding methods for improving services without increasing administrative costs. With financial constraints an ever-present condition, cooperative programs are a strong force in support of library service to the deaf and hearing impaired.

RESOURCE CENTERS

Resource centers within a cooperative program or independently developed are vital to the continuing progress of a nationwide library program. These centers can be developed within any geographical delineation. With rapid communication available, proximity to the libraries served ceases to be the important factor it once was.

A resource center which was developed in the early 1970s and continued into the 1980s has been recognized as an important element in the development of library service to the deaf and hearing impaired. The Resource Center, Library Service to the Deaf and Hearing Impaired, served people with a hearing loss throughout the greater Los Angeles area. The library was based on the already existing Metropolitan Cooperative Library System (MCLS), a cooperative system made up of 25 libraries. The goal of the service was to bring the people it served into the mainstream of library service. Emphasized was the use of libraries as information and social centers. Its training emphasis was to make libraries responsive to the needs of people with a hearing loss and to sensitize the hearing population to the problems of the nonhearing. The center provided toll-free typewriter (TTY) service in southern California for reference service, interlibrary loan, and general information. Included in the resource center were books, films, periodicals, videocassettes, and other visual materials on subjects of interest to its clientele. The center interacted closely with other agencies and maintained an extensive publicity program through speaking engagements, brochures, and a monthly newsletter, *Fingertips*; the developing and monitoring of the center was done by an effective advisory board. The resource center helped to develop a model plan of service within the 25 MCLS member libraries. Programs included a community survey, reference service and interlibrary loan, captioned film programs, programs for children, rotating loans and displays, collection development, workshops on communication modes for staff members, and exploration of the possibility of public TTYs in member libraries.

The project began in 1975 and continued as a unit into late 1981. It was initially funded as a federal program through the California State Library. The center served as a national clearinghouse for use by the "invisibly handicapped"—the deaf and hearing impaired. Its collection of captioned films served a large population area and the center worked closely with other agencies for the deaf and hearing impaired. Another purpose of the center was to establish a service which could be duplicated in other locations in its entirety or in part.

One of the things the center did was to develop a packet of materials on subjects such as:

- A resource guide to the deaf community.
- Videocassettes.
- Story hours for deaf and hard-of-hearing children.
- A programing primer.
- 16mm films.
- Definitions relating to deafness and hearing impairment.
- Language and electronic communications.

- Captioned films.
- Producers on distributors of materials relating to deafness and hearing impairment.
- Bibliographies on deafness and hearing impairment.

The packet was frequently updated. Inquiries came to the resource center from libraries and other agencies from around the country.

A strength of this resource center was the Greater Los Angeles Council on Deafness, Inc. (GLAD). This group consists of both deaf and hearing organizations within the metropolitan Los Angeles area, including MCLS. The members of the organization are nonprofit groups working directly or indirectly with the deaf and hearing impaired. GLAD was involved with the center from its beginnings, as was a Los Angeles County public school educational program for the deaf and hearing impaired—SELCO. Among the nonlibrary groups within the Los Angeles area involved from the beginning were the John Tracy Clinic and the Center on Deafness at California State University–Northridge.

Similar resource centers for library service to the deaf and hearing impaired would provide assistance to all libraries everywhere. Although each resource center will differ, depending on the community, the need for service, other institutions and agencies in the area providing service, and the level of government concerned, some of the characteristics of any resource center are:

- Users. This group includes the deaf and hearing impaired people in the community; children and their parents; adults and friends; and associates and relatives of the deaf and hearing impaired. It would also include libraries, institutions, agencies, and organizations concerned with this part of the population.
- Materials. Among the materials included are signed, captioned, and nonverbal films; print materials, including periodicals, books, pamphlets, and government publications on the subject of deafness and hearing impairment; and picture books, in wordless, Signed English, and signed text forms.
- Equipment. Included in the equipment are TTY/TDD and amplified sound equipment including telephones and equipment necessary to ensure hearing within meeting rooms. Equipment for the use of nonprint materials is also needed as are television sets and decoders.
- Facilities. Meeting rooms are necessary for the continuing usage by those groups of people who have a hearing loss. Such use will

include film showings of captioned films and classes in sign
language and other communication modes.

- Services. These would be primarily of an informational and referral nature relating to the library needs of deaf and hearing impaired people; they would have priority in library services offered.
- Financial Requirements. Adequate financing would be allotted initially in this priority order: (1) equipment; (2) materials; (3) personnel; and (4) operating expenses. On an ongoing basis, the priority of allocation would be as follows: (1) materials; (2) personnel; (3) operating expenses; and (4) equipment.
- Evaluation. Members of the advisory board can provide the evaluation and the monitoring of the program. Among the considerations in the evaluation should be the progress being made, the effectiveness of the work as perceived by the deaf and hearing impaired, the response of the people to the center, contacts for advice and assistance by libraries and other agencies, use of the TTY/TDD, use of resources in the collection, and attendance at program activities.

Before developing a resource center on library service to the deaf
and hearing impaired, some considerations need to be studied carefully
to help ensure its success. Among these considerations are:

- The concentration of the deaf and hearing impaired in the area to be served by the resource center.
- The establishing of close contact with the deaf and hearing impaired community and obtaining their participation in planning, developing, and implementation of the service through the advisory board or in a comparable capacity.
- The availability of adequate funding for collections, program development, personnel, equipment, and facilities needed to serve the area. Consideration should also be given initially to the ongoing availability of the funding.
- Participation of all libraries in the area to be served by the resource center.
- The ability to provide a 24-hour TTY/TDD service.
- The ability to provide a communication network on whatever level the center operates—local, regional, state, or national.

Resource center staff members should be knowledgeable about
deafness and hearing impairment and be able to communicate with the
deaf and hard of hearing in many ways. Needed also are people who
have a strong interest in library service to people who are deaf or hear-

ing impaired and who have an enthusiasm for their work. On the staff should be individuals who can assess the needs of the group to be served and act as a liaison between these people and the library. Organizational abilities are needed among the staff as well as the skill of identifying sources of materials and selecting and acquiring them. An ability to develop effective publicity and public relations is another important trait for staff members. The center should include both librarians and support staff as needed. Because the center personnel will act in an advisory capacity to other libraries, staff members are needed who can consult effectively with librarians in assisting in the development of total programs or segments of programs.

As programs for library service to the deaf and hearing impaired are developed throughout the United States and other countries, the role of the resource centers will change. They will become more predominantly centers for materials and equipment which do not need to be maintained within each individual library. A strong emphasis will continue to be on its activity as a clearinghouse and on its capacity to monitor research in the field of deafness and hearing impairment. The centers will also place a high priority on maintaining currentness in technological advances and assisting in technological development as it applies to libraries and people with a hearing loss. The resource centers will be catalysts in the development of materials and equipment which will provide improved library service to the deaf and hearing impaired.

CLEARINGHOUSES

A clearinghouse for library service to the deaf and hearing impaired is essential if the programs for such service are to be developed in all libraries. There are presently many unanswered questions nationwide relating to the effective development and implementation of a program. It is not the type of service that can be provided through a model plan or by the use of a manual of information. While these would definitely be of assistance, an ever-current, all-encompassing clearinghouse of information and materials is needed to answer the many questions which now exist and which will continue to be asked. The economy of such a service is a strong point in its favor. Presently, an informal clearinghouse situation does exist through one library contacting another and through conference and workshop programs. But, to meet the need for accurate and up-to-date information dealing with the service, a centralized source of information is a necessity.

The clearinghouse can provide specific answers to questions through letters, fact sheets, brochures, bibliographies, and computerized printouts. It can become a depository of materials locally developed and found effective to serve as a materials and program exchange. The center can also be a source of information on questions concerned with deafness and hearing impairment, technology and its use with the service, barrier-free design, environmental problems in providing the service, demographics in relation to deafness and hearing impairment, publicity and publications which have been effective, sources of materials for the service, and evaluation methods which successfully measure the effectiveness of the service.

The information and materials in the clearinghouse may come from many sources. One responsibility of the clearinghouse is to search constantly for resources which can provide information and library service to the deaf and hearing impaired as well as to hearing persons who are interested in deafness and hearing impairments. The search for information is an important activity of a clearinghouse. It is, however, a 2-way responsibility. Libraries should also be active in providing information to the clearinghouse for the use of other libraries or to nonlibrary agencies and organizations. The staff of a clearinghouse is also an all-important segment of its planning and implementation. The work of the staff cannot be passive; the staff must make known the materials available and those needed. To be effective in such an operation, the staff must be proactors as well as reactors.

The clearinghouse cannot know every resource available locally but can provide the information which has been collected. It is incumbent on the clearinghouse to maintain current and detailed information; updating materials is extremely important. Also of high priority in the functions of the clearinghouse is that of referral. The ultimate goal of the agency will be that of providing the information needed either directly or through referral to another source.

Sources of information and referral do exist, although on a more limited basis than a national, state, or regional clearinghouse. Among the existing services are:

- The American Library Association's unit on Library Service to the Deaf, which is a part of the Association of Specialized and Cooperative Library Agencies Division, provides information and materials to its members and to others who are interested in the deaf or hard of hearing. This unit disseminates information through its programs at the ALA summer conferences. *Interface,* the ASCLA newsletter, provides current information on books, films, and activities concerned with library service to the deaf and hearing impaired.

- *The Red Notebook: Communicating with Hearing People,* is an information source book published by the National Association of the Deaf. It is a depository for information about deafness, services for the deaf, and library services which help people who are deaf and their families to function in the mainstream of society. Through scheduled updating, this loose-leaf book provides information on deafness and 2-way communication.[1]
- Gallaudet College, the only liberal arts college for the deaf, provides information and materials relating to deafness and hearing impairment. Such information is readily available from many offices in the college, located in Washington, DC. Some of its materials are concerned with library service to the deaf and hearing impaired or include information on current activities in libraries in this area of service.
- An outstanding, ongoing program at the Center on Deafness, California State University–Northbridge, is the National Leadership Program for both deaf and hearing students. The program has as a completion requirement the development of a graduate project. This requirement has been in effect since the first class was held in 1962; the first deaf students came to the campus in 1964. The projects developed in this program cover a wide range of subjects. Among the ideas considered by the program have been community service for the deaf, laws and legislation, sign language/linguistics/total communication, communication devices, and parent information. A key to the success of the education of deaf students and hearing students together is the program of interpreting.
- The National Technical Institute for the Deaf, Rochester Institute of Technology, Rochester, New York is the only postsecondary technical college for the deaf. The institute shares with others the data, skills, and insights which are needed by the deaf and hearing impaired population. It offers interested organizations and individuals information about education, rehabilitation, accommodation, and employment of persons who are deaf. Some publications focus solely on the subject of library service to the deaf and hearing impaired; other publications include information on this subject within a larger framework.

Many other centers on deafness exist throughout the United States, some on a statewide basis. Schools which have a program on teaching the deaf and hearing impaired often have a center on deafness. Much information is available through these centers; however, the best approach is a national approach which specifically relates to library service as well as deafness and hearing impairment.

In addition to national resource centers are bibliographic centers on the subject of disabilities, including deafness and hearing impairment. These are very valuable. One of these bibliographic centers is the National Rehabilitation Information Center (NARIC), based at the Catholic University of America in Washington, DC. This center is invaluable to those working in the field of disabilities, including deafness and hearing impairment. Many people need frequent information about rehabilitation concerning the work being done by and for the deaf and hearing impaired, and one of the best sources is NARIC. It provides bibliographies on rehabilitation in all areas of this subject. REHAB-DATA is its database and is updated monthly. Among the subjects available are deaf-blind; deaf or hearing impairments, 1950–1980; deaf or hearing impairments, 1980–1982, 1982–1984; devices for the deaf or hearing impaired; and employment of the deaf or hearing impaired. Users can visit NARIC's facility to use the print and nonprint sources of information. Specialists and brokers are on duty during office hours. Information requests can be made by telephone, letter, or in person. Many requests can be handled immediately while more comprehensive in-depth requests take more time.

NARIC is designed to help many groups of people, including librarians. NARIC's services include custom literature searches, user training, a rehabilitation network, and a variety of publications. The collection consists of research reports, print and audiovisual materials and reports relevant to professional and administrative practice in the rehabilitation field. Bibliographic information and brief abstracts are available for each item and are maintained in an online computer system, available internationally through standard telecommunication links. NARIC also publishes the *NARIC Thesaurus*, a list of descriptors with definitions used in organizing the center's collection. Its periodical list contains over 200 journals and newsletter titles. Proceedings, rehabilitation information, network conferences, and accessibility maps are available.

Anyone can use the NARIC services, but they are of particular help to disabled individuals and rehabilitation professionals, as the center contains information on library services relating to deafness and hearing impairment. In addition to these many research services, NARIC is managing a significant program, ABLEDATA. This is a data bank of adaptive equipment and devices designed for the disabled.

The manufacturers, the location, and the price of the equipment are held in the ABLEDATA system, as well as evaluations with user comments included whenever possible. This unique resource includes more than 4,000 commercially available aids and equipment useful to disabled persons, including the deaf and hearing impaired.

Another essential source of information in the area of library service to the deaf and hearing impaired is the Educational Resources Information Center (ERIC). This network of information sources offers access to the literature on education and related fields. ERIC collects and indexes a wide variety of materials, including periodical articles, theses, workshop proceedings, bibliographies, and many other materials that are difficult to locate. *Resources in Education* (RIE) is a monthly abstracting service announcing recent report literature. The *Current Index to Journals in Education* (CIJE) is a monthly index to over 700 periodicals in education and related fields.

ERIC collects a significant amount of sources concerning the disabled, including the deaf and hearing impaired. Material is also included about library service to people with hearing loss. Among the other subjects included are daily living skills; counseling; and rehabilitation and education. One clearinghouse, the ERIC Clearinghouse on Handicapped and Gifted Children, has as its primary purpose the acquisition of documents on special education and where these documents can be found. The aurally disabled are included in this group as well as people who are multiple disabled.

Many other data banks exist which are useful sources for information on deafness and hearing impairment. Libraries and resource centers need to explore the field to determine how they can access relevant information in addition to NARIC, ERIC, and ABLEDATA. Librarians should constantly be aware of new developments in data banks and the kinds of materials available relating to deafness and hearing impairment.

BIBLIOGRAPHIES

In addition, many bibliographies have been issued which are specifically directed to library service to the deaf and hearing impaired. These materials are usually of an ephemeral nature but can be effective tools. Examples include:

- *The Heritage of Deaf People.* A collection of books, articles, and moving image videotapes for enjoyment and enlightenment as researched and compiled by Margaret Myhre. A special publication of the San Francisco Public Library, San Francisco, CA. 1982.

- "Hearing Impairment." *Disabled People*. A select list of recent books. Margaret Gibson Smith. Auckland Public Library. Auckland, New Zealand. 1981, pp. 108–11.
- *Audio-Visual Services for the Deaf and Hearing Impaired*. Contra Costa County Library System. Pleasant Hill, CA. 1983.
- Cooperative Library Services for the Deaf. San Francisco Public Library and Oakland Public Library, 1981–1982 (San Francisco and Oakland, CA). Offers *Deaf Awareness Videotapes*, Sources of Video Materials by and for the Deaf, *Deaf Characters in Literary Classics*, and *Books by Deaf Authors*.
- *Deafness and Hearing Impairment: A List of Materials*. Selected and compiled by Bonnie Bassis and Karen Mitchell. Houston Public Library. Houston, TX. 1981.
- *Sounds of Silence: Books about the Hearing-Impaired at Mid-Manhattan Library*. The New York Public Library. New York, n.d.
- *A Silent World*. Compiled by Steve Brown. Washington State Library. Olympia, WA. 1980.
- *Deafness: The Invisible Handicap*. Compiled by Barbara Brower. The Farmington Community Library. Farmington, MI. 1981.
- *Reaching Out: Books and Films on Deafness for Children*. Cuyahoga County Public Library. Cleveland, OH. 1980.
- *Great Directors; Great Films; Notable Foreign Films with English Subtitles*. Queens Borough Public Library. Jamaica, NY. 1983.

These are only a few examples. Many other bibliographies have been issued by other libraries on the specific subject of library service and deafness and hearing impairment. Many of these were issued in the 1970s with some continuing into the 1980s.

Book stores and distribution centers specializing in books for, by, and about the deaf and hearing impaired are excellent resources. Some particularly worthwhile sources are the Communications Center of the San Francisco Public Library; Gallaudet Media Distribution Center; Joyce Media, Northridge, CA; National Association of the Deaf, Silver Spring, MD; National Center on Deafness, California State University–Northridge; National Technical Institute for the Deaf, Rochester, NY; Sign Language Store, Northridge, CA; T-J Publishers, Silver Spring, MD; Alexander Bell Publications, Washington, DC; John Tracy Clinic, Los Angeles, CA.

Resources of all kinds are available: clearinghouses, data banks and retrieval systems, publications, catalogs, and bibliographies. Some overlap, while some are directed to the disabled and include the deaf and hearing impaired. Some are concerned with library service to the deaf and hearing impaired. While searches for materials need to be wide-ranging in order to ensure that adequate information is obtained, information is already available to help support a library program on service to the deaf and hearing impaired. Through the use of all sources which can be located, a librarian increases the options available. Although a national clearinghouse does not exist for library service to the deaf and hearing impaired, progress has been made toward that goal. The Library Service to the Deaf Forum (formerly Section) of the Association of Specialized and Cooperative Library Agencies serves in that capacity to some extent. *The Red Notebook* makes the concept a reality. The White House Conference on Library and Information Services addressed the possibility on several levels of government. The federal legislative policy in ALA's 1983 statement continued the progress through its support of the establishment of a national library for the deaf and hearing impaired.

While much remains to be accomplished, significant progress has been and is being made in providing access to the resources which are needed to support library services to the deaf and hearing impaired. In addition, cooperative programs have been developed to make the use of these resources an economic reality.

NOTE

1. National Association of the Deaf. *Communicating with Hearing People: The Red Notebook*, orig. Alice Hagemeyer (Silver Spring, MD: National Association of the Deaf [1980]. (Loose-Leaf.)

REFERENCE LIST

ABLEDATA. Washington, DC: National Rehabilitation Information Center, n.d. (Brochure.)

ALA World Encyclopedia of Library Information Services. Chicago: American Library Association, 1980.

"Aids Data Base (ABLEDATA) Now Available Online in Australia." *Link-up* (22) (September 1983): 2.

California Library Association. *Strategies for Service.* Sacramento, CA: California Library Association, 1982.

"Deaf Network: The Red Notebook, First Stop for Information on Deafness." *The Pathfinder* 2 (4) (July–August 1981): 1.

"ERIC for Information on the Disabled." *Link-up* (10) (July 1982):2–4.

Greater Los Angeles Council On Deafness, Inc. Los Angeles, CA: Greater Los Angeles Council on Deafness, Inc., n.d. (Brochure.)

Guella, Bernard. "Short Stories with Fictional Characters." *American Annals of the Deaf* 125 (1) (February 1983): 25–33.

John Tracy Clinic. Los Angeles: John Tracy Clinic, n.d. (Leaflet.)

Library Service to the Deaf. Chicago: Association of Specialized and Cooperative Library Agencies, n.d. (Brochure.)

A Library System Meeting Challenges: Goals for Clark County Library District, 1983–1988. Las Vegas, NV: Clark County Library District, 1983. (Brochure.)

"Microcomputers in Education of the Hearing Impaired." (National Conference.) *American Annals of the Deaf* 127 (5) (September 1982).

National Center on Deafness. *National Leadership Training Program. Area of the Deaf; Area of the Deaf-Blind Projects.* National Center on Deafness Publication Series. Northridge, CA: California State University–Northridge, 1982.

National Rehabilitation Information Center. *ABLEDATA.* Washington, DC: National Rehabilitation Information Center, n.d. (Brochure.)

Takahashi, Keith. "Clearinghouse for Materials: Library is Center of Project for Deaf." *Los Angeles Times* (September 17, 1978): 6.

Chapter 15
Equipment to Support the Library Services Program

In the search for a means to help the deaf and hearing impaired with 2-way communication, people have always relied on mechanical devices to complement or replace manual communication modes. Among a few of the early equipment items were ear trumpets (some also served as the head of a cane), talking gloves, the hearing aid, and the telephone. Of these, the hearing aid and the telephone survived. Each had its successes and each had its limitations. Great advances are now being made to help those with a hearing loss better understand communication taking place in the mainstream of society. Also important is the development of new products that can easily be used by a library. Such devices can be used within the library itself or loaned to improve service to people with a hearing loss. Having come through a long period where few breakthroughs in technology benefited those who are hearing impaired or deaf, we now have effective technology which is being used by them every day. Although still out of the economic reach of many, these tools are now available through libraries.

As we leave the industrial age and move into the information age, librarians, as information providers, need to be aware of the technology in relation to communication characteristics between deaf and hearing impaired people and those who can hear. While printed books, magazines, and other visual materials in various formats remain important media, they are now being supplemented by electronic products. The future will be a challenging time as is the present for all people concerned with deafness and hearing impairment. Because of this, it is important to look to the future as libraries plan for the present. This new direction must be taken into consideration at all times so that libraries' actions will not only be responding to changes in the future but will also play a role in shaping the future for service to the deaf and hearing impaired. Awareness alone will not enable libraries to help shape the new information society for hearing impaired and deaf people. As technology develops and the electronic age of information comes into focus, public policy will, of necessity, be altered. It is incumbent on libraries to assist in setting priorities in policy determination because decision making is becoming more and more complex. As technology is utilized to enable the hearing impaired and the deaf to become a part of the mainstream of library service, librarians need to maintain the concept that service is the *goal* with the technological developments a *means* to reach that goal more effectively and perhaps more economically.

Librarians must recognize that, although the new technology as it affects people with a hearing loss may have its limitations, it is important to people with this type of disability. There is a need to respond to the fact that each deaf or hearing impaired person is different from another. It must be recognized also that problems encountered by the deaf in the electronic world are different from those of the hard of hearing or from those with other types of hearing impairments. Each may have a totally different need. However, all of their needs can be satisfied through the understanding of the library, the cooperation of the consumer, and the accomodations of the people involved in developing technology for these people. The cost must be taken into consideration constantly in determining whether the new developments are "everyday use" items or economically unavailable to deaf and hearing impaired persons on an individual basis. Thus, there is no solution which is all-encompassing and which will provide communication to all people with all types of hearing loss, through an electronic means. But continued technological advances can bring people closer together through better communication.

TELECOMMUNICATION DEVICES

The International Year of Disabled Persons 1981 brought into the forefront various types of library systems, equipment, and supplies which can assist the deaf and hearing impaired in using the library. Probably one of the first pieces of equipment a library acquires in its effort to communicate with deaf and hearing impaired persons is a TTY/TDD. This piece of equipment is as essential to a library as a telephone in total communications. A person who is deaf and has a TTY/TDD available for use can communicate with the library like a hearing person does by telephone. Also, with this device, a person who is deaf can communicate with other persons who have access to the same equipment by typing messages which are transmitted by telephone. With a TTY/TDD 24-hour service, attended by staff during library hours and by volunteers after hours or put on automatic during that time, the deaf person can receive the same reference and information service as hearing persons. Because many people find it difficult to afford a TTY/TDD, obtaining a machine on loan from the library is a welcome service. Another important service a library can provide through this equipment is the relaying of TTY/TDD and telephone calls.

Many types of TTY/TDDs are available and are widely advertised in publications for, by, and about the deaf. The machines are available in portable, lightweight models; the heavier, stationary models are also on the market. Some have a tape printout, some have a display unit, and some have both. All of them, like the telephone, simply send and receive messages. They are available from a variety of suppliers who, in addition to advertising in publications directed to the deaf, also display their equipment at exhibits such as those held at the Annual Meeting of the President's Committee on Employment of the Handicapped. In many instances, the suppliers can give librarians the names of libraries already using the product so that the librarians can get direct information on the machine's capability, durability, and usefulness. Many organizations other than libraries are using the TTY/TDD, including organizations of the deaf, hospitals, vocational rehabilitation offices, schools, government agencies, police and fire stations, and private individuals, as well as colleges, stockbrokerages, and utility companies. New types of agencies and organizations are continually being added to the list of users.

To determine the kind of TTY/TDD needed in the library on a permanent basis will require a review of the characteristics of each type of equipment in relation to the needs of those who will use it. In this decision-making process, deaf users should be consulted. They should also be consulted about the choice of those machines purchased for loan by the library to deaf individuals. Perhaps a variety of TTY/TDDs will be required to meet the diverse needs. Because each machine is a major investment, special care should be taken to ensure the purchase of the best equipment in relation to the need.

Telecommunication devices, such as the TTY/TDD, are invaluable in the library. With such a device, anyone can communicate anywhere in the world. Hearing people can use the TTY/TDD to communicate with family members and friends who are deaf, and the device also allows the individual to communicate on a one-to-one basis without having to involve a third person. Conducting training programs on the use of the machine will increase users' skills and will increase the machine's popularity as an easy and effective means of communication. When this electronic device is widely available in libraries, businesses and industry, and in government offices, its use will increase dramatically. When it is available to individuals at a reasonable cost, this device will really make an impact on the lives of people who are deaf, hearing impaired, and the hearing.

There are still some constraints on telecommunication devices, namely the initial cost and the fact that communicating a message by TTY/TDD takes longer than communicating by voice over the telephone. However, the use of this equipment will assist those who live in remote locations and it will simplify communication with hearing people. Using TTY/TDDs in libraries promotes the social and linguistic growth of the individual user as well as expanding library usage.

The TTY/TDD has many benefits, including a news and weather service presented 24 hours a day, 7 days a week. News is directed primarily toward those people who are deaf. The content of the news ranges from announcements of meetings within the deaf community to items of personal interest. The news is changed several times a week. No special competency or involved training is needed to operate the equipment for the news service.

Another service of value is the relaying of TTY/TDD telephone conversations between hearing and deaf users (the *International Telephone Directory for the Deaf* is a necessary item for a library). TTY/TDDs provide an invaluable service to deaf people in the development of their careers and in the opening of opportunities to them as far as all employment is concerned. Through the TTY/TDD, people who are deaf can communicate readily with prospective employers just as a hearing person can by using the telephone. This method of communication opens many new types of employment opportunities for deaf people. They can communicate rapidly and effectively through a TTY/TDD and no longer need to be relegated to positions where communication is not a requirement.

There are some disadvantages to TTY/TDDs, such as cost, but they are far outweighed by the freedom from dependence on others in making telephone calls and in the ability to make business and social contacts by telephone. The ability to handle an emergency with the help of a TTY/TDD also provides peace of mind to the individual.

Training is helpful to all people who use the equipment. The National Technical Institute for the Deaf has developed a packet of training materials to help the person who is deaf to learn to use this device. Materials show how deaf persons can make the best use of TTY/TDDs.

There are many resources to assist people in their use of telecommunication devices. One of these is Teletypewriters for the Deaf, Inc. In addition to publishing an annual directory of TDD numbers, it provides consultation, information, and assistance on communication issues. Libraries can assist by providing brochures on subjects such as guides for TTY/TDD/telephone communication, where to purchase the equipment, and what to look for when purchasing or renting it. Library training classes would also be helpful to all users of the system.

Significant progress has been made in some areas relating to TTY/TDDs. The state of California allows speech or hearing impaired residents to receive a free TDD from their local telephone company. California legislation passed in 1979 requires equal access to telephone networks by all hearing and speech impaired people who are certified. The law requires the statewide emergency service number (911) to be available to TTY/TDD users as well.

Connecticut became the second state to pass a free TDD law. Patterned after the California law, the Connecticut legislation instructs the Southern New England Telephone Company to set aside funds for this purpose, while the State Commission on the Deaf and Hearing Impaired is charged with the distribution responsibility. When TTY/TEL-MED can be provided to the deaf as a prerecorded health information service, the library can be the sponsor of this program. Through this service, information on a variety of subjects, such as child care, family planning, dental care, first aid, and nutrition, will be available.

Many of the TTY/TDD services are not available to people who are deaf, according to the first statistically valid and reliable survey of telecommunication device usage by persons in Texas. In 1982, the Texas Association of the Deaf sent out 11,000 survey forms. They found that only 30 percent of those responding to the questionnaire owned a TTY/TDD; more than 63 percent did not. About 25 percent of the owners said they owned donated equipment similar to that used by telegraph offices more than 50 years ago. Many indicated that they borrowed TTY/TDDs when necesssary. The 2 reasons given most often for borrowing the equipment were that they were needed for emergencies and for special communication needs. Only 2.6 percent responding to the survey said they rented TDDs. The survey did indicate that the purchase of TDDs is on the rise, but a great majority said the TDD equipment was too expensive for purchase. Most respondents believe that TTY/TDDs are needed and desirable to improve communication. Following the release of the recommendations made by the Texas Association of the Deaf, the Texas Commission for the Deaf called for a united effort to make TDDs affordable and available to every deaf household in Texas.

In 1982, as part of a federal grant to the New Jersey Library for the Blind and Physically Handicapped, 17 public libraries in that state received and are using TTYs. Part of the requirement for receiving them was that at least 2 staff members in each library had to study sign language for a minimum of one year. All libraries receiving the equipment agreed to extend their normal geographic service perimeters in order to make their facilities and the TTYs available to as many people as possible. An extension of the original grant is being used to obtain additional TTYs and staff training.

It is essential that the request for a TTY/TDD come from the deaf population itself whether the device is a gift or a purchase. Without this initial request from the consumer group, the TTY/TDD usually sits idle because of the lack of their involvement in its acquisition. The same request and/or consultation is important with the user groups in all special equipment acquisitions. The deaf and hearing impaired are not accustomed to having specialized equipment for their use in libraries or to having library service which is usable by them. Because they are accustomed to the lack of the service and equipment, the reality of its presence will not result in its use unless the deaf and hearing impaired make the request or are consulted in the developmental stages. This lack of communication will result in lack of use even though a TTY/TDD is as necessary to people who are deaf as a telephone is to the hearing. While the equipment is still quite expensive, many service clubs and other organizations make a TTY/TDD available to people through libraries.

CLOSED CAPTIONING

A new technology which is as valuable as the TTY/TDD is the closed-captioning decoder. Prior to closed captioning and the decoder, people who are deaf or hard of hearing did not have the opportunity to hear or to read television. Only an occasional interpreted program was available to them. Now, through closed captioning and decoders, these people can know what is happening when it happens, while other programs are available on a delayed basis. With closed captioning, the dialog on television appears in the form of subtitles. It is unlike the open captions where the subtitles appear on the screen for all audiences. Closed captioning requires special decoder devices which receive an electronic code and translate it into subtitles. Decoders come in many different forms. Some are color television sets with built-in television circuitry. Others are adapters which, when attached to any ordinary television set, enable them to receive closed captions.

The programing for closed-captioned television is provided by the National Captioning Institute. Many television program listings indicate the closed-captioned programs. Because the captions are coded electronically, they are visible only on television sets equipped with the special decoding units.

Real-time or instant captioning has fine potential for the deaf and hearing impaired. Live programs can now be captioned, providing the deaf and hearing impaired with the same opportunities available to those who can hear. Captioned programs not only provide entertainment but are educational as well. They improve reading skills, increase the vocabulary, and provide a better understanding of the hearing world. The library can play an active part in providing this type of information, recreation, and education to deaf and hard-of-hearing people. Deaf and hearing impaired people watch approximately as much television as the general population. The success with live captioning paves the way for real-time captioning, providing deaf and hearing impaired viewers with access to televised up-to-the-minute news and many hours of closed-captioned program entertainment.

COMMUNICATION WITH DEAF-BLIND PEOPLE

Another technological advance allows communication with people who are deaf-blind. With teletouch interpreting, the interpreter types what is being spoken onto braille tape. The deaf-blind person feels the tape and receives the message.

Other types of hearing loss have been helped extensively through advances in technology. In many instances, hearing aids may be helpful to people with a hearing loss. There is no one type of hearing aid suitable for all types of hearing losses—much depends on the nature and extent of the hearing loss. Trying to decide which hearing aid to buy becomes a problem with which many people need help. Not every person with a hearing loss necessarily needs, or can use, a hearing aid. Many factors are involved. A competent audiologist, otolaryngologist, or otologist can evaluate whether or not a hearing aid is needed. If it is determined that a hearing aid will be helpful, they can also prescribe the kind of hearing aid needed. If the individual is fitted for a hearing aid, s/he should have a trial wearing period to ensure its capability and usability. A hearing aid is designed to make sounds louder and easier to hear.

Hearing aids vary in size. Some can be small enough to be concealed in the ear or in eyeglass frames. Librarians should understand the nature and the use of hearing aids so that they can work effectively in communicating with people who are hard of hearing. They need to know that a hearing aid does not ensure normal hearing; that the hearing aid does not correct but can improve hearing in some instances. It may enable a person to hear a voice even though the words spoken may not be understood. Some people need the power that only a larger hearing aid can supply. It is important that library staff working with people who wear hearing aids enunciate clearly in order to be understood. A hearing impaired person experiences a period of adjustment during which time increasing benefit from hearing aid use will develop. The hearing aid, however, actually introduces a new series of problems which can be overcome with experience. It is important when talking with a person with a hearing aid not to speak in an unusually loud voice but rather converse in a normal tone.

Hearing aids cannot solve all of the problems of hard-of-hearing people, however, they are continuously being improved upon just as the current models were improvements on the telescopic ear trumpet of the 1800s, the speaking tube of the late nineteenth and early twentieth centuries, the vacuum tube hearing aid of the mid-1940s, and the transistor hearing aids of the 1960s. However, no matter what improvements have been made over the years, getting used to a hearing aid is never easy. Learning to use a hearing aid is something like learning a new language. An aid does not always make all sounds or speech clearer—visual clues are still needed.

Great progress has been made in the use of the telephone by those who wear a hearing aid. A volume control handset is helpful to people with a hearing loss. This handset has a built-in amplifier in the earpiece which increases the volume of what is heard and an amplifier in the mouthpiece which increases the sound that is spoken. An adjusting wheel on the handset amplifies the voice being received. For hearing impaired persons using a public telephone, a switch on the handset for modified coin telephones amplifies the voice being received. The switch automatically returns the volume to normal when the receiver is hung up. Telephones also have a ringer available which concentrates all of the sound energy in a frequency range which the majority of persons with impaired hearing can hear.

A person who is deaf can carry on a telephone conversation with the aid of a third person. This person uses an auxiliary receiver to listen to the person at the other end and then repeats the words for a lipreader or uses sign language, if preferable. Either the person who is deaf speaks to the person at the other end of the line or the third person on the extension speaks as is appropriate.

New products are being introduced at a phenomenal rate, making constant monitoring of the innovations necessary to maintain current information in this field. Libraries can provide the latest information on hearing aids and the use of the telephone by hearing impaired people so that all can be aware of the new advances. They can also be kept informed on legislation affecting them such as P.L. 97-410, the "Telecommunications for the Disabled Act of 1982," which was signed into law in January 1983. This new law, regulated by the Federal Communications Commission, helps to ensure that public telephones and other essential telephones, such as those used frequently by hearing aid users, continue to be compatible with the telephone switch on most hearing aids. This special telephone reduces background noises and eliminates feedback. Hearing aids that do not have the telephone switch can be modified to include this switch. Also included in the law is a provision allowing state public utility commissions to require that telephone companies offer special telephone equipment for disabled customers. This authority had been temporarily lost under the deregulation of telephone services. Although the law represents a big step forward for hearing impaired users of telephones, it has its limitations. Because of these limitations, a bill, HR 210, was introduced into Congress requiring that all telephones be made compatible with hearing aids when the telephones are *manufactured.* The present goal is to ensure that all telephones everywhere are compatible with hearing aids. Most hearing aids are designed for use in telephone conversation, however, not all telephones are compatible with hearing aids. As a result, more than 2,000,000 hearing impaired Americans are unable to use telephones. When enacted, HR 210 would amend the Communications Act of 1934 to state that telephone receivers may not be sold in interstate commerce unless they are manufactured in a manner that permits their use by persons with hearing aids. The Organization for Use of the Telephone (OUT) has played an important role in ensuring that such legislation is passed to benefit people who are presently prevented from using the telephone.

Libraries need to ensure that their telephones are usable by people with hearing aids. They also need to provide an amplification of sound for people who can use a telephone through a simple amplification adjustment.

There still remains a group of hearing impaired people who cannot be assisted by hearing aids and who may or may not be helped by amplification of sound by telephone. Some of these people are those who have tinnitus—a constant ringing in the ears. There is no way to measure people with tinnitus but almost all who do have it have some form of hearing loss. Also, there is a large group of people who have a nerve deafness hearing loss. Most of them cope as best they can with this difficulty because their understanding is that nothing can be done for them. However, some cases are treatable; there is promise for the future. The number of people with some type of hearing loss is great—most of them are invisible to other people. Librarians need to understand these losses so that they can communicate in a variety of ways with those deaf and hearing impaired persons who come into the library.

Another effort to respond to these people is to develop a collection of always-current materials to assist them. This collection should include pamphlets, brochures, government publications, films, television programs, and other types of materials of current and immediate assistance to people with hearing problems. Among the subjects which can be included in such an important collection are:

- Hearing loss.
- Facts about hearing aids.
- Communication services available.
- Communication services to meet special needs.
- Research in progress on hearing loss.
- Helping the child who has a hearing loss.
- Special materials on deaf-blind and communication.
- Using a hearing aid and a hard-of-hearing amplifier.
- Students with a hearing disability.
- Legislation relating to deaf and hearing impaired people.
- Public telephones and the hard of hearing.
- Public TTY/TDDs.
- Alternative listening devices.
- Television captioning.
- Microcomputer applications.
- Types of hearing impairment.
- Hearing health.
- Technology and hearing.

Because so many of these subjects are ever-changing, the library will find it necessary to keep materials in these areas current. Some of the subjects will fade in appeal, to be replaced by new topics. The goal should be to offer information of immediate and practical value to the consumer. Assistance from those with hearing problems is vital in building and maintaining such a file. This will help to ensure that these materials are relevant to their needs and are used by the people who need them.

To assist all hard-of-hearing people who use the library, including staff members, modified telephones are a necessity. Coin-operated telephones which can be used by people who wear hearing aids should be available on the same basis as coin-operated telephones for the hearing. Amplification handsets are also needed within the library for staff members who need them or by library users as the situation requires, as well as telephones that are compatible with hearing aids.

These are just a few types of telephone equipment which will make communication by telephone easier for those with a hearing loss who either work in the library or are library users. Other modifications which will be necessary when hard-of-hearing people are members of the staff are:

- Increasing the volume of the telephone bell.
- Installing a tone ringer—a ringer that concentrates more of the sound energy in a frequency range which the majority of people with impaired hearing can hear.
- Installing a flashing light that indicates that the telephone is ringing; for a deaf-blind person, a small electric fan can signal the ringing of the telephone.
- Amplifying the person's voice through the use of a telephone handset if the individual also has a speech impairment.

Amplification will be needed elsewhere in the library, particularly for audio equipment.

Special sound systems are necessary in rooms in the library where people gather for a program or a meeting to provide accessibility to the spoken word. These systems require little modification of the places where they are used, and they are nearly maintenance free. They can permit those who can still benefit from amplification to participate in library meetings and programs. A great advantage of all of these systems is that all background noise is eliminated. Portable sound systems are also available, which are wireless and require no modification of the place where the individual or individuals are using their portable devices.

For people who have a total hearing loss, amplification provides no answer. Visual counterparts are needed such as signs, interpreters, and the TTY/TDD. These all increase the deaf person's ability to cope independently. For those who have poor vision as well as deafness or hearing impairment, both disabilities must be taken into consideration in providing equipment for their use. Tactile communication is the basis of equipment which can be readily used by deaf-blind persons.

OTHER TECHNOLOGICAL ADVANCES

An excellent method of communicating is through electronic mail. Through electronic mail, a person who is deaf or hard of hearing can send a message long distance without making a long-distance call. The messsage is delivered instantly, or it can be held by the computer for delivery at a specific time when so instructed. A carbon copy can be sent to as many people as needed without making several long-distance calls. To use the service requires a telephone, a computer terminal, and a mailbox. Using this system, people who are deaf or hard of hearing can send and receive messages, share information, and hold conferences by computer. The number called to send the message initially is a local number so that long-distance charges are not involved. Electronic mail for deaf people allows messages to be sent to about 300 different locations. Included in the group of people who subscribe to electronic mail for the deaf are:

- Individuals who are deaf.
- Hearing associates, friends, and relatives of the users who are deaf.
- Schools for the deaf.
- Organizations of, by, and for the deaf.

Electronic mail provides a usable means by which people who are deaf can communicate with many people. It also provides them with much information and material otherwise inaccessible to them.

An interesting and attractive development in the world of the deaf and the hearing impaired is videotext. While the Line 21 system (closed captioning for hearing impaired and deaf people) primarily performs captioning, a videotext system can provide virtually unlimited services. The National Captioning Institute demonstrated compatability between closed captioning presently being used and teletext when Line 21 captions were successfully transcoded on to the teletext signal and both were broadcast simultaneously.

Compatability is important so that closed captions and teletext can be viewed on the same receiver. Telecaption decoding devices, with about 60,000 now in use, enable television viewers to read subtitles which are closed captioned and appear as subtitles (captions) on the screen. These captions are inserted on Line 21 of the television picture, a line which does not carry picture information. Captions do not appear on sets that are not equipped with a decoder. Teletext is a system which was developed several years ago in Great Britain. This provides viewers with printed information on a screen of a specially equipped television set with captioning as one type of service.

Closed captioning is well known and enjoyed by American audiences. Videotext as a visual presentation, designed to be read in pages or in screens, has exciting possibilities. Prestel, a British-based electronic utility, is the most comprehensive videotext information service presently available in the United States or anyplace in the world. Canada's Telidon and France's Antiope are not yet ready to offer their services in the United States as is Prestel. The disadvantage once again is the cost. Of all present Prestel users, 87 percent are businesses, so the price presently is a business, not personal, expense. Probably neither Prestel nor any other viewdata service will take over in the immediate future, but it will develop as have other technological means and methods.

A statewide, state-funded news service was implemented by the State of Nebraska in late 1982. It is a cooperative project of 3 state agencies: the Nebraska Commission for the Hearing Impaired, the Nebraska Educational Television Commission, and the University of Nebraska Television Station. This service has done much to narrow the gap between the hearing and nonhearing societies. This Hearing Impaired Video Information Service is called HI-VIS and makes state, local, and national news available to an estimated 96,000 hearing impaired and deaf people in Nebraska.

A teletext news and information service is available in Nebraska 7 days a week. This continuous text appears on the television screen and is visible only to viewers who have a special adapter connected to the television set. The adapter, which is marketed under the trade name "TeleCaption," is the same piece of equipment used to receive closed-captioned television programing. This teletext is made possible through the use of Line 21, the same one used for closed captioning.

Technological advances such as videotext are taking place at a rapid rate. Library staff members must regularly read newspapers, government publications, and magazines pertaining to the deaf and hearing impaired in order to keep current on developments in this area. It is vital that the deaf and hearing impaired work with the library in order that advances in technology are reviewed carefully and that the right decisions to purchase such devices are made. Every technological advance may not be applicable to library service to the deaf and hearing impaired. However, enough background should be obtained about each alternative to make an informed decision. Any progress which has a positive effect on the lives of the deaf and hearing impaired should be reflected in library service. Keeping in close touch with the people themselves will enable the library to be closely involved in the world of the deaf and hearing impaired. News items may not be evaluative but the people with a hearing loss, collectively, will have an evaluative opinion on the changes being made.

Use of the ABLEDATA system will be helpful also. Although not dedicated to the deaf and hearing impaired, the data bank does contain much information on how new equipment is affecting the lives of this group of people. Of special value, with so many new and so many competitive aids and equipment coming on the market, are the evaluative abstracts and the comments of informal evaluations from users.

One of the most difficult problems for libraries in acquiring the necessary equipment is the cost. So much of the special equipment is needed by the deaf and hearing impaired and they, as much as anyone, wish to keep library costs reasonable. However, much of the equipment is a necessity for the library and must be acquired regardless of cost. Because the majority of the programs are in the infant stages of development, librarians should make every effort to avoid large investments and instead obtain the equipment by means of a gift or a grant. Although the original investment in equipment may come from outside of the library's ongoing budget, the maintenance of the equipment and the subsequent expenses become the library's financial responsibility. Because of the large investment in initial purchase, librarians should strive, also, to ensure that the equipment acquired is of the quality that will withstand extensive use and is usable by the consumer. Technology is always changing, so some means of updating the equipment is essential. As new features come on the market, changes should be able to be made at a minimal cost to the library; such a condition should be a part of the original agreement. As with all equipment, the service agreement is extremely important—how quickly will the service response be and of what quality is the service? As purchasers of library equipment become more familiar with machines such as TTY/TDDs, they will be able to purchase as easily in these areas as in any others. The same care must be taken if the equipment is acquired as a gift or through a grant.

It is incumbent on a library to install this equipment in order to provide basic services to the deaf and hearing impaired. Technological advances should make certain that the quality of library service to this group will improve as time passes.

REFERENCE LIST

All Telephones Must Work with Hearing Aids Everywhere. Owings Mills, MD: Organization for Use of the Telephone, Inc. OUT, 1983.

Becker, Gaylene. *Growing Old in Silence.* Berkeley, CA: University of California Press, 1980.

Bell, Trudy. *Technologies for the Handicapped and Aged.* Washington, DC: National Aeronautics and Space Administration, Office of Space and Terrestrial Applications, Technology Transfer Division, 1979.

Bellefleur, Philip A., and Breunig, H. Latham. *Telecommunications: A Telephone System for the Deaf.* Washington, DC: Teletypewriters for the Deaf, Inc., 1977.

"Beyond the Hearing Aid." *Shhh* 3 (6) (December 1982): 1–4.

Bishop, Thomas G. "Hearing Aid Hall of Fame, A Future Look into the Past." *Disabled USA* (Fall 1982): 28–29.

Brown, Dale. "Communicating with Deaf-Blind Persons." *Disabled USA* (Spring 1982): 20–21.

The College Student with a Disability: A Faculty Handbook. Washington, DC: HEATH for the American Council on Education, 1980.

"Connecticut Passes Free TDD Law." *The Silent News* 14 (2) (February 1983): 4.

Cylke, Frank Kurt, et al. "Research to Develop Information Aids and Programs for Handicapped Individuals." *Drexel Library Quarterly* 16 (2) (April 1980): 59–72.

Dalton, Phyllis I. "Library Service to the Deaf and Hearing Impaired." *Library Technology Reports* 17 (6) (November–December 1981): 491–93.

"Deaf Resources." *Keystone. Technical Bulletin* 13 (1–2) (January–April 1984): 5–9.

"Deafnet Offers Electronic Mail." *Gallaudet Alumni Newsletter* 17 (2) (January 15, 1983): 1–2.

Del Polito, Gene A. "Common Questions about Hearing Aids." *Shhh* 4 (6) (November–December 1980): 3–4.

Dubuque, Jeanne. "Deaf Center Fights for Funds." *Las Vegas Review Journal.* (January 7, 1983): 10.

"FCC Mandated to Make Pay Phones Accessible." *Newsounds* (April 1983): 2.

Garstecki, Dean. "Adjusting to the Use of Your Hearing Aid." *Shhh* 4 (1) (January–February 1983): 9–11.

Hagemeyer, Alice. "Library Service to the Deaf and Outreach Programs for the Deaf." *Illinois Libraries* 63 (7) (September 1981): 530–34.

Knight, Nancy H. "Library Service to the Disabled: Survey of Selected Equipment." *Library Technology Reports* 17 (6) (November–December 1981): 497–622.

Kriesler, Nancy, and Kriesler, Jack. *Catalog of Aids for the Disabled.* New York: Mc-Graw-Hill Book Company, 1982.

"Law Enacted for Phone Use with Hearing Aids." *The Silent News* 15 (2) (March 1983): 27.

"Line 21 Telecaption Demonstrated: Compatible with Teletext." *The Silent News* 15 (3) (March 1983): 15.

"Line 21 TeleCaption/Teletext Compatible: Combination Cable Converter/Decoder Unveiled." *Caption. News about National Closed-Captioning Service* (Winter 1982): 4.

Long, The Honorable Clarence D. "Telephone for Hearing Impaired People. The 1-Penny Bargain." *Congressional Record* (June 23, 1981).

McCarroll, Jane. "Innovative Technology: Improving Access to Information for Disabled Persons." *Drexel Library Quarterly* 16 (2) (April 1980): 73–80.

"Nerve Deafness." *Shhh* 4 (1) (January–February 1983): 4,14.

"Reach Out and Touch Someone...with a Compatible Phone, of Course." *Shhh* 4 (3) (May–June 1983): 3–5.

Remarks of Vice President George Bush before the President's Committee on Employment of the Handicapped. Washington DC, May 5, 1983.

"TDD Boosts Career." *The NAD Broadcaster* 5 (10) (November–December 1982): 13.

"The Telecommunication for the Disabled Act of 1982." *Congressional Record* (May 10, 1983).

Telecommunication Services for Special Needs. Bell System, 1982. (Brochure.)

Telecommunication Training for the Deaf. Rochester, NY: National Technical Institute for the Deaf, 1982.

"Texas Survey Leads to the Formation of TDD Committee." *The Silent News* 15 (21) (February 1983): 2.

"TTY's in New Jersey Libraries." *The Silent News* 15 (4) (April 1983): 8.

What Are TTD's? Washington, DC: Gallaudet College, 1982. (Brochure.)

What You Should Know about TDD's. Rochester, NY: National Technical Institute for the Deaf, n.d. (Brochure.)

Chapter 16
Environmental Setting for the Service

In addition to having a collection of adequate to excellent resources, services, and programs, a library must also have an inviting and accessible environment. Although the physical setting of library service is important to the general public, it is even more important to the deaf and hearing impaired user. The physical attributes of the building, both inside and out, make the difference between nonusability, modified usability, and total usability of the library with enjoyment. For people with a hearing loss, the total physical accessibility must be considered also because some of them have multiple disabilities, and many are elderly. Many libraries have developed and implemented plans to ensure physical accessibility. Much has been done in this area particularly during the International/National Years of Disabled Persons, 1981–1982. Accessibility continues to be a priority concern during the Decade of Disabled Persons, 1983–1992. However, in spite of these advances, some libraries and their programs are not yet accessible to all disabled persons. They are not as readily usable for the disabled person as for the able-bodied individual.

Libraries are just now beginning to modify buildings or construct them to eliminate environmental barriers for those who are deaf or hearing impaired. Some overall accessibility improvements have been made for all users of the library which benefit people who are hard of hearing or who are deaf. Examples of such improvements are increased lighting and signage. Conversely, as libraries improve the environment for people with a hearing loss, they will, in many respects, improve it for all users.

USE OF SIGNS IN THE LIBRARY

To use a library effectively and with a sense of satisfaction, the consumer needs to be able to use resources and services with a certain degree of independence. For people with a marked degree of hearing loss, such an ability to be self-reliant in a library depends, to a great extent, on the visual clues available, both inside and outside of the building. Asking directions is merely a nuisance to hearing people; it is almost an impossibility for deaf and hearing impaired people. To encourage these people to use library services, libraries must make sure that all basic signs are in place and readable. To improve the situation further, signs that may not be basic but which are attractive and informative should also be incorporated into the building and the library program.

Basic signs which should be on the outside of the library are the name and address of the library in letters which can be read from the street. Also, directional signs should be in place along the routes to the library telling people that they are on the right route. On an educational campus or in an industrial or governmental complex, maps of the area with the library located are essential. The parking area and the parking spaces for people who are physically disabled should also be clearly marked. Any library service located outside the library, such as bookmobile stops, should be designated. In all signage, libraries need to be careful to use terminology which is easily identified by people who do not have a special knowledge of libraries. To test the comprehensibility of the signs, both users and nonusers should be consulted. Symbols can be used, with or without wording, but they should be tested prior to being permanently installed.

The signs within the library are guides to needed services such as the location of adult services, the children's area, and location of magazines and films and other visual equipment. The signs should be as specific as necessary for the size of the library. They should be placed at a height that can be easily read and should be placed far enough ahead of the destination to avoid wasted effort on the part of the user. The colors selected should allow easy readibility within the interior setting. Some signs will be permanent while others will be temporary or set up for a special occasion. Prior study and consultation will help to prevent error in developing signs, and usage will determine their adequacy. Signs should be made of materials that will be as maintenance-free as possible. Sign maintenance includes cleaning, revision, and repair.

While it is true that signs cannot make a user entirely self-sufficient, they can minimize the need for people with communication problems to ask questions of others who may or may not be able to communicate with them.

A directory at the entrance of the building will be of assistance as will giveaway maps depicting locations within the building. Because some words will not be understood by the library user with a hearing loss, symbols should be used along with the printed word on both signs and maps. Some points to consider in determining sign effectiveness are:

- People have a minimum of difficulty in locating each sign.
- The sign is easily read in both symbols and print.
- The sign is well illuminated to accommodate those with low vision.
- A sign is visible at the entrance of the library that indicates locations within the building.
- Elevators and stairs are well indicated.
- The message is communicated readily.

In addition, the following should be included for deaf-blind people:

- Braille on signs when possible and always on signs in elevators and rest rooms.
- Braille on maps of the facilities in the library.
- Raised or indented letters in addition to braille.
- Raised or indented letters on signs throughout the library.
- Placement of signs at a level at which deaf-blind persons can feel them. Such placement also accommodates people in wheelchairs and those who have usable but limited vision who can move close enough to read the signs.

The usual standards for developing signage for people who are sighted and hearing should be followed in the library. The additional visual cues are needed for people who have a hearing problem; the tactile features are needed for those who have both a visual and a hearing loss. To ensure that the libray is as barrier free as possible through a signage system, the library needs to involve deaf and hearing impaired people in its development. The noninvolvement of these consumers is a barrier to library use in itself. Because most of the people who plan and work in libraries have not experienced deafness or hearing impairment, they approach the development of a signage system from the point of view of a hearing person. For this reason, it is essential that people who have a hearing loss be involved.

The development of a signage system is made easier because there are suppliers who work with total signage systems. However, while signs are a necessity, care must be taken that visual bombardment does not occur. Suppliers can be helpful in both interior or exterior installations of both lighted and nonlighted signs. Also, special symbol signs may often be needed on a special basis, such as the sign to indicate that a program is interpreted. To achieve the desired level of information to the deaf and hearing impaired, librarians must consider many factors and seek the advice of other competent people in the signage program. Concurrently, care must be taken that there are no visual barriers to the signage system. To ensure that signs will be effective, a survey can be taken by putting the signs in place for a period of time and then having them reviewed by deaf and hearing impaired people and with others. More than one set of signs should be reviewed.

Because library buildings and programs are designed for users, it is important that they are usable by the maximum number of people with a minimum amount of difficulty. By providing visual and tactile signals for the deaf and hearing impaired and the deaf-blind, a large group of people will be accommodated. It is important that signs be clear either in symbol or in simple wording, or both. In this way, language limitations become less important as the need to ask for directions and understand responses diminishes. All those with a limited command of English will be helped through this signage.

ELEVATORS

Other types of signage are also important. For example, it is important that a building of more than one floor be equipped with elevators, however, they must be accessible to deaf and hearing impaired people. Elevators should be well marked and located so that they are visible upon entering the building. Because people with a hearing loss cannot hear the bell which signals that an elevator is coming, a visible signal is needed, such as a light which goes on at the same time as the bell sounds. This system will help those who cannot hear to have sufficient time to enter the elevator before the door closes. It is important, too, that the doors have a photosensing device which will not allow the doors to close when the doorway is occupied. Such a device will assist the deaf and hearing impaired people who have trouble ascertaining that an elevator is arriving.

Another important consideration is the method a deaf or hard-of-hearing person can use to signal trouble on an elevator, such as getting stuck between floors. The telephone with which elevators are often equipped cannot be used by people with a hearing loss. Even if they can speak into the telephone, they cannot hear a response so there is no way for them to know that the message has been received and help is on the way. The person should be able to send a signal to a central office without the need to use speech or hearing. This signal would be notification that a problem exists. The answer indicating the message has been received could be in the form of a signal light, with or without words. For people who have both a visual loss and a hearing loss, the activation of a fan to give the message to a deaf-blind person can be used.

Because deaf and hearing impaired persons must, of necessity, be visually oriented, color is very important in the library. Library accessibility can be improved in a variety of ways through the use of color. Some examples are:

- Using color-coded symbols designating the buildings on a map for a multibuilding complex.
- Displaying signs and symbols in light colors on a dark field for the best visibility.
- Eliminating patterned wall covering and conflicting color schemes.
- Using color coding to indicate different areas, groups of books, and paths to given areas.
- Decorating each building level with a different color code to facilitate location of services.

LIGHTING

Lighting of the building is related closely to the use of color and the usability of the library by deaf and hearing impaired people. Lighting outside the building should be at a level which will allow the building to be identified easily at night. The name of the library should be clearly visible. Lighting to assist people in entering the building should be continuous diffuse light. Intense light in darkness should be avoided. Such diffuse light is of assistance to people who have a balance problem. Because many people with impaired hearing have balance difficulties, easy visual orientation is essential.

In designing rooms such as conference rooms, librarians should take into consideration the lighting features in relation to the deaf and hearing impaired. Lighting should be adjusted to avoid glare. Lighting should also be designed so that reading lips and signs is easier. To do this, avoid placing the lights in such a way that backlighting of the speaker or interpreter is eliminated. Even lighting rather than uneven lighting assists people who are reading lips and signs; distinct contrasts between light and dark areas can be eliminated through diffused lighting. Light dimmer switches are of assistance and ball and socket adjustable lighting is desirable so that the location of speakers and interpreters in a room can be changed without losing the lighting necessary for lipreading and signing. For the lighting of the entire library, natural light plus general ambient lighting and a task-ambient lighting system should provide desirable light for deaf and hearing impaired people within the library building. The overall lighting of the room has a special importance for the deaf and hearing impaired because they must rely so heavily on vision. Proper lighting also reduces eyestrain.

ACOUSTICS

Another environmental concern of librarians in providing library service to deaf and hearing impaired people is that of acoustical considerations. In a meeting room, this consideration is of utmost importance. People rely on their residual hearing as well as their visual clues. In locating such a room, library staff should make sure that it is away from any area which is the source of continuous noise. This is important because sound within the room can be controlled through sound absorption methods; however, sound from outside the room cannot be controlled the same way. Within the meeting room itself, noise should be controlled to allow people to use residual hearing to the greatest extent possible. It is important also that there be no static emanating from the carpet as build-up of static interferes with hearing aid operation. Also, since hearing aids not only amplify speech but also all other sounds, the reduction of sound is most important. Sound reverberations can be controlled with carpeting and with ceilings with acoustical absorption qualities. Walls should also have absorption treatment to eliminate transmission of sound. No 2 opposite walls should remain untreated because sound will reverberate between them within a room.

SAFETY

Safety considerations for the deaf and hearing impaired in the library environment must also be examined. Some problems occur because in an emergency, the telephone cannot be used independently by many of the people. People who are deaf or have a severe hearing loss cannot hear a fire alarm or any other type of signal which relies on sound to alert people of danger. Any security system involving inter- coms or other such devices cannot be used to communicate with deaf and hearing impaired people. Announcements made over a loudspeaker will not be heard by many. Therefore, visual alarm signals must be used in addition to audible alarms. One problem, however, is that visual sig- nals are not multidirectional. While auditory signals can be heard throughout a building, visual signals are restricted by barriers and are less effective. Some signals which can be used to alert nonhearing peo- ple to danger include smoke detectors and security alarm equipment which uses lights. Such a system requires that lights be visible in every area of the library to ensure that all people who cannot hear can be alerted. For reporting emergencies, when the telephone or intercom cannot be used, a system of emergency reporting devices which do not require communication by voice should be available. Visible and tactile procedures should be developed within the library so that people who cannot hear and those who are deaf-blind are alerted to any general information or to any emergency situation. While it will not be known who among the people in the library are so disabled, staff members can observe the people to determine whether the message has been heard or the emergency signal received. While this is not a foolproof method, it can be a valuable adjunct to mechanical means. When a group of deaf and hearing impaired people are meeting in the library building, those responsible for building security and safety should be alerted. Those who are handling the meeting, themselves, can take responsibili- ty for alerting deaf and hearing impaired people in the event of an emer- gency. These precautions can be incorporated into the regular library procedures. They will assist in providing the library not only with an environment which promotes use of its resources and programs but which also provides a safe environment for deaf and hearing impaired people.

MEETING ROOMS

There are other factors to be considered relating to the develop- ment of an environment enabling deaf and hearing impaired people to use the library effectively. Steps taken by libraries to accommodate deaf and hearing impaired people will have a definite impact on overall ac- cess to library resources and services. Deafness and hearing impairment is a major issue which should be addressed. The range of impairment which will have the most effect on libraries is that of the profound to the moderately severe hearing loss, a disability correlated with age. This is a growing problem and one which will continue to be a concern as older people make up a larger part of the population. Because deafness and hearing impairment are so prevalent in the population, certain other considerations should be taken into account when planning or modifying a library building. When designing accommodations for any meeting room, librarians should consider the seating arrangements carefully. Those who lip-read must be close enough to the speaker to do so effectively and without undue strain. A group of seats close to the speaker and/or interpreter should be available to people who lip-read or read signs. Accommodations should be available so that, if the meeting is one in which discussion takes place, movable chairs can be set up in a circle or semicircle. It is important that this type of seating be available so that participants can communicate through lip-reading and signing during the group discussion. In story telling situations, such a circular fashion of seating is also desirable. When visual materials are used in a meeting, the screens used for display should be large enough so that the display can be easily read. Information should be kept on the screen long enough to permit reading all of it without undue haste. It is helpful to provide the script to the people in advance with the indication that the meeting is for the deaf and hard-of-hearing people as well as the hearing. Unless this information is widely publicized, it may be assumed that the meeting is for hearing people only, and the deaf and hearing impaired will not be able to understand what is taking place. If that assumption is made, they will not come to the meeting.

The library may wish to have the capability of captioning videotapes for audiences so that deaf and hearing impaired people can be included in a program. Videotapes can be open captioned, so that all viewers see the words, or closed captioned. The closed captioning requires a decoder. This form is useful when the hearing audience may be annoyed by the captions appearing on the screen. Libraries will find, in most instances, that open captioning on the videotapes they produce will be satisfactory and that closed captioning will not be required. The use of advance scripts and scripts acquired at the time of the meeting will, however, undoubtedly be found to be most satisfactory.

For those whose language capability is limited and who have low vocabulary skills, the library may wish to augment its program services by rewriting the material in simple language and omitting idioms. Social service agencies, people in education, and others may be able to provide this service. They may be able, also, to attend the event and explain what is being said or shown to the people who cannot hear. Sign language interpreters will be helpful to some. To others, a summary of the material to be presented will be helpful if provided in advance. People will then be able to follow the presentation with much less difficulty if they know the content of the presentation as it is being made. Another technique is the nonverbal acting out of the event. This method is known as modeling; it shows people information rather than tells them and then asks them to repeat the acting out of the information. Such repetition helps people to comprehend the meaning of the actions. This technique can be used when the people have very limited linguistic skills. It is important that the library take into consideration these many forms of communication in designing the rooms where programs will take place. Where such accommodations are possible, deaf and hearing impaired people can always be included. They can be sure that they will be able to understand the materials being presented; they will know, too, that they can be understood. Finally, the hallways throughout the library should be wide enough to allow deaf and hearing impaired people to walk side by side and converse through lipreading or signing. It is not possible to hold such conversations when the building has narrow corridors.

WORK ACCOMMODATIONS FOR STAFF MEMBERS

When staff members are deaf or hard of hearing, some of the same environmental considerations are necessary for them as for the library user. Additional procedures should be added when necessary. However, before special accommodations are made, it is important that the employee be consulted individually to determine what his/her specific needs are. In telephone usage, it is usually helpful if a hearing person is trained by the employee to handle the largest part of the telephoning. This person can write out the message so that the employee who is deaf can respond or the communication can take place through lipreading or signing. If the employee is in a position where a secretary is assigned, a secretary who has interpreting skills is invaluable. The time period for calling the employee can be arranged so that the interpreter is available at the same time. A TTY/TDD should be available, but to use that equipment, the person at the other end of the line must also have a TTY/TDD; or a voice/TDD conversation can take place if hearing employees listen to the voice conversation and type it onto a TTY/TDD. The employee can respond by typing and the hearing employee can then speak the words into the telephone. For the hard-of-hearing employee, a telephone with a telephone switch for a hearing aid and/or amplification will be required. Because each situation is different, the equipping of the office and the establishing of procedures must be done in full consultation with the employee.

Because deaf or hard-of-hearing people are visually oriented, the work area design is important. Lighting should be even and should be at a level to prevent eyestrain. Supplies of notepaper should be readily available so that that employee may write to others and receive written messages easily. Employees who have a hearing loss should be assigned to work in areas where they can be seen by others in order to prevent accidents. When the employee has a private office, the door should include some glass space so that the person can see and be seen. Deaf or hearing impaired persons can often "hear" people approaching, but they need to see them also. Personal tactile alarms are available, and the employee may wish to have them as emergency signals, but they should never replace the general emergency setup for all deaf and hearing impaired people in the library. As part of the emergency procedure, coworkers and security personnel need to take specific responsibility for helping to ensure the employee's safety in an emergency. Some provision must also be made for the deaf employee who needs to call in sick to the office or for some other reason. TTY/TDDs are suitable for such calls.

OFFICE DESIGN CONSIDERATIONS

For overall use of the library by deaf and hearing impaired people, individual study carrels are desirable. Visually oriented people tend to be visually distracted. The carrels provide a privacy which helps to eliminate this problem. They should be well and evenly lit. Temporary office space can also be included in the library for those working on special projects. The information desk and other areas of public contact should be equipped at all times with pencil and paper to facilitate communication, and library staff should make telephone calls for people who cannot use the telephone. Telephones can be equipped with a flashing light signal in addition to an audible signal, and the telephone bell can be adjusted to a tone that can be heard by the majority of people. In areas in which hard-of-hearing people will engage in extensive telephoning, an area enclosed on 3 sides can act as a telephone booth. The booth can be made of sound-absorbent panels which will help to control noise. Additional sound absorption objects which can be used are extensive carpeting; upholstered furniture; draperies or other soft, fibrous materials which have noise-absorption qualities; and other materials such as cork or acoustic tile. A closed-circuit television system can be used for communicating messages. Individual vibrating pagers can be used to contact nonhearing employees who cannot be reached by other communication systems.

The following points should be observed in developing environmental design guidelines to be followed:

- Clear lines of vision are needed to interpreters, speakers, and to the people with whom they are communicating.
- Films require captioning to be understood unless they are nonverbal.
- Seating in a circular fashion is desirable in a group where discussion takes place. Swivel chairs are also helpful in assuring clear vision lines among participants. Visual distractions need to be avoided in a meeting room.
- Informational signage should be provided in a prominent place near the entrance of the library.
- Directional and procedural information should be provided in writing or graphics. This should be available to reduce, as much as possible, the need for deaf and hearing impaired people to question others.
- In designing a meeting room, visual noise in the environment should be reduced as much as possible.
- Deaf and hearing impaired people need to orient themselves visually in relation to the activities within or without a room. Vision panels in doors to offices, meeting rooms, and similar areas are desirable.
- For group discussion, round or oval tables provide the best vision lines among the participants.
- Because audible signals for elevators cannot be heard by some people, signal lights operating concurrently with the bells are necessary.
- An adequate signage system is necessary for ensuring direction, identification, and location.
- Sound is especially disturbing to deaf and hearing impaired people and is amplified through hearing aids. Acoustic panels help to absorb sound and reduce noise.
- People with auditory/visual impairments require tactile clues to their environment rather than auditory or visual ones.

COST AND IMPLEMENTATION OF ACCOMMODATIONS

A consideration in all of the modifications of the library building is cost. Modifications can range from low-cost adjustment to a fairly high investment. As new buildings are constructed, the elements that will eliminate barriers for deaf and hearing impaired people to buildings and programs of libraries should be incorporated. In the meantime, some modifications can be accomplished within an ongoing budget and many of these modifications will be helpful to all library users. In assessing the cost, the library staff should review both the outside and inside of the building to determine the accommodations that are needed immediately and that will require low financing. In the interim, while decisions are being made and the budget is being planned, library staff can revise library procedures so that they can make the library usable to the deaf or hard-of-hearing consumer.

One important service which can be provided within a short period of time is the preparation and distribution of a guide to library access for the deaf and hearing impaired. Such a directory is of greatest value if it encompasses a large geographic area such as a library region, a large city, or a county. It is most helpful, too, when it includes all types of libraries in the area. Although the arrangement and content will vary from area to area, some of the points to be included are the following:

- The type of library.
- The name and address of the library.
- The name of the librarian.
- Telephone and TTY/TDD numbers.
- A map of the general geographical area, showing the library and landmarks which will assist in determining the exact location of the library buildings.
- Physical accessibility of the library building through words and the use of the access symbol when appropriate.
- Telephone accessibility, including the accessibility by means of a TTY/TDD.
- Resources available, such as captioned films, amplified audiovisual material, collections of materials on deafness and hearing impairment, and children's picture books and signed stories.
- Services available, such as story telling, puppet shows, programs of information and recreation, and reference and referral library services. All services are accessible to the deaf and hearing impaired through various communication methods. TTY/TDDs

available for loan and programs for special groups as requested are provided.
- Description of accommodations for people who are deaf-blind such as maps and directional signs that can be understood by touch.

This directory would only be an interim tool; the information it contains would be included in the ongoing library directory once the service to the deaf and hearing impaired becomes a recognized part of the library program.

To accomplish all of these modifications requires an organized approach. One method is to do an initial assessment by conducting an on-site review of the library building(s) now in use and reviewing the plans of those under construction or scheduled for construction. This review of existing buildings should help to determine which modifications have already been accomplished to make the library usable for deaf and hearing impaired people. Some of the items to be reviewed are:

- Directional information outside of the building.
- Signage and directional information within the building.
- Elevator signal lights and closure of doors.
- Meeting rooms for visibility and acoustics.
- Lighting outside and within the building.
- Accessibility of library resources.
- Accessibility of library programs.
- Equipment to ensure safety of users and staff.

Once an initial assessment has been made, short-term planning should follow. This phase incorporates the following steps:

- Make the decision to make access to the library and its programs and resources by hearing impaired people a priority.
- Develop a document setting forth the modifications needed to achieve this accessibility.
- Determine which modifications can be accomplished readily at an affordable cost.
- Set priorities for accomplishing these modifications.
- Publicize those services and resources which are presently accessible to deaf and hearing impaired people.
- Make changes in procedures which will help ensure that library services are usable to people with a hearing loss.
- Make sure that hearing loss is included whenever planning is being done in relation to accessibility for people with disabilities.

- If the building is under construction or in the planning stages, incorporate the needs of people with a hearing loss into the accessibility requirements.

The final phase of the modification program is to do some long-term planning. This phase consists of the following actions:

- Determine the remaining modifications needed to make the library building and programs totally accessible to deaf and hearing impaired people.
- Establish the priorities of these final modifications.
- Develop a schedule for completion of each modification.
- Budget for and secure the funding necessary to accomplish these objectives.
- Complete the modifications to establish total accessibility to the library for the deaf and hearing impaired user.
- Establish contact between the library and people who have a hearing loss to assure all people with a hearing loss that they have library services readily usable.
- Make other modifications as they become necessary, including the acquisition of new equipment which comes on the market and is proved to be useful in library service to deaf and hearing impaired people.

It is most important that the library administration handles the review, does the planning, and makes the modifications in conjunction with deaf and hearing impaired people. Their involvement includes that of policy decisions as well as procedural changes and modifications. The deaf and hearing impaired people may well make the first move to ensure their involvement. They have an information need that makes the use of libraries essential. Communication works 2 ways. Libraries and people with a hearing loss can best be served when communication is flowing freely between them; the breaking down of barriers to library use will make this easier. Through this interaction, programs for library service which are easily accessible to people with a hearing loss will become the usual rather than the unusual. The changes brought about by the combined efforts of the deaf and hearing impaired community and the library will benefit all users. The environmental setting for the service will lead to easy and self-reliant usage of libraries by hearing people and those who have a hearing loss. All groups will move forward to eliminate the barriers to free and complete use of all libraries.

REFERENCE LIST

Abend, Allen C. "Design Criteria for Educational Facilities for Special Education Services." *Journal of Research and Development in Education* 12 (4) (1979): 23–25.

American National Standards Institute, Inc. *American National Standards: Specifications for Making Buildings and Facilities Usable by the Physically Handicapped. ANSI A117.1-1980.* New York: American National Standards Institute, Inc., 1980.

Begg, Robert T. "Disabled Libraries: An Examination of Physical and Additudinal Barriers to Handicapped Library Users." In *The Mainstreamed Library: Issues, Ideas, Innovations*, edited by Barbara H. Baskin and Karen H. Harris, pp.11–21. Chicago: American Library Association, 1982.

Bennett, Philip M. "Users Come First in Design." In *The Mainstreamed Library: Issues, Ideas, Innovations*, edited by Barbara H. Baskin and Karen H. Harris, pp. 231–33. Chicago: American Library Association, 1982.

Bowe, Frank A., Ph.D., consultant to United Nations Industrial Development Organization (UNIDO). *Access for Deaf and Hearing Impaired Persons. Final Report of the Study of Access to United Nations Buildings.* Washington, DC: National Rehabilitation Information Center, 1982.

Castle, Diane L. *Signaling Devices for the Hearing Impaired.* Rochester, NY: National Technical Institute for the Deaf. Rochester Institute of Technology, n.d. (Brochure.)

Cohen, Aaron, and Cohen, Elaine. *Designing and Space Planning for Libraries: A Behavioral Guide.* New York: R. R. Bowker, 1979.

Engelbert, Alan. "Library Service to the Deaf and Hearing Impaired." *Show-Me-Libraries* 33 (5) (February 1982): 20–24.

"Gallaudet Learning Center." *Gallaudet Today* 11 (3) (September 1981): 1–9.

Hagemeyer, Alice. "Accessibility at Libraries." In *Communicating with Hearing People: The Red Notebook*, by the National Association of the Deaf. Silver Spring, MD: National Association of the Deaf, 1981.

Library Access for the Handicapped. A Guide to Materials, Services and Physical Accessibility of Public and Academic Libraries in New York Metropolitan Area. New York: New York Metropolitan Reference and Research Library Agency, 1979.

Mallery, Mary S., and De Vore, Ralph. *A Sign System for Libraries.* Chicago: American Library Association, 1982.

Miller, Richard T., Jr. "Library Services with Deaf People." *Show-Me-Libraries.* 32 (4) (January 1981): 34–35.

Morgan, Michelle. *Notes on Design Criteria for People with Deafness.* (A research project funded through the Institute Scholar Program.) Washington, DC: The American Institute of Architects, 1976.

National Library Service for the Blind and Physically Handicapped. *Planning Barrier Free Libraries.* Washington, DC: National Library Service for the Blind and Physically Handicapped, Library of Congress, 1981.

"The Office that Changes Gracefully." (A reprint from *Office.*) Zeeland, MI: Herman Miller, Inc., n.d.

Opening Library Doors. A library-accessibility workshop sponsored by Central ALSA, Indiana Central University, and the Indiana State Library. Made possible through a grant from the Commissioner on Higher Education, 1981.

Pollet, Dorothy, and Haskel, Peter C. *Sign Systems for Libraries: Solving the Wayfinding Problem.* New York: R. R. Bowker, 1979.

Radocy, Robert. *An Accessibility Study of Boulder, Colorado.* Boulder, CO: Western Interstate Commission for Higher Education, 1976.

Stephens, Suzanne. "Hidden Barriers." In *The Mainstreamed Library: Issues, Ideas, Innovations*, edited by Barbara H. Baskin and Karen H. Harris, pp. 31–33. Chicago: American Library Association, 1982.

U.S. Congress. *The Architectural Barriers Act PL 90-480 1968 as amended.* Washington, DC: U.S. Congress, 1968.

Velleman, Ruth A. "Architectural and Program Accessibility: A Review of Library Programs and Facilities Publications for Librarians Serving Disabled Individuals." *Drexel Library Quarterly* 16(2) (April 1980): 32–57.

Chapter 17
Personnel Training and Employment

A serious problem deaf and hearing impaired individuals have is their inability to keep up-to-date with current events. As our environment changes, hearing people keep up-to-date with those changes, but people with a hearing loss must make a continuous special effort to know all that is taking place around them. The library can be a great asset in this respect. As the library, with its resources, services, and programs, takes on the responsibility for informing hearing people, it can widen its range of activities to include deaf and hard-of-hearing people as well. Although people with a hearing loss differ in their everyday-life backgrounds, their level of education, their social interaction, and their beliefs, one characteristic is common to all—each faces some sort of communication barrier. This barrier makes the use of traditional library service more difficult for them than for hearing people and, in some instances, causes some parts of the library service to be totally unusable.

Deaf and hearing impaired people meet all of the problems that hearing people do in their lives with the additional problem of communicating with others. Library administration can take a responsibility in 2 areas to ensure that deaf and hearing impaired people become a part of the mainstream of the library: (1) personnel training and (2) employment. All of the resources and services planned, developed, and implemented fall into place when the following occurs:

- Attitudinal barriers no longer exist in libraries.
- Libraries include deaf and hearing impaired individuals among their personnel.
- Libraries provide resources and programs to other members of society which will help to remove *all* attitudinal barriers.

- Libraries make resources and services available which will aid deaf and hearing impaired people to find employment within the working world.

The personnel training within a library has, as its goal, the development of a good working relationship with deaf and hearing impaired people based on a knowledge of deafness and hearing impairment. To know how to provide service to deaf people equal to that for hearing people requires a training program enabling the library staff to understand the characteristics of deaf and hearing impaired people. Knowing the facts about the variations in hearing loss and its effect on people will assist librarians and other library staff members in knowing how to work with deaf and hearing impaired people effectively. Because there is such wide variation in ways to communicate with people who have a hearing loss, the staff needs information on what those communication techniques are and how to achieve 2-way communication regardless of the barrier which may seem to exist. This type of awareness and information training can greatly reduce the possibility of misunderstandings and can also assist in eliminating myths and stereotypes about deaf and hearing impaired people.

Besides the facts about deafness and hearing impairment, special training should also be provided on how to develop the needed communication skills. All staff members will not become proficient in all types of communication, but they need to be familiar with every means which will facilitate effective 2-way communication.

Library personnel should also learn about the agencies and organizations that work with the deaf. A knowledge of the special services available in the community will help facilitate the total program of library service to deaf and hearing impaired people. A clear understanding of the work of national as well as international organizations of, by, and for deaf and hearing impaired people is also of assistance in working with them on the local level as library users or potential users. Part of the training program should include guidelines on how to communicate, on architectural access, and on environmental access. General information on technology and library service to the deaf and hearing impaired should be provided to all staff on a current basis. In short, personnel should build up a well-rounded store of information on the deaf community.

As with communication, some staff members will become skilled in using the latest technological equipment, but the majority will have only a knowledge of its existence and its effectiveness. It is important that library personnel become accustomed to including deafness and hearing impairment in any library program relating to greater accessibility and service to all disabled people. The mission of the training will be realized when the library staff becomes aware of the needs of the deaf and hearing impaired—when they gain the competencies, through information and understanding, needed to provide quality effective service to this group.

TRAINING PROGRAMS

When some of the staff members are deaf or hard of hearing, this training takes on additional dimensions. Staff members will need to know how to communicate with hearing people—both the library users and their coworkers. They will also need to know how to communicate with people with different types of hearing loss and different methods of communicating. An important part of the training session will take place when the time comes for the staff to ask questions. The session, made up of deaf, hard-of-hearing, and hearing people will provide a laboratory in which to develop communicative skills; it will also provide a working situation in which these skills can be tested. A program of staff training is presented below.

I. Goal
   A. To sensitize all staff members to the characteristics of deaf and hearing impaired people with which the staff may not be familiar.
II. Objectives
   A. To provide information to the staff on how deaf and hearing impaired people can effectively use the library.
   B. To answer questions staff members have relating to people with a hearing loss and library service for them.
III. Resources
   A. *The Red Notebook*, pamphlets, books, films, bibliographies, guides, TTY/TDD, and captioned films and television.
   B. Educators from schools teaching deaf and hearing impaired children and adults.
   C. Members of the local chapters of national associations of the deaf, local organizations, and social clubs.
   D. Parents of children who are deaf or hard of hearing.
IV. Program
   A. Presentations by resource people.
   B. Questions by the staff.

C. Showing of a film.

D. Time to review the materials, technological aids, and equipment.

Employing deaf and hearing impaired people on the library staff is an important part of bringing them into the mainstream of the library. In a fully accessible library, staff members who are deaf or hard of hearing are physically different from hearing staff in communicative ability, but they are not disabled if the following are true:

- The library administration and staff have the awareness and information needed concerning the capabilities of deaf and hearing impaired people and make the accommodations necessary for them to function effectively in their work.
- The attitude of the deaf and hearing impaired people includes the belief that alternative methods of dealing with obstacles can be successfully integrated into the job to be done.
- The emphasis in employment is on the *ability* of the deaf or hard-of-hearing person just as with the hearing.
- The concepts of individual differences, job satisfaction, and career planning are a part of the employment procedure and the development on the job.

ACCOMMODATIONS IN THE WORK ENVIRONMENT

Some modifications of the work environment and other accommodations may need to be made in order to overcome obstacles to employment. Because each position is different and each employee has different capabilities, accommodations need to be made on an individual basis. The employer and the employee working together can determine the best way to modify the job and/or make accommodations.

Some points to be stressed in ensuring a satisfying working relationship between hearing impaired and hearing employees are:

- One-to-one communication. There may be an initial problem in communication. The person with the hearing loss, however, knows the best method to establish 2-way communication. Sometimes an interpreter is required to facilitate 2-way communication, as the person may be difficult to understand initially. Again, the person whose speech has been affected by a hearing loss knows best how to ensure that the other person will understand the message.

- Communication in meetings. In a group of people, an interpreter may be needed. The method of communication used will depend upon the individual needs of the employees who have a hearing loss. A note taker is also effective because the deaf or hard-of-hearing person can review the notes before the close of the meeting to ask informed questions.
- Work accommodations. A conventional job description seldom analyzes specific tasks in relation to their corresponding specific physical requirements. An analysis of the job, with the aim of restructuring it for a qualified person with physical disabilities which include deafness and hearing impairment, should be made. The specific goal to be reached in this restructuring is to develop or modify job descriptions for library positions in order to make them accessible to people who are deaf or hearing impaired. In making this review, library personnel should (1) inventory the present job descriptions in the library for each class of positions; (2) develop for each such class of positions a model job description with the suggested salary for each; (3) modify model class specifications to make them accessible to individuals who are deaf or hard of hearing. If any other physical disability is present, an additional modification should be made; and (4) accommodate any modifications in work site, reassignment of a task to another employee, and additional time needed to perform the work. The work may also be accomplished in an alternate way such as through the assistance of a coworker, an interpreter, or special technology.

The problem areas for the deaf and hearing impaired in employment are centered around communication and the quality of sound. The amount of accommodations necessary varies from job to job according to the nature of the work and the specific disability of the employee. The 4 main types of reasonable accommodations are:

- Modification of work site and commonly used areas.
- Use of assistive devices.
- Provision of interpreters or other aids for communication for deaf and hearing impaired persons.
- Adoption of flexible personnel policies including such elements as flextime, reduced hours, job restructuring, reassignment of nonessential tasks, and work trading.

In developing job analysis with the aim of modification of jobs, the following points are important:

- Title of job.
- Purpose. What is the reason for the job? Why does the job exist? Can the goals of the organization be attained without the job?
- Major tasks. What are the really essential tasks to accomplishing its purpose? What are the minimum standards? Must the tasks be performed in a certain order?
- Job setting. What are the work situations and conditions where the major tasks are performed? How is the work area organized for safety and efficiency? What are the physical and social conditions?
- Worker qualifications. What are the minimum requirements a worker must meet to perform the tasks? What are the physical requirements of the job? What special training is needed? What experience is essential and what are the personality characteristics required?

It is important to know that job modifications are not necessary in all cases; sometimes a minor change will suffice.

Throughout the process of restructuring jobs to enable deaf and hearing impaired people to be employed, the library management should keep in mind the need for independence and self-reliance. This factor is very important as it relates to deafness and hearing impairment and the work that the individual with this disability will perform; such an emphasis enables the employee to be productive and satisfied with the restructured job. In the process of employing deaf and hearing impaired people in library positions, library management needs to take into account their individual capabilities in order that they might achieve the limits of their abilities. Many people in this group are not employed to their full capacity. This is not because they do not have the skills but because of the lack of understanding in the hearing world.

THE LIBRARY AS A CLEARINGHOUSE

The library can provide an important service in the areas of deafness and hearing impairment by becoming a clearinghouse and resource center for employment of deaf and hearing impaired individuals. Much information is available in the area of employment of people with disabilities. These disabilities cover a wide range of physical differences, and the accommodations which need to be made for some disabled individuals may differ from those individuals with other disabilities. This adaptation is not a one-time activity but a continuing need as changes occur in the environment, technology, legislation, and in the personal needs of the employee. All the people involved have a continuing need for new information. This kind of clearinghouse and resource center would need to be in touch with the national employment scene as well as with that of the local community; it would require a working relationship with educational institutions, service agencies, and employers in the geographical area served by the library. Among the materials needed in such a clearinghouse/resource center are:

- Legislation relating to deaf and hearing impaired persons.
- Educational information on possible careers for deaf and hearing impaired people.
- Types of employment opportunities available in the community.
- Information on how deaf and hearing impaired people have secured and retained a variety of jobs and work in them successfully.
- Information on programs which have been successful in employing deaf and hearing impaired people.

The library can also take an active part in the job fairs held in many communities to provide greater employment opportunities for people with disabilities. Workshops on employment of disabled persons can also be organized by the library. Deaf and hearing impaired people can be part of a larger group, or the emphasis can focus only on people with this disability.

To assist in the career development of people who have a hearing loss, it is important that the library have a collection of materials on career education and have a librarian who is knowledgeable both in the area of hearing loss and in career education. Included in the materials should be catalogs and information about the following educational institutions:

- Gallaudet College in Washington, DC. This school is the only accredited liberal arts college for the deaf in the world.
- National Technical Insitute for the Deaf (NTID) in Rochester, NY. The institute was established to provide technical education and training to deaf citizens. Special services are geared to the needs of the deaf and are easily accessible. Successful employment is the goal of the courses taught, which are supplemented by culturally enriching courses.
- California State University–Northridge, National Center on Deafness. The center enables its deaf students to have full access to classroom and extracurricular activities. The support units offer class note taking, tutoring, counseling, speech, and conver-

sation and interpreting for deaf undergraduates and graduates in various academic studies.

- SUNY LaGuardia Community College, Long Island City, NY. This school has a special program of credit and noncredit for students who are deaf.
- J. Sargeant Reynolds Community College, Richmond Center for the Deaf, Richmond, VA. The center serves deaf students on campus and members of the community as well.
- Madonna College, Livonia, MI. This school set up a program for deaf students and also offers a degree program in sign language studies primarily for hearing students.
- Mount Aloysius Junior College, Cresson, PA. The college offers 6 academic majors for deaf and hearing impaired students.
- Northwestern Connecticut Community College, Winsted, CT. This institution has set up a support service for deaf persons which includes classes in sign language, interpreting, note taking, and audiovisual programing.
- Oregon College of Education, Monmouth, OR. The college houses the Regional Resource Center on Deafness, which provides resources for deaf and hearing impaired people.
- Tampa Technical Institute, Tampa, FL. This institute trains and finds jobs for deaf students in the computer, electronics, drafting, and commercial arts fields.
- University of Maryland–Baltimore, MD. The school has the Center for Graduate Social Work Education of the Hearing Impaired.
- Utah State University, Logan, UT. Utah State coordinates support services and provides auxiliary assistance to hard-of-hearing and oral-deaf students.
- Waubonsee Community College, Sugar Grove, IL. Hearing impaired students are enrolled in the vocational and technical training programs, among others.
- Miami-Dade Community College, Miami, FL. The school has adapted its humanities course to serve deaf students who are homebound.
- University of Minnesota, Minneapolis/St. Paul, MN. At this university, prelingually deaf students complete 4-year undergraduate programs and enroll in graduate school.
- Johnson County Community College, Overland Park, KS. The college has developed, for classroom use by deaf students, a series of technical language books depicting hand signs for techni-

cal terms and vocabulary. The college also acts as a midwestern center for deaf student services offered by Gallaudet College.
- Community College of Philadelphia (CCP) Center on Disability. The college has opened all classes to deaf students. There are more than 40 areas of study related to certification of completion or to the Associate Degree.
- Temple University, Philadelphia, PA. This is the home of the National Theater of the Deaf, which highlights the special talents of deaf students.
- University of Iowa, Iowa City, IA. The university offers its hearing impaired students auditory training aids.
- El Camino College, Torrance, CA. This college offers hearing impaired students support services.

These cited educational institutions are some of the schools which focus specifically on deaf students.

Another area a library can assist through its resources is financial support of deaf and hearing impaired students. Any source of funding should be included, but those which are directed specifically toward assisting deaf and hearing impaired students should be emphasized in the collection. The number of deaf and hearing impaired students obtaining college degrees and securing professional positions has increased over the last several years. There are still, however, too few who go to college. Of those who do, many experience difficulty finding related employment. By providing material on education and careers, libraries can help make higher education a reality to the deaf and hearing impaired and to their parents. The information can motivate students to obtain undergraduate and graduate degrees with the hope that they will find employment in their chosen fields. One type of material which will help deaf and hearing impaired students is a collection of descriptions of programs in which college students can gain related work experience in addition to their course work.

By examining the resources provided by the library on education and employment, deaf and hearing impaired people will be able to think broadly about their future, see the career choices open to them, and follow their personal interests and aptitudes to find a satisfying career. These resources can also help deaf and hearing impaired persons in career growth and advancement; upward mobility has been difficult in general for people who are deaf or hard of hearing. In addition, the library can maintain a current file on workshops and continuing education opportunities which can assist the deaf or hard-of-hearing person find employment, change jobs, or move up in a current job.

It is important that the library know about and inform the public of the rights of deaf and hearing impaired people relating to education and employment. There are federal rules and regulations as well as those implemented by local government. For example, the Department of Justice and Presidential Task Force on Regulatory Relief decided on March 21, 1983, to retain the Section 504 coordination guidelines under the Rehabilitation Act of 1973, P.L. 93-112. As stated, Section 504 prohibits discrimination against disabled persons in employment—including deaf and hearing impaired people. Under this act, the deaf and hearing impaired are entitled to federally supported programs and facilities. As a result, many colleges and universities began to provide educational programs to deaf and hearing impaired students. Now, in an information- and service-oriented society, with an economy which is increasingly influenced by technology, more employment opportunities are open to deaf and hearing impaired people than in the past.

Problems still exist in attitudes of employers and potential employers. Some of them resist the employment of deaf and hearing impaired people. Others are permissive in their attitudes as long as they can fit into the job and into the organization as they stand. Some employers are ready to accommodate qualified deaf and hearing impaired applicants. Still another group of employers institutes recruitment programs for qualified applicants for positions in the organization. It is important for library management and management in services, business, and industry to have positive attitudes toward accommodation and recruitment of deaf and hearing impaired people. It is more important, however, to translate those philosophies into action. The laws which now exist to bring deaf and hearing impaired people into the mainstream of employment are only symbolic unless employers recruit qualified applicants from among the deaf and hearing impaired population and are accommodating as far as the jobs themselves are concerned.

Many of the problems encountered by people with a hearing loss in the area of employment can be overcome. It is difficult for a person, psychologically, to transfer from an educational situation to the working world. This is especially true for people from an insular environment, such as a school for the deaf. The work-experience program is an especially important service in 2 respects: (1) the hearing employer overcomes any apprehension about hiring deaf or hard-of-hearing people and (2) the employee gains confidence that s/he can do the job. Libraries can assist by becoming a part of a work-experience program and by providing materials for and about such programs. Personnel administration for middle management and training programs for deaf personnel can help change the attitudes of the hearing employer regarding the deaf and hearing impaired employee and provide a learning experience on both sides. Such activities give all of the people the opportunity to find out for themselves what they can do. Such activities help to blend the hearing world and the deaf world.

THE WORK ENVIRONMENT AND OPPORTUNITIES

While entering the working world is important, job mobility is equally important. There is a need to enhance career opportunities and job mobility. It is important for people with a hearing loss to become politically aware in the environment in which they are working. Because they have only themselves to rely on for advancement, they need to understand clearly the possibilities for advancement in their own organization, at another organization, or even in another field of work. Flexibility and common sense work as well for deaf and hearing impaired employees as for those who can hear. These individuals work well in libraries as they do in other fields of employment. There is a need to put forth ideas as suggestions, to determine which ones to accept, and to follow those selected. Following these precepts helps people who are deaf or hard of hearing attain job mobility in a hearing environment. There are new career horizons; they do not have to settle for limited employment opportunities. Important points for people who have obtained the work they want are to:

- Take on only as much as can be done and thus eliminate pressure from the job.
- Develop self-confidence in the work and avoid tension.
- Learn to concentrate on the work.
- Develop a pleasant and stable attitude rather than one of restlessness and irritability.
- Become involved in activities to prevent loneliness and discouragement.

While such points as these are helpful to all people, they are especially important to deaf and hearing impaired people in order to succeed in the working world in the hearing environment.

The first national survey of how employers modify jobs to disabled people was made in 1982 for the U.S. Labor Department's Employment Standards Administration. The report, "A Study of Accommodations Provided to Handicapped Employees by Federal Contractors," had 3 primary objectives: (1) to find out how many federal contractors are making accommodations, (2) to learn the range and cost of modifications employers are making, and (3) to understand the decision-making process for determining whether an accommodation is "reasonable." Among the findings were the following:

- The accommodations were not prohibitively costly.
- Responses to employees making requests for accommodations were encouraging.
- The companies and the employees did not feel that accommodations either helped or hindered upward mobility.
- A major factor in encouraging accommodations is the affirmative action commitment of top management.

The library can provide information on surveys such as this and can make available other information concerning the effects of rules and regulations and compliance or noncompliance on the working lives of deaf and hearing impaired people. Everyday information can be included on a variety of subjects relating to the current needs of people with a hearing loss. Among these are facts about income taxes, social security, insurance, and consumer problems. Information can be included for TTY/TDD users; many programs can be accessible by this means of communication. College courses for credit can be set up through this type of communication; tips on gardening and other consumer needs can be included. The script for these programs should change at least weekly. The script writing can be done by the consumer groups providing the information. A similar plan can be used to make available information on employment concerns such as job availability. This information can be provided by establishing job lines listing available jobs—either limited to library positions or more extensive positions.

A strong force in the employment of people with disabilities, including problems of communication, is the President's Committee on Employment of the Handicapped. The purpose of this committee is to promote a climate of opinion nationally which will bring about full acceptance of physically and mentally disabled people in the work place. It also works toward the elimination of environmental and attitudinal barriers which impede their opportunities.

The committee gathers, produces, and disseminates information with the goal of gaining employment for disabled persons. Within each state, there is also a similar organization which has these goals, known in many states as the Governor's Committee on Employment of the Handicapped.

An important committee of the President's Committee on Employment of the Handicapped is the Library Committee. This committee encourages the participation of American libraries in serving the needs of disabled people. One of the outstanding meetings of this committee was "Target '83, Technology, Attitudes, Resources, Growth, Employment, Training," held at the 1983 Annual Conference of the President's Committee on Employment of the Handicapped. The Library Committee's program was on the subject of "Images of Disability through the Printed Word." Three distinguished writers spoke about their books, their experiences in writing them, and their hope that the material would influence the development of a positive image of disabled people. Irving Zola spoke about an autobiographical story, *Missing Pieces: A Chronicle of Living with a Disability*[1]; William Roth spoke on his book, *The Handicapped Speak*[2]; the stories of 13 people he interviewed; and Jack Gannon spoke on the writing of his book, *Deaf Heritage*[3], a detailed history of the deaf community. Four newsletters which focus on disabled people—*In the Mainstream*; *Human Services Insider*; *Information from HEATH Resource Center*; and *Handicapped Americans Reports* —were discussed by their editors. Similar meetings can be held at the state and local level by identifying local authors or other creative artists and encouraging them to participate.

The goals of the Library Committee are:

- To assist libraries in better serving people with disabilities.
- To encourage disabled people to use libraries as resources in finding and keeping jobs. The use of libraries is encouraged also to improve the quality of life and to secure needed information.
- To encourage the development of literature by, about, and for disabled people and to publicize existing literature.

The projects of the Library Committee are both practical and creative. The committee works closely with the American Library Association, especially with the Association of Specialized and Cooperative Library Agencies. Articles are written and sponsored by the committee on such subjects as literature on disabilities or library service to disabled people. Bibliographies, such as *The World of Work*, are also sponsored by the Committee. Deaf and hearing impaired people are included in all of the activities of the committee, and librarians who have shown national leadership in the field of making libraries accessible to disabled people also volunteer time to its work.

The deaf and hard-of-hearing individual has more learning opportunities and communication aids available now than at any other time in history, as well as new employment opportunities. It appears that it is the communication barrier which hearing people are unable or unwilling to overcome that stands in the way of employment of people with a hearing loss. There is a need for hearing people to be aware of both the public and the private resources available to both employers and to applicants which can aid in job placement. Knowledge needs to be disseminated concerning the vocational abilities of deaf and hearing impaired people and about their careers. Employers and applicants need to be able to open and conduct an interview comfortably to assist in communication. Through changes in attitudes, there will be more extensive opportunities for students to work in their chosen fields. Through work-experience, cooperative education, and internships, deaf and hearing impaired people will have an opportunity to try out their skills in their chosen work before graduation. However, more needs to be done to enable them to enter the mainstream of the economy. They should be able to think broadly about their futures and to select from alternative careers based on their interests and aptitudes, not on what positions hearing people allow them to hold. As more and more deaf and hard-of-hearing people secure and succeed in a variety of fields, they can serve as models for others seeking a wider range of employment. With undergraduate courses, graduate courses, seminars, workshops, and continuing education available, people with a hearing loss can prepare for employment through education. Such programs will assist the employees in their careers and will aid upward mobility.

Libraries can be a vital influence in the development of positive attitudes toward the employment of deaf and hearing impaired people. Banks have been one of the leading services which have proved the ability of deaf or hard-of-hearing people to work with the public as tellers or in other public and behind-the-scenes capacities. Libraries can also provide a wide variety of opportunities to deaf and hearing impaired people in employment. Just as important is providing resources to people in the area of employment possibilities, both for the employer and the applicant or employee. With material in personnel training and employment widely available, the horizons for people who have a hearing loss can be expanded far beyond their present limits. Libraries have a vital part to play in this continuing expansion.

NOTES

1. Irving Zola, *Missing Pieces: A Chronicle of Living with a Disability.* Philadelphia, PA: Temple University Press, 1982.

2. William Roth, *The Handicapped Speak.* Jefferson, NC: McFarland and Company, 1981.

3. Jack Gannon, *Deaf Heritage.* Silver Spring, MD: National Association of the Deaf, 1981.

REFERENCE LIST

California Department of Rehabilitation. *Guide for Reasonable Accommodations in Employing the Handicapped.* Sacramento, CA: California Department of Rehabilitation, 1980.

California State Personnel Board. Cooperative Personnel Services. *Job Restructuring to Employ the Handicapped.* Sacramento, CA: California State Personnel Board, 1979.

Careers and You. Washington, DC: Gallaudet College, 1978. (Brochure.)

"Deaf Executive Opens Doors for Others." *The NAD Broadcaster* 34 (10) (October 1982): 3,13.

"Employment of Disabled Person." *Interface* 4 (1) (Fall 1981): 3–4.

"Fact Sheet—Employment of Deaf People." *Fingertips* (May 26, 1976): 2.

Goode, Nancy. "Hearing Aids and Lip-Reading Make Difference for Bank Teller." *The Nevada Informer* (Summer 1983): 5.

Levinson, Ken. "Expert Gives Tips on Job Mobility." *The NAD Broadcaster* 34 (10) (October 1982): 9.

Lowman, Rex P. *Implications of Deafness for Education.* Speech given at Gallaudet College, July 4, 1974. Washington, DC: Gallaudet College.

McLaughlin, William P. "The Deaf, the Law and Higher Education." *Volta Review* 84 (6) (October–November 1982): 275–83.

Metcalf, Mary Jane. "Library Service for the Hearing Impaired." *Illinois Libraries* 63 (8) (October 1981): 626–32.

National Technical Institute for the Deaf. *A Workshop on Improving Support Services for Hearing Impaired Students.* Rochester, NY: National Technical Institute for the Deaf, Rochester Institute of Technology, 1983.

Office of Demographic Studies. *Guide to College/Career Programs for Deaf Students.* Washington, DC: Gallaudet College, n.d.

Pati, Gopal C.; Adkins, John I., Jr.; with Morrison, Glen. *Managing and Employing the Handicapped: The Untapped Potential.* Lake Forest, IL: The Human Resource Press, 1981.

President's Committee on Employment of the Handicapped. *Hiring Persons with Hearing Impairments.* Washington, DC: President's Committee on Employment of the Handicapped, n.d.

————.*So You've Hired Someone with a Hearing Impairment.* Washington, DC: President's Committee on Employment of the Handicapped, n.d. (Brochure.)

Rawls, Rebecca L. "Easing the Way for Handicapped in Science." *Chemical and Engineering News* 56 (4) (January 23, 1978): 25–27.

"Reasonable Accommodations in Employment." *The Nevada Informer* (Summer 1983): 4.

Ritter, Audrey. *An Annotated Bibliography of Literature Related to the Employment of Deaf Persons.* Rochester, NY: National Technical Institute for the Deaf, Rochester Institute of Technology, 1980.

Santos, K. Dean. *Preparation for a Career: Roles and Functions of Educational Specialists.* Rochester, NY: National Technical Institute for the Deaf, Rochester Institute of Technology, 1982–83.

Scharfenberger, Julie. "Section 504: Employer-Employee Relations." In *Opening Doors*, a library-accessibility workshop sponsored by Central Indiana ALSA, Indiana Central University, and the Indiana State Library through a grant from the Commission on Higher Education, 1981: A11-A12.

Tickton, S. G.; Kinder, W. A.; and Goley, A. S. *1981 Idea Handbook for Colleges and Universities. Educational Opportunities for Handicapped Students.* Prepared in recognition of UNESCO's International Year of Disabled Persons. Washington, DC: Academy for Educational Development, September, 1981.

U.S. Office of Personnel Management. Selective Placement Program Office. *Work Disability in the United States. A Chartbook.* Washington, DC: Government Printing Office, 1980.

————.*Handbook of Job Analysis for Reasonable Accommodations.* Washington, DC: Government Printing Office, 1982.

Warren, George G. *Career of the Handicapped Librarian.* Metuchen, NJ: Scarecrow Press, 1979.

West, L. *Breaking the Sound Barrier: Working with Hearing Impaired Adults in an Educational Setting.* Beverly, MA: North Shore Community College, 1979.

Chapter 18
Economics of Providing the Service

Library services, resources, and programs for the general public, for all special populations, and in all types of libraries require financial support. This support may take the form of public monies, private funds, donations, grants, gifts, and complimentary services. Whatever the funding, each source must be sought by the library. A strong consideration in all programing of library service to deaf and hearing impaired people is its cost. Such cost has to be assessed on an individual library basis but can be fairly easily determined if the program is broken into its several components. While no part of the program will be cost-free, some will require only the expenditure of time, the reordering of priorities, the addition of new priorities, or an exchange of priorities.

Because many service organizations see library service to the deaf as a program in which they wish to be involved, equipment such as TTY/TDDs are usually available in varying numbers from these organizations. Usually a fully developed program will require more TTY/TDDs than can be acquired through gifts, so the additional equipment needs to be included in the cost estimate developed by the library. The same will be true, to some degree, of other equipment which is developed especially for the people who are deaf or hard of hearing.

COST CONSIDERATIONS

The development of a collection of materials on deafness and hearing impairment, as well as materials especially purchased for people with a language difficulty, requires an initial outlay of funds plus a continuing budget. While some materials or funding for these materials may be donated by interested and concerned people and/or organizations, the larger part of funds requires a special financial commitment in the form of ongoing funding from the library's regular budget, although the initial investment to purchase the collection in the quantity and quality needed will undoubtedly require a commitment of funds over and above the budget. To achieve the continuing resources necessary requires either additional funds or a reordering of priorities of expenditures or both.

Staffing presents the same kind of financial considerations. Either additional staff or redeployment of staff or both is required to achieve adequate staffing of the service. While all ongoing staff and new staff will require training in working with people who have a hearing loss, some of the members will need special training to develop the skills necessary to communicate with all people who have any type of hearing loss. As new librarians and support staff are employed who are deaf or hard of hearing, they, too, will require training. Their training will involve developing the skill necessary to communicate with hearing people. Some of this training can be accomplished in-house and will require, primarily, an expenditure of time. Funds should be set aside, however, for special seminars and workshops to be held on a local, state, regional, or national basis and for the purpose of bringing specialists into the library to provide additional staff training.

Funding from grants is invaluable in offering training workshops in the community. One type of workshop, which is effective and needed and can be funded from grants, is that of training parents to advocate effectively for their children's educational needs. Another is the development of an information center where people who are deaf or hard of hearing can turn for referral service in solving their problems. A third type of workshop can train a younger deaf or hard-of-hearing person in self-advocacy. Young adults who are going to use community services need to know how to do so effectively.

If the service is being provided in a new library building with the architectural and environmental barriers, as they relate to deafness and hearing impairment, considered in the construction, the cost of the actual start-up of the service will be reduced. These costs are a one-time investment in the library building and, in a new building, the construction costs to eliminate such barriers are a small percentage of the overall cost of the building. If, however, the building requires remodeling to make it architecturally acccessible and environmentally modified, money will need to be budgeted. The cost will be dependent on the specific changes which need to be made; however, even with an existing building, the changes necessary to accomplish these goals can be relatively inexpensive. Making rest rooms accessible, however, can be costly as can installing ramps or even accessible doors.

Throughout all of the modification, all alternatives should be considered to achieve the goals at a reasonable cost. These costs are, for the most part, one-time investments requiring a minimum of upkeep. With such accommodations as using new technology in an auditorium so that deaf and hearing impaired people can use it effectively, it will be necessary to keep abreast of new developments in the field; existing equipment will be improved upon and new equipment will be available.

The accommodations made in the job for deaf and hearing impaired employees will be, for the most part, negligible in cost. Many of the job modifications are related only to the shifting of duties or to making changes in the job requirements. Most of the other requirements for modification will be accomplished when the building is architecturally accessible, environmentally modified, and all attitudinal barriers have been dissipated.

Development of a new program or the extension of a current program does involve spending additional library funds. The program will require extra funding because it is in an area which, in most libraries, has not yet been fully developed. It requires equipment which may never before have never been purchased by the library, or like TTY/TDDs, have never been purchased in quantity for use in the library and for loan. Staff have been employed without a special search for those qualities and skills which make them fully capable of working effectively with deaf and hearing impaired people. Jobs have seldom required modification to accommodate to the needs of deaf and hearing impaired employees. Books, films, and other materials usually have not been purchased with deaf and hearing impaired people in mind. Architectural, environmental, and attitudinal barriers have not been considered in relation to deaf and hard-of-hearing people. In those libraries which now have an ongoing program of service, the initial investment will be only in the area of the expansion and the extension of the service program.

All of these changes are costly in both time and money. How much it will cost depends on whether the program already has a healthy start and is strong in its relationship to other programs in the library. Each library administration needs to assess the cost of the program in relation to the overall library needs of the deaf and hearing impaired community.

FUNDING SOURCES

Ideally, a basic part of the funding should come from an ongoing library support source. It may come from a reordering of priorities or from additional funding provided from the basic source. Such funding signifies a commitment from library management, the funding body, and the staff who will work with the program. In most instances, however, the funding for the entire program will require funds in addition to those sources which provide the basic funding for all of the library programs.

A significant source of funds in library service to deaf and hearing impaired people has been and is being provided by the Library Services and Construction Act (LSCA), a federal funding program for libraries. Funding is available through this source for services, resources, and equipment, and to make buildings physically accessible. This act (P.L. 84-597), as amended, is a state formula grant program. One of the purposes of the grants is to extend and improve public library services in areas which are without such services or in which such services are inadequate. Another purpose is to promote interlibrary cooperation among all types of libraries. Many of the states have used these varying levels of funding to develop library service to the deaf and hearing impaired. While the grants were not always large, they provided the additional funds needed to institute services or to extend programs already established. Represented among these programs of service are:

- Training library staff in sign language.
- Offering awareness training.
- Providing reference and information service through a TTY/TDD.
- Showing captioned films.
- Making available captioned television.
- Purchasing titles in signed English for children.
- Acquiring titles for adults with low verbal skills.
- Having interpreters sign programs held in the library.
- Giving an overview of the service through programs.
- Printing out all news of interest, including the weather forecast, to the deaf and hearing impaired communities by means of the TTY/TDD.
- Purchasing a definitive book collection to serve people who are deaf and hearing impaired or who have an interest in this subject.
- Producing an annotated film catalog.

- Publicizing "Deaf Awareness Week."
- Publishing bibliographies and brochures on deafness and hearing impairment.
- Improving communication between the staff and the patron with a hearing loss.
- Providing signed story hours for children.
- Holding workshops on special problems of the deaf and hearing impaired.
- Surveying needs by questionnaire.

Other public funding sources are available which can assist in programs developed for consumers who are deaf or hard of hearing. LSCA is especially valuable, however, because it is designed for libraries.

Many types of grants are provided by the private sector. As with the proposals for public funds, the requests for private gifts and grants begin with the knowledge of exactly what will be done with the grant funds—what services, resources, programs, or equipment the funds are intended to provide. All requests for funds must be clearly stated in order to enhance the chances for acceptance. There is a need for self-examination within the library itself before turning to outside funding sources. It is not only important that the requester has clearly in mind the purpose for which the funds are being sought, but that it is clearly stated in the proposal in easy-to-understand language. The people who read the requests for public or private funds may know nothing about the library requesting the funds or may not be acquainted with the program of service presented. In applying for a grant, a library must assess the community in relation to the needs of people who have a hearing loss. This can be done through study and through determining the community's perception of those needs. The people who will be receiving the library service must be involved in the writing of any grant proposal—in this instance, the people who have a hearing loss.

Because library service to the deaf and hearing impaired is an identifiable service, the grant proposal may well be designed for the development of that specific service with good chances of its being favorably received by the granting source. Before seeking funding from a specific granting source, it is first necessary to determine the interest of the funding source. Does it include in some of its aspects library service to people with a hearing loss? With the dwindling of monies for the basic funding of libraries, other types of funding sources are more vital than ever before. Before searching for funds from either the public or the private sector, it is necessary to take the following steps:

- Identify that part of the library service to be funded which is unique.
- Be able to demonstrate the need for the library service to be funded.
- Learn how to write an application or secure the services of a writer who can produce a professionally designed proposal.
- Develop a budget which is realistic.
- Write a proposal for the program which includes: a description of the basic and continuing funding available for the library service presented in the proposal; estimation of the number of people who will be served as a result of the program presented; statement of the objectives of providing the service with a highlighting of their significance in the lives of the people in the community in which the service is to be provided; identification of qualifications of the people to work in the library service to be funded and highlighting of those qualifications which are unique to the service; description of how such a program of service relates to the overall mission, goals, and objectives of the library; and an explanation of the cost-effectiveness of providing the service and delineation of the community benefits.
- Study carefully all sources of funding available to determine which ones are most likely to be interested in the program described in the proposal.
- Present the completed proposal to the funding source which has been selected.

If the funds are granted for the program, immediate detailed planning can begin. If the funds are not granted, the library should review the proposal for flaws and shortcomings. When the proposal has been revised, it should be submitted to other funding sources.

Many sources exist that have a direct interest in projects providing benefits to people who have a hearing loss. Even though it has been determined that a financial source has a definite interest in benefitting people with a hearing loss, it is necessary to study the specific interests of that source in this area of disability to determine their geographical or other restrictions. One good source is the National Endowment for the Humanities' Program Development Division. This division assists in fulfilling the endowment's purpose of increasing the public's understanding of the humanities. The National Endowment for the Humanities and the National Endowment for the Arts were originally created in 1965 by Public Law 89-209, known as the National Foundation on the Arts and Humanities. Their publications are *Humanities* and *Cultural Post.*

A project that was funded by the National Endowment for the Humanities in the area of library service and people with a hearing loss was that of "American Culture: The Deaf Perspective." Through this project, the San Francisco Public Library in cooperation with the Fremont Public Library, Fremont, California, and the Oakland Public Library, Oakland, California, presented a program which included the following subjects: "The Heritage of Deaf People;" "The Folklore of Deaf People;" "Deaf Literature;" "Classics in American Sign Language;" and "Minorities within the Deaf Community." One of the programs was presented at the California School for the Deaf in Fremont. In addition to these programs, a series of videotapes was included in the plan to provide a visual introduction to deaf heritage.

Another part of the private sector which can provide funding is that of corporations. Corporate giving may be in the form of monies or services. Corporations have made progress in accommodating deaf and hearing impaired employees. They have also made great advances in technology relating to employment of people with a hearing loss. By making specific requests for funds for library services to people who are deaf or hard of hearing, libraries can explore the effectiveness of proposals to corporations.

Libraries should also find out the type of service they can provide to a program of library service to people with a hearing loss. In many situations, a cooperative approach to grants is a practical way to secure funding and to initiate a service program which will serve a wide community of needs and concerns. Other service agencies which have an interest in the deaf and hearing impaired can add a new dimension to the service and be influential in securing a grant which will benefit all of the people served by the libraries and other organizations involved. They will provide a wider base of support in securing funding and in implementing the program. They will also add the support needed to continue the project after the expiration of the special funding.

Libraries can develop their own funding sources which will provide continuing supplemental support. Some of these can be developed by the library itself and others can be developed by Friends groups or advisory groups. A foundation can be established which will provide continuing support for a program. Because it is a legal entity, the foundation can become the manager of the funds it receives for the long-range support of the library program. A foundation with a board of trustees can make both investments and disbursements. Foundations receive both large and small financial contributions to a library program, part of which could be devoted to library service to deaf and hearing impaired people. Funding from a foundation would act as a supplement to the basic financial support and would provide relatively stable financing. A foundation provides an alternate means of supplemental support for any type of library or any kind of library program. An advantage of this type of foundation funding is that the funds are readily accessible, and the income from the funds can be projected for any given time span.

The decision makers in a foundation established to support library programs should come from the area in which the library is located. With representatives of the deaf and hearing impaired community concerned with this decision making, the needs of people with a hearing loss can be easily and quickly translated into programs and resources.

Fund raising is a coordinated, well-planned and implemented continuing program. The many aspects of fund raising and programs will vary from library to library; however, some elements of fund raising are common to all such efforts. They include:

- Determining the specific purpose of raising funds and the benefits to be received by the people in the community.
- Developing a budget for the program to be funded.
- Determining the time span for the fund-raising project.
- Assessing the urgency for the program.
- Deciding on a working group to implement the fund-raising effort and the chairperson of the group.
- Securing an honorary chairperson for the fund raising.
- Organizing the fund-raising project in relation to types of donations to be sought and the organizations and people to be contacted.
- Estimating the number of people needed as fund raisers in the project.
- Recruiting volunteers from various segments of the population and from various geographical locations in the area to be covered by the service.
- Planning publicity for the fund-raising project in advance of the actual request for funds.
- Securing the funds through appearances before organizations, a direct mail campaign, personal visits, and by telephone.
- Making the appeal to a wide group of interests with the goal of broad participation.
- Informing the people that the funds will be used directly for the program as presented to the public.
- Explaining that the program of library service to be funded has been well planned and that the people to be served by the program have been involved.

- Showing that the basic library funding cannot adequately support the service program.
- Explaining that the need for service is not being met by any other organization in the community.
- Developing an identifiable theme for the fund-raising project.
- Keeping the public informed on the progress of the project.
- Arranging for special messages of appreciation to be sent out for donations.
- Securing widespread publicity concerning the success of the campaign and information about the next fund-raising project.

In applying these aspects of fund raising for library service to the deaf and hearing impaired, it is essential that the library involve people with a hearing loss in every phase of the project.

Another type of fund-raising effort is the special project. Such an effort can be an ongoing project such as a bookstore. A bookstore may be located within a library and sell books, magazines, phonograph records, tote bags, and other donated items. Such a project can provide a steady source of income. An annual book sale held in an accessible area for a period of several days can also be profitable. Wide publicity is important to its success. Raffles, tours, services, publications, and entertainment can also provide some fund-raising revenue.

Donated services such as technical assistance, printing, equipment, or personnel are valuable in moving forward library service to the deaf and hearing impaired. A cost-effective community approach for solving problems is also invaluable. Libraries, for the most part, are not doing well in the competition for the local tax dollar when compared with other people-oriented activities such as schools, hospitals, health, police, and parks and recreation. Support for libraries can come from all levels of government and from private funding as well. With an improved balance of financing from all of these sources, service programs improve both in quality and in the number of programs which can be offered.

While grant funds are a fine source of supplementary financing, regular operating funds must be budgeted into the program. It is difficult to anticipate grant funding; libraries can approach it in 2 ways: a library can develop hypothetical plans based on grants and other supplementary funding. If the supplementary funding is not forthcoming, the plans will require adjustment in relation to the financial situation. Another way supplementary funding can be approached is that of stretching the basic available funds. Some of this planning will result in reducing present costs so that additional or alternate services can be added. Cost-avoidance can broaden the limits of financial support and/or increase the quality of service. Long-range planning for library service for hearing impaired and deaf people will result in a program-oriented budget which anticipates needs for funding for the services. It will also result in a sound financial foundation for the program and the supplementary funding needed to support it.

PLANNING—FUNDING—EVALUATION

The search for adequate funding for library service to the deaf and hearing impaired is a never-ending process. The planning and funding continually move through the following phases:

- Planning of a library service to meet the needs of people who are deaf, hard of hearing, or who have any type of hearing loss.
- Development of a workable methodology to secure funds to obtain the service and to make that service worthwhile and meaningful to users.
- Designing of a proposal for funding—a written, well-organized document which describes the plan for the service, the methodology to be used in achieving the desired results, and the resources required for its development. Included, also, are the results of the service which are expected and the benefits to be obtained by the people served and by the community.
- Commitment of resources to support the plan for library service to the deaf and hearing impaired. These may come from any source and may be in the form of funds, donated services, or both.
- Management and direction of the service, using the methodology developed in the designing of the proposal.
- Evaluation of the service provided to people who are deaf and hearing impaired to determine its usefulness. The analysis of the results of the service will be used to make modifications in the following year.
- Reporting in writing on the findings of the analysis. Such a report can be developed along the same lines as the original proposal. It will differ in that this document reports findings while the proposal presented ideas and conjectures.
- Dissemination of the results of the service through publication to deaf and hearing impaired populations and organizations, to the library community, and to the general public.

- Planning of library service to the deaf and hearing impaired based on the findings reported from the evaluation of the service being provided and on new and/or additional needs of the people being served.

This planning will go through the same cycle of development in securing the resources needed to support the program on a continuing basis.

To live effectively requires access to adequate information and to satisfying recreation. Deaf and hearing impaired people require accessible library services and the motivation to use them. To reach this ideal, libraries must provide appropriate resources and services; people who have a hearing loss must know about the services offered and how they can access them. Funding is required to achieve the planning and implementation for eliminating physical, environmental, and attitudinal barriers. Such an achievement will make the library, for people with a hearing loss, a pleasant and usable place to enjoy. Financial resources are required to effectively disseminate public information concerning the availability of these resources and services and to evaluate the program for improvements. The funding sources are many, but they require constant vigilance on the part of the library and the people for and with whom the services are developed. Only through this continuing effort can libraries present the programs which will effectively provide appropriate resources and programs for the deaf and hearing impaired.

REFERENCE LIST

Bonnell, Pamela G. *Fund Raising for the Small Library.* (Small Libraries Publications, No. 8. Library Administration and Management Association). Chicago: American Library Association, 1983.

Brevick, Patricia Senn, and Gibbon, Burr E. *Funding Alternatives for Libraries.* Chicago: American Library Association, 1979.

Corry, Emmett.*Grants for Libraries: A Guide to Public and Private Funding Programs and Proposal Writing Techniques.* Littleton, CO: Libraries Unlimited, 1982.

Eckstein, Burton, ed. *Handicapped Funding Directory.* Oceanside, NY: Research Grants Guide, 1983–1984.

"Financing the Library Operation." In *The Librarian and the Patient*, edited by Eleanor Phinney, pp. 263–67. Chicago: American Library Association, 1977.

Flanagan, Joan. *The Grass Roots Fund Raising Book: How to Raise Money in Your Community.* Chicago: Contemporary Books, 1982.

"For Your Reading: Fund Raising." *The NAD Broadcaster* 4 (1) (January 1982): 12.

Funding Sources Bulletin. Sacramento, CA: California State Library, 1983.

Grant Money and How to Get It: A Handbook for Librarians. New York: R. R. Bowker, 1980.

McGovern, Gail. "Alternative Sources of Library Funding." *Interface* 4 (4) (Winter 1983): 7–9.

———."Getting Grants and Gifts." *Interface* 5 (2) (Winter 1983): 1–3.

"Humanities Programs." *Focus: Library Service to Older Adults, People with Disabilities* (5) (1983): 1.

"National Endowment for the Arts Wins Grants." *The NAD Broadcaster* 4 (11) (November–December 1982): 9.

Robertson, Linda. "Finding Funding Resources." In *Opening Library Doors*, a library-accessibility workshop sponsored by Central Indiana ALSA, Indiana Central University, and Indiana State Library through a grant from the Commmission on Higher Education, 1981: D1–D3.

Tested Ways to Successful Fund Raising. New York: Anacom, 1980.

Van Betten, Herman. "Why a Foundation for Public Libraries?" *The Bookmark* (June 1983): 5.

Part IV: Evaluation of Library Service to the Deaf and Hearing Impaired

Chapter 19
The Effectiveness of the Service

As libraries develop programs to meet the needs of all the people in their areas of service, there is increasing concern with the need to measure precisely and objectively the effectiveness of a certain program within the entire service. When that program is a new one, the need for knowing its effectiveness is of even greater importance to ultimate success. The very fact that it is new allows a greater opportunity to change, redirect, strengthen, or abandon methods, services, resources, or procedures as the evaluation progresses. The fact that library service to the deaf and hearing impaired is of recent concern to libraries allows planners of the program to use innovative ideas and the newest technology and library techniques. Such an approach allows, too, for alternative actions. With continuing evaluation of effectiveness, alternative actions can be employed if the patterns originally selected do not produce the desired results. These measures of effectiveness will demonstrate the level of success of the program.

The definition of success in a program of library service to people with a hearing loss needs to be determined before an evaluation is made. It is important to know that there can be many kinds of success in a given program. There are also different degrees of success. Evaluation does not determine only success or failure. What is most important is the assessment of the relative effectiveness of alternate kinds of service to the people in the deaf and hearing impaired community. Positive results are helpful but so are the negative results in an evaluation. The negatives are important for future modification.

Basically, the evaluation is concerned with determining how well the service works. It should answer the following questions:

- How are we doing?
- Are we accomplishing what we planned to do?
- Should we reexamine our plans and try a different approach?
- How can we improve our effectiveness?

METHODS OF EVALUATION

Many methods can be used in measuring this effectiveness. One that is helpful is to ask questions of the staff involved in the program, of the members of the advisory group, and of the deaf and hearing impaired people themselves—both library users and nonusers. It is important in this type of evaluation, also, to talk with parents of deaf and hearing impaired children, with other family members, and with hearing advocates for deaf and hearing impaired people. Involved in this type of evaluation is a review of reports of activities of the service and its use by deaf and hearing impaired people. An on-site observation of the work and participation in work sessions can also be a part of an evaluation. While such an assessment is subjective to a great extent, it is valuable in this particular service since little evaluative materials of any kind exist. Because deaf and hearing impaired individuals, for the most part, are not accustomed to using a library, the potential users will be slow to respond to the library program developed for and by them. The number of users is always important in any service but in this particular area, the quality and appropriateness of the program transcend quantity. This investigative approach will assist in assessing the quality in relation to what the individual wants and needs.

Another technique commonly used to assess effectiveness is that of a questionnaire and structured interviews. The purpose is to ascertain whether the program is doing what the users want it to do. Because the evaluation will be more effective if the questionnaire is returned by a large number of consumers and potential consumers, it should be carefully designed. Some people within the deaf and hearing impaired population have a language difficulty which hinders their understanding of complicated sentence structure. Points that should be considered in the development of the questionnaire include the following:

- The language level should be considered carefully. The level selected should not be too easy but neither should it be too difficult for complete understanding.
- The sentence structure should be simple and not ambiguous. The sentences should be declarative or interrogative rather than conditional. "When" should be used instead of "if."
- The page should be well designed with a careful consideration as to the density of the page and the size of type used as well as the color of the paper. The page should be clear, easily readable, and attractive.

- An example should be given, when appropriate, to explain the question asked or the statement made.
- Vocabulary should be used which will be understood by all of the respondents. Many people do not understand library terminology such as "bound periodical," "title," and "reference." Alternate words should be used for such terms. If there is need to use them, they should be defined.
- The terms used in the questionnaire should be consistent throughout the document.
- The questions related to a certain subject should be grouped so that the individual answering can concentrate on one subject at a time.

Such an evaluation will provide information on both the strengths and weaknesses of the program.

In some areas within the library field, there are fairly well-developed and well-accepted standards which can form the basis for yet another type of program assessment. However, standards have not yet been developed in a field of service as new as library service to the deaf and hearing impaired. So, techniques and guidelines that have been determined for the service should be used in a survey of the program. A composite library program can be developed by bringing together those components of the service which have demonstrated their effectiveness in libraries. The specific service can then be measured against the composite to show how the program stands in relation to demonstrated performance. It will not show whether the specific program is reaching the goals set for it, but it will assess whether its direction and approach are valid.

Some of the questions which should be answered concerning a library program for people who have a hearing loss are:

- Should the program be continued in its present form?
- Should the program be continued but modified?
- Should it be extended and broadened?
- Should it be terminated?
- What parts of the program are successful?
- Can the program be improved?

In evaluating such projects, it is necessary for librarians to work in well-defined program and time increments because the reaching of the ultimate goal of the program lies far in the future. Immediate results are needed, however, to justify the program's existence and to confirm that the program is going in a direction which will result in achieving the ultimate goal. Intermediate goals can be set along the way. The program should be measured on a continuing basis to ensure that it moves steadily toward the end goal. Periodic evaluation will also show whether the ultimate goal is still a valid one. It is important to know what is actually happening in the program rather than only to know what has been planned.

In looking at its service to the deaf and hearing impaired, the library needs to determine the service's awareness level among the people it is designed to serve. Before an individual who is hard of hearing or deaf can make use of the services the library offers, that individual must be made aware of their usability and quality. After that has been accomplished, the library can measure what use is now being made of the service by the people. Questions to ask include:

- How well is the library satisfying the consumers in terms of service?
- How efficiently are the activities of the program being performed?
- Does the service justify its existence?

The level of performance is measured in relation to use and potential use. Other questions which need to be answered about use are:

- How good is the service?
- How much good is the service doing?

One of the ways to measure the service's effectiveness is to conduct an intensive user study. Such a study will tell the library whether it is meeting the needs and interests of deaf and hearing impaired people. It will also tell the library what the users really need and desire. It is not really possible for a library specifically to determine what people want and need without consulting them on a continuing basis. The library will learn from the study who, among the deaf and hearing impaired community, uses the library. It will also learn what the consumers use, how the library is used, and why it is used. If such a survey is extended to nonlibrary users among deaf and hearing impaired individuals, it will, as a result, be an extension of awareness of the service among the potential consumers. The evaluation is important, too, because it reinforces, or establishes for the first time, a communication link between the library and the deaf and hearing impaired users and nonusers. Such a study will result in an increased awareness among all of the people concerned, including the library staff.

To determine more accurately the characteristics of the library user and nonuser in the deaf and hearing impaired community, the information secured during the survey of both can be separated into data concerning those who have used the library and those who have not. A profile of the user and of the nonuser can then be developed from the responses received. The 2 groups can be studied on such measures as age, sex, educational level, economic level, occupation, distance they must travel to the library, access to transportation, and general mobility. If questions are included as to what positive factors influence their use of the library, some insight can be gained in the following areas:

- The quality of the materials provided.
- The general appropriateness of the service to the needs and interests of deaf and hearing impaired people.
- The effectiveness of the communication modes used.
- The convenience of the library hours.
- Whether library use by one individual stimulates others in the deaf and hearing impaired community to use the library.

The same type of questions can be included concerning the negative aspects of library use to gain additional information about the program.

A detailed user evaluation of specific areas of the service can be acquired by asking questions about service or particular aspects of a service such as:

- TTY/TDD reference service.
- TTY/TDD story time.
- Telephone relay service.
- Captioned film collection.
- Captioned television in the library and/or through the lending of decoders.
- TTY/TDD accessibility to the user in the library and/or through loan.
- TTY/TDD news service.
- Accessibility and usability of amplified telephones and audio equipment.
- Signed story hours.
- Communication modes used.
- Directional signs and instructional materials.
- Overall accessibility of the library and its materials.
- Appropriateness of the collection to reading levels, needs, and interests.
- Programs developed for and by deaf and hearing impaired people.
- Displays and exhibits.

Throughout any evaluation of use, the library should focus on identified needs as set forth in the goals and objectives for the service. The measurement will then be directed in the progress made in achieving these goals and objectives. User activity will be measured as well as user satisfaction. To do this, both numbers and written or verbal statements can be a part of the evaluative process. A part of the survey can be statistical, and a part can be presented in essay form. The purpose of gathering this information is to gain data which assess the effectiveness of a program which is new and which has had a much shorter existence than other library programs. To use such evaluation methods means that it must be possible to gather this information from people who have a hearing loss. In some instances the data can be gathered from the total community. In others, because of the size of the population involved, it may be possible only to sample this special population. The information gathered will be supplemental to the regular statistical reporting system of the library.

Because there are so many areas of use to be examined in library service to deaf and hearing impaired people, librarians need to determine the specific areas of the total program they wish to evaluate in terms of effectiveness. Areas which can be used as the base for the survey are:

- Appropriateness of resources, materials, and equipment for deaf and hearing impaired individuals.
- Accessibility of the library and its program to the user.
- Communications available through the library staff and through visual directions and instructions.

Library users can be asked to assess their ability to find and use materials they want, to comment on the accessibility of the building, to assess their ability to communicate with staff members, to measure their ability to find the way independently through visual instruction and direction, and to assess the effectiveness of their 2-way communication with library staff.

MEASUREMENT OF THE SERVICE

Effective measurement of library service requires some knowledge of the people who come to the library. The knowledge of who uses the libary and when is of value. Also important is how long the visits are and what takes place during those visits. Through a brief questionnaire, a profile of the library users surveyed emerges. Responses to such questions as to what degree the user was satisfied during the visit and the length of time spent in the library can be very helpful in assessing program effectiveness. The time spent in the building affects the use of materials and equipment within the library, available seating space, and staffing needs. The use of materials both in circulation and within the library can be estimated through an outside-the-library count and an inside-the-library estimate. An accurate count can be made of the use of equipment designed especially for the deaf and hearing impaired individuals. It can be determined what equipment is being used on what days and at what times. Other areas of service can be described statistically through such questions as:

- How many reference questions were answered by TTY/TDD?
- How many captioned films were used?
- What other special materials were used and how many times?

Through these measures, library service can be assessed from many points; however, some areas of the service will remain unmeasured. These aspects can, for the most part, be estimated or their value assessed through observation.

Another area of the library service to deaf and hearing impaired people which requires periodic user evaluation is that of programing. Although certain aspects cannot be statistically determined, some can be described and the value of the total programing evaluated. The following are aspects of programing for deaf and hearing impaired people which can be measured:

- The number of programs presented.
- The variety of the programs.
- An estimate of the number of people served who have a hearing loss.
- The satisfaction level of the attendees.
- The number of organizations of and for the deaf and hearing impaired who use the library for meetings and programs.

Each program presented by the library for people with a hearing loss has a goal. Staff members can, through observation, ascertain the success of the program in relation to the goal. Some of the successes may come at a much later date. A signed story hour can be rated as immediately successful in relation to the established goals and objectives. Added benefits may come later when participants who are deaf become regular library users as a result of the story hour. Programs should be interpreted in a broad sense so that any formal activity of the library which is designated for and with deaf and hearing impaired people is included.

Through the overall measurement of the service's effectiveness on library usage, the following information can be compiled:

- Description of the user.
- The time of use.
- The satisfaction of the user.
- Outside-the-library use of special materials and special equipment.
- In-library use of special materials and special equipment.
- The kinds of special materials and equipment used.

Although only a partial profile of library usage will emerge, it will be an indicator of the program's effectiveness. From all of the data collected, a profile can be developed to be used in future decision making.

Why is it necessary to do a user study of library service to the deaf and hearing impaired? The study has, as its goal, the determination of the level of use, the pattern of that use, and the levels of service awareness among consumers and potential consumers. Through such knowledge, the success or nonsuccess of the service as presently constituted can be assessed. The results will also indicate that adjustments are needed in the resources, programs, services, equipment, facilities, staffing, public relations, communication, and interaction with individuals and organizations in the deaf and hearing impaired community.

The importance of such a survey to the continued existence of the service cannot be overemphasized. A pattern of short-term programs of library service to deaf and hearing impaired individuals has been developing since libraries became aware of the need for the service. Evaluative materials delineating the effectiveness of the service are essential to the increased longevity of the programs. A factor which must be included in evaluating a new program established to provide service to people with a hearing loss is that of time. The time span between the establishment of the program and the substantiated use will, in all probability, be longer than that for other types of service because of the communication barrier. Successful programs minimize this barrier, but it must be a recognized factor in measuring the effectiveness of the total program.

There will be a cost, in both staff time and additional funds, involved in any type of user survey developed. However, these costs can be kept to a minimum through careful planning with people who are deaf or hard of hearing. After a pattern of user evaluation has been established and tested, it can be reused periodically by the library, with modifications as necessary, to measure the effectiveness of the service in relation to the user. It is important in developing and using such a survey to know what information is wanted by the library, what information can be realistically gathered, and for what the information will be used. All of this will be determined based on what the library knows about the service and what it will find out in the regular course of business. The survey should be supplemental to information already gathered by the library on a continuing basis.

Administering the survey requires a broad knowledge of who the people are who are deaf or hard of hearing. Many individuals can be reached through organizations of and for deaf and hard-of-hearing people. Churches, rehabilitation agencies, schools, senior citizen centers, and other local formal groups can be selected for dissemination of survey materials. Articles about the survey in the local newspapers will inform people about it. In addition, information can be included in library leaflets and brochures and other publications. If nonusers of the library are to be surveyed also, the same methods can be used. An especially good channel to pass information through is local publications of organizations for and of deaf and hearing impaired people as well as those of agencies serving this group. The survey can be effectively highlighted in these publications. With wide and effective publicity, the library can be successful in encouraging deaf and hearing impaired people to request the survey form. If the forms are easily available in the library and at other distribution points, a large part of the population will be included. Such an approach will broaden participation in the survey. Other agencies and organizations related to people with a hearing loss can be helpful in compiling data received by the library and in interpreting it. The results of the survey should be made available to the deaf and hearing impaired community as soon as possible after the results have been compiled so that they can react to the results while the survey is still fresh in their minds. It also will provide a useful method of letting all people know of the service and how it is being used. If the use appears to justify the cost in time and money, the service will be considered essential. If the results are less than positive, the service will be viewed as marginal. It will then require the creativity of the library, the deaf and hearing impaired community, and the organizations and agencies involved to determine how the program can be redesigned to make it essential in the lives of the people it serves and essential to the library management.

Through the assessment of the use and nonuse, the library can explore alternative methods of providing service to people who are deaf or hard of hearing. It is important to compile information immediately because it is a reflection of the present and will soon become dated as changes take place in the library and in the community. The reporting should not be complicated in its sentence structure and difficult in its vocabulary but should be at a reading level acceptable to all. The reporting will need to appeal to several audiences and may need to be issued in several formats. It is important to highlight the results which are most important for people to know.

The survey can be done by the library itself, or it can be conducted by an outside consultant. Because the evaluation of the service is a continuous process, the library staff will be involved with this activity on a continuing basis. The broader evaluation conducted on a periodic basis, which includes formal recommendations, may well be done by an outside agency or person. An outside evaluation at regular intervals adds a new, objective approach to the review of the service and the use made of it by the people by and for whom it was developed. Such an evaluation will assist in determining this service's present status and future direction by those who have not been previously involved with the program. The goals and objectives will be assessed as well as the success of the service from the viewpoint of the user. It will be determined, also, why nonusers are not availing themselves of a library service specifically designed to meet their needs and interests. The evaluation should be constructed so it will tell library management how well the service is fulfilling its present goals and objectives and what new directions should be considered in the next given time span.

In summarizing the results of the survey, noting the major points of agreement of the users with the service offered is an effective way of presenting the outcome of the survey. A second summary can be developed stating some of the areas of concern with the service as presented by the users. It can be assumed that, with most library services, the users as a group will overwhelmingly favor certain components of the service. It can also be assumed that some components of the service will be questioned and suggestions made for modification of the services and additional or alternative services. The library and the advisory group need to turn their attention to these areas. These concerns may not represent disagreement with the service so much as doubt that all needs are being met by it in its present form. Both summaries should be carefully considered by the library and by the advisory group.

A part of the evaluation will determine how well each part of the service is operating in practice and discover where problems have developed and why. The evaluation will also determine the degree of success obtained with the service's present goals and objectives. Once this has been accomplished, a recycling program can begin to determine the validity of the goals and objectives. When this has been accomplished, additional emphasis can be given to those parts of the program which have been less than successful.

Such an evaluation of the users and nonusers of the serivce will not truly assure that a measure has been taken of the service's educational, informational, recreational, and cultural benefits. The only way in which it will is by measuring the degree to which the goals and objectives are being met. It can be presumed that the goals and objectives of the service are of an educational, recreational, informational, and cultural nature. To the degree that they are being met, the library user is benefitting, and the library can estimate or infer a great deal about those social and individual benefits. Also, through the evaluation, the service can reflect more accurately the wishes of the consumer and the potential consumer. This can be accomplished when the library and the advisory group respond to the results of the survey by accommodating the preferences of the public being served—people with a hearing loss.

ASSESSING THE RESULTS

It is necessary to assess the achievements of the library service to deaf and hearing impaired people as the program develops over time. Through such an evaluation, this new program can become responsive to the people throughout the process of establishing it as a permanent program. The efficiency of the program, its effectiveness in making the service available to the people concerned, as well as its impact on the community served, are all a part of the total service. The library management should know, at any given time, the following facts, obtained from the continuous evaluation:

- How well the service is meeting the needs of the people.
- How accessible the service is to the people.
- How active the program is in seeking out the people who need and want the service.
- How many people are using the service.
- What the satisfaction level of the user is.

In its effort to achieve these goals, the library can rate each component of the service program as follows: 1–2 below average; 3–4 average; and 5– above average. From such a rating, the total program can be assessed. Each part can be examined, also, to see how it can be improved, eliminated if not necessary, or substituted with an alternate means if deemed to be a necessary service.

The importance of knowing the total effectiveness of a library service to the deaf and hearing impaired, on a continuing basis, is essential to a successful program. It is mandatory if the service is to be maintained on a permanent basis that the uses and benefits be known in relation to the cost of the service. Many programs have been developed throughout the United States, established and operated for the period of the grant funding, but have not been maintained as permanent services. For the service to flourish as it should, to accommodate the people who have a hearing loss, and to be responsive in their needs requires a continuing knowledge that the service is accomplishing its goal. If the service is begun as a grant project, it is essential that the evaluation be continuing. The library cannot wait until the close of the project to do an evaluation if that project is to be of continuing benefit to the people it is designed to serve. At any time, any part of the service that is not producing desired results should be redesigned. The refinement can take place at any point along the time line of the project before the end is reached.

MAKING A REPORT

A useful report reflects the effectiveness of the program provided in relation to the ultimate goals and objectives. Such a report undoubtedly will find some parts of the project rejected or in need of major recycling. If the entire report is favorable, the service will be retained as is, and the findings will be considered in the ongoing evaluations and in subsequent periodic ones.

PLANNING AND IMPLEMENTING THE EVALUATION

Specific points which should be incorporated in planning and implementing an evaluation are the following:

- Evaluation should involve consumers of the library services to the deaf and hearing impaired.
- The advisory group—a citizen group—should have a clearly defined role in the evaluation process and have adequate background information.
- The library must go out to the consumer and potential consumer to secure an adequate assessment of how service is progressing.

- The people who are involved in the evaluation from the beginning should be involved in the implementation of the evaluation recommendations.
- Adequate time should be blocked out for the evaluation to allow for the involvement of many groups of people in the assessment of the services.
- Simple data collection and analysis methods should be used which are easy to understand and self-explanatory.
- Information should be integrated with routine program activities whenever possible so that the data are current and always available.
- Subject analysis of the program should be used to fill out areas where data gathering and analysis are not possible to accomplish.
- The information acquired should be understandable and meaningful to the decision makers.

Because the use of an effective evaluation is as important as the results themselves, a library should provide training in evaluation for staff members. In addition, a specialist in evaluation should be employed on a periodic or retainer basis. The evaluation must have acceptance and credibility to be of value to decision makers, and the results of the report should be understandable to all people concerned.

One effect of such an evaluation report will be to ensure informed decision making concerning the status of library service to deaf and hearing impaired people. When the original planning of this library service has been effectively accomplished, continued and periodic evaluations will allow the library to adapt to changing situations and rectify errors in the original plans. It will also provide the information needed in time of crisis. If budgetary problems arise which result in decisions to cut back on services, the data acquired in the evaluations can substantiate the need for the service. It can also indicate how the program can be maintained at a lesser cost since the priorities of the users of the service will be known. If the library is examining its priorities for a reordering, the evaluation report will indicate that the service is high among the priorities of the deaf and hearing impaired community. Through such an indication, the service can remain high on the list of priorities of the library.

To achieve such a status, however, the service must be well planned and well executed. It must show positive use and positive benefits by and to the deaf and hearing impaired. The one element for library management to consider in the program of service is time. When a population has been neglected as far as library service is concerned, the members of that group will not immediately begin using the library as soon as it opens its doors. The development of a pattern of library use is slow to occur even though the service may be excellent and the publicity widespread. It may be necessary to subsidize the service for a period of time before it becomes cost-effective. Intensive programs provided by grants do provide the opportunity to experiment with innovative services or to establish services for the first time, using those services which have proved effective in other libraries.

All of these projects add to our body of knowledge concerning library service to deaf and hearing impaired people. Such projects are needed because for such a long period of time, library service, outside of schools for the deaf, did not exist. It is through such projects, usually funded by grants, that librarians now know how to set up a program, what components to provide, and how to proceed in making the service possible.

The problems which arise, however, from this approach are many. Probably the most serious one is that of providing excellent library service to the deaf and hearing impaired in a locality for a period of time and then having it cut off entirely or reduced to a minimal and/or diffused service. Such an approach raises people's expectations, meets those expectations for a period of time but does not provide an acceptable level of continuing service or any service at all. An evaluation cannot prevent this from happening; some programs which are excellent in terms of concept, planning, and implementation have not continued for a variety of reasons. The evaluations can, however, give the program a better chance of survival if a continuing refinement has taken place during its established lifetime.

When the time comes to decide whether to continue the program or not, the people making the ultimate decision will have data on which to make an informed decision. Throughout all of the programs of library service to deaf and hearing impaired people which have been established, some evaluation has been done concerning the components of the programs. Many of these evaluations have taken place in the area of education. Some evaluations have been made of entire programs. These have been done primarily to meet requirements made by funding sources when the programs have been funded initially, all or in part, by grants. All of these evaluations provide valuable information on approaches to be used, services to establish, resources to buy, and technologies to use.

If the program is started as a part of the total library service, using the continuing budget as its support, the use of evaluation is just as important as with grant funds. The program of library service to the deaf and hearing impaired must be, in the long run, just as cost-effective as any other program in the library. To be considered a basic library program, it must, on a continuing basis, operate under the same constraints and the same opportunities as all other continuing programs. A difference does exist initially, however, in that deaf and hearing impaired people are, for the most part, members of a group who do not use the library. From past experience with the library and with other service agencies, many are convinced that libraries cannot provide them with information and recreation in a form they can use and enjoy. They will use the library only if they have a part in making its resources and services appropriate to their use. Even then, the development of a pattern of service will be slow.

Granting agencies need to also have an evaluation of the services, resources, equipment, and facilities provided to the deaf and hearing impaired as a result of the funds provided by that agency. Such an evaluation may include the measurement of input as well as output. This would then include assessments of the total number of materials, number per capita, and other statistical measurements in addition to information about usage levels and the satisfaction of the user. A measure of nonuse of the library in relation to the potential of users is also often needed.

An important result of an evaluation is that of relevant planning. In the original planning for a new service, many of the decisions were made on conjecture and were, of necessity, hypothetical. Even with the most representative and informed advisory committee assisting in the developmental stages, this will be true. A survey of the deaf and hearing impaired will result in decisions which have more validity than they would have had without it. However, much still remains unknown until it has been tested. The planners can still only project what the needs and interest will be and how the service will affect the community. They can only estimate what the use will be and have little basis for estimating user satisfaction. The relative effectiveness of the components of the service can be predicted, primarily, from the experiences of other libraries in providing the specific parts of the service.

After continuing and periodic evaluations have taken place, planning can be done with greater confidence, now that something is known of the users and the nonusers. Their satisfaction or dissatisfaction with the service will be somewhat predictable now, based on past experience. The service has been modified and alternatives have been employed as a result of an evaluation indicating that another method is needed. When an evaluation of the overall service and of its parts has been completed, librarians and the advisory group can work with the entire service and its components to move ahead in this cycle of developing a library service which is appropriate to the needs of deaf and hearing impaired people.

REFERENCE LIST

Beeler, M. G. Faucher, et. al. *Measuring the Quality of Library Service: A Handbook.* Metuchen, NJ: Scarecrow Press, 1974.

DeProspo, Ernest R.; Altman, Ellen; and Beasley, Kenneth. *Performance Measures for Public Libraries.* Public Library Association. Chicago: American Library Association, 1973.

Dugdale, Sharon, and Vogel, Patty. "Computer-Based Instruction for Hearing Impaired Children in the Classroom." In *The Mainstreamed Library: Issues, Ideas, Innovations,* edited by Barbara H. Baskin and Karen H. Harris. Chicago: American Library Association, 1982: 162–72.

Guba, Egon G., and Stufflebeam, Daniel L. *Strategies for the Institutionalization of the CIPP Evaluation Model.* Columbus, OH: The Ohio State University Evaluation Center, 1970.

Lancaster, F. W. *The Measurement and Evaluation of Library Service.* Washington, DC: Information Resources Press, 1977.

Murphy, Marcy. "Measuring Library Effectiveness: A Prelude to Change." *Special Libraries* 70 (1) (January 1979): 18–25.

Public Management Institute. *Evaluation Handbook.* San Francisco, CA: Public Management Institute, 1982.

Serving Deaf Students in Academic Libraries. Association of Specialized and Cooperative Library Agencies, Library Service to the Deaf Section; and the Association of College and Research Libraries, Community and Junior College Libraries Section. American Library Association Annual Conference in Los Angeles, 1983. Chicago: American Library Association, 1983. (Cassettes.)

Weiss, Carol. *Evaluting Action Programs.* Boston: Allyn and Bacon, Inc, 1972.

Wood, Judith B.; Bremer, Julius J.; and Saraidaridis, Susan A. "Measurement of Service at a Public Library." *Public Library Quarterly* 2 (2) (Summer 1980): 49–57.

Zweizig, Douglas, and Rodger, Eleanor Jo. *Output Measures for Public Libraries.* Chicago: American Library Association, 1982.

Chapter 20
Planning through Evaluation

The relationship between the evaluation of the users, nonusers, and the program to that of planning is a direct and valuable one. With both the organization providing the service and the users of that service participating in the assessment, the planning by these groups is a natural outgrowth of the evaluation. It is a part of the cycle of planning-evaluation-planning. The results of both continuous and periodic evaluation of the program of library service to the deaf and hearing impaired should be used to make the program relevant to the needs and wants of those people.

The information discovered in the assessment is essential to raising the level of the effectiveness of the program. It can also be used to inform others about the value of the program and its relevance to the deaf and hearing impaired community. Such planning will take time and well-developed methods to accomplish changes which will result in satisfying service to the users. The library and the community must be realistic about how much can be accomplished and in what time frame. The results of the evaluation should be approached creatively, also, so that the planning for the future will improve on that of the past. Using the evaluation to improve the program helps to ensure that the services provided are actively used and found to be satisfying and of value. A program of service can never be perfect; however, it should be one which can be justified as a program which deaf and hearing impaired people consider to be important in their lives, indicating that the service is worth the funds used in supporting it.

It is important for the library staff not to become discouraged by negative findings in the evaluation. Negative findings are just as important to improved service as positive findings. If the findings indicate that few people are making use of the TTY/TDD either within the library or through loan, the library staff needs to find out the cause of the low use and make changes in the service which will result in an increasing level of use. The library staff and the community can then monitor the program to see whether the nonuse pattern will return or whether the program will develop as an essential one. If the attendance at the signed story hour is smaller than it should be for the number of deaf and hearing impaired children in the library's area of service, the library can determine why this is the case and at the same time, determine whether the number of children in attendance is a true measure of the importance of the story hour.

At this point in the development of the service, it may be that the measure of accomplishment is the very existence of the program even though the attendance is small. If few people are using the TTY/TDD to ask reference questions, the library can develop a program which gives people information on the kinds of questions the library can answer. Positive results are easier to build on than negative because only improvement or accommodation is needed. If the people are enthusiastic about captioned films but specify changes they would like to see in the program such as frequency of showings, hours and days of showings, and subjects covered, the library administration and staff have information on which they can take action to meet the needs and wishes. If the users like the library's directional signs and instructional material but would like some changes or additions, the library can consider the requests and act on the information provided.

IMPLEMENTING THE SURVEY

There will be conflicting responses in many areas. The library needs to resolve any conflicts before action is taken on the recommendations. In all of the changes made in the program of service, the expectations of the library and of the consumers should remain realistic. Some changes can be accomplished immediately. Other changes may require a waiting period because they cannot be initiated until the new fiscal year. Those making the decisions may not wish to use all of the evaluation data at one particular time. If the data will remain relevant for a period of time, it need not be used right away. As a result, information from the evaluation can be used at many points in the long-term planning process.

In the planning for library service to people with a hearing loss, the information gained from evaluation will undoubtedly be new data. Therefore, it will take time, in some instances, to determine its value and to reconcile it with information from other sources which may be conflicting. The purpose of the evaluation is to provide information to help guide future actions concerning library service to the deaf and hearing impaired.

Using the evaluation findings will be easier if data on the potential users have been gathered before, as well as after, the library service has been implemented. If that information is not available, it will be difficult to reconstruct what existed before the program began. A comparison of the 2 sets of data will be valuable in the redesigning of the service.

A comparison of user satisfaction as indicated by the evaluation outcomes can be made with that of other services in the community. The user level of satisfaction with services such as recreation, rehabilitation, and public transit can be compared with the level indicated for the library. This comparison can assist in determining whether the facts gained in the evaluation concerning user satisfaction follow a pattern of satisfaction and dissatisfaction with other services in the community.

The availability of preimplementation data concerning potential consumers of the service will make the postimplementation evaluative data more reliable. In reviewing the evaluative data before application to the program already in place, it is important to compare the preprogram and postprogram evaluation outcomes. This, in addition to the comparative evaluation data from other service programs with similar goals and objectives, can provide a basis for judging the level of the satisfaction of the user with the program of library service to the deaf and hearing impaired.

In working toward the goal of increasing the effectiveness of library service to people with a hearing loss, the library decision makers should be concerned with those aspects of the service which may require changes in design and changes in direction. They should also consider those parts of programs in which changes need to be made to reach goals and objectives. It is important to consider which accommodations will have the most influence on the goals and objectives of the entire program. For example, it may be that a change in the library hours will have a beneficial effect on the use of the library and on the level of user satisfaction.

Sometimes a conflict will exist between a change which is certain to increase both the use of the program and the user satisfaction but is infeasible for implementation. It may be that the evaluative data indicate that a doubling of the number of captioned films would be of great assistance in reaching the goals and objectives of the program. However, in the process of planning, the decision makers may find that such an increase is not feasible for a variety of reasons, such as scarcity of staff and a conflict with other film showings which are of importance to the goals and objectives of the library's program of service. The planners must then determine whether any modification of the number of captioned films will be effective in increasing user satisfaction with that part of the program of service. This must be done in relation to a consideration of other programs which may be adversely affected by the decision. They must also ascertain whether the constraints cited in the evaluation data concerning staff and other programs are valid ones. It may be necessary for the library to go back to the consumers with the data from the evaluation to determine the priorities which should be used as a guide in determining the changes to be made, those which should be made in modified form, and those which should be avoided. They can be asked to rate the possible changes in relation to whether they would use or not use them or make modified use of them.

Such a determination needs to be repeated periodically because changes take place both in the library and in the community. Opinions, too, change within the same people and within the same group. It is important for the planners to know where they should apply resources and funds. It is essential, also, to know when to use an alternative procedure to improve the effectiveness of the service.

THE PLANNING PROCESS

During the planning process, it is important for those who are making decisions concerning library service to the deaf and hearing impaired to know the current status of the service and where it should go in the future. Some of the questions to be asked about the planning for the future include the following:

- What is the service accomplishing for the deaf or hard-of-hearing user?
- What proportion of the library funding and time should be allocated to this service?
- What determines whether individuals will decide to use the library, will decide not to use it, or will never consider use as a possibility?
- How can library service to people with a hearing loss best be evaluated on a monitoring and/or periodic basis?
- To what extent is the program serving individuals in the deaf and hearing impaired community, such as oralists (lip readers), American Sign Language users, bilingual language users-ASL/English, deaf individuals, hard-of-hearing individuals, elderly people with a hearing loss, children with a hearing

loss, hearing people with deaf or hard-of-hearing family members, and hearing employers of deaf and hard-of-hearing individuals?

- To what extent does the library have service or access to service appropriate to specific needs of all deaf and hearing impaired individuals?
- To what degree should the library design its programs to dovetail with programs of other service agenices to the deaf and hearing impaired on the local level?
- How can these services be provided effectively on a cooperative basis with other libraries in the area regardless of type of library?

A strategic part of the planning is to develop the practical and realistic steps necessary to achieve the purpose for which the service was originally developed. These strategies, if carefully designed, will bring about the desired modifications in the service. It is during this part of the planning that alternatives should be considered in making the service relevant to the needs and desires of the people it serves.

In small libraries, the planning can rapidly integrate changes indicated by the evaluation results into the present service. In larger libraries, the process will take longer but should be expedited so that consumers can benefit immediately from the assessment. Communication will continue to be predominant among library management, library staff, and the deaf and hearing impaired because of the involvement of all in the evaluation process.

This pattern can be carried easily into the redesigning and refinement of the service when carried out as part of the planning cycle. It brings together the people who are essential to the service. Such an effective situation will result when the decision makers use the outcomes of the evaluation in setting future directions for the library programs already in action. There is need to rethink the programs of service so that any changes made are those which allocate resources effectively and channel them to the user realistically. When the evaluations are done on a continuing basis, along with periodic evaluations, the changes will be less drastic than when evaluations are done less frequently. In most instances, the program of library service will be relatively new and amenable to modification without undue disruption of other programs. Through the recommendations provided in the evaluation, the decision makers will have guidance in the replanning for more effective library service to the deaf and hearing impaired.

COMMUNITY INVOLVEMENT

All those involved in the evaluation process should also be involved in the planning process so that the resulting service will reach all deaf and hearing impaired people in appropriate form and with satisfying results. Many methods can be used to ensure that the planning reflects the consumers' wants and needs.

One method is for the library and the library advisory group to the library service to the deaf and hearing impaired to develop plans for a community meeting after the results of the evaluation have been widely disseminated and publicized. Such a meeting should focus on how the results can become a part of the service and what the new service should look like. The meeting should involve as much community participation as possible with appropriate interpreters and examples of the new technology available. The meeting should be as free as possible of communication barriers so that thoughts can be freely exchanged. All people who are deaf or hard of hearing should have information about the date, place, and subject of the meeting as should other people with an interest in deafness and hearing impairment. The recommendations of the evaluation should be available at the meeting as a basis for discussion and conclusions.

In a community which has a small number of deaf and hearing impaired people, the attendees at the meeting can act as a committee of the whole and work in one group. This group, along with the library and advisory group, can look critically at the recommendations from the evaluations and decide where, in their opinion, changes should be made to achieve a more effective service. In large communities where interests are diverse and capabilities are many, the large group, after an initial general presentation of the recommendations, should disperse into predetermined subject groups to discuss the issues in which they have recognized competencies or which are important to them. After these groups have examined the issues thoroughly, resolved problems, and have developed a course of action with a time frame for accomplishment, they should report back to the entire meeting. The reports can be summarized and incorporated into a document for planning action.

Through this means, the library will have a statement from which it can plan a more effective service. Additional meetings may be required to develop the strategies further, but they should be kept to a minimum in the interest of time. It is important that the results of the evaluation and the planning are put into effect as soon as possible. Such involvement of consumers and potential consumers is most important in this type of service because librarians need guidance in effectively serving the members of a population group which have had little recognition as a library consumer group.

A more formal type of involvement of deaf and hearing impaired people in the community in the planning can result from an invitational meeting. The library and the advisory group should determine who, among the population group to be served and other interested people, should be invited. The purpose of the meeting is to acquire guidance in using the evaluation outcomes to bring about changes which will make the program more effective. A cross section of the people involved should make up the group. A meeting with as many as 50 participants can work effectively with one leader and appropriate interpreters. The group members in this type of meeting will relate more closely with the leader than with each other.

Each person invited should receive the written results of the evaluation outcome and a brief description of the present program prior to the meeting. The question to be addressed is: How can the library serve deaf and hearing impaired people more effectively? These 2 documents will be the basis for comments from the participants—comments that should be directed toward coming up with a plan of action. A definite time limit should be set for the meeting (such as 2 hours); within that time, each member of the group should be given an opportunity to comment to the leader concerning what should be done to improve service. If there is time, members of the group can then make additional suggestions to the leader. When suggestions are made for a specific course of action to be taken, the group member making the suggestions should provide written material describing the changes to be made, the alternate services to be provided, or other information relevant to the program. A time period of not more than one week should be allowed for members of the group to send to the library, in writing, further suggestions or comments concerning the service. A written document should evolve from the meeting, which will form the basis for the plan of action.

A completely formal approach involves the employment of a planning consultant and an advisory planning group. This group should study the outcomes of the evaluation and develop a planning document(s) for the library's use. Through a series of 3–4 meetings, the planning group and library management should review and redirect the mission of the service itself or its components. They should also review goals and objectives. If new objectives are developed, the planning group and library management should make sure that they are measurable in time and/or performance. In developing the total plan, the library, the library staff, and the deaf and hearing impaired should be involved. They should have the opportunity to interact with each other concerning the mission, goals, and objectives.

PLAN OF ACTION

The action plan itself should be developed through the cooperative efforts of all 3 groups. Those members of library management involved with the service and staff members of the service should individually develop the strategies needed to accomplish the changes deemed necessary by the evaluation. The members should work in their own areas of responsibility for the service. After the review of the mission, goals, and statement of objectives, the staff members should develop the strategies necessary to achieve the goals and objectives. The strategies are a set of options or activities to improve the library service to the deaf and hearing impaired. The strategies are the alternatives which can be used in developing the action plan. To determine whether a strategy is appropriate to the objective supported, the following considerations should be reviewed:

- The contribution of the activity to the goals and objectives.
- The cost in staff time and other resources.
- Its effect on other services and programs of the total library program.

Such a development of strategies will provide the options from which activities can be selected to achieve the purpose of the programs of service. The costs in money and in other resources should be considered, and the activity should be examined as to its effect on programs already in place and successful, on the total program, and on other changes in programing. A time frame should also be included in the strategy for putting the activity into effect and in measuring its achievements. When the development of strategies has been completed, the library management, the planning group, and the staff should meet together to develop the written plan. When completed, it will consist of a mission statement for the service and a set of goals within the mission. For each goal, there should be an objective or set of objectives. Each objective should be measurable by number, degree, and/or time. The action plan will then include the following:

- The mission statement, which includes information concerning the people the program is serving and the kinds of services provided.

- The goals, which are the ends toward which the service should move to accomplish the mission.
- The objectives, which are specific and measurable activities designed to fulfill the goals. They indicate the particular outcomes desired and how their achievement will be measured.

REDESIGNING THE SERVICE

The action plan redesigning the service should be accomplished within 2 months after the evaluation outcomes are known. It is important to follow such a time schedule so that the momentum begun by the evaluation will be maintained.

From each approach to the planning, a new design for the program of service will evolve. This design becomes the current plan for action. The plan, whether for one year or 5 years, should be available in writing so that the library management, advisory committee, and the staff will have a guide for the next time span of the service. Such a document will assist in monitoring progress toward the goals and objectives. In order that all who were involved in the evaluation and planning know how the plan has been developed, a summary should be available in leaflet form for everyone—especially for people in the deaf and hearing impaired community. Copies of the total plan should be available in the library, also, for anyone to review or take home for study. Many other approaches to planning can be used, but it is important, whatever approach is used, to involve the consumer in the evaluation and in the planning. The depth and breadth of involvement in the redesigning of the service will need to be decided by each library in relation to the size of the community and the complexity of the organization providing the service.

Areas of service and programs which should be considered in the redesigning of the service are those in which deaf and hearing impaired people are adversely affected in their everyday lives. These undoubtedly will be indicated in the evaluation outcomes. If they are not, they should still receive consideration by the staff and the advisory group. The following areas should receive special attention:

- Information for parents of deaf or hard-of-hearing children.
- Careers for people who are deaf or hard of hearing.
- Education for people with a hearing loss.
- Employment for people who have hearing difficulty.
- Legislation related to deafness and hearing impairment.
- Deaf studies.

In the majority of these areas, currentness is all important. Even though these concerns have been a part of the total service from the beginning, they are so important that each should be reviewed in relation to the appropriateness of the materials and effectiveness of the service.

In the area of library information available to parents of deaf or hard-of-hearing children, the library should involve the parents in the development and design of the program. This should include their participation in the development of any service program, in the setting of goals and objectives, and in determining the means for reaching them. Parents can assist in the planning for meeting the needs of education and recreation for the children, also. There should not be just one voice in this planning group; librarians will need to work with parents to determine what should be accomplished and what can be accomplished. Together they must establish priorities as well as resolve differences.

Careers are now broadening for people who are deaf or hard of hearing. As new opportunities open, libraries should make sure that related materials are available. A career service can be developed with deaf and hearing impaired young people, with educators, with people in the field of career development, and with people who have been successful in a variety of careers. The materials in the collection should range from pamphlets and catalogs to books and films. Seminars and workshops on careers should be a high priority in this area of service. In such a meeting, special attention should be paid to providing the opportunities for asking questions and to examine materials relating to careers in general and to specific careers. This will greatly enhance the service for young people and for adults who are changing careers.

Closely allied to career materials are educational materials. Because many people will not go on to college, materials on education should include secondary school materials and materials concerning technical and professional schools. The range of choices in colleges and universities has been increasing rapidly in the last several years. Catalogs from all colleges for deaf and hearing impaired students should be included in the collection. These should include colleges which provide support services even though they may have a small enrollment of students with a hearing loss. In planning such a program of service to students, the students themselves should develop plans for the service and be involved in its implementation from the beginning. Local educators should also become a part of the planning group.

Employment is of high concern to many deaf and hearing impaired people. Underemployment is also a serious problem. Business and industry have begun to recognize the abilities of deaf and hearing impaired people and to accommodate to any special needs they may have on the job. The advancements in technology broaden the employment opportunities for people with a hearing loss. Again, the participation of deaf and hearing impaired people in developing a program in this area is essential. Important as participants, also, are employers from business, industry, services, and government. The plan for developing a service for employment does not include placement of people in jobs but rather provides them with materials which show them what is possible and what is available in the job market.

Legislation—both favorable and unfavorable—at all levels of government has been important in the past to people with a hearing loss. It will undoubtedly continue to be important. Along with the legislation itself are regulations which implement the laws and which affect the lives of hearing impaired and deaf people. Because this is an unexplored area, for the most part, for people with a hearing loss, they may not be as familiar with the means of securing desired legislation and defeating unwanted legislation as are the people in the agencies which serve them. Providing service in this area can offer new opportunities for the deaf and hearing impaired to be effective in the legislative process. Librarians should become familiar with laws and regulations which apply to people who are deaf and hearing impaired. It is important, too, that they know the laws that affect people with other disabilities because deaf and hearing impaired people are often included in such broader legislation. Information on federal, state, and local laws, as well as regulations and ordinances, should be kept current. Deaf and hearing impaired people, advocates for the deaf, people in agencies serving the deaf, legislators, city and county commissioners, and other public officials will all be of value in the planning and implementation process.

Advocacy is relatively new in the lives of deaf and hearing impaired people. It is, however, important in effecting changes in services, legislation, and other aspects of the day-to-day living of people who have a hearing loss. Deaf and hearing impaired people will be helpful in planning this service, but other people and other groups which have long been involved in advocacy are necessary to give it the strength it needs. The thrust of advocacy is ever-changing as is the approach which advocates take in relation to issues. This area is one where currentness is of great importance to the effectiveness of the program.

An aspect of service in which the past is as important, or more so, than the present or future is that of deaf studies. While every library will not want or need to be involved in deaf studies, at least one library in a community should be able to provide people who are deaf with information on their heritage. Planning for this service should involve both people who are deaf and hearing impaired and historians. The field has not yet developed on a broad basis among libraries; many libraries will be entering into a new and important area of service. This is one type of planning which may well go beyond one particular library or type of library. It is particularly well adapted to cooperative planning and implementation. All planning should be done in relation to larger collections in other libraries which are accessible.

REVIEW OF THE PLAN

In all of the planning it is necessary to:

- View the service in relation to other services needed.
- Identify the services that can be modified or which are new.
- Evaluate the alternatives which could be used.
- Develop the services and resources selected.

The plan should be compatible with the overall mission of the library and should be incorporated into the complete library plan. Such planning will demonstrate that the library service to the deaf and hearing impaired is a part of the mission of the library—to provide library service to all people in its service area. The financial details should be incorporated in the budget document of the library. If outside funding is required in addition to the ongoing library budget, the plan for library service to the deaf and hearing impaired can become the basis for a grant proposal. Because of its positive impact on library service to the deaf and hearing impaired, the planning-evaluating-planning method is of vital importance in the developing of this service. The planning for each component should include the following:

- Program goals—purpose of the service.
- General means of how these programs for the service can be accomplished.
- Objectives—measurable by amount, degree, and/or time.
- Description of current program—what exists now.
- Description of future program—what is planned.
- Major activities of the program.
- Plan for implementing each major activity.
- Other activities of the program with statements of time of accomplishment.

Dynamic leadership needs to be involved in all aspects of the total library planning with as broad as possible participation by the user and the potential user. Evaluation and planning as included in these chapters are designed to improve the services offered. These activities should have, as a by-product, a continued high degree of involvement of people with a hearing loss.

An advisory group which truly represents the deaf and hearing impaired community enables the library to obtain an objective view of how to revitalize a library program through new activities and modification of established ones. The involvement of the advisory committee and the community in the development of the evaluation is all important as is their involvement in acting on the evaluation recommendations for the future. Keeping what is good from the past is just as important as eliminating that which has been less than effective and making accommodations in those services which need to be changed. By discovering ways to improve on the original plan of service, more and more people will become committed to it. As a result, the service can have increased vitality and become more realistic and effective than it would have been with less involvement by the deaf population. It is possible that, after the evaluation participation, the people in the deaf and hard-of-hearing community will take the initiative to get involved in the planning. If they do, the library should welcome them eagerly. With total community involvement, the library has a built-in support for the program's goals and objectives.

It is important, also, for the library to inform the community in general about plans for service to the deaf and hearing impaired. Governmental bodies should be included in this publicity program as should business, industry, and service organizations. Public relations should include, also, people in the political field and in labor and management. In presenting the informational programs, speakers from the library and from the community it serves should be readily available to groups and organizations. Through a widespread publicity effort, nonlibrary users will become aware of the library and its service to the deaf and hearing impaired. Parents of deaf and hearing impaired children may also become interested in a program of which they did not have prior knowledge. Community apathy can be turned into community support through such an informational program.

Meeting the library needs of deaf and hearing impaired people is not easy. It will continue to be ever-changing while effective methods of service continue to be explored. The changing technology is also an important factor because of its strong impact in this area of library service. User satisfaction with the service will also be a factor in the development and growth of the program. When the evaluation indicates there is need to make changes in service because of the level of user satisfaction, the library can make those changes.

The program of library service to the deaf and hearing impaired should have as its concern the individual. This is true whether that individual is a library user or a nonuser. The informational and recreational library needs of all the people in the deaf and hearing impaired community should be the concern of the library. So that individuals will use the library to its fullest extent, education in library use is needed for all people in the deaf and hearing impaired community. The library must become and remain current on how libraries can update services. They have an ongoing responsibility to be aware of ways in which they can provide a more satisfying service to people with a hearing loss. The users will know best what their needs and wants are. The librarian should know the resources available to meet those needs and wants and how to provide them so that the people can use them.

Deaf and hearing impaired people need to know that the library has something of value for them and in a form they can use and enjoy. Special funds have provided the largest part of the funding of library service to hearing impaired and deaf people. Through emphasis on evaluation and planning, librarians will be better able to determine how these special projects can become an integral part of library service. When the acceptance of library service to deaf and hearing impaired people is seen as an essential part of library service, planning and evaluation will have played a major part in establishing a level of service that becomes the standard rather than the exception.

REFERENCE LIST

Ackoff, R. L. *Redesigning the Future.* New York: John Wiley and Sons, 1974.

Attkisson, C., et al., eds. *Evaluation of Human Services Programs.* New York: Academic Press, 1978.

Campbell, H. C. "Methods of Evaluation of Public Library Systems." *Public Library Quarterly* 2 (2) (Summer 1980): 35–48.

Detweiler, Mary Jo. "Planning is More Than a Process." *Library Journal* 108 (January 1, 1983): 23–26.

Drucker, Peter. *Management: Tasks, Responsibilities and Practices.* New York: Harper and Row, 1974.

Institute of Governmental Research. *Project: Close Gap.* Seattle, WA: University of Washington, 1978.

Jackson County Library System. *Goals Report.* Medford, OR: Jackson County Library System, 1979.

Miller, Edward P. "User-Oriented Planning" *Special Libraries* 64 (11) (November 1973): 479–82.

Norton, Alice. "Public Relations—Its Meaning and Benefits." In *Local Public Library Administration*, edited by Ellen Altman, pp. 47–60. Chicago: American Library Association, 1980.

Oklahoma Department of Libraries. *Statewide Performance Guidelines for Oklahoma Public Libraries.* Oklahoma City, OK: Oklahoma Department of Libraries, 1982.

————.*Performance Measures for Oklahoma Public Libraries.* Oklahoma City, OK: Oklahoma Department of Libraries, 1982.

Palmour, Vernon E.; Bellassai, Marcia; and DeWath, Nancy V. *A Planning Process.* (Public Library Association). Chicago: American Library Association, 1980.

Shaw, Jane B. "How Do I Get from Today to Tomorrow?" *Illinois Libraries* 66 (3) (May 1984): 226–29.

Zweizig, Douglas L. "Community Analysis." In *Local Public Library Administration*, edited by Ellen Altman, pp. 38–46. Chicago: American Library Association, 1980.

Part V: Potential for Library Service to the Deaf and Hearing Impaired

Chapter 21
Factors to Be Considered in the Future of the Service

In comparison with many other library programs, library service to the deaf and hearing impaired individual is in the infant stage. Although an estimated 7 percent of the population have a hearing impairment, ways to provide library resources in a form in which people with a hearing loss can use them have developed slowly. In some areas of the United States, the problem has even yet to be considered. In others, some attempt is being made to provide the service. In a few libraries, a program exists which is as fully developed as programs of service to hearing people and is funded through the ongoing library budget. For the most part, however, the goal of providing library service to nonhearing people equal to that for hearing people universally has not yet been achieved.

AWARENESS AND UNDERSTANDING

The fact that libraries have successfully demonstrated that resources and services can be provided to people who are deaf or hard of hearing and that they can and do use them is encouraging for the future. The public is being educated about deafness and hearing impairment, also, through the success of these programs. There are, however, many factors that limit the rapid development of the service in the breadth and depth needed.

Undoubtedly the strongest deterrent to a rapid development of library service to the deaf and hearing impaired is the lack of awareness of the implications of hearing loss and a lack of understanding that those who have a hearing loss need and want information and recreation just as much as the hearing population. There is also a widespread lack of understanding concerning the reading ability of people with a hearing loss. It is a widely held belief that being deaf has no effect on the ability to read. While it is true that many people who are deaf can read, it is not true for all. Also, there is a lack of understanding concerning the severity of the disability that results from a hearing loss. This disability results in definite barriers to successful communication and, because library service consists of communication, the barrier is especially drastic in its effect on the ability of deaf and hearing impaired people to use the library.

Because people with a hearing loss are often isolated and hesitant about using a library, librarians need to take the first step in seeing that they are served equally well as those who can hear. If the service is to be developed successfully in the future, that equality of access must be kept in mind as the plans for the years ahead are put together. The early intervention of the library in the lives of deaf or hard-of-hearing people helps to minimize their unwillingness to use the services and resources of a library and, as libraries employ more and more people who have a hearing loss, hearing people will better understand nonhearing people.

There is little homogeneity among the deaf and hearing impaired just as there is among people who have normal hearing. If the deaf and hearing impaired community can be seen as being comprised of people with individual characteristics, the stereotypes will disappear and libraries will, as a matter of course, include all people in their service. It is the lack of opportunity for interaction between hearing people and those with a hearing loss that strengthens the stereotype of deaf and hearing impaired people and propagates their status as "outsiders" as far as many service agencies, including the library, are concerned.

Much of this misunderstanding arises from the communication barrier—a very real and serious problem. The very invisibility of deafness and hearing impairment is a strong deterrent in developing library service to people who have a loss of hearing. Although an estimated 17.7 million people have some type of hearing loss, they are an unidentified part of the population of every community.

Even when identification is made of individuals as being deaf or hard of hearing, the communication barrier is still there. Speaking clearly can assist communication in some instances. Communication between hearing and nonhearing people can be facilitated through written messages. Also, manual communication can assist in mutual understanding. None of these methods, however, enables communication to move smoothly in library usage by deaf and hearing impaired people. Few library staff members are skilled in manual communication, and many people who are deaf are not skilled in its use. Lipreading is sometimes effective but not always. While technology now enables people who are deaf to use the telephone system, TTY/TDDs are not yet as widely used as telephones either by individuals or by libraries. Libraries, as leaders in the field of communication, are especially adversely affected by the communication barrier. The library collection is made up of print, video, and audio communication. Much of this material cannot be used by deaf and hearing impaired people unless accommodation of some kind has been made by the library. The availability of information by telephone or by means of a visit to the library is hampered by the barrier which exists between hearing people and those with a hearing loss. By eliminating or minimizing these barriers, deaf and hearing impaired people can successfully use the library. Such experiences will be encouraging to hearing library staff members and also to library staff members who have a hearing loss as they develop self-confidence in their ability to work with hearing people.

One reason that library service to the deaf and hearing impaired has developed so slowly is the lack of emphasis on the service on either a national or a state level. A national library service to the deaf and hearing impaired does not exist except for the service to the deaf-blind provided by the National Library Service to the Blind and Physically Handicapped, Library of Congress. At the state and regional levels, the same is true with a few exceptions. Some state libraries have developed services to deaf and hearing impaired people or have provided assistance in the development of a statewide service. The 1979 White House Conference on Library and Information Services resulted in the adoption of resolutions concerning national and state responsibilities in this area. These recommendations still await implementation.

INFORMATION SOURCES

National leadership in library service to the deaf and hearing impaired has come from Gallaudet College and from the National Technical Institute for the Deaf. The Learning Center at Gallaudet College provides library service to students attending the college. Much useful material can be obtained from various offices and organizations at Gallaudet College.

The National Technical Institute for the Deaf was established by an Act of Congress, and it is funded by the U.S. Department of Education. It is one of 10 schools at the Rochester (New York) Institute of Technology. The library for the students is the Wallace Memorial Library. Special bibliographic instruction and communication assistance are available to students who are deaf and the institute produces a wide variety of information on deafness.

The material from both of these schools is very helpful to librarians who are developing or expanding a program of library service to deaf and hearing impaired people. It is because their first responsibility is to their students that they do not provide national library service.

One group concerned with library service to all people is the American Library Association (ALA), a membership association which was founded in 1876. The association is the oldest and largest national library association in the world. Through its divisions, primarily the Association of Specialized and Cooperative Library Agencies (ASCLA), ALA makes available information on library service to the deaf and hearing impaired. A primary outlet for this information is the publication *Interface*, issued by ASCLA.

ALA includes library service to deaf and hearing impaired individuals in its concern for all library interests. Information sources such as Educational Resources Information Center (ERIC), National Rehabilitation Information Center (NARIC), and ABLEDATA have sources of information and materials available which are valuable to libraries working in the area of library service to the deaf and hearing impaired. Materials and sources are available through these information centers which would be difficult, if not impossible, to access elsewhere.

With persistence and initiative, librarians can acquire the information needed. Some sources of information are listed in the "Resource List" at the end of this chapter. Such organizations all have material and information available in the field of deafness and hearing impairment. Taken together, they can provide any kind of information needed concerning people with a hearing loss. There is not, however, any one organization devoted to library service to the deaf and hearing impaired. Some of them do carry in their publications articles or regular features concerned with library service. Through these organizations and information centers, plus others, they can find out about deafness, hearing impairment, and library service. Information includes background materials as well as current activities. There is no central national source, however, to which librarians can turn to for information, service, or referral. To maintain currentness in the many aspects of deafness or hearing impairment in relation to library service is a very time-consuming, uncertain, and intensive project.

NEED FOR A CLEARINGHOUSE

The development of services is seriously hampered by the lack of a central national point of service and information. The fact that a national clearinghouse of information is not available is a constraint on the service's development. Such a clearinghouse which would be concerned only with enabling libraries to serve people who are deaf and hearing impaired would bring together the many activities and informational sources available. Development of a national clearninghouse that could provide information on successful techniques of service, on materials needed, on new technologies which can be employed, and on advances in research as well as on communication and environment, would benefit libraries. Through its ability to make this information available, the clearinghouse would do what is impossible to accomplish presently—secure information, service, or referral from one central agency. Needed also are clearinghouses at the state level devoted solely to the advancement of library service to deaf and hearing impaired people.

Libraries need assistance within their own localities in setting up these programs—assistance from a central point within their own geographical area. In addition, there is a need for stimulating local library service to the deaf and hearing impaired by an agency of the state. The clearinghouse could be located within the state library, within an agency serving the deaf and hearing impaired, or within a private organization with funding and responsibility for statewide service. Large states, when necessary, could have 2 such agencies to give impetus to this aspect of library service.

Such a clearinghouse would not be passive in its activities but would be promotional in efforts to ensure that library service is available and accessible to all people with a hearing loss. Without such a state and/or national service, the programs of library service to the deaf and hearing impaired will have less chance of being universally available and accessible to all deaf and hearing impaired people. The library service of the future will continue to be unevenly provided throughout the United States. It appears that, in order to achieve library service which is available and accessible to all deaf and hearing impaired people, agencies at the state and national levels will need to assume some responsibility for providing that service. Professionally, there is a need for librarians to accept responsibility to serve deaf and hearing impaired people as part of the commitment to assure availability and accessibility of all library services to all people.

To achieve such service will also require a community attitude which is supportive of libraries. Barriers such as communication still exist for deaf and hearing impaired people within the community in which they live. Problems still exist in the employment of people with a hearing loss as well as with their choices in education. There also still exist stereotypes about this population group.

However, positive changes are taking place. The deaf and hearing impaired are benefitting, to a certain extent, from changes in community attitudes toward people with disabilities. Established education for the deaf began about 200 years ago in this country. It has only recently been broadened so that the deaf and hearing impaired now have several educational institutions to choose from. Such opportunities indicate that the hearing community is developing an understanding about hearing loss. The broadening of employment opportunities, also, is an indication of a better understanding of deaf and hearing impaired people by hearing people. However, to assist the libraries in their efforts to include appropriate services and resources for people with a hearing loss, the community needs to broaden its understanding further. Libraries receive their support from the people in the community—either from the public or private sector or both. Both financial and attitudinal support is needed to enable libraries to offer consistently good service to people with a loss of hearing.

Within the total community, the hearing and nonhearing people have difficulty in communicating. As a result, information transmitted between them is sometimes fragmentary, misunderstood, or does not get through at all. This situation has an adverse affect on library service to deaf and hearing impaired people. When library service is established, it is important that there be a reasonably good flow of information between the library and the people for and by whom the service is being developed. Because the majority of librarians and library staff members are people with normal hearing, there is a built-in barrier in communication. The message concerning what the library is, what it can do, and how they can use it does not reach the deaf and hearing impaired in a form which they can completely understand. Some programs of services, resources, and equipment which have been made available in a usable form for deaf and hearing impaired people have had little use; the programs have not received support from the people they were designed to serve.

Such lack of use can occur for a variety of reasons. A part of the problem can, however, be attributed to the difficulty of 2-way communication. Many hearing impaired and deaf people are isolated from the hearing community. They are not aware of library services and resources which they can use; use of a library for information and recreation purposes is foreign to them. For information to flow freely between the library and the people to be served requires time, effort, and understanding.

Probably the greatest and most successful communications medium is learning about successful library experiences from deaf people themselves. Once the attitudinal barrier built by the potential users is broken down, the communication problem will diminish. People in the community who are deaf or hard of hearing can promote the development of library service by using the service and by informing other people in the community about it. They can also initiate a service program themselves by letting the library know that the service is wanted, needed, and will be used.

Basic to the development or nondevelopment and the continuing or not continuing of all library programs are the economic conditions in the nation, in the state, and in the locality. Many libraries are supported by taxes; others are privately supported. Adverse economic conditions have a direct adverse effect on libraries. Libraries are seldom mandated services even in areas where services are mandated by law. Their local priority among other services depends on the community which they serve. Their state priority depends upon the state's attitude toward libraries, its financial condition, and its concern with other issues and agencies. Their national priority depends on the emphasis which is currently being placed on libraries as well as financial considerations and other issues and agencies which may have a higher priority.

For poor economic conditions not to have a devastating effect on library service to deaf and hearing impaired people requires a strong effort on the part of libraries and the people to be served to demonstrate the need of the program and its benefits. Because of their many concerns, people in government and in the community they represent have given little or no thought to library service to deaf and hearing impaired people.

To get what they need, the library and the deaf and hearing impaired must be vocal about their needs. The community of people who have a hearing loss is not a homogeneous one. In most localities, it is not a unified group. The people tend to be invisible in the political community; therefore, the library and the people they are serving or hope to serve need to explain to the public the problems that exist in providing and in using the service. They need to impress upon the people in government that solutions must be found for these problems and that the solutions must be financed. While existing organizations for and of the people who are deaf and hearing impaired are helpful in making library needs visible, local groups are needed also.

The people who will benefit by the service, along with the people who will provide it, are best able to translate needs and priorities into facts. These facts can then be presented to the people who will support or not support library service to people with a hearing loss. In some areas of the United States, the effort is a pioneering one—it has never been tried before. The library entering into a field which has never before been considered for ongoing funding faces some difficult problems. There is a need to work from a unified position to be successful in the establishment of the service.

LIBRARY FINANCES

Taxpayer revolts and a widespread reluctance to raise taxes are affecting financial conditions at all levels of government. Funds available for services such as library service to people who are deaf or hard of hearing are being reduced as efforts are made either to maintain or reduce current levels of taxes. Tax shifts have also resulted in lower tax revenues. Escalating costs make the situation even more serious because an increase in financial support can most often be attributed to increased costs rather than to an increase in the quality or quantity of service. Private funding agencies are not set up to absorb the financial loss which results. The use of federal funding to make up the loss of revenues at the state and local level is precarious. In most instances, in funding library service to deaf and hearing impaired people, federal funds are used for only a given number of years. The service is then usually reduced in level of service or eliminated. The same is usually true with grant funds. Libraries have not been in a preferred position to prevent this erosion of their financial support. Because the financial situation of many libraries does not allow them to expand services, it is essential that deaf and hearing impaired people give them their full support in the planning and implementing of library services developed by and for them. It is only through such a demonstrated need that libraries will be able to provide library service to all the people.

Another factor affecting library service to deaf and hearing impaired people is the "new federalism." This concept has a definite meaning for libraries and to people with a hearing loss. Under this philosophy, the state and local governments are given responsibility for many services which were formerly administered by the federal government. As far as libraries are concerned, state and local governments are reluctant to replace federal funding with state and local funds. Because of the lower priority of libraries in comparison with many other services, it is doubtful that the state/local responsibility for the service will be accompanied by funds to maintain or increase the level of service. With the rising costs which libraries are facing and the reduction in state and local resources, libraries have a problem in maintaining their services.

Libraries are, to a great extent, supported all or in part by state and local funding. So if the people who receive service from the library, such as the deaf and hearing impaired, make their wants and needs known to the funding authorities, libraries will stand a better chance of retaining their present funding and increasing it in the future. Through their organized efforts, library service has a chance of securing initial and/or continued funding. With the responsibility of programs turned back to the state and local governments, each state or locality will determine the priority that those services will have. It is important that people who are deaf or hard of hearing successfully emphasize to the state and local government authorities the need for library service to people with a hearing loss. This type of local and state support is also vital when a partnership program exists with the federal government for financial support.

State and local financial support will vary; levels of funding will depend on the total funding available and the value which is placed on library services compared with other services to be supported. Because of differences among states and localities, the quality and level of library service will vary even more. Multistate programs will undoubtedly also be affected by this situation.

Library service to deaf and hearing impaired people has lacked, for the most part, the awareness and support of other agencies of and for the deaf and hearing impaired. This situation exists primarily because each agency is concerned with carrying out the responsibilities assigned to that agency, rather than also being concerned with the activities of others in the same field. The deaf and hearing impaired are the responsibility of other service professionals in the areas of rehabilitation and education just as they are of the library. Some of these responsibilities and services are overlapping, some duplicate each other, while others are unique to a specific agency.

The library service to deaf and hearing impaired people will be improved if all of the agencies join together to consider how they can work together. Through such cooperation, they can reduce duplication and eliminate the overlapping of services. The resulting benefit to people with a hearing loss will be improved service. Such efforts will also help to stabilize costs.

Through the professional interrelationship established, all groups can benefit despite the leveling out or reduction of financial support. When federal or grant funding is available, the agencies can develop planning which will use the best each agency has to offer. This will result in an improved delivery system to deaf and hearing impaired people in the community.

NETWORKS

The independent action of a library in initiating library service to deaf and hearing impaired people places an ongoing responsibility on that library which cannot, many times, be sustained at a continuous, high-quality level. That is why library service to people with a hearing loss lends itself well to a cooperative approach. Interagency cooperation is especially well-suited to multitype library service programs because so much of their success is based on effective communicating. For example, one library could assume responsibility for being the link to all other libraries in the network. It could be the reference center for calls coming in by means of a TTY/TDD. It could provide a telephone relay system. Within the network, libraries could provide, according to their abilities and interests, collections of wordless, signed, or captioned videotapes and films. Also, the libraries could develop information on employment, education, deaf culture, and deaf awareness. Through cooperation, the group of libraries could develop educational programs providing information on the materials held in all of the libraries, how those materials can best be used by the people in the community, and the kinds of information they can provide. The network could give the people the information on location of all resources and on the status of their availability which could be accessed at any location and at any time.

Classes on sign language and lipreading could be offered on a cooperative basis. This would enable people in a large geographical area to learn to communicate with each other effectively. Signers and oral interpreters as well as note takers could be available on a larger population base than when each library works independently. Conference facilities equipped with the newest in technology could be available in the network of multitype libraries. The employment of librarians who are deaf or hard of hearing could be facilitated because staff members could be easily trained in communication on a cooperative basis.

Cooperative training could also be available for the purpose of sensitizing people in 2-way communication between hearing and nonhearing people. The establishing of a clearinghouse of information about deafness and hearing impairment would enable all members of the library staffs to be constantly informed. Because each library would need to provide its own local service, the clearinghouse would include an exchange of both ideas and materials. Such a cooperative arrangement would enable a group of librarians to provide programs to acquaint people who are deaf or hard of hearing with what the library has to offer and show them how they can acquire information from it. As a result, they will learn to depend on the library, and it will become an important part of their daily lives.

It requires creativity to develop a network of library services to people who have a hearing loss. However, through this means, resources and services can be shared by all types of libraries. Each library would, however, offer, a direct service to the people in its community. It would, as a result, have a broader base of services and resources from which to draw. If, along with this group of libraries, the other professional services are involved, the deaf and hearing impaired people can benefit greatly.

One problem which continues to slow down library service to people with a hearing loss is that alternatives for hearing and speech are not as widely used as they should be to facilitate communication. With a greater availability of TTY/TDDs at a lower unit cost, libraries can communicate as successfully with deaf and hearing impaired people as they can by telephone with people who do not have a hearing loss nor impaired speech. Signed books and other such materials for people who are deaf provide a written means of communication. With a wide availability of captioned films, hearing is compensated for through captioning. Interpreters can compensate for both hearing and speech. They can expand the informational opportunities for people who are deaf and be of assistance in communication in a library setting. They can expand the social and educational opportunities of these people and widen the choices which people with a hearing loss have in selecting and following a career.

To compensate for not being able to engage fluently in 2-way communication, visual displays can be used in libraries for informational purposes. Captioned television programs are valuable and, as videotext becomes available for wide use, television sets will be modified for videotext and another information facility will be available in the library for the use of deaf and hearing impaired individuals.

In spite of the large number of people with a hearing loss, that number remains small when compared with the total population. The deaf and hearing impaired depend, for the most part, on the limited awareness of the public concerning their needs and priorities. Some advocacy is taking place among deaf and hearing impaired people through organizations of and for people with a hearing loss. This is augmented through the efforts of relatives, friends, and other advocates. The benefits gained through the activities pursued, such as that of library service, enables people to add a new quality to their lives. It also enables them to participate more fully in the life of the community.

With adequate state and local funding available, libraries can continue to use federal and grant funding. These funds can be used successfully to initiate service which can then be supported by the ongoing library budget. Even more important, such funds can enhance a service already firmly in place within the library program and can encourage resource sharing. Sign language books can be purchased with federal or grant funds as can other appropriate materials. Books for adults with low verbal skills can be added to the resources through outside funding. Deaf Awareness and Deaf Heritage weeks as well as other special months and weeks can be observed by programs developed with special funding.

There are many barriers to overcome in developing such a service. There are also many factors which, taken together, form an excellent base from which to continue on a positive course in developing library service to deaf and hearing impaired people. Through the efforts of many people, the negative factors can be minimized and the positive factors emphasized to make the library service available, accessible, and effective on a universal basis.

RESOURCE LIST

Organizations of and for the deaf and hearing impaired can provide information in a variety of areas to librarians who are working in the field of deafness and hearing impairment. Some of them are:

- The National Association of the Deaf, an organization founded in 1880, which provides information concerning all types of programs and services for people who are deaf. It is a nonprofit consumer-oriented organization, especially helpful because of its 50 state chapters. NAD publishes *The NAD Broadcaster* and *The Deaf American*.

- The Alexander Graham Bell Association, a nonprofit membership organization, founded in 1890, which promotes the teaching of speech and language through maximizing the use of residual hearing. The publications of this association are the *Volta Review*, *Newsounds*, *OK Magazine*, and *ODAS Newsletter*.
- American Deafness and Rehabilitation Association, an organization which has information on adults who are deaf and on the subject of employment. They are also concerned with rehabilitation services. Their publications are the *Journal of Rehabilitation* and *ADARA Newsletter*.
- Convention of American Instructors of the Deaf, an organization promoting professional development. The organization also emphasizes communication and information among educators of the deaf. Their publication is *American Annals of the Deaf.*
- Helen Keller National Center for Deaf-Blind Youth and Adults, an organization which provides comprehensive evaluation and prevocational rehabilitation training. The organization maintains the National Register of Deaf-Blind Persons. Their publication is *Nat-Cent News.*
- American Society for Deaf Children, a membership organization providing information and support to parents and to families of children who are deaf or hard of hearing. They publish *Endeavor.*

National organizations concerned with people who are hard of hearing include:

- Self Help for Hard of Hearing People, Inc. (SHHH), a recently established volunteer organization devoted to the welfare and interests of people who are hard of hearing. The organization is especially helpful on a local basis because of its chapters in over half of the states. The organization became a member of the President's Committee for Employment of the Handicapped in 1983. The publications of the organization are *SHHH* and *Special Reports.*
- Better Hearing Institute, a private, nonprofit educational organization which provides information on hearing loss. Its publication is *Communication.*
- American Tinnitus Association (ATA), a nonprofit corporation which makes information about tinnitus available as well as information concerning other hearing problems. The organization publishes *ATA Newsletter* and brochures.

• The Suzanne Pathy Speak-up Institute, Inc., an organization devoted to facilitating communication between hearing and hearing impaired people. The institute has compiled rules for the general public to use in communicating with hard-of-hearing people. Newsletters and pamphlets are issued by this organization.

REFERENCE LIST

Biehl, Jane, comp. *Staff Sensitivity Workshop. Helping the Deaf Patron in the Library.* Canton, OH: Stark County District Library, 1984.

"Building Bridges." *Shhh* 4 (4) (July–August 1983): 3–7.

California State University–Northridge. *Can Deaf Students Succeed?* Northridge, CA: California State University–Northridge, 1979.

"Colleges for Deaf Taxed by '60's 'Rubella Bulge.' " *The NAD Broadcaster* 5 (12) (November–December 1983): 3.

Dugan, Robert. "How the States are Faring." *Interface* 4 (4) (Summer 1982): 4–7.

Firestone, George. "The New Federalism and Libraries." *Interface* 4 (4) (Summer 1982): 2–3.

Kennedy, Senator Edward M. "A Vow to Fight Back." *Interface* 4 (4) (Summer 1982): 1–2.

Naisbitt, John. *Megatrends. Ten New Directions Transforming Our Lives.* New York: Warner Books, 1982.

"New Federalism." *Las Vegas Review Journal* (May 29, 1983): 11A.

O'Halloran, Charles. "Could New Federalism Bring New Freedom?" *Interface* 4 (4) (Summer 1982): 3–4.

"Physical Disability and Public Policy. *Scientific American* 248 (6) (June 1983): 40–49.

"Stereotypes Handicapped's Biggest Obstacle." Report of speech by Vice President George Bush. *The President's Committee on Employment of the Handicapped Conference Daily* (May 6, 1983): 1.

Chapter 22
The Promise for the Future

Awareness, understanding, concern, and action are key words in fulfilling the promise of library service to deaf and hearing impaired people in future. A part of future success is concerned with providing library service without unnecessary restrictions. People with a hearing loss are restricted as to the number of television programs they can understand because only a limited number are closed captioned. They are restricted in the number of films they can enjoy because dialog and narration play such an important part in most movies. They are also restricted in their choice of books as many cannot be used successfully by people who are deaf because the level of the language is too difficult for their reading skills. The availability of high interest/low level reading material is limited. The list of restrictions on information and recreation as traditionally provided by a library is a long one. Will the future provide a lessening of those restrictions and open the doors of libraries to all deaf and hearing impaired people?

During the last decade, there has been a realization and awareness of a need for communication with and an understanding of deaf and hearing impaired people by hearing people. The fact that they are not in the mainstream of American life is, as a result, being considered and remedied. This attitudinal change has come about, to some extent, through the overall recognition given to the rights of all people with disabilities. The International Year of Disabled Persons, 1981, and the National Year of Disabled Persons, 1982, had a positive effect on the lives of people with all types of disabilities. The main thrust of these 2 years was to make all people aware of the need to bring people with disabilites into the mainstream of society and to develop an understanding and a concern for the continued improvement of their quality of life. Much action took place in partnerships throughout the United States. These partnerships were between many organizations and agencies; there were also partnerships between able-bodied and disabled persons. Libraries participated actively in the programs of these 2 years.

Some services were initiated for the first time, and some were expanded. Programs of library service to hearing impaired and deaf people were a part of this mainstream movement.

FUTURE TRENDS

The future holds the promise of the Decade of Disabled Persons, 1983–92. The General Assembly of the United Nations released the proclamation on the Decade of Disabled Persons on April 19, 1983. On July 25, 1983, both Houses of the United States Congress passed Concurrent Resolution #39 in support of the Decade of Disabled Persons and asked that the American people work together in partnership in achieving the decade's goals. On November 28, 1983, President Ronald Reagan issued a proclamation declaring 1983–92 as the National Decade of Disabled Persons. The American Library Association was one of the first national organizations to declare its support of the Decade of Disabled Persons.

As with the international and national years, the decade is dedicated to full participation and equality in society of persons with disabilities. The progress toward the goals in relation to library service will depend on the leadership and commitment of librarians throughout the United States. The decade promises to equal the International/National Years, 1981–82, in reaching its goals. Deaf and hearing impaired people can benefit directly through this emphasis on library service throughout the 1980s and into the 1990s.

Nationwide, positive and negative trends in library service to the deaf and hearing impaired were apparent in these dedicated years. According to the statistics of the Library Services and Construction Act for fiscal 1981 and fiscal 1982, the number of projects concerned with library service to deaf and hearing impaired people dropped from 28 projects in 16 states in 1981 to 7 projects in 7 states in 1982. At the same time, however, the comparison showed that 13,894 more people were served with projects of library service to deaf and hearing impaired people in 1982 over 1981—a substantial increase.

The improved environment developing in overall services for the deaf and hearing impaired is exemplified by the activities of Coeur d'Alene, Idaho, in its first year of the decade program. Although all disabilities were included in the program, special emphasis was placed on library service to hard-of-hearing and deaf people. Much of the leadership came through a local chapter of Self Help for Hard-of-Hearing

People (SHHH), which worked with the mayor's committee and with all community organizations.

There are many crucial issues ahead but none that cannot be overcome or accommodated so that library service to people who have a hearing loss can move ahead. To do this mandates that libraries and people in the deaf and hard-of-hearing community become aware of and involved in the political process at all levels of government. They must be realistic in working for programs and services but, at the same time, be creative. Funding support of governmental bodies is most important, but it needs to be supplemented with private funding and support. Both library-related people and those who are concerned with their needs must ask themselves the following questions about the program of library service:

- Do we know the services, programs, and resources we want to include in this library activity?
- Do we know who the people are in government who will make decisions concerning the funding and other support of the services, programs, and resources?
- Are they aware of the specific needs of people who are deaf or hard of hearing in relation to library service?
- Do they have adequate information about the library programs so they can make informed decisions concerning the library program for people who have a hearing loss?
- What are the critical issues which we should present to the people in government?
- How can we best work together to accomplish our goals?
- What other groups or individuals can we involve in our advocacy for library service to people who have a hearing loss?
- What other sources of support do we need to inform concerning the need for and the priority of library service to deaf and hearing impaired people?

Adequate answers and solutions to all of these questions will help to ensure a positive future for library service to people with a hearing loss. All of the questions are important, but one which is vital is "What other groups or individuals can we involve?" The future will reflect the past. Deaf and hearing impaired people and librarians cannot achieve the positive results needed alone. A broad base of community support is essential.

Several other groups of people can help build a coalition of strength. The many professionals, in addition to librarians, working with deaf and hearing impaired people are knowledgeable about the needs and priorities of people with a hearing loss. They can be a strong component of the cooperative effort to let government officials know that these people need library service. Along with the professionals are the several local and state associations as well as local chapters of national associations. They can all be very convincing in their presentations because they are made up, for the most part, of deaf and hearing impaired individuals.

A group of people who usually know library service firsthand are the parents of deaf and hearing impaired children. Many of the parents are already library users and may already be politically active. They may already be influential in the community on the subject of deafness and hearing impairment. Other relatives of people who have a hearing loss can be helpful as well as other interested people. The total disabled community can be a strong force in influencing those who make decisions about library service to hearing impaired and deaf people. This is especially true during the Decade of Disabled Persons. People who have a hearing loss may have other disabilities, permanent or temporary, which also need accommodation. This requires the development of broader goals, but the benefits gained will benefit all.

COOPERATION

Through cooperation with other groups, deaf and hearing impaired consumers and potential consumers and librarians can be prepared to deal with the issues concerning problems of the future as they relate to library service. Although economic conditions at any given time may threaten development of library service, its development cannot be put aside until the conditions improve. Deaf and hearing impaired people are part of the tax-paying public and are entitled to the benefits provided by society—including library service. The time to act is at the time the service is needed and not wait for some better day in the future. The future will have its challenges, its victories, and its defeats. Many positive results have been achieved in the past several years in library service to people with a hearing loss. The future developments will be that much easier because of the success of the past. Some of the future concerns include the following:

- Are we meeting the basic library needs of the many individuals in the deaf and hearing impaired community?
- Does the general public understand what these needs are?

- Are the public officials aware of the effect of deafness and hearing impairment on 2-way communication? On using traditional library service?
- How should the library service accommodate deaf and hearing impaired people?
- What are the best means of establishing effective communication between hearing and nonhearing people?
- How can we promote the availability of better career opportunities? What is the library's role in this issue?
- How can we increase the choices in educational opportunities? Does the library have a role to play in this question?
- What can we do to increase the number of employment opportunities as well as the variety of choices in jobs? What is the most effective role for the library in this issue?

Facing these issues positively requires broad-based support and an informed public. The potential for success is apparent; the past has indicated that library service can be effectively provided and profitably used. It is important that librarians and hearing impaired and deaf people know what is needed so that they can remain current with the changes in society and yet reach the goals for the service. It is important to be vocal, but it is also important to be sure that people who will make the final decisions are listening. An active role will help to ensure that library service is continually available.

REPRESENTING THE VIEWS OF THE DEAF AND HEARING IMPAIRED

The people who represent the views of the deaf and hearing impaired in the future can make sure they are truly representing their views if they:

- Consult regularly with the organizations of and for the deaf and hearing impaired and with individuals who are deaf or hard of hearing.
- Inform the people about pending or future issues and obtain their views.
- Report back to the organization and individuals concerning the activities relating to the status of the issues.
- Make sure that the views and ideas presented represent the entire community.

Any opinions concerning libraries and the need for service by hearing impaired and deaf people expressed by representatives must be informed ones. It is time-consuming to gain information from many and to report back, but it is only through that process that credible information can be presented on behalf of the library and the people it serves. In most localities, there are more deaf and hearing impaired individuals who are out of the mainstream of organizations than are in it. To consult with and report back requires the utilization of many formats and many sources to reach all of the people involved. It is of utmost importance, however, that this communication with the nonhearing people and with the decision makers takes place. With the many issues that are and will be facing the people who make the final decisions about library service to deaf and hearing impaired people, it is essential that the support for the service be visible and articulate.

A factor which has had an influence on the development of library service has been the independent living movement for people with disabilities, which began in the early 1970s with independent living centers in Berkeley, California, and Boston, Massachusetts. There are now many such centers throughout the United States. Independent living is based on the attitude that more self-help initiatives are needed to remove barriers and allow full participation in society by people with disabilities. It does not include the attitude of paternalism. It is based, rather, on the traditional values of self-reliance and the freedom to be independent. As far as nonhearing people are concerned, the practicality of independent living is enhanced by the use of new technology.

ACADEMIC LIBRARIES

Activities in library service to hearing impaired and deaf people are taking place presently that indicate that the future will provide some of the accomplishments people have sought in the past. It appears that the development will be ongoing and will follow new patterns as well as carrying on those which have been successfully established in the past.

One such program is that of "Serving Deaf Students in Academic Libraries," presented by the Library Service to the Deaf Section of the Association of Specialized and Cooperative Library Agencies (ASCLA) and the Community and Junior College Section of the Association of College and Research Libraries (ACRL) at the American Library Association Conference in Los Angeles in 1983. This was a significant program because it included a nationwide representation of well-developed academic programs for students who are deaf and hearing impaired. The range of colleges and universities participating included California State University–Northridge; Gallaudet College; Austin (Texas) Community College; Golden West Community College, Huntington Beach, California; Pasadena (California) City College; Rochester (New York) Institute of Technology; and the University of Scranton (Pennsylvania). Information was also available concerning other academic institutions, including Chemeketa Community College, Salem, Oregon; Seattle (Washington) Community College; Seattle Central Community College; and Lenoir-Rhyne College, Hickory, North Carolina.

The program included guidelines and approaches to be used in academic library settings. Resource persons were available both in the library field and in companies which serve the library field in the area of service to deaf and hearing impaired people. The program emphasized that, in the last 20 years, the number of colleges and universities which serve the deaf in some way has grown dramatically. Students can now choose from the many colleges and universities offering programs and/or support services. Because libraries are becoming more complex, students who have a hearing loss will be asking more and more questions of the library staff. As a result, it will become even more important to post explanatory signs and make instructional materials available.

The unique aspects of providing library service to deaf and hearing impaired students in academic libraries were presented and discussed at this conference. Even though librarians and other library staff members do not communicate through signing or lipreading, they can communicate through writing. Interpreters are also provided by the college so that the librarian can ask for an interpreter when necessary to achieve 2-way communication. Self-guided tours of the library are provided to the students, and handbooks describing the library and how to use it are available. Videotapes are often in the library collections which give signs for unique vocabulary on certain subjects such as history, mathematics, and drafting. The goal is to enable students to use the library independently. It is important that the library staff use any technique possible in teaching them to do this.

Students need to know that the library is there and ready to serve them. Because deaf or hearing impaired students do not overhear conversations about what the library can do for them as do hearing students, they need written materials. Group instruction can include a hands-on experience. If librarians and other staff members learn basic finger spelling, they will find it to be helpful in communicating with students. In some colleges, a tutor-liaison system is available so that the students can receive individual instruction on how to use the library. In some instances, a panel of students who are deaf or hard of hearing attend the library staff meetings and have an opportunity for 2-way communication and information exchange. This enables librarians to interact with deaf and hearing impaired students. It also educates the nonhearing students about the library. They can then share this information with other students. Many of the colleges have deafness collections and resources on careers and employment. In some of the colleges, a course is given to the librarians on how to communicate successfully with deaf and hard-of-hearing students.

Considered also in the program was the evaluation of the materials provided to deaf and hearing impaired students—can they be understood? Are they helpful? Librarians may find that the materials on how to use the library are not as effective as they seemed to be when designed because of a variety of reasons. They may be too difficult because of the level of vocabulary used and the sentence structure or may present too much information at one time. In such cases, the material can be redesigned and adapted so that it is more appropriate to student needs. While these services to students are always important, they are especially significant now that a larger number of college-age young people are deaf. This is due to the German measles epidemic which swept the United States in 1964–65, which has resulted in higher enrollments of students who are deaf in the colleges and universities.

VIDEOTAPES IN TRAINING

Another positive development in library service to deaf and hearing impaired people presented at this program included 2 videotapes. One was developed by the National Academy of Gallaudet College and the other by the Austin Community College Media Center. The title of the videotape from Gallaudet College is "027.6 Access: Deaf Patrons in the Library." The tape is made up of a series of scenes in a general library setting. The emphasis is on how to recognize that people are deaf, how to communicate with them, and how to provide the library service they want and need. The tape can be used in any type of library. The Austin Community College tape was made by the library staff for in-service training. Both actions are positive developments for the future of library service to deaf and hearing impaired people.

The program "Serving Deaf Students in Academic Libraries" presented many ideas for the future concerning library service which can be provided in academic libraries. Described also were the support services to deaf and hearing impaired students in colleges and universities. Although the program was directed toward the student in an academic setting, the services described and the techniques used have a much wider application.

ESTABLISHMENT OF A CLEARINGHOUSE

A development in the providing of library service to people who have a hearing loss which has significance for the future is that of a clearinghouse established at the St. Mary's School for the Deaf in Buffalo, New York. In the evaluation of 3 workshops conducted by the New York State Library, in cooperation with St. Mary's School for the Deaf, many of the 160 librarians attending indicated their need for continuing information. They indicated that the establishment of a clearinghouse would assist libraries in their service to deaf and hearing impaired people. They felt it would also respond to the recommendation pertaining to deafness and hearing impairment that came out of the White House Conference on Libraries and Information Service in 1979.

The St. Mary's School is, as a result, cooperating with the New York State Library to provide that service. This school is now the Northeastern United States Demonstration School in the Gallaudet College-Kellogg Foundation's Special School of the Future Project. As such, it maintains contact with programs for the deaf throughout New York State.

The clearinghouse was a natural outgrowth of the extensive specialized collection at St. Mary's. The school, in cooperation with a local college, has a graduate program for teachers of deaf children. Their collection includes the following materials:

- A list of national, state, and local resource agencies serving deaf and hearing impaired people.
- A collection of materials which includes captioned films, Signed English books, books of signs, and publishers' catalogs.
- A reference file for devices and equipment such as signaling devices, alarms, TTY/TDDs, and manufacturers' catalogs and specifications.
- Information on access to public buildings by the removal of barriers—acoustic and visual.
- Research materials on medical, social, and educational aspects of deafness.

St. Mary's also conducts workshops for librarians and other professionals on materials and services available as well as on deaf awareness. Funding for the entire program comes from the ongoing budget. This clearinghouse is a positive indication of what the future can bring at the state and national levels as far as clearinghouses are concerned.

Another important area of service being addressed by St. Mary's School for the Deaf through a grant is that of a parents' library. This library contains a special collection of material for use by parents. A wide variety of materials are offered through this program including:

- Books and pamphlets on language and speech development.
- Communication and sign language.
- Parenting and child development.
- Child management.
- Legislation affecting deaf persons.
- Impact of deafness on the family.
- Career options for deaf persons.
- Community services for deaf persons.

The library has also prepared special kits which include games, tapes, and books. These are designed to enhance language, speech, and motor coordination development in young deaf children. Two bibliographies have been issued. One is on the deafness collection and includes information on how to use the Parent Lending Library and covers such subjects as anatomy/audiology, causes of deafness/genetics, deafness in later life, information by and about deaf people, materials for children, psychological/social implications on deafness, and telecommunication devices. The second bibliography is concerned with parenting.

COMMUNITY INVOLVEMENT

Involving a community's public services in a total program for the deaf and hearing impaired is a hope for promoting the mainstreaming of the deaf and hearing impaired into society and into the library. An example of this involvement was demonstrated in Phoenix, Arizona, in 1983. The Phoenix Mayor's Committee on Employment of the Handicapped sponsored a "Festival for Speech and Hearing Awareness." A day of festivities was held at the central branch of the Phoenix Public Library in the art/museum/ theatre complex. Activities included dance performances, music, mimes, and plays; the events were signed when appropriate. Exhibits of community services for hearing and speech impaired persons were provided with free, long-distance

TTY calls. Silent movies and captioned films were provided as entertainment for all participants. Such a program brings the total community together and makes it aware of the needs and priorities of deaf and hearing impaired people. It can also demonstrate how agencies are meeting these needs.

An activity linking a publisher of books for and about deaf and hearing impaired people with library collections has been established through the A. G. Bell "Book Share-A-Thon." Through this plan, packages of selected titles on deafness and hearing impairment are available for specific types of libraries. Through the share-a-thon, individuals and groups can donate these titles to local libraries, complete with a specially designed bookplate.

A unique contribution to assisting those with a hearing loss is the video program "What Is a Bank?" This is a tape which explains basic banking service to deaf and hard-of-hearing people. It is signed in American Sign Language with voice narration for hearing audiences. Key information is captioned. The program was initiated by the Bank of America's Social Policy Department. The project was designed and the script written by the San Francisco Public Library's Deaf Services Department in cooperation with individuals who are deaf and with agencies for deaf people. The tape provides information to enable anyone unfamiliar with banking to visit a bank confidently to ask for further details.

A project of the present and the future which responds to needs and sets a trend is Project ACCESS. During the fifth anniversary of the street fair "New York Is Book Country," the New York Public Library sponsored its 1983 poster sale to benefit children's library services including children who are deaf or hearing impaired. Thousands of dollars were raised to support such programs as signed story hours, mime, and captioned films. Volunteers knowing American Sign Language were stationed at each of the NYPL's 4 booths. In addition, the same volunteers are "Friends" of Project ACCESS—a service designed to link people who have a physical disability with the full range of library services. With the help of the "Friends," Project ACCESS is exploring ways to meet the special needs of the deaf library users. The service lends books on a wide variety of reading levels, provides career information, and answers reference questions over TDD. All services are by appointment so that individual assistance can be provided.

SOME POSITIVE SIGNS

The use of microcomputers is a step forward in the education of deaf and hearing impaired individuals in the schools and in libraries. Because the microcomputer is primarily visual, people with a hearing loss do not have auditory restrictions in its use. The adaptability of computers to basic research is an asset to libraries and to people who are deaf or hard of hearing. Microelectronic aids to speech and comprehension may enable people who have a hearing loss to hear better; in the future, it may be possible to construct hearing aids which alter speech as needed by a hearing impaired individual. Microcomputers are having a positive effect on TTY/TDDs, and rapid communication through electronic mail allows rapid communication for the deaf and hearing impaired.

These are all significant events, programs, services, and breakthroughs because they indicate the possibilities in broadening library service to deaf and hearing impaired people; technological advances will continue to improve library service to deaf and hearing impaired people.

Probably as important is a more widespread usage of present technology in libraries and throughout the community. In some areas of the country, TDD customers have the option of listing their names and telephone numbers in the telephone directory with "TDD only" or "TDD and voice" after their names. They may also list them in the directory assistance records. Such listings will be helpful to libraries in making initial and continuing contact with people who are deaf.

Some states which have not yet developed programs at the state level are assessing the present services provided in libraries throughout the state. Promotional and informational materials have been developed to tell libraries about how important the program of library service to deaf and hearing impaired people is and how it can be developed. Others have developed a statewide plan with a measurable objective of serving a given number of deaf and hearing impaired people in a given time span. Much of this work has been accomplished through cooperation with the Governor's Committee on Employment of the Handicapped, state commissions on deaf service, and other comparable agencies at the state level. An encouraging development is the inclusion of all types of libraries in this information and promotion. While all programs will not be developed by all libraries, the libraries do have the opportunity of making an informed decision on which programs are applicable to their communities. Such promotion also provides an opportunity for librarians to decide cooperatively which programs can best be developed on a state or regional basis for the benefit of all libraries and their deaf and hearing impaired users.

Libraries will be important in the future because of the part they will play in facilitating research in the area of deafness and hearing impairment just as they are in the present. Research is being carried on in many aspects of deafness and hearing impairment. Work is being done in the area of implants. Infants and adults affected with nerve deafness may still have some hearing sensitivity for greater and more effective use in reception. Modern technology may be able to provide an electronic substitute for the poorly functioning inner ear auditory nerve. Advances are being made in the area of research in hearing in the young. Hearing loss in the elderly caused by nerve deafness is common and at present cannot be reversed; however, research is being done in this area also. Middle ear infection, Meniere's disease, and tinnitus (ringing in the ears) are all being researched to find an initial or more effective treatment. Research is being done to determine which drugs damage the auditory system. Excessive noise, the most common external cause of hearing loss, is being studied to determine the precise effect of severe and continuing noise on the auditory system. Librarians can assist in providing materials for research in these areas. They can also be of assistance in providing current information on the progress of medical research for people who are deaf or hard of hearing.

Legal and legislative actions related to hearing impaired and deaf people will also have an impact on library service. All legal, legislative, and governmental advances make possible further advances in library service to deaf and hearing impaired people. The lessening of attitudinal barriers in any aspect of the lives of deaf and hearing impaired individuals helps programs of library service to develop and flourish, so that they become essential services in all libraries.

An ongoing service to both nonhearing and hearing people is the information contained in *Communicating with Hearing People: The Red Notebook.* The information about activities, captioned films, laws and issues, TTY/TDD, and captioned TV, among other subjects, is helpful to librarians working with people with a hearing loss. It provides a bridge between the user who is deaf or hard of hearing and the library and provides a basic source of information with continuous updating.

Library associations are developing a continuing awareness of library service to the deaf and hearing impaired. Librarians, in turn, are translating this awareness into action. The Pennsylvania Library Association, in its 1983 meeting, held a sign language workshop. Its purpose was to enable conference attendees to learn the hand alphabet, a few pertinent signs, and to have the opportunity to use what they learned. The Midwest Federation of Library Associations, at its conference in 1983, included a program on library service for deaf and hearing impaired people. The activities included presentation of a model for integrating deaf and hearing impaired people into a total library program. This model included plans for using existing staff, sign language, TTY/TDD, and videotaped instruction.

This trend of increasing awareness was confirmed in the visits made by Alice Hagemeyer, librarian for the deaf community, District of Columbia Public Library, in 1983 to many libraries throughout the United States. While much remains to be done in developing library service to the deaf and hearing impaired, positive trends are indicated by increased awareness and the interest of library associations in service to people who are deaf or hard of hearing. It is also demonstrated by the participation of associations of the deaf and hearing impaired in library advocacy.

At the national level, a Working Group on Handicapped Policy was established under the United States Cabinet Council on Human Resources. This group was responsible for developing a national policy on the disabled. The policy was to:

- Foster independence and dignity in the lives of disabled persons.
- Encourage care for the disabled within the context of the family and school.
- Promote integration of the disabled into society, school, and the work place.

A major step forward was the approval on August 29, 1983, of the proposed National Policy for Persons with Disabilities by the National Council on the Handicapped, a group established under Title VI of the Rehabilitation Act of 1973. A further impetus was added on January 5, 1984, when President Ronald Reagan assured full cooperation in achieving both the short- and long-term goals of this policy. In developing the national policy, the working group consulted with a large number of leaders among disabled persons and providers in each of the 50 states and the District of Columbia in both the public and the private sectors. Within the policy are statements and discussions of the following:

- Education
- Attitudes
- Responsibilities of disabled persons
- Employment
- Demographic information

- Single point of entry
- Law
- Accessible communities
- Fiscal responsibility
- Independence
- Incentives
- Research
- Prevention
- Coordination
- Evaluation
- Private Sector
- Involvement
- Volunteers
- Qualified personnel
- Continuum of support services
- Rural areas
- Ethnic and social minorities
- International cooperation

The document is designed to change as society changes. People who are deaf or hard of hearing are included in the policy.

A continuing leader in motivating libraries to make their services accessible to people who are deaf or hard of hearing is the state of Florida. In August 1983, the State Library of Florida sponsored a workshop, "Improving Library Service to Florida's Population." The workshop was held at the Tampa/Hillsborough County Public Library, located in an area where a large number of people with some type of hearing loss live (Florida ranks seventh in the United States with its population of 750,000 people with a hearing loss of some degree of severity). The workshop considered the practical aspects of providing library service to this group and discussed such subjects as communication, environment, equipment, resources, and services.

Another positive indication of the future of library services to the deaf and hearing impaired is the fact that it was included in the Ethnic Materials Information Exchange Round Table during the American Library Association's annual conference in Los Angeles in 1983. In the program, "Ethnicity and ALA," it was emphasized that the first language of people who are deaf is American Sign Language (ASL) and that English is a second language. Thus, the people who are deaf are actually bilingual. Many hearing people are not familiar with deaf culture, but the award-winning Broadway play "Children of a Lesser God" in itself made positive changes in the attitudes of the general public toward deaf culture. The right to be bilingual as emphasized in ethnic materials in libraries can be a model in the community.

A second presentation in this program highlighted the trend toward treating sign language as a written language. Through The Center for Sutton Movement Writing, a newspaper, *The Sign Writer*, is available internationally. The newspaper is written in sign writing and is used in 41 countries. It is issued 4 times a year and is added to ethnic materials in many libraries which provide library service to the deaf and hearing impaired.

The future for library service to the deaf and hearing impaired is embodied in the expansion of Gallaudet College services at additional centers throughout the United States. The first extension center was opened at Johnson County Community College in 1977 in suburban Kansas City and serves a 6-state midwestern region. The second was opened north of Boston at Northern Community College in 1980, serving the New England region. The third was opened in the fall of 1983 at Ohlone College, Fremont, California for the western part of the United States. Each center's activities include educational programs in a variety of areas of interest to people who are deaf, to the parents of children who are deaf, and to professionals who provide services to deaf individuals.

Public libraries are continually expanding their services for deaf and hearing impaired people by making available, for home use, closed-captioned videocassettes of recent movies as well as telecaption decoders. It is estimated that about 50 libraries are involved in this particular program. New cassette offerings are constantly being added.

Finally, the trend toward providing TTY/TDD reference service is a positive one. The *American Library Directory*,[1] 35th edition, lists the libraries which have TTY/TDD reference service available. Included are 179 libraries which represent 38 states.

An example of employment trends of the deaf and hearing impaired is exemplified by the Pacific Gas and Electric Company's San Francisco District Office. Deaf students from Laney Junior College in Oakland, California, visited the office to see the special telephone equipment installed for service customers who are deaf. They also explored job opportunities with the company. The tour was interpreted through the signing of a company employee.

A directory of resources and services for adults with disabilities was issued by the U.S. Department of Education in 1983, and a network of adult education programs serving disabled persons was also established in the department. Its purpose is to facilitate, coordinate, and disseminate information on adult education programs serving the disabled in order to improve program practice and effectiveness. The network provides information and assistance on adult education programs through correspondence, telephone calls, and technical assistance bulletins and products. Services and resources for deaf and hearing impaired people are included.

In 1978, the District of Columbia Public Library began a newsletter designed to help serve the library and information needs of people in the District of Columbia who were deaf or had some hearing loss. The newsletter was titled *Cross Roads*. It ceased publication for a time but resumed in late 1983. Part of the reason was that, because of the increased deaf and library awareness of deaf and hearing impaired people, their need for information about library service became more acute. *Cross Roads* provides the information they need. *Red Notebook* owners in the District of Columbia receive the publication free; *Red Notebook* owners from each state—the state library and the statewide deaf services—also receive free subscriptions.

A movement which will have a long-term effect on library service to the deaf, nationwide, is the push for national recognition of "Deaf Heritage Week." Deaf culture is a subculture within the general culture with its own language—American Sign Language (ASL).

In the District of Columbia, the Martin Luther King Memorial Library was the center of activity as the District of Columbia Public Libraries observed the 10th anniversary of Deaf Heritage Week in 1983. A proclamation was issued by Mayor Marion S. Barry, Jr., of Washington, DC and a deaf-talk marathon was held during one of the days of the dedicated week. These annual celebrations have had as their purpose the closing of gaps between deaf and hearing people, between deaf and hard-of-hearing people, and between deaf groups and hard-of-hearing groups. Another achievement in the recognition of Deaf Heritage Week is the promotion of deaf culture through the library. Because the month of December contains so many important dates in the deaf heritage in America, a week in December is proposed to be observed as National Deaf Heritage Week. In 1984, the U.S. Congress enacted a law declaring April 8–14 as National Hearing Impaired Awareness Week.

To assist with this national recognition, the Library Service to the Deaf Section of the Association of Specialized and Cooperative Library Agencies (ASCLA) presented a resolution on Deaf Heritage Week to the American Library Association Council in January 1984. The supporting resolution was passed first by the ASCLA Board and then by the ALA Council. The resolution, entitled "National Deaf Heritage Week," urged the President of the United States to declare December

2–9, 1984, National Deaf Heritage Week. It also urged that the week be celebrated throughout the United States by libraries in cooperation with the deaf community. It is significant in the future of library service to the deaf and hearing impaired that this resolution was developed cooperatively between librarians and the deaf community.

One of the long-range activities taking place in the American Library Association, especially in ASCLA, which demonstrates a positive trend in the future of library service to people with disabilities, is the establishment of a committee on the "Decade of Disabled Persons" within the ASCLA division. Another long-range activity is the organizational streamlining of the division, bringing together all of the sections of the division devoted to specific disabilities into one section, Library Service to Special Populations. This newly formed unit is concerned with all types of disabilities in relation to library service. The ability to program for library service to the deaf—an important part of the work of the Library Service to the Deaf Section—continues in the new unit in the Library Service to the Deaf Forum. Reorganization began June 28, 1984. Those ASCLA members interested in these programs of service will now be able to devote their association time to this activity and not be concerned with the organizational details of the unit.

Another organization exemplifying the trend toward a strong emphasis on programing is the President's Committee on Employment of the Handicapped Library Committee. With the change in name to the PCEH Committee for Libraries and Information Services in 1984, the committee broadened its representation and its interests. One activity being carried on throughout the Decade of Disabled Persons, 1983–1992, by the committee is a program of recognition of authors of books on disability. This recognition was begun during the International Year of Disabled Persons, 1981. Jack Gannon, author of *Deaf Heritage*, was one of the authors recognized.

The need for an information center to assist libraries and other community services as well as disabled people themselves is a continuing one. In October 1983, the Columbia Broadcasting System announced the establishment of a grant to the National Organization on Disability to develop a national data bank of information on disability and related issues.

A decision by the Public Library Association of the American Library Association on measuring library service has implications for future public library development in the area of library service to the deaf and hearing impaired. This decision will result in the development of new performance standards which determine libraries' effectiveness in relation to many services including those to people who are deaf or hard of hearing.

In general, increased attention and concern is being demonstrated in creating a barrier-free environment for people who are deaf or hard of hearing. Hearing dogs are becoming more readily available and are helping to bridge the communication gap between deaf and hearing people. Improvements in hearing aids are constantly being made, and more people are using them to hear more clearly. Progress is also being made in the area of the development and use of the cochlear implant.

INTERNATIONAL TRENDS

On the international level, notable events are also taking place. Prior to the 49th International Federation of Library Associations and Institutions (IFLA) Council and General Conference in Munich, Federal Republic of Germany, a discussion document was sent out on library service to people with a hearing loss. The document was entitled "Working Group on Library Needs of the Deaf: Discussion Document." It was distributed to members of the section on Library Service to Patients and Handicapped Readers of the Division of Public Libraries. Included in the points to be discussed were the following:

- The role of the working group. Possibilities include the collection of facts and library practices; promotion of library service both for libraries and deaf people using the library; and the responsibility for supplying a means of exchanging information.
- The need for libraries to encourage deaf and hearing impaired people to use the services because they may not think of the library as a resource they would automatically use. Library staff are not specifically trained to serve deaf and hearing impaired individuals. As a result, they may not be able to communicate successfully.
- The importance of identifying the library needs of the deaf. The promotion of the idea of service and its availability to deaf and hearing impaired people.
- The need for discussion with librarians who are deaf. The deaf community itself and those working with deaf and hearing impaired people such as rehabilitation agencies need to be included among a larger working group.
- The collection of examples of library practice, the planning of projects to assist in the development of library service to the

deaf, and the organizing of discussion groups concerning the service.

This was the basis for the first open meeting of the Working Group on Library Needs of the Deaf. The meeting was held on August 23, 1983, at the 49th Conference of IFLA. The meeting was well attended with many countries represented, and discussion, based on the discussion document, was enthusiastic. Each of the countries represented volunteered a person to be responsible for keeping other countries informed about the activities within that country related to library service to people who are deaf; the vehicle for transmitting information would be the working group. Possible ways of broadening the activities of the group in the future include the participation of more members and of corresponding members, distribution of a questionnaire assessing the work presently being done, and issuance of a newsletter which would act, to a certain extent, as a clearinghouse. The Working Group on Library Needs for the Deaf will correlate its activities with other international groups concerned with the deaf such as the World Federation of the Deaf.

Countries involved in the provision of library service to deaf and hearing impaired individuals include Sweden, Holland, Denmark, the United Kingdom, Australia, and Japan. The publication in March 1984 of the first issue of the *Deaf Newsletter* [2] is an international accomplishment in the development of this service. The newsletter provides an exchange, internationally, on activities in the area of library service to the deaf and hearing impaired—an important element in the future of the service.

One example of library service provided in countries other than the United States is that of Sweden. Sweden has about 9,000 people who are deaf from birth and about 5,000 who became deaf after they had had some experience with spoken and written language. The Swedish Association for the Deaf publishes, with financial support from the state, a journal in sign language, titled *Video Journal*. It also produces videograms; among its purchasers are a few libraries. When those who are deaf have video equipment of their own, libraries will be able to lend them videograms for home use.

For a number of years, libraries have distributed "easy-to-read" books to deaf people who have difficulty reading. These books are produced in Sweden with state grants. Some libraries in Sweden offer significant services to the deaf. The Swedish Council of Cultural Affairs supported a library project of recording, through video, books translated into sign language. Videograms in sign language have been shown to elderly deaf people in leisure centers. A book-lending service is operated on the premises of the deaf association, and a reading circle has been formed. Libraries invite the organizations of the deaf and other groups to the library for informational programs in sign language, and some library staff members have learned sign language to improve the library services to people who are deaf. The text-telephone is a new communication development for the deaf in Sweden and is available in some libraries. It is often placed at the information desk so that people who are deaf can use the library's information services.

In Australia, a library listing of films suitable for people who are deaf or hard of hearing has been compiled by the State Film and Video Library of South Australia. Among the categories included are:

- Early feature and short films made in the "silent" era.
- Foreign language films which are subtitled.
- Animated and educational films in which visuals are the main feature.
- Geographical films.
- Mime films.

A course which has also established, internationally, a positive trend for the future was held in the fall of 1983 at the School of Librarianship, Leeds Polytechnic Institute, Leeds, England. Because people who are deaf are a "hidden group" in society, libraries have been slow in England in recognizing their needs for library and information service. This course was designed to raise the awareness of libraries to recognize and respond to expressed and defined needs. The subject content of the course recognized that there are deaf people in society, considered that visual materials are vital to them, and studied the unique needs of deaf persons in relation to library service. These recognitions were then related to the resources and services of the library.

These international trends are very important to library service to the deaf and hearing impaired everywhere. The Working Group established in the Section on Library Service to Hospital Patients and Handicapped Readers in the International Federation of Library Associations and Institutions will have an increasingly positive effect on library service to the deaf and hearing impaired worldwide.

The future of library service to deaf and hearing impaired people will be influenced by the positive and negative factors which can be seen now. Many unseen factors will also be influential. Library service to people with a hearing loss is becoming a reality even though the progress is slow. The future must ensure that it exists permanently at a high level of quality and is available to all. It is a new service with all of the uncertainties associated with newness. Many steps will be taken forward but occasionally there will be a backward movement. Its continuance and continuity forward depend greatly on a widebased community awareness and understanding of its need. The service depends upon the professionalism of all librarians for its solid and welcoming implementation so that its offering is inviting to and well-received by the people for whom the service is developed—the deaf and hearing impaired.

NOTES

1. *American Library Directory.* 35th edition. Chicago: American Library Association, 1982.
2. *Deaf Newsletter,* IFLA Working Group on the Library Needs of the Deaf, Leeds, England.

REFERENCE LIST

A. G. Bell BOOK-SHARE-A-THON. Washington, DC: Alexander Graham Bell Association for the Deaf, Inc., 1984.

Anderson, William. *Libraries for the Deaf—The Hidden Society.* Paper presented at the IFLA Council and General Conference. Leipzig, East Germany, 1981.

Bolt, Nancy M. *Should There Be New National Standards for Public Libraries?* Presented at the California Library Association Annual Conference, Oakland, CA, 1983. Sacramento, CA: California Library Association. (Cassette.)

Byrne, Richard. *Communications—Technology—Motivation.* Presented at the California Library Association Annual Conference, Oakland, CA, 1983. Sacramento, CA: California Library Association. (Cassette.)

College and Career: Programs for Deaf Students. Rochester, NY: National Technical Institute for the Deaf, 1983.

"Cooperatives and Networks." *Interface* 5 (4) (Summer 1983, Special Issue).

Correspondence with Gunilla Malgrem-Neale, hospital librarian, Biblioteket Lasarette, Helsingborg, Sweden, 1983.

"Cross Roads Resumes." *Cross Roads.* November 22, 1983.

Crowley, Carolyn. "A Hearing Dog Story." *Disabled USA* March 1983: 33–36.

Dalton, Phyllis I. "Focus on Service to the Disabled." In *The ALA Yearbook, 1983.* Chicago: American Library Association, 1983: 69–71.

"Deaf Librarian Promotes Library Use." *Sioux City Journal* (July 15, 1983): A10.

"Deaf People Need Barrier Free Environment." *Disabled USA* March 1983: 30–31.

"Doctors Seeking Ear Implants." *The Silent News* 4 (1) (January 1984): 1.

Ethnic Materials Information Round Table. *Ethnicity and ALA.* American Library Association Annual Conference, Los Angeles, CA, 1983. Chicago: American Library Association, 1983. (Cassettes.)

Gallaudet College. *Media Distribution.* Washington, DC: Gallaudet College, January 1984.

"A Group of Deaf Students." *P. G. and E. Week* IV (23) (November 8, 1983): 2

Hagemeyer, Alice. "Deaf Heritage Week Urged by National Groups." *The President's Committee on Employment of the Handicapped Conference Daily* (May 6, 1983): 4.

————."Sowing Libary Seeds and Letting Others Move On." *The Silent News* 15 (10) (October 1983): 19.

————."Yes Virginia, There is Library Service for Deaf Communities in Ohio." *The NAD Broadcaster* 5 (11) (November–December 1982): 13.

Letter from Collette Sangster. St. Mary's School for the Deaf. Buffalo, NY: June 20, 1983.

Letter on the National Policy on Disability. Justin W. Dart, Jr., Vice Chairperson. National Council on the Handicapped. Austin, TX: 1983.

Letter on the National Policy on Disability. Suzanne Thomas, Regional Representative. Governor's Committee on Employment of the Handicapped (Nevada). Las Vegas, NV: 1983.

"Libraries Lend Decoders, Videocassettes, Movies." *Caption* (Fall 1983): 3.

Lindberg, Kerstin. "Video—A Revolution for the Deaf." *Scandinavian Public Library Quarterly* 14 (2) (1981): 56-57.

Marshall, Mary R. *Libraries and the Handicapped Child.* Leeds Polytechnic School for Librarianship. Leeds, England, 1981.

Minor, Dorothy, comp. *The World of Work. The Handicapped Person's Guide to Finding a Job: A Bibliography.* ASCLA occasional paper number 2. Chicago: Association of Specialized and Cooperative Library Agencies, American Library Association, 1984.

National Center for Law and the Deaf. *Legal Rights of Hearing-Impaired People.* Washington, DC: Gallaudet College, 1982.

National Library Service for the Blind and Physically Handicapped. *A Research Guide on Computer Applications for Visually and Physically Handicapped Individuals.* Washington, DC: National Library Service for the Blind and Physically Handicapped, 1984.

"New Extension Center Opens on West Coast." *Outreach* (October 1983): 1.

Organization for the Use of the Telephone (OUT). "FCC Regulations Implementing PL 97-410. Brief Analysis of the Regulations." Owings Mills, MD: Organization for the Use of the Telephone, 1983.

"President Reagan Forms Working Group on Handicapped Policy." *Programs for the Handicapped* (May–June 1983): 2.

St. Mary's School for the Deaf. *Parent Lending Library. Deafness Collection.* Buffalo, NY: St. Mary's School for the Deaf, n.d.

"Serving Florida's Hearing Impaired Population." *Keystone. Technical Bulletin* 12 (2) (September–October 1983).

SHHH, Self Help for Hard of Hearing People. *Communications Systems for Groups and Large Rooms.* Bethesda, MD: SHHH, Self Help for Hard of Hearing People, October 1983. (Chart.)

Sundstrom, Susan C. *Understanding Hearing Loss and What Can Be Done to Help.* Danville, IL: Interstate Printers and Publishers, Inc., 1983.

Trubo, Richard. "Have You Heard the Latest?" *50 Plus* 24 (1) (January 1984): 35–36.

U.S. Department of Education. Office of Vocational and Adult Education Services. *Directory of Resources for Adults with Disabilities.* Edited by William R. Langer. Washington, DC: U.S. Department of Education, 1983.

U.S. National Council on the Handicapped. *National Policy for Persons with Disabilities.* Washington, DC: U.S. National Council on the Handicapped, 1983.

Yglesias, H. *Starting Early, Anew, Over and Late.* New York: Rawson Wade Publishers, 1978.

027.6 Access: Deaf Patrons in Libaries. National Academy of Gallaudet College. Washington, DC: Gallaudet College, 1983. (Videocassette.)

Appendices

Appendix A
Population Breakdown of the Deaf and Hearing Impaired

Table 1. Number and percent distribution of persons 3 years of age and over by age and sex, according to hearing ability: United States, 1977

[Data are based on household interviews of the civilian noninstitutionalized population. The survey design, general qualifications, and information on the reliability of the estimates are given in appendix I. Definitions of terms are given in appendix II]*

			Hearing ability						
				Hearing trouble					
					Bilateral hearing trouble				
Age and sex	All persons 3 years of age and over	No hearing trouble	All levels of hearing trouble[1]	All speech comprehension statuses[2]	At best, can hear words shouted in ear	Can hear words shouted across a room	Can hear words spoken in a normal voice	Unilateral hearing trouble, all levels	Hearing trouble borderline or unclear whether unilateral or bilateral
Both sexes				Number of persons in thousands					
All ages 3 years and over	202,936	188,696	14,240	7,208	842	2,310	3,984	5,969	985
3-16 years	50,692	49,868	824	379	36	96	242	308	135
17-44 years	86,620	83,688	2,933	986	82	230	668	1,631	297
17-24 years	31,340	30,699	642	199	*24	46	127	376	66
25-44 years	55,280	52,989	2,291	787	58	183	541	1,255	230
45-64 years	43,357	38,705	4,652	2,178	149	646	1,346	2,143	301
45-54 years	23,191	21,237	1,954	836	50	228	547	974	136
55-64 years	20,166	17,468	2,698	1,342	99	418	799	1,168	165
65 years and over	22,266	16,435	5,831	3,665	576	1,339	1,730	1,886	252
65-74 years	14,259	11,276	2,983	1,696	196	566	922	1,138	132
75 years and over	8,007	5,159	2,848	1,969	380	773	807	749	120
3-14 years	42,330	41,653	677	324	*28	88	203	231	119
15-44 years	94,982	91,902	3,080	1,041	89	237	707	1,708	312
Males									
All ages 3 years and over	97,680	89,548	8,131	4,282	429	1,322	2,483	3,178	621
3-16 years	25,843	25,369	474	215	*15	61	137	189	67
17-44 years	41,940	40,084	1,856	660	38	141	475	970	213
17-24 years	15,233	14,884	349	112	*11	*28	71	198	40
25-44 years	26,707	25,200	1,507	548	*28	113	404	773	174
45-64 years	20,700	17,781	2,920	1,508	91	451	938	1,182	211
45-54 years	11,181	9,946	1,236	563	*25	164	369	574	97
55-64 years	9,519	7,835	1,684	944	66	287	569	608	114
65 years and over	9,197	6,315	2,882	1,899	286	670	933	837	129
65-74 years	6,196	4,574	1,623	1,006	111	319	569	533	73
75 years and over	3,000	1,741	1,259	894	174	351	363	304	56
3-14 years	21,590	21,203	387	187	*13	55	117	139	58
15-44 years	46,193	44,250	1,943	687	40	147	495	1,021	222

*See footnote at end of Table. *Source:* p. 626.

Table 1. (Continued)

| Age and sex | All persons 3 years of age and over | No hearing trouble | Hearing trouble | | | | | | | |
| | | | Bilateral hearing trouble | | | | | Unilateral hearing trouble, all levels | Hearing trouble borderline or unclear whether unilateral or bilateral |
			All levels of hearing trouble [1]	All speech comprehension statuses [2]	At best, can hear words shouted in ear	Can hear words shouted across a room	Can hear words spoken in a normal voice		
Females									
All ages 3 years and over	105,256	99,148	6,108	2,927	413	988	1,501	2,790	363
3-16 years	24,849	24,499	350	164	*21	35	104	119	67
17-44 years	44,680	43,604	1,076	326	43	88	192	661	83
17-24 years	16,107	15,815	292	87	*13	*18	55	179	*27
25-44 years	28,573	27,789	784	239	*30	70	137	482	57
45-64 years	22,657	20,925	1,732	670	58	195	408	961	90
45-54 years	12,010	11,292	718	273	*25	64	178	400	40
55-64 years	10,647	9,633	1,015	398	*34	131	229	560	50
65 years and over	13,070	10,120	2,950	1,766	290	669	797	1,050	122
65-74 years	8,063	6,703	1,360	691	85	247	353	605	59
75 years and over	5,007	3,417	1,589	1,075	206	422	444	445	64
3-14 years	20,740	20,450	290	137	*15	*33	85	92	61
15-44 years	48,789	47,653	1,136	353	49	91	212	687	90
Both sexes				Percent distribution					
All ages 3 years and over	100.0	100.0	100.0	100.0	100.0	100.0	100.0	100.0	100.0
3-16 years	25.0	26.4	5.8	5.3	4.3	4.2	6.1	5.2	13.7
17-44 years	42.7	44.4	20.6	13.7	9.7	10.0	16.8	27.3	30.2
17-24 years	15.4	16.3	4.5	2.8	*2.9	2.0	3.2	6.3	6.7
25-44 years	27.2	28.1	16.1	10.9	6.9	7.9	13.6	21.0	23.4
45-64 years	21.4	20.5	32.7	30.2	17.7	28.0	33.8	35.9	30.6
45-54 years	11.4	11.3	13.7	11.6	5.9	9.9	13.7	16.3	13.8
55-64 years	9.9	9.3	18.9	18.6	11.8	18.1	20.1	19.6	16.8
65 years and over	11.0	8.7	40.9	50.8	68.4	58.0	43.4	31.6	25.6
65-74 years	7.0	6.0	20.9	23.5	23.3	24.5	23.1	19.1	13.4
75 years and over	3.9	2.7	20.0	27.3	45.1	33.5	20.3	12.5	12.2
3-14 years	20.9	22.1	4.8	4.5	*3.3	3.8	5.1	3.9	12.1
15-44 years	46.8	48.7	21.6	14.4	10.6	10.3	17.7	28.6	31.7
Males									
All ages 3 years and over	100.0	100.0	100.0	100.0	100.0	100.0	100.0	100.0	100.0
3-16 years	26.5	28.3	5.8	5.0	*3.5	4.6	5.5	5.9	10.8
17-44 years	42.9	44.8	22.8	15.4	8.9	10.7	19.1	30.5	34.3
17-24 years	15.6	16.6	4.3	2.6	*2.6	*2.1	2.9	6.2	6.4
25-44 years	27.3	28.1	18.5	12.8	*6.5	8.5	16.3	24.3	28.0
45-64 years	21.2	19.9	35.9	35.2	21.2	34.1	37.8	37.2	34.0
45-54 years	11.4	11.1	15.2	13.1	*5.8	12.4	14.9	18.1	15.6
55-64 years	9.7	8.7	20.7	22.0	15.4	21.7	22.9	19.1	18.4
65 years and over	9.4	7.1	35.4	44.3	66.7	50.7	37.6	26.3	20.8
65-74 years	6.3	5.1	20.0	23.5	25.9	24.1	22.9	16.8	11.8
75 years and over	3.1	1.9	15.5	20.9	40.6	26.6	14.6	9.6	9.0
3-14 years	22.1	23.7	4.8	4.4	*3.0	4.2	4.7	4.4	9.3
15-44 years	47.3	49.4	23.9	16.0	9.3	11.1	19.9	32.1	35.7
Females									
All ages 3 years and over	100.0	100.0	100.0	100.0	100.0	100.0	100.0	100.0	100.0
3-16 years	23.6	24.7	5.7	5.6	*5.1	3.5	6.9	4.3	18.5
17-44 years	42.4	44.0	17.6	11.1	10.4	8.9	12.8	23.7	22.9
17-24 years	15.3	16.0	4.8	3.0	*3.1	*1.8	3.7	6.4	*7.4
25-44 years	27.1	28.0	12.8	8.2	*7.3	7.1	9.1	17.3	15.7
45-64 years	21.5	21.1	28.4	22.9	14.0	19.7	27.2	34.4	24.8
45-54 years	11.4	11.4	11.8	9.3	*6.1	6.5	11.9	14.3	11.0
55-64 years	10.1	9.7	16.6	13.6	*8.2	13.3	15.3	20.1	13.8
65 years and over	12.4	10.2	48.3	60.3	70.2	67.7	53.1	37.6	33.6
65-74 years	7.7	6.8	22.3	23.6	20.6	25.0	23.5	21.7	16.3
75 years and over	4.8	3.4	26.0	36.7	49.9	42.7	29.6	15.9	17.6
3-14 years	19.7	20.6	4.7	4.7	*3.6	*3.3	5.7	3.3	16.8
15-44 years	46.4	48.1	18.6	12.1	11.9	9.2	14.1	24.6	24.8

[1] Includes 78,221 persons who did not respond to either hearing scale. Excludes persons reporting tinnitus only
[2] Includes 71,144 persons who did not respond to the Gallaudet scale.

* *Source*: National Center for Health Statistics, P.W. Ries: "Hearing Ability of Persons by Sociodemographic and Health Characteristics: United States." *Vital and Health Statistics*. Series 10. 140. DHHS Pub. No. (PHS) 82-1568. Public Health Service. Washington, D.C. U.S. Government Printing Office, August 1982. pp. 23–24.

Appendix B
Effects and Treatment of Hearing Loss*

IMPLICATIONS OF HEARING LOSS

Degree of Loss	Description	Children		Adults	
		Effect	Referral	Effect	Referral
0–15 dB.	Normal	None	None	None	None
15–25 dB.	Slight	May have difficulty with faint or distant speech and in group situations. May result in delay in speech and language acquisition for very young children and/or learning disability, inattention.	Frequent otologic and audiologic monitoring; consideration of need for hearing aid; may need speechreading, auditory training, speech therapy and/or language therapy; preferential seating. Family counseling may be indicated.	May have problems in difficult listening situations (group, noise).	Consideration of need for hearing aid; may need speechreading, auditory training, speech therapy and/or language therapy; preferential seating.
25–40 dB.	Mild	Difficulty with faint or distant speech and in group situations; may have speech problems, or language delay and/or learning disability; inattention.	Frequent otologic and audiologic monitoring; consideration of need for hearing aid, speechreading, auditory training, speech therapy, language therapy; preferential seating. Family counseling may be indicated.	May have problems in difficult listening situations.	Frequent otologic and audiologic monitoring; consideration for hearing aid, speechreading, auditory training, speech therapy, language therapy; preferential seating.
40–65 dB.	Moderate	Speech problems, language retardation, learning disability, inattention, conversation must be loud to be understood, difficulty in group situations, increasing difficulty in school.	Hearing aid, auditory training, speechreading, speech therapy, language therapy. May need tutoring and/or special educational placement. Family and individual counseling may be indicated.	May have speech problems; conversation must be loud to be understood, problems in group and other difficult listening situations, dependence on visual cues.	Consideration for hearing aid, speech therapy speechreading, special consideration (seating, lighting, noise, other). Family and individual counseling may be needed.
65–95 dB.	Severe	May hear only loud speech; may be able to identify environmental sounds; may be able to discriminate vowels but not consonants; speech and oral language may not develop spontaneously if loss occurs prior to age 3; speech and language problems.	Hearing aid. Special educational placement with emphasis on language development, concept development, speechreading, speech, auditory training. May need total communication. Early education program indicated. Family and individual counseling may be needed.	Will not hear conversational speech, may be able to identify environmental sounds, speech may deteriorate, heavy reliance on visual cues.	All of above. Personal counseling, vocational evaluation and rehabilitation may be indicated. Interpreting and other accommodations may be necessary. Family counseling may be needed.
95 dB+.	Profound	May hear some loud sounds but more aware of vibration; vision primary avenue for communication; speech and oral language will not develop spontaneously.	Special education program with emphasis on language skills, concept development, speechreading, and auditory training. May need total communication. May benefit from hearing aid. Family and individual counseling may be needed.	May hear some loud sounds but more aware of vibration; vision primary avenue for communication; speech may deteriorate.	All of above.

*From training materials developed by The National Academy of Gallaudet College. Used with permission. Also appears in *SHHH*, November–December 1982. pp. 4–5.

Appendix C
National Deaf Heritage Week

In January 1984, the "Resolution for National Deaf Heritage Week," developed by the Library Service to the Deaf Section, Association of Specialized and Cooperative Library Agencies, was presented to the ASCLA Board of Directors by LSDS Chairperson Mary E. Flournoy. It was adopted by the ASCLA Board and presented to the American Library Association Council by ASCLA Councilor Barratt Wilkins and seconded by Stefan B. Moses, councilor-at-large. It was then adopted by the ALA Council and transmitted by the secretary of the council, Robert Wedgeworth, to the president of the United States, Ronald Reagan.

AMERICAN LIBRARY ASSOCIATION
50 EAST HURON STREET · CHICAGO, ILLINOIS 60611 · (312) 944 6780

NATIONAL DEAF HERITAGE WEEK

WHEREAS,   Approximately 17 million persons in the United States are hearing impaired; and this number will increase due to illness, noise, accident, heredity, greater longevity, and ironically, better medical care which now saves the lives of children but may leave them with a hearing impairment; and

WHEREAS,   Deafness is an invisible disability which is unrecognized and misunderstood by most hearing people; it is not only the handicap of not being able to hear, but also the disability of communication, which, in the words of Helen Keller, "separates people from people";

WHEREAS,   The term deaf community implies uniformity in disability, the deaf community consists of individuals from varying backgrounds, who have different types of hearing loss and different needs and limitations but all share the common characteristics of hearing loss and communication disability; and

WHEREAS,   The general public has become more aware of the deaf community and deafness through such efforts as:

- The National Theater of the Deaf, which has toured throughout the United States and appeared on television;
- "Children of a Lesser God," the Tony-Award winning play about deafness which starred a deaf actress;
- closed captioning of television programs; and

WHEREAS, Libraries have been instrumental in Deaf Awareness and Deaf Heritage, such as:

. Since 1974, the Libraries of the Washington, DC metropolitan area have annually observed a week of special recognition for the deaf community; now called Deaf Heritage Week, it is celebrated in December;

. The Free Library of Philadelphia coordinated the first celebration of Deaf Awareness Week in Philadelphia and has helped with all succeeding activities;

. The San Francisco Public Library is conducting a special project on Deaf Heritage and Culture;

. Public, school and academic libraries are acquiring literature and media on deafness and deaf individuals as well as materials presented in formats which are accessible to the deaf community;

. The Library Services to the Deaf Section of the Association of Specialized and Cooperative Library Agencies, a division of the American Library Association, was formed in 1978 "to promote library and information service to deaf persons; by fostering deaf awareness in the library community at large and the deaf and hearing populations at large..."; and

WHEREAS, The heritage of deaf people in America has been recognized in the recent publication of Deaf Heritage, the first history of the deaf community in America and American Sign Language has been acknowledged as a true language and is taought throughout the United States; and

WHEREAS, Deaf, and hard of hearing persons and hearing persons alike, need to know and understand the heritage of the deaf community; and

WHEREAS, The month of December contains these important dates in the Deaf Heritage of America:

. Thomas Hopkins Gallaudet, the founder of America's first permanent school for the deaf, one of ten educators honored in the Library of Congress and for whom Gallaudet College was named, was born on December 10, 1787;

. Laurent Clerc, the first deaf person to teach deaf children in America, was born on December 26, 1785;

. Laura Bridgman, the first deaf-blind person to be successfully educated and who served as a model for Helen Keller and many other deaf-blind persons, was born on December 21, 1829;

. Henry C. Rider, founder of the Deaf Mute's Journal, the publication which served as the spring board leading to the founding of the National Association of the Deaf, was born December 14, 1832;

. The first transistorized electronic hearing aid was offered for sale on December 29, 1952;

. December 1982 was proclaimed as "National Closed Captioned Month" by the President of the United States; NOW, THEREFORE, BE IT

RESOLVED, That the Council of the American Library Association urge the President of the United States to declare a National Deaf Heritage Week to be held December 2-9, 1984, and to be celebrated by libraries, especially public libraries, in cooperation with the deaf Community throughout the nation.

ADOPTED BY THE
COUNCIL OF THE AMERICAN LIBRARY ASSOCIATION
January 11, 1984 in Washington, DC
Transmitted by

Robert Wedgeworth

Robert Wedgeworth, Secretary of Council

Appendix D
ALA's Role in Deaf and Hearing Impaired Services

Library Service to the Deaf Section
Association of Specialized and Cooperative Library
Agencies
A Unit of the American Library Association*

Goals:

To promote library and information service to deaf persons by: fostering deaf awareness in the library community and in the deaf and hearing population at large; monitoring and publicizing legislation and funding developments related to library and information services for deaf persons; encouraging their participation in the American Library Association; stimulating the production, distribution, and collection of materials in formats that are readily accessible to deaf persons and that accurately portray deaf persons; and developing and operating a clearinghouse of information on services for deaf persons to assist libraries in collection development and programing.

In the discharge of this purpose, the Section shall work through specialized and cooperative library agencies and in cooperation with other American Library Association units and national organizations as appropriate.

Responsibilities and Interests:

The Section has general responsibility for those functions and services relating to library service to deaf persons. The Section has specific responsibility for:

A. Planning and developing programs, policies and studies for the development of library service to the deaf and encouraging greater use by the deaf community.

---

*Source: By-laws of the Library Service to the Deaf Section, Association of Specialized and Cooperative Library Agencies.

B. Encouraging librarians to work toward effective coordination of library resources and services for deaf persons through the ALA and its membership.
C. Working with other units in the Association for Specialized and Cooperative Library Agencies and in the American Library Association to coordinate activities that promote library service to the deaf, including encouraging the formation of inter-divisional committees or the appointment of liaisons, when appropriate.
D. Contributing to the development of guidelines and standards through active participation on any ASCLA committees or subcommittees in this area and assisting in the dissemination of those standards and guidelines.
E. Continuously encouraging employment opportunities for deaf librarians and library workers in all types of libraries and in all functional areas within libraries.
F. Developing and assisting in the maintenance of a clearinghouse for the exchange of information and encouraging the development of materials, publications, and research within the areas of concern of the Section.
G. Studying and recommending needed legislation for improving library and information services to deaf persons.
H. Representing the interests of librarians and staff working with deaf persons to all relevant agencies, governmental or private, and to industries that serve deaf persons as clients or consumers.
I. Encouraging awareness among librarians of the special needs and problems of deaf persons.

The Deaf Community Has Varying Library and Information Needs*

Over 6 percent of the general population has some hearing impairment. Categories include:

> Oralists (lip readers)
> American Sign Language Users
> Bilingual Language Users (ASL/English)
> Minimal Language Users
> Deafened Adults

---

*Source: *Library Service to the Deaf*; Section of Association of Specialized and Cooperative Library Agencies, Division of the American Library Association.

Hearing Impaired Elderly
Hard-of-Hearing Individuals
Hearing People with Deaf Members in the Family

Each category has varying degrees of hearing loss: mild, considerable, or profound, regardless of whether or not they are a hearing aid wearer; whether or not they know sign language.

They are of all ages, races, and nationalities. Some of them have additional disabilities such as blindness, orthopedic problems, cerebral palsy, mental retardation, and others. They have all levels of educational backgrounds and come from differing political, social, religious, and economic perspectives.

GOALS OF LSDS INCLUDE:

- fostering awareness
- studying legislation and funding sources
- encouraging career opportunities for the deaf in libraries
- stimulating the production and distribution of materials
- developing an information clearinghouse for librarians and others who work with the deaf
- coordinating interpreter services at ALA conferences
- working through specialized and cooperative library agencies
- cooperating with other local and national organizations for the deaf and hearing impaired

AREAS OF EXPERTISE

- Laws and Legislation
- Communication Skills
- Library Resources and Programing

COMMITTEES

- Nominating: selects candidates for Section offices
- Planning, Organization and Bylaws: does long range planning; determines structure of Section
- Legislation and Funding: monitors and investigates status of deaf with regard to laws, regulations and grant-giving agencies

- Relations with Outside Organizations: works with many library and other agencies to share information and coordinate activities
- Programs and Activities: plan programs and conferences and ongoing endeavors which channel the individual assets and energy of members toward achievement of Section goals
- Publications: produces materials for librarians serving the deaf; stimulates the production of publications for use with the deaf.

The Section was formed on September 1, 1978.

Appendix E
A Library Media Center at a Residential School for the Deaf

Many things happen at the library media center. In addition to the traditional book and materials cataloging, shelf-reading, and card catalog filing, audiovisual software and equipment are used. Instructional, production, and consulting services are provided for the classroom programs and the library media center. Materials are developed for use in the library as well as in the classroom and the dormitory.

First priority is given to library media services for each class. The class comes to the library at a regularly scheduled time each week to reinforce the students' learning processes that occur in the classroom. Other students come to the library for free reading as a reward for completing homework. The students are given student passes from classrooms for study hall.

Part of the library period is used to develop reading skills, audiovisual skills, and/or library skills. Part of each session also allows students to select books or periodicals to be read in the library, classroom, and dormitory. Students should make use of skills learned here when they go to the public library.

Also, the students make use of the reference section to research selected topics for term papers. Periodical collections and reference collections do not need to be altered for deaf and hearing impaired students. However, these students may seek help in understanding the language in the periodicals and in reference books. Audiovisual collections should be supplemented with films which have been captioned for the hearing impaired.

Numerous books on deafness will be needed for the professional shelves. These books given an overview of the pathology of deafness, the methods of instruction and communications, and relevant topics to inform teachers, parents, college students, and others working with the hearing impaired.

Students and staff use all areas of the library media center. Many students have become library aides as part of their vocational education. The center offers unlimited opportunities for learning experience.

Irene Hodock
Librarian
Indiana School for the Deaf
Indianapolis, IN

Appendix F
International Federation of Library Associations. Section of Library Services to Hospital Patients and Handicapped Readers.

49th IFLA Council and General Conference—Meeting 103a.—Working Group on Library needs of the deaf Discussion Document.

A. Terms of reference for the Working Group on the Library needs of the deaf.
These are suggestions which need confirmation, discussion and expedition:
- to collect information (i.e. facts and library practices);
- to promote library service—to both libraries and deaf patrons;
- to serve as a means for the exchange of information.
B. They are based on several assumptions, viz:
  1. the deaf are physically able to use normal public library services (though the multiply handicapped may have difficulty).
  2. library resources are already provided i.e. information sources, staff resources and library services.
  3. libraries make no special efforts to encourage the deaf to use their services;
  4. the deaf may not think of using libraries as a resource to which they would turn naturally;
  5. library staff are not trained specifically to serve deaf patrons (this relates especially to communicative abilities);

6. library service is disproportionately available to the deaf—they are not using them as they could.
C. The necessary steps begin with the objective of the Working Group, as follows:
  1. identify the library needs of the deaf.
  2. promote the idea of service provision to libraries and librarians.
  3. promote the idea of service availability to the deaf.
D. Achievement of these successive steps: e.g. by
  1. reviewing the librarianship literature—this is almost complete.
  2. discussing this between:
    i. interested parties:
      a) deaf librarians need to be identified and asked for their view.
      b) the deaf themselves need to be surveyed or their views obtained—individuals and organizations.
      c) those in close relationships with the deaf—e.g. deaf center social workers.
    ii. between members of a larger Working Group.
  3. collecting current examples of library practice.
  4. planning projects to assist in development of library services for the deaf.
  5. organizing forums for the discussion of the whole idea.

Appendix G
Decade of Disabled Persons (1983–1992)*

 DECADE OF DISABLED PERSONS (1983–1992)
MESSAGE OF UNITED NATIONS
SECRETARY-GENERAL PEREZ DE CUELLAR

The General Assembly has proclaimed the period 1983–1992 as the United Nations Decade of Disabled Persons.

This proclamation underlines the determination of the international community to carry forward the impetus given by the International Year of Disabled Persons in 1981 towards the prevention of disability and the equalization of opportunities for disabled persons, as well as their rehabilitation in society.

I am therefore fully confident that during this decade efforts will be intensified for the implementation of the world programme of action concerning disabled persons, the primary aim of which is to realize the rights of as many as 500 million disabled persons around the world to contribute to and benefit from the economic and social progress of their countries. However, this cannot be achieved unless society changes its attitude towards people with disabilities. Indeed, we should focus on their abilities and the contribution they can make.

We bear the responsibility to encourage and assist disabled persons to lead useful and meaningful lives. This is not to be done as an act of charity but because it is their right and because society as a whole can progress only if each of its members is given full recognition and respect for his or her own inherent dignity and worth.

I appeal to all governments, concerned organizations and individuals alike to contribute to the implementation of the world plan of action during this decade and beyond, and thereby demonstrate our commitment to the "full participation and equality" of persons with disabilities.

Released in New York, Geneva, and Vienna—April 19, 1983.

Source: National Organization on Disability Report. Summer 1983. p. 1.

Congressional Record

United States
of America

PROCEEDINGS AND DEBATES OF THE 98^{tb} CONGRESS, FIRST SESSION

Vol. 129	WASHINGTON, MONDAY, JULY 25, 1983	No. 106

U.S. House of Representatives
Concurrent Resolution #39
Decade of Disabled Persons (1983–1992)

H. CON. RES. 39

Whereas, a new era in recognition of human rights and universal respect for these rights has begun;

Whereas, The United Nations General Assembly has declared 1983 through 1992 as the United Nations Decade of Disabled Persons;

Whereas, The United States has made great strides during the last decade in improving the lives of thirty-five million American citizens with physical and mental disabilities;

Whereas, there is still much to be done to open doors to the full participation and equality of disabled persons in society throughout the world;

Whereas, handicapped individuals should be able to participate fully in the mainstream of society through education, employment and community living opportunities;

Whereas, the United States recognizes the need for further progress in strengthening public understanding and awareness of the needs and aspirations of disabled persons;

Whereas, there is hope that this spirit of carrying out the goals of the International and National Years in 1981 and 1982 will continue through this decade;

Whereas, a framework for national action has been established by these previous initiatives and the improvement of programs for the disabled over the last decade; and

Whereas, further progress should be made in the United States toward achieving the following long-term goals of and for disabled persons promoted during the International Year of Disabled Persons: (1) expanded educational opportunity; (2) improved access to housing, buildings, and transportation; (3) expanded employment opportunity; (4) expanded participation in recreational, social, and cultural activities; (5) expanded and strengthened rehabilitation programs and facilities; (6) purposeful application of biomedical research aimed at conquering major disabling conditions; (7) reduction in the incidence of disability by expanded accident and disease prevention; (8) expanded application of technology to minimize the effects of disability; and (9) expanded international exchange of information and experience to benefit all disabled persons: Now, therefore, be it

Resolved by the House of Representatives (the Senate concurring), That it is the sense of the Congress that the President should take all steps within his authortiy to implement, within theUnited States, the objectives of the United Nations Decade of Disabled Persons (1983–1992), as proclaimed by the United Nations General Assembly on December 3, 1982.

SEC. 2. The President should report to the Congress annually during the United Nations Decade of Disabled Persons on the plans developed by the executive branch in accordance with United Nations General Assembly Resolution 37/53 to implement, within the United States, the objectives of the United Nations Decade of Disabled Persons and on the steps taken pursuant to those plans.

SEC. 3. The Clerk of the House shall transmit a copy of this resolution to the President.

National Decade of Disabled Persons

By the President of the United States of America

A Proclamation

During the 1981 International Year and the 1982 National Year of Disabled Persons, we learned about the many accomplishments of disabled persons, both young and old. We also gained vast new insights into the significant impact that access to education, rehabilitation, and employment have on their lives.

The progress we have made is a tribute to the courage and determination of our disabled people, to innovative research and development both in technology and training techniques to assist the disabled, and to those—whether in the private or public sectors—who have given so generously of their time and energies to help enrich the lives of disabled persons.

We must encourage the provision of rehabilitation and other comprehensive services oriented toward independence within the context of family and community. For only through opportunities to use the full range of their potential will our disabled citizens attain the independence and dignity that are their due.

In furtherance of the initiatives encouraged by observance of the International Year of Disabled Persons, the United Nations General Assembly has proclaimed the years 1983 through 1992 as the United Nations Decade of Disabled Persons. The Congress of the United States, by House Concurrent Resolution 39, has requested the President to take all steps within his authority to implement, within the United States, the objectives of the United Nations Decade of Disabled Persons as proclaimed by the United Nations General Assembly on December 3, 1982.

NOW, THEREFORE, I, RONALD REAGAN, President of the United States of America, do hereby proclaim the years 1983 through 1992 as the National Decade of Disabled Persons. I call upon all Americans in both the private and public sectors to join our continuing efforts to assist disabled people and to continue the progress made over the past two years.

IN WITNESS WHEREOF, I have hereunto set my hand this twenty-eighth day of November, in the year of our Lord nineteen hundred and eighty-three, and of the Independence of the United States of America the two hundred and eighth.

Ronald Reagan

In January 1983, the "Resolution, Decade of Disabled Persons" was developed by the Association of Specialized and Cooperative Library Agencies Committee on the International/National Years of Disabled Persons, 1981–1982. It was presented to the ASCLA Board of Directors by IYDP/NYDP Chairperson Phyllis I. Dalton and adopted by the ASCLA Board. It was then presented to the American Library Association Council by ASCLA Councilor Barratt Wilkins, with a second by Sharon A. Hammer, councilor-at-large, and adopted by the ALA Council. It was transmitted by the secretary of the council, Robert Wedgeworth, to the chairman of the board of directors, Richard M. DeVos, of the National Organization on Disability, Washington, DC.

AMERICAN LIBRARY ASSOCIATION

50 EAST HURON STREET   CHICAGO, ILLINOIS 60611   (312) 944 6780

RESOLUTION DECADE OF DISABLED PERSONS

WHEREAS, The United Nations has officially proclaimed the period 1983-1992 as the Decade of Disabled Persons and has urged all nations and organizations to continue the momentum of the 1981 International Year of Disabled Persons in improving the quality of life for the world's half-billion persons with disabilities;

WHEREAS, the International Year of Disabled Persons led to widespread commitment and action to further the full participation of America's 35 million persons with disabilities in all aspects of national and community life;

WHEREAS, the International Year observances led to the proclamation by the President and the Congress of the United States of 1982 as the National Year of Disabled Persons, to the formation of the National Organization on Disability and to the widespread use of the slogan, "Meeting the Challenges Through Partnerships";

WHEREAS, these partnerships between persons with and without disabilities; between government and the private sector; and among state, local and national organizations are continuing to improve the lives of Americans with disabilities; and

WHEREAS, further progress should be made in the United States toward increasing understanding of the unmet needs and potential contribution of America's disabled citizens in furtherance of the following long-term goals of and for disabled persons as set forth during the 1981 and 1982 observances:

-Expanded Educational Opportunity

-Improved Access to Housing, Buildings and Transportation

-Greater Opportunity for Employment

-Greater Participation in Recreational, Social and Cultural Activities

-Expanded and Strengthened Rehabilitation Programs and Facilities

-Purposeful Application of Biomedical Research Aimed at Conquering Major Disabling Conditions

-Reduction in the Incidence of Disability through Accident and Disease Prevention

-Increased Application of Technology to Ameliorate the Effects of Disability

-Expanded International Exchange of Information and Experience to Benefit All Disabled Persons, BE IT THEREFORE

RESOLVED,   That the Board of Directors of the Association of Specialized and Cooperative Library Agencies at its meeting on January 8, 1983, in San Antonio, Texas, and the Council of the American Library Association at its meeting on January 12, 1983, in San Antonio, Texas, support the Decade of Disabled Persons of the United Nations and join in furthering the above long term goals of and for Americans with disabilities, and that same be transmitted to the National Organization on Disability, 1575 I Street, NW, Washington, DC   20005.

ADOPTED BY
THE ALA COUNCIL
January 11, 1983
TRANSMITTED BY

Robert Wedgeworth

ROBERT WEDGEWORTH
SECRETARY
OF THE COUNCIL

Appendix H
Symbols Related to Library Service to the Deaf and Hearing Impaired

International Symbol of Deafness

© NATIONAL ASSOCIATION OF THE DEAF

The concept of the symbol was originated by the World Federation of the Deaf. Each member country holds its own copyright and promotes appropriate use of the symbol. In the United States, the National Association of the Deaf holds the copyright.

The following policies have been set to govern the use of the symbol:

1. The symbol should be used in the design and proportions approved by the World Federation of the Deaf. The colors used for the symbol should be white on a dark blue background unless there are special reasons to use other colors. The white on blue coloring conforms with international road sign requirements.
2. The symbol should not be changed or added to. The basic symbol can be used along with other symbols or with text as long as the integrity of the symbol is not distorted.
3. The symbol should be used to identify, mark, or show the way to buildings, facilities, and devices that are accessible to and usable by deaf or hearing impaired people. For example, the symbol could be used to mark:
    a. Information offices which have TDDs or other devices for deaf and hearing impaired people and/or interpreters at such places as railway stations, airports, first aid stations, etc.
    b. Offices, hospitals, or institutions concerned with deaf persons, and cultural centers, clubs, and sports facilities sponsored by deaf groups.
    c. Conference or meeting rooms, theatres, and auditoriums which have interpreter services, induction loops, or special amplification for deaf and hearing impaired people, or special seating arrangements.
    d. Identification such as drivers' licenses.
    e. Membership cards issued by organizations of deaf or hearing impaired individuals.
4. Reproduction of the symbol is prohibited except in publications and media intended to promote popularization and universal recognition of the purpose and function of the symbol.
5. Use of the symbol for commercial purposes is *not* authorized. It is not intended for uses such as advertising, as a trademark, on a letterhead design, or on articles and productions made by or for the handicapped. It may, however, be used to identify or advertise the accessibility of commercial premises or devices in commercial premises intended for the use of deaf customers or patrons.

National Library Symbol

Copr. © 1980, WCFL

The national library symbol was first launched at the 1982 American Library Association Annual Conference for libraries throughout the United States to promote awareness of their services. Originally developed by the Western Maryland Public Libraries for systemwide use, this symbol is recommended for national use by the ALA Council.

The purpose of a national library symbol is to increase public awareness of libraries through widespread use of a standardized symbol on library directional signs and promotional materials. The symbol is designed primarily for use on exterior library signs appearing on streets, highways, campuses, and buildings, but it can also be used by individual libraries on promotional materials.

Impetus for adopting a national symbol developed from a recommendation of the 1979 White House Conference on Library and Information Services which suggested the adoption of a national library symbol to increase the public awareness of libraries. The Western Maryland symbol was selected for national use because it was designed as a part of a total coordinated sign system and because it meets the criteria for a good library symbol. This library symbol is:

- Readily understood by the average person without the need of text;
- Easily reproduced for both large and small application;
- Universally recognized and associated with a library;
- Suggestive of the active use of information by library patrons;
- Aesthetically pleasing, clear, and simple in design, similar to the graphic style of international symbols already in widespread use;
- Capable of modification by libraries should they change significantly in the future.

Development of this library symbol in Maryland included the preparation of an excellent sign system manual which gives specifications for using the symbol independently or as a part of a total sign system for a library. *A Sign System for Libraries* has been published by the American Library Association. The manual specifies a standard shade of blue (PMS 285) as the background color for exterior use of the symbol on directional and building signs.

**Libraries . . .
For Fun and
Information**

Reproduced with permission
of the District of Columbia Public
Library, Washington, DC.

"Libraries...for fun and information" was developed by the District of Columbia Public Library. It is an attractive logo which has many uses in promoting library service to deaf and hearing impaired people. It is an excellent example of a logo which can be developed and one which is in use.

Ann Silver's Sign Language Interpreting (Accessibility) Logo Design

Ann Silver's sign language interpreting (accessibility) logo design can be used for program brochures, flyers/mailers, identification badges, desk and wall display signs, reserved seat signs for special sections, signage, calendars of events, etc. The logo is attractive and easily visible. It is designed especially for announcing sign language interpreted events. Originally commissioned by the Museum Program for the Deaf in New York City, the logo has also been used by the Mark Taper Forum in Los Angeles, the Goodman Theater in Chicago, and the National Endowment for the Arts.

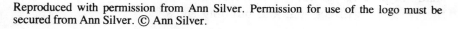

Reproduced with permission from Ann Silver. Permission for use of the logo must be secured from Ann Silver. © Ann Silver.

International Symbol of Access*

The international symbol of access was adopted by Rehabilitation International in 1969 at its 11th World Congress on Rehabilitation of the Disabled. Rehabilitation International is a federation of national and international organizations providing rehabilitation services for the disabled in more than 60 countries.

The symbol tells a disabled person, particularly one using a wheelchair, that a building or facility is accessible and can be entered and used without concern of being blocked by architectural barriers.

To use this symbol for reasons other than to denote an accessible building or facility intended for use by the disabled is prohibited because such use confuses the symbol's meaning. Wherever it is displayed,

Source: The President's Committee on Employment of the Handicapped and the National Easter Seal Society for Crippled Children and Adults.

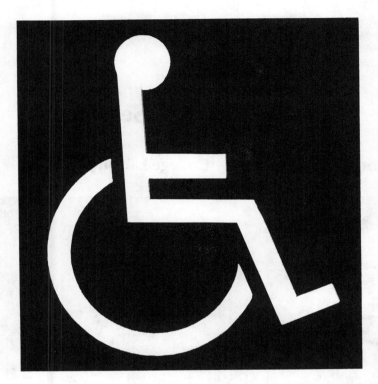

the disabled can be assured that they will not be barred by thoughtless obstacles or prohibited from participating in the mainstream of society.

To preserve the meaning of the symbol, to maintain the dignity of the disabled individuals, and to avoid confusing the public at large, the symbol must be displayed correctly and properly at all times. Its use must never be associated with commercial promotion of any product or service. Under no circumstances should the design of the symbol be changed or altered.

Several states have passed legislation setting forth the criteria for accessibility in buildings constructed with public funds and providing that the symbol be displayed prominently in such buildings.

The correct color for the symbol of accessibility is similar to the blue used on international road signs indicating hospitals and parking. This blue should be the background color for a white wheelchair figure when used without a border, or as the color for the border and wheelchair figure on a white background.

Reproduced with permission of The President's Committee on Employment of the Handicapped, Washington, DC.

Appendix I
Specific Library Services

Austin (TX) Community College Library

Photo by Austin (TX) Community College Library. Used by permission.

Reference librarians trained in the techniques of courteously and effectively interacting with deaf persons are always on duty at the Austin (Texas) Community College Library. These librarians helped with the production of ACC's videotape on working with deaf patrons, "Breaking the Sound Barrier."

Clark County Library District, Las Vegas, Nevada

Photo by Patricia Mortati. Used by permission of the Clark County Library District.

In addition to offering a wide range of materials for the visually and physically disabled, the Clark County Library District is now able to provide information to the hearing impaired with a telecommunication device for the deaf. Persons who have a similar device in their homes can now "talk" to Library Assistant Mary Anne Morton and have their reference questions answered, find out when captioned films for the deaf are scheduled, or check on the availability of a best-seller.

Contra Costa County Library, Pleasant Hill, California

Photo by Contra Costa County Library. Used by permission.

Young deaf employee Candy McCullough (left), receives instructions in sign language from her supervisor, Bettye Morgan (right), in Contra Costa County Library's circulation department.

Gallaudet College Learning Center, Washington, DC

Photo by Gallaudet College Library. Used by permission.

One of the several lounges in the Gallaudet College Learning Center in which library, educational technology, and instructional areas are integrated.

Indiana School for the Deaf Library/Media Center, Indianapolis, Indiana

Photo by Indiana School for the Deaf. Used by permission.

A fine selection of books, both fiction and nonfiction for all ages, along with newspapers and magazines, makes library visitation an enjoyable part of the student's day. Reference and audiovisual collections are available to assist the students and teachers. The addition of professional books which are relevent to deafness, methods and communication, and similar topics to inform teachers, parents, college students, and interested public is essential to the library collection. The activities and the accumulation of education materials that stimulate learning, assist instruction, and provide recreation by the staff, in addition to the attractive appearance of the center, are aimed to support the whole school.

Queens Borough Public Library, Jamaica, New York

Photo by Queens Borough Public Library. Used by permission.

Eileen Gellman and Antonio Martin use *The Red Notebook* at the Queens Borough Public Library, Central Library.

Appendix J
Samples of Library Promotion

Albany Public Library, Albany, New York

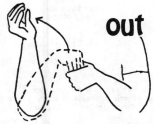

Deaf Awareness check it out

Albany Public Library
161 Washington Avenue
Albany, New York 12210

Telephone: 449-3380 ◆ Teletype: 449-8402

PERIODICALS

AMERICAN ANNALS OF THE DEAF
DEAF AMERICAN
GALLAUDET TODAY
ROCHESTER ADVOCATE

VERTICAL FILE

SEE

DEAFNESS
HEARING
HANDICAPPED

CAPTIONED FILMS
FILMS ON DEAFNESS
PLAYING CARDS AND GAMES
BOOKS FOR CHILDREN

◆   ◆   ◆   ◆

Meeting rooms for library and community-sponsored events — parking lot — conference rooms — elevators — barrier free access — children's room, young adult lounge — job information center — adult independent study room — Pruyn Library of Albany History — cable television public access studio — exhibit space — framed art print collection for lending — film lending service — periodicals and books — interlibrary loan service — video tape facilities —

at the **Albany Public Library**
161 Washington Avenue
Albany, New York 12210
Telephone: 449—3380
Teletype :   449—8402

The library offers programs for children and adults, and sometimes interpreters are present to sign for the deaf. If you would like a special kind of program to meet your needs, please contact the Library.

Used by permission of the Albany Public Library.

This brochure describes library services available to persons who are deaf. The Albany Public Library provides equal access and acts as a "communication satellite" by delivering information to the deaf via their TTY. The use of the TTY brings deaf individuals into the mainstream of library service. It provides an effective link to students in classrooms and helps them use the library as a center for information, education, and recreation throughout their lives.

Anderson, Anderson & Stony Creek Township Public Library, Anderson, Indiana

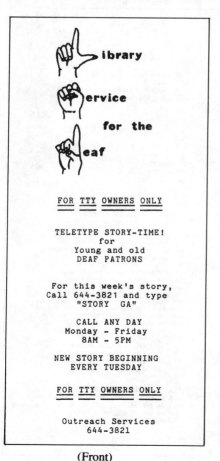

library

ervice

for the

eaf

FOR TTY OWNERS ONLY

TELETYPE STORY-TIME!
for
Young and old
DEAF PATRONS

For this week's story,
Call 644-3821 and type
"STORY GA"

CALL ANY DAY
Monday - Friday
8AM - 5PM

NEW STORY BEGINNING
EVERY TUESDAY

FOR TTY OWNERS ONLY

Outreach Services
644-3821

(Front)

OTHER
LIBRARY SERVICES
for
DEAF PATRONS

- Library Reference

- Community Information

- Sign Language

- Telephone Relay Service
   Monday - Friday 8AM-5PM
   CALL
   Outreach Services
   644-3821

   After hours, on weekends
   or holidays
   CALL
   Contact-Help
   649-5211

- Teletype Story-time

A service provided by
Anderson, Anderson & Stony Creek
Township Public Library

Outreach Services Office
815 Jackson
Anderson, IN 46016
644-3821
(Voice or TTY)

(Back)

Used by permission of the Anderson, Anderson & Stony Creek Township Public Library.

The bookmark tells people about the library services for the deaf. The teletype for the deaf, using regular telephone lines, allows the deaf to communicate with and between the deaf and hearing communities. The outreach office acts as liaison for deaf persons for making doctor appointments, answering tax questions, contacting services, and other situations.

Cuyahoga County Public Library, Cleveland, Ohio

To the deaf and hearing impaired . . . .

THE
CUYAHOGA COUNTY
PUBLIC LIBRARY

is as close as your
telephone

WELCOME TO
Cuyahoga County Public Library

we have
5 TTY Units
to serve you

For faster service, please be ready to provide your name, phone number, community, and the questions you would like answered.

Bay Village, 502 Cahoon Road
✱ BEACHWOOD, 25501 Shaker Boulevard 831-6868
Bedford, 155 Center Street
Berea, 7 Berea Commons
Brecksville, 8997 Highland Drive
✱ BROOK PARK, 6155 Engle Road 267-5250
Brooklyn, 4480 Ridge Road
Chagrin Falls, 100 East Orange Street
✱ FAIRVIEW PARK REGIONAL, 4449 West 213th Street 333-4700
Garfield Heights, 5409 Turney Road
Gates Mills, Old Mill & Epping Roads
Independence, 7121 Valley View Drive
Lyndhurst, 5389 Mayfield Road

✱ MAPLE HEIGHTS REGIONAL, 5225 Library Lane 475-5000
Mayfield Regional, 6080 Wilson Mills Road
Middleburg Heights, 15600 East Bagley Road
North Olmsted, 27425 Butternut Ridge Road
North Royalton, 14600 State Road
Olmsted Falls, 7850 Main Street
Orange, 31300 Chagrin Boulevard
Parma Heights, Greenbrier Commons, 6206 Pearl Road
Parma Regional, 5850 Ridge Road
Parma-Snow, 2121 Snow Road
Solon, 33800 Inwood Road
✱ SOUTH EUCLID, 4645 Mayfield Road 382-4880
Strongsville, 13213 Pearl Road
Warrensville, 22035 Clarkwood Parkway

* COUNTY LIBRARIES
WITH TTY UNITS

C
A
L
L
U
S

Used by permission of the Cuyahoga County Public Library.

This brochure describes the services offered by the library, including TTY units in 5 branches, staff members who are skilled in sign language, free sign language classes, signed story hours, sign language materials available for loan, and captioned films shown in the library and available for loan through the system's extensive 16mm film library.

Phoenix Public Library, Phoenix, Arizona

How does the TTY/TDD service work?

1. From a TTY/TDD phone, call the library —

   **TTY/TDD NUMBER
   254-8205**

2. The library will answer —
   HELLO. THIS IS PHOENIX PUBLIC LIBRARY. SAY YOUR NAME, TELEPHONE NUMBER, AND QUESTION. GA

3. You then type your question, name and telephone number —
   THIS IS TOM JONES AT 123-4567. WHO ARE MY U.S. SENATORS? GA

4. The library will respond —
   I WILL LOOK THAT UP FOR U AND CALL U BACK. GA

CONNECT WITH THE LIBRARY by TTY/TDD

Phoenix Public Library

Used by permission of the Phoenix Public Library.

The Phoenix Public Library offers library services to the speech and hearing impaired community through their telecommunications device for the deaf.

Rockford Public Library, Rockford, Illinois

The Rockford Public Library is

as close as your telephone!

TTY

Telephone

Telegraph

Communications

PURPOSE:

--to provide telephone
    information to the
    hearing-impaired

--to provide facilities for
    local and long distance
    communication for the
    hearing-impaired
    community.

SPONSORED BY QUOTA CLUB

and

ROCKFORD PUBLIC LIBRARY

TYPES OF QUESTIONS

"Does the library have a book on
jogging? Is it in the library to
be borrowed?"

"What hours is my branch library
open?"

"What is the address of the Better
Business Bureau?"

"How do you remove a coffee stain
from clothing?

"Does the library have any books
about sign language?"

"Does the library have any books in
signed English?"

"Do you have any books to help
children learn their ABC's?" (or
colors, or numbers)

"Does the library loan framed art
reproductions?"

"Do you have Westerns in large print?"

"Am I eligible for a free library
card?"

Used by permission of the Rockford Public Library.

The Rockford Public Library provides library service for the deaf and hearing impaired with a TTY donated by the Quota Club.

Prince George's County Memorial Library System, Hyattsville, Maryland

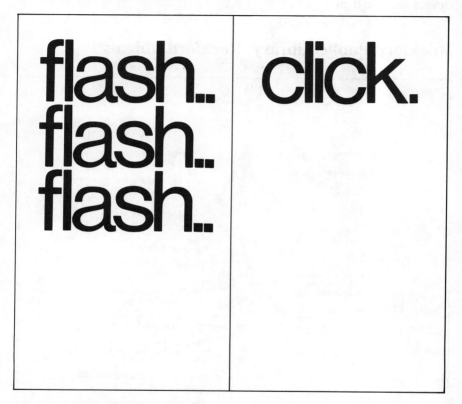

flash.. flash.. flash..

click.

Used by permission of the Prince George's County Memorial Library System.

"Total Communication—Prince George's County (MD) Memorial Library System's Services for the Deaf": This leaflet describes the many services of the library system including: TTY/TDD at each of 9 locations; TEL-MED, a prerecorded health information bulletin for voice and TDD callers; films/videocassettes, books, magazines, and pamphlets on subjects of deafness/hearing impairment and sign language available for children and adults, as well as Signed English children's books; multimedia kits; interpreted programs; and CLIC! (Community Library Information Centers), offering information on area organization/agency services. Funding, begun as a 5-year LSCA-funded demonstration project (1975–80), is now totally integrated within PGCMLS budget.

Fairfax County Public Library, Springfield, Virginia

How can you call?
Hearing-impaired patrons with access to a Teletypewriter (TTY) can call the Kings Park Library (978-2209) on special TTY telephone lines and communicate with us by typing back and forth. An acoustic coupler is used to cradle the telephone receiver and connect the phones.

Why call the Library?
Because it is an information/ referral resource center in this area for the hearing-impaired. Now the hearing-impaired can have the same quick access to information via the telephone that the hearing have long enjoyed.

We can answer your questions.
Whatever you need to know, we can find the answer. We can tell you about résumé writing, and building sundecks and buying a used car and lots of other things too! Call the Library and find out.

We can contact individuals or community groups for you.
We can explore available resources and services, and in an emergency, we may be able to help with a "voice call."

We can share ideas.
The hearing-impaired community can help the library with designing and planning programs such as story hours in sign language, captioned films and craft activities. We'd like to know what YOU want! TTY Us!

Used by permission of the Fairfax County Public Library.

A bookmark developed by the Fairfax County (Virginia) Public Library to publicize TTY service.

School of Librarianship, Leeds Polytechnic, Leeds, England

Course discussions offered by the library include: "Deaf People in Society"; "A National Deaf Video Service"; "The Deaf Person in the Library: A Vignette"; "Resource Implications"; and "Service Im-

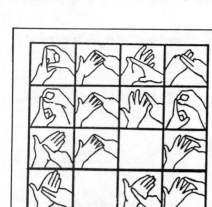

Deaf People in Libraries

WEDNESDAY

12th OCTOBER 1983

at

Brunswick Building
Leeds LS2 8BU

Course Organizer: Bill Anderson
School of Librarianship Leeds Polytechnic

DEAF PEOPLE IN LIBRARIES

This one-day exhibition and conference is organized on behalf of the Medical Health and Welfare Libraries Group of the Library Association.

Deaf people may use all types of libraries, and therefore library staff from public and academic libraries, and from medical health and welfare libraries are encouraged to attend.

Non librarians - social workers and social services administrative staff - are also invited to attend. The client group of deaf people will be welcomed - at no cost.

The exhibition comprises examples of publications by the British Deaf Association (print and A/V) RNID, recently published Shell films (signed) and material from publishers.

This will be complemented by examples of library initiatives from a wide range of libraries.

The deaf are a 'hidden' group in society - maybe for this reason libraries have been slow to respond to their library and information needs. Yet libraries can have a role to play.

Services of information for the deaf <u>do</u> exist - A/V resources especially can be exploited more fully for the deaf.

Used by permission of the School of Librarianship, Leeds Polytechnic.

plications." The brochure describes the course, which was designed to help in raising consciousness about the library needs of the people who are deaf.

Glossary

AM System. *See* Sound systems.

Audio Loop System. *See* Sound systems.

Closed Captioning. A process by which the audio portion of the television program is translated into subtitles (captions) which appear on the screen. These hidden subtitles (closed captions) can only be seen on a television set equipped with a decoding device.

Decoding Device. A piece of equipment required to receive closed-captioned television programs. The device may be an adapter unit for a conventional television set or may be built into a special television set.

FM System. *See* Sound systems.

Hearing Dog. A dog trained to assist an individual who cannot hear. With hearing dogs, also known as audio dogs and hearing ear dogs, people who are deaf can be alerted and respond to the everyday sounds of life. The dog's training is tailored to the individual needs of the owner.

Individualized Educational Program (I.E.P.). A program that includes all activities and services needed to provide appropriate education for children who are disabled, including those who are deaf or hard of hearing. It is a part of the mandated appropriate education program provided for by P.L. 94-142, the Education for All Handicapped Children Act.

Infrared System. *See* Sound systems.

Line 21. A line of the television picture that does not carry any picture information. Subtitles (captions) are inserted on this line in the form of an electronic code. With a decoding device, the hidden subtitles (closed captions) on Line 21 appear on the screen.

Residual Hearing. The amount of hearing that remains with any individual who has a hearing loss of some degree.

Rochester Method. A communication based on the English language, fingerspelled, written, and spoken.

Sound Systems. Amplification systems for hard-of-hearing people for use in communicating in meeting rooms are of several types. With the audio loop system, a loop of wire (electrical cord) is placed around a designated area of a room and is connected with the public address system. A user must sit in the area around which the loop is placed and have a hearing aid with a telephone switch (T). With the infrared system, the rays are emitted from a transmitter connected to the public address system. A special portable receiver picks up the signal. No special seating is required. With the AM system, the individual uses a portable radio with an earplug to receive the AM radio signal from the public address system. With the FM sound system, the sound is conducted from a wireless FM transmitter directly to the user's wireless receiver which consists of a headset and a small unit of pocket size.

TDD. A telecommunication device which allows a person who is deaf to make telephone calls without using an interpreter. The messages are typed and read rather than spoken and heard.

TTY. A term that refers specifically to the original mechanical teletypewriters, both the old and the new models. With this device, people who are deaf may converse through typing and reading.

Total Communication. The use of all communication modes to ensure clarity and understanding in giving and receiving messages. All language modes are used, including speech, lipreading, pantomime, gestures, signing, writing, reading, and fingerspelling. All types of media are also used as is any residual hearing obtained through hearing aids and amplification.

Videogram. Videotape.

Suggested Resources

Association of Specialized and Cooperative Library Agencies. Library Service to the Deaf Section. *Basic Sources of Serving Deaf Library Users.* Chicago: Association of Specialized and Cooperative Library Agencies, 1983.

Baskin, Barbara Holland, and Harris, Karen H., eds. *The Special Child in the Library.* Chicago: American Library Association, 1976.

Batson, Trenton W., and Bergman, Eugene. *The Deaf Experience.* South Waterford, ME: Merriam-Eddy Company, 1976.

Benderly, Beryl L. *Dancing without Music: Deafness in America.* Garden City, NY: Anchor Press/Doubleday, 1980.

Bowe, Frank. *Handicapping America: Barriers to Disabled People.* New York: Harper and Row, 1978.

Castle, Thomas H. *Deaf People are People Too.* Rochester, NY: Rochester Institute of Technology, 1981.

Cohen, Elaine, and Cohen, Aaron. *Automation, Space Management and Productivity: A Guide for Libraries.* New York: R. R. Bowker, 1981.

Dequin, Henry C. *Librarians Serving Disabled Children and Young People.* Littleton, CO: Libraries Unlimited, 1983.

Duncan, Jack G. "Recent Legislation Affecting Hearing Impaired Persons." *American Annals of the Deaf* 129 (2) April 1984: 83–94.

Gannon, Jack. *Deaf Heritage: A Narrative History of Deaf America.* Silver Spring, MD: National Association of the Deaf, 1981.

Greenberg, Joanne. *In This Sign.* New York: Holt, Rinehart and Winston, 1970.

Griffin, Betty F., ed. *Family to Family.* Washington, DC: Alexander Graham Bell Association for the Deaf, Inc., 1980.

Harrington, Thomas R., comp. *Mediagraphy on Deafness and the Deaf.* Arlington, VA. ERIC document ED 169 721, 1979.

Huffman, Edythe S. *Library Services for Deaf, Blind and Physically Handicapped People in the United States, 1977–1979: An Annotated Bibliography.* Chapel Hill, NC: University of North Carolina, 1980. ERIC document ED 189 816.

Jacobs, Leo. *A Deaf Adult Speaks Out.* Revised and expanded second edition. Washington, DC: Gallaudet College, 1980.

Katz, Lee; Mathis, Steve L., III; and Merrill, Edward C., Jr. *The Deaf Child and the Public Schools.* Danville, IL: Interstate Printers and Publishers, Inc., 1978.

Klima, Edward, and Bellugi, Ursula. *The Signs of Language.* Cambridge, MA: Harvard University Press, 1979.

Library and Information Service Needs of the Nation. Proceedings of the Conference on the Needs of Occupational, Ethnic and Other Groups in the United States. Washington, DC: Government Printing Office, 1974.

Lucas, Linda, and Karrenbrock, Marilyn. *The Disabled Child in the Library: Moving into the Mainstream.* Littleton, CO: Libraries Unlimited, 1983.

McGeough, Charles S.; Jungjohan, Barbara; and Thomas, James, eds. *Directory of College Facilities and Services for the Handicapped.* Phoenix, AZ: Oryx Press, 1983.

Mindel, Edward C., and McCay, Vernon. *They Grow in Silence.* Silver Spring, MD: National Association of the Deaf, 1971.

Moores, Donald F. *Educating the Deaf: Psychology, Principles and Practices.* Second edition. Boston: Houghton Mifflin Company, 1982.

National Library Service for the Blind and Physically Handicapped, The Library of Congress. *That All May Read: Library Service for the Blind and Physically Handicapped.* Washington, DC: National Library Service for the Blind and Physically Handicapped, Library of Congress, 1983.

National Rehabilitation Information Center. *Deaf and Hearing Impairments. Bibliography, 1981–1984.* Washington, DC: National Rehabilitation Information Center, 1984.

Neeham, William L., and Jahoda, Gerald. *Improving Library Service to Physically Disabled Persons. A Self-Evaluation Checklist.* Littleton, CO: Libraries Unlimited, 1983.

Neisser, Arden. *The Other Side of Silence: Sign Language and the Deaf Community in America.* New York: Alfred A. Knopf, Inc., 1983.

Ohio Legislative Commission. *The Use of a Commission to Address the Needs of the Deaf and Hearing Impaired.* Columbus, OH: Ohio Legislative Commission, 1984.

Parlato, Salvatore J., Jr. "Captioned and Nonverbal Films for the Hearing-Impaired." *Library Trends* 27 (1) (Summer 1978): 59–63.

Robinson, Luther D. *Sound Minds in a Soundless World.* Washington, DC: U.S. Department of Health, Education and Welfare, 1978.

Rosenthal, Richard. *The Hearing Handbook.* New York: Schocken Books, 1978.

Schein, Jerome, and Delk, Marcus T. *The Deaf Population of the United States.* Silver Spring, MD: National Association of the Deaf, 1974.

Schein, Jerome D. *A Rose for Tomorrow: A Biography of Frederick C. Schreiber.* Silver Spring, MD: National Association of the Deaf, 1981.

Spradley, Thomas S., and Spradley, James F. *Deaf Like Me.* New York: Random House, 1978.

Sundstrom, Susan C. *Understanding Hearing Loss and What Can Be Done to Help.* Danville, IL: Interstate Printers and Publishers, Inc., 1983.

Thomas, James L., and Thomas, Carol H. *Academic Library Facilities and Services for the Handicapped.* Phoenix, AZ: Oryx Press, 1981.

————.*Library Services for the Handicapped Adult.* Phoenix, AZ: Oryx Press, 1982.

Turock, Betty. *Serving the Older Adult: A Guide to Library Programs and Information Services.* New York: R. R. Bowker, 1982.

U.S. Commission on Civil Rights. *Accommodating the Spectrum of Individual Abilities.* Clearing House Publication 81. Washington, DC: U.S. Commission on Civil Rights, 1983.

U.S. Department of Education. *Resource Guide, Employment of the Handicapped.* Washington, DC: U.S. Department of Education, 1982.

U.S. Department of Labor. Employment Standards Administration. *A Study of Accommodations Provided to Handicapped Employees by Federal Contractors.* Final Report, Volume I. "Study and Findings." Volume II. "Ten Case Studies." Berkeley, CA: Berkeley Associates, 1982.

Velleman, Ruth A. *Serving Physically Disabled People: An Information Handbook for All Libraries.* New York: R. R. Bowker, 1979.

Wright, Kieth C., and Davie, Judith F. *Library and Information Services for the Handicapped.* Second edition. Littleton, CO: Libraries Unlimited, 1983.

Index

Compiled by Linda Webster